BIG IDEAS MATH®
Modeling Real Life

Grade K

Volume 1

Ron Larson
Laurie Boswell

Big Ideas Learning™
Erie, Pennsylvania
BigIdeasLearning.com

Big Ideas Learning

Big Ideas Learning, LLC
1762 Norcross Road
Erie, PA 16510-3838
USA

For product information and customer support, contact Big Ideas Learning at **1-877-552-7766** or visit us at ***BigIdeasLearning.com***.

Cover Image:
Paul Lampard /123RF.com, bgblue/DigitalVision Vectors/Getty Images

Printed in the U.S.A.

ISBN 13: 978-1-64727-872-4

2 3 4 5 6 7 8 9 10—25 24 23 22 21

One Voice from Kindergarten Through Algebra 2

Written by renowned authors, Dr. Ron Larson and Dr. Laurie Boswell, *Big Ideas Math* offers a seamless math pedagogy from elementary through high school. Together, Ron and Laurie provide a consistent voice that encourages students to make connections through cohesive progressions and clear instruction. Since 1992, Ron and Laurie have authored over 50 mathematics programs.

"Each time Laurie and I start working on a new program, we spend time putting ourselves in the position of the reader. How old is the reader? What is the reader's experience with mathematics? The answers to these questions become our writing guides. Our goal is to make the learning targets understandable and to develop these targets in a clear path that leads to student success."

Ron Larson

Ron Larson, Ph.D., is well known as lead author of a comprehensive and widely used mathematics program that ranges from elementary school through college. He holds the distinction of Professor Emeritus from Penn State Erie, The Behrend College, where he taught for nearly 40 years. He received his Ph.D. in mathematics from the University of Colorado. Dr. Larson engages in the latest research and advancements in mathematics education and consistently incorporates key pedagogical elements to ensure focus, coherence, rigor, and student self-reflection.

"My passion and goal in writing is to provide an essential resource for exploring and making sense of mathematics. Our program is guided by research around the learning and teaching of mathematics in the hopes of improving the achievement of all students. May this be a successful year for you!"

Laurie Boswell

Laurie Boswell, Ed.D., is the former Head of School at Riverside School in Lyndonville, Vermont. In addition to authoring textbooks, she provides mathematics consulting and embedded coaching sessions. Dr. Boswell received her Ed.D. from the University of Vermont in 2010. She is a recipient of the Presidential Award for Excellence in Mathematics Teaching and later served as president of CPAM. Laurie has taught math to students at all levels, elementary through college. In addition, Laurie has served on the NCTM Board of Directors and as a Regional Director for NCSM. Along with Ron, Laurie has co-authored numerous math programs and has become a popular national speaker.

Contributors, Reviewers, and Research

Big Ideas Learning would like to express our gratitude to the mathematics education and instruction experts who served as our advisory panel, contributing specialists, and reviewers during the writing of *Big Ideas Math: Modeling Real Life*. Their input was an invaluable asset during the development of this program.

Contributing Specialists and Reviewers

- **Sophie Murphy**, Ph.D. Candidate, Melbourne School of Education, Melbourne, Australia
  Learning Targets and Success Criteria Specialist and Visible Learning Reviewer
- **Linda Hall**, Mathematics Educational Consultant, Edmond, OK
  Advisory Panel
- **Michael McDowell**, Ed.D., Superintendent, Ross, CA
  Project-Based Learning Specialist
- **Kelly Byrne**, Math Supervisor and Coordinator of Data Analysis, Downingtown, PA
  Advisory Panel
- **Jean Carwin**, Math Specialist/TOSA, Snohomish, WA
  Advisory Panel
- **Nancy Siddens**, Independent Language Teaching Consultant, Las Cruces, NM
  English Language Learner Specialist
- **Kristen Karbon**, Curriculum and Assessment Coordinator, Troy, MI
  Advisory Panel
- **Kery Obradovich**, K–8 Math/Science Coordinator, Northbrook, IL
  Advisory Panel
- **Jennifer Rollins**, Math Curriculum Content Specialist, Golden, CO
  Advisory Panel
- **Becky Walker**, Ph.D., School Improvement Services Director, Green Bay, WI
  Advisory Panel and Content Reviewer
- **Deborah Donovan**, Mathematics Consultant, Lexington, SC
  Content Reviewer
- **Tom Muchlinski**, Ph.D., Mathematics Consultant, Plymouth, MN
  Content Reviewer and Teaching Edition Contributor
- **Mary Goetz**, Elementary School Teacher, Troy, MI
  Content Reviewer
- **Nanci N. Smith**, Ph.D., International Curriculum and Instruction Consultant, Peoria, AZ
  Teaching Edition Contributor
- **Robyn Seifert-Decker**, Mathematics Consultant, Grand Haven, MI
  Teaching Edition Contributor
- **Bonnie Spence**, Mathematics Education Specialist, Missoula, MT
  Teaching Edition Contributor
- **Suzy Gagnon**, Adjunct Instructor, University of New Hampshire, Portsmouth, NH
  Teaching Edition Contributor
- **Art Johnson**, Ed.D., Professor of Mathematics Education, Warwick, RI
  Teaching Edition Contributor
- **Anthony Smith**, Ph.D., Associate Professor, Associate Dean, University of Washington Bothell, Seattle, WA
  Reading and Writing Reviewer
- **Brianna Raygor**, Music Teacher, Fridley, MN
  Music Reviewer
- **Nicole Dimich Vagle**, Educator, Author, and Consultant, Hopkins, MN
  Assessment Reviewer
- **Janet Graham**, District Math Specialist, Manassas, VA
  Response to Intervention and Differentiated Instruction Reviewer
- **Sharon Huber**, Director of Elementary Mathematics, Chesapeake, VA
  Universal Design for Learning Reviewer

Student Reviewers

- T.J. Morin
- Alayna Morin
- Ethan Bauer
- Emery Bauer
- Emma Gaeta
- Ryan Gaeta
- Benjamin SanFrotello
- Bailey SanFrotello
- Samantha Grygier
- Robert Grygier IV
- Jacob Grygier
- Jessica Urso
- Ike Patton
- Jake Lobaugh
- Adam Fried
- Caroline Naser
- Charlotte Naser

Research

Ron Larson and Laurie Boswell used the latest in educational research, along with the body of knowledge collected from expert mathematics instructors, to develop the *Modeling Real Life* series. The pedagogical approach used in this program follows the best practices outlined in the most prominent and widely accepted educational research, including:

- *Visible Learning*, John Hattie © 2009
- *Visible Learning for Teachers*
John Hattie © 2012
- *Visible Learning for Mathematics*
John Hattie © 2017
- *Principles to Actions: Ensuring Mathematical Success for All*
NCTM © 2014
- *Adding It Up: Helping Children Learn Mathematics*
National Research Council © 2001
- *Mathematical Mindsets: Unleashing Students' Potential through Creative Math, Inspiring Messages and Innovative Teaching*
Jo Boaler © 2015
- *What Works in Schools: Translating Research into Action*
Robert Marzano © 2003
- *Classroom Instruction That Works: Research-Based Strategies for Increasing Student Achievement*
Marzano, Pickering, and Pollock © 2001
- *Principles and Standards for School Mathematics*
NCTM © 2000
- *Rigorous PBL by Design: Three Shifts for Developing Confident and Competent Learners*
Michael McDowell © 2017
- *Universal Design for Learning Guidelines*
CAST © 2011
- Rigor/Relevance Framework®
International Center for Leadership in Education
- *Understanding by Design*
Grant Wiggins and Jay McTighe © 2005
- Achieve, ACT, and The College Board
- *Elementary and Middle School Mathematics: Teaching Developmentally*
John A. Van de Walle and Karen S. Karp © 2015
- *Evaluating the Quality of Learning: The SOLO Taxonomy*
John B. Biggs & Kevin F. Collis © 1982
- *Unlocking Formative Assessment: Practical Strategies for Enhancing Students' Learning in the Primary and Intermediate Classroom*
Shirley Clarke, Helen Timperley, and John Hattie © 2004
- *Formative Assessment in the Secondary Classroom*
Shirley Clarke © 2005
- *Improving Student Achievement: A Practical Guide to Assessment for Learning*
Toni Glasson © 2009

Instructional Design

A single authorship team from Kindergarten through Algebra 2 results in a logical progression of focused topics with meaningful coherence from course to course.

FOCUS

A focused program dedicates lessons, activities, and assessments to grade-level standards while simultaneously supporting and engaging you in the major work of the course.

The **Learning Targets** in your book and the **Success Criteria** in the Teaching Edition focus the learning for each lesson into manageable chunks, with clear teaching text and examples.

Learning Target: Write related addition and subtraction equations to complete a fact family.

Laurie's Notes

Preparing to Teach

Students have heard about time and the language of time. Most students do not understand time or know how to tell time on an analog clock. In this lesson, students are introduced to telling time to the hour. They learn about the hour hand and telling time as o'clock.

Laurie's Notes, located in the Teaching Edition, prepare your teacher for the math concepts in each chapter and lesson and make connections to the threads of major topics for the course.

Think and Grow

$$\underline{4} + \underline{7} = \underline{11} \qquad \underline{7} + \underline{4} = \underline{11}$$

addend addend sum

Changing the order of the **addends** does not change the **sum**.

The **expressions** 4 + 7 and 7 + 4 are both equal to 11.

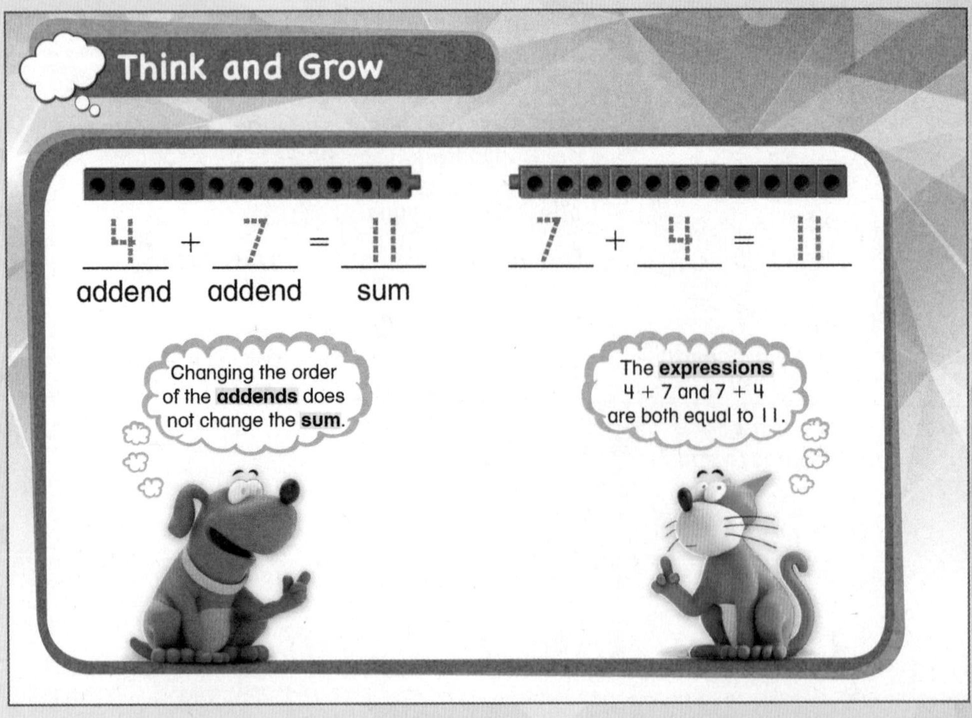

a Single Authorship Team

COHERENCE

A single authorship team built a coherent program that has intentional progression of content within each grade and between grade levels. You will build new understanding on foundations from prior grades and connect concepts throughout the course.

The authors developed content that progresses from prior chapters and grades to future ones. In addition to charts like this one, Laurie's Notes give your teacher insights about where you have come from and where you are going in your learning progression.

Through the Grades		
Kindergarten	**Grade 1**	**Grade 2**
• Represent addition and subtraction with various models and strategies. • Solve addition and subtraction word problems within 10. • Fluently add and subtract within 5.	• Solve addition and subtraction word problems within 20. • Fluently add and subtract within 10. • Determine the unknown number to complete addition and subtraction equations.	• Solve addition and subtraction word problems within 100. • Solve word problems involving length and money. • Solve one- and two-step word problems. • Fluently add and subtract within 20.

One author team thoughtfully wrote each course, creating a seamless progression of content from Kindergarten to Algebra 2.

	Grade K	Grade 1	Grade 2	Grade 3	Grade 4	Grade 5	Grade 6	
Number and Quantity	**Number and Operations – Base Ten**				**Number and Operations – Base Ten**		**The Number System**	
	Work with numbers 11–19 to gain foundations for place value. *Chapter 8*	Extend the counting sequence. Use place value and properties of operations to add and subtract. *Chapters 6–9*	Use place value and properties of operations to add and subtract. *Chapters 2–10, 14*	Use place value and properties of operations to perform multi-digit arithmetic. *Chapters 7–9, 12*	Generalize place value understanding for multi-digit whole numbers. Use place value and properties of operations to perform multi-digit arithmetic. *Chapters 1–5*	Understand the place value system. Perform operations with multi-digit whole numbers and with decimals to hundredths. *Chapters 1, 3–7*	Perform operations with multi-digit numbers and find common factors and multiples. *Chapter 1* Divide fractions by fractions. *Chapter 2* Extend understanding of numbers to the rational number system. *Chapter 8*	Perfor ration Chapt
				Num. and Oper. – Fractions	**Number and Operations – Fractions**		**Ratios and Proportional Relation**	
				Understand fractions as numbers. *Chapters 10, 11, 14*	Extend understanding of fraction equivalence and ordering. Build fractions from unit ... mal notation ... d compare	Add, subtract, multiply, and divide fractions. *Chapters 6, 8–11*	Use ratios to solve problems. *Chapters 3, 4*	Use pr to solv Chapt

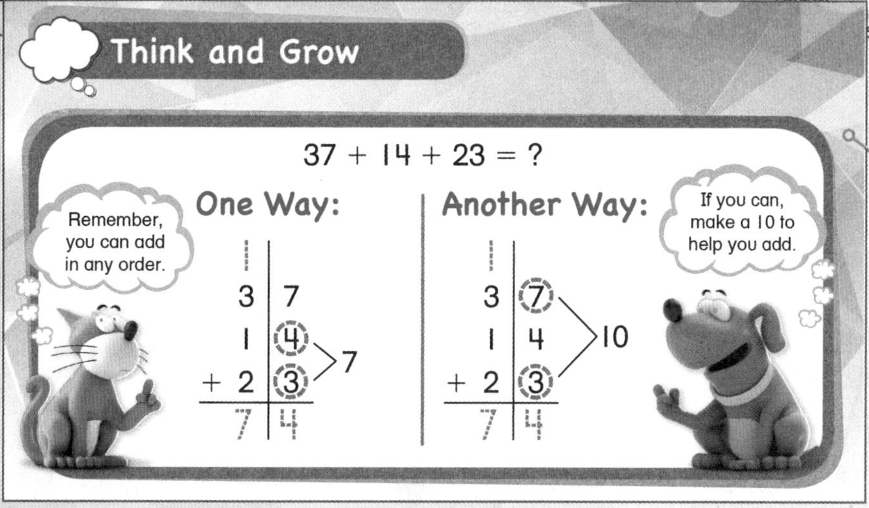

Think and Grow
37 + 14 + 23 = ?
Remember, you can add in any order.
One Way:
Another Way:
If you can, make a 10 to help you add.

Throughout each course, lessons build on prior learning as new concepts are introduced. Here you are reminded of rules and strategies that you already know to help solve the addition problem.

Rigor in Math: A Balanced Approach

Instructional Design

The authors wrote each chapter and every lesson to provide a meaningful balance of rigorous instruction.

RIGOR

A rigorous program provides a balance of three important building blocks.

- **Conceptual Understanding** Discovering why
- **Procedural Fluency** Learning how
- **Application** Knowing when to apply

Conceptual Understanding
You have the opportunity to develop foundational concepts central to the *Learning Target* in each *Explore and Grow* by experimenting with new concepts, talking with peers, and asking questions.

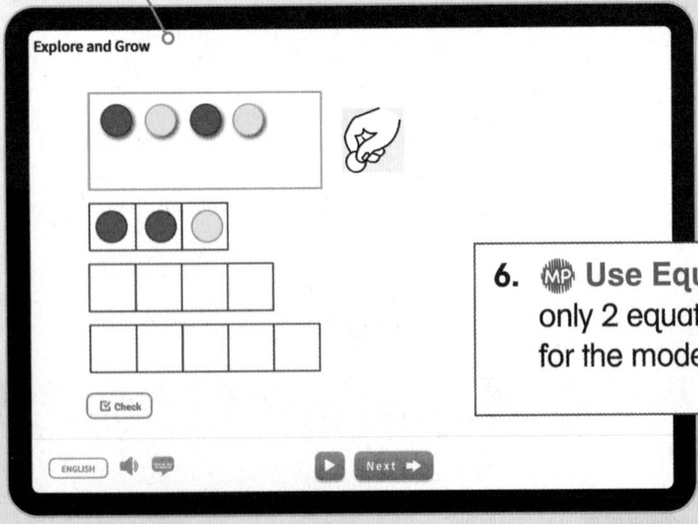

Conceptual Thinking
Conceptual questions ask you to think deeply.

6. **Use Equations** Your friend uses only 2 equations to write the fact family for the model. Is this reasonable?

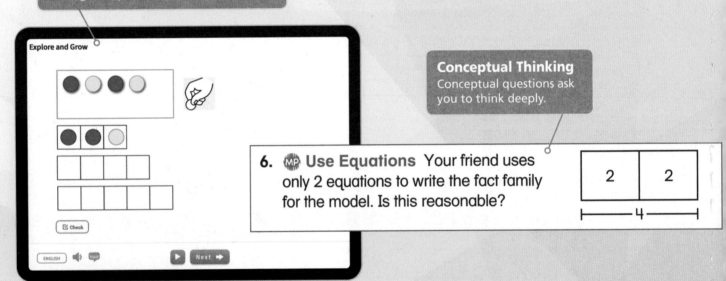

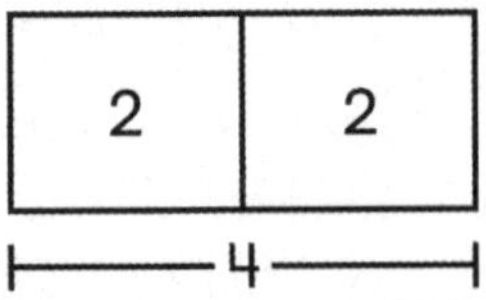

Procedural Fluency
Solidify learning with clear, stepped-out teaching in *Think and Grow* examples.

Then shift conceptual understanding into procedural fluency with *Show and Grow, Apply and Grow, Practice*, and *Review & Refresh*.

5

Subtract Numbers within 20

- What do bees make?
- How many bees do you see? 7 of them fly away. How many bees are left?

Chapter Learning Target:
Understand subtraction strategies.

Chapter Success Criteria:
- I can identify counting back strategies.
- I can describe subtraction equations.
- I can explain the subtraction strategy I used.
- I can compare addition and subtraction strategies.

Connecting to Real Life
Begin every chapter thinking about the world around you. Then apply what you learn in the chapter with a related *Performance Task*.

Name ________________

Performance Task 5

1. You keep track of the number of honeybees and bumblebees you see.

Day	Honeybees
Monday	12
Tuesday	6
Wednesday	13

Day	Bumblebees
Monday	5
Tuesday	14
Wednesday	

a. How many more honeybees did you see on Monday than on Tuesday?

____ more honeybees

Daily Application Practice
Modeling Real Life, *Dig Deeper*, and other non-routine problems help you apply surface-level skills to gain a deeper understanding. These problems lead to independent problem-solving.

15. **Modeling Real Life** Your magic book has 163 tricks. Your friend's magic book has 100 more tricks than yours. How many tricks does your friend's magic book have?

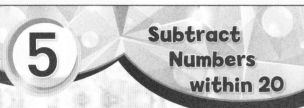

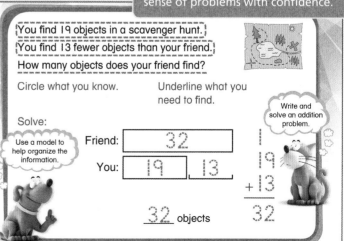

_____ tricks

16. **DIG DEEPER!** You have 624 songs. Newton has 100 fewer than you. Descartes has 10 more than Newton. How many songs does Descartes have?

_____ songs

Problem-Solving Plan
Walk through the Problem-Solving Plan, featured in many *Think and Grow* examples, to help you make sense of problems with confidence.

THE PROBLEM-SOLVING PLAN

1. **Understand the Problem**
   Think about what the problem is asking. Circle what you know and underline what you need to find.
2. **Make a Plan**
   Plan your solution pathway before jumping in to solve. Identify any relationships and decide on a problem-solving strategy.
3. **Solve and Check**
   As you solve the problem, be sure to evaluate your progress and check your answers. Throughout the problem-solving process, you must continually ask, "Does this make sense?" and be willing to change course if necessary.

You find 19 objects in a scavenger hunt. You find 13 fewer objects than your friend. How many objects does your friend find?

Circle what you know. Underline what you need to find.

Solve:

Use a model to help organize the information.

Friend: 32

You: 19 | 13

Write and solve an addition problem.

$$\begin{array}{r} 19 \\ +\ 13 \\ \hline 32 \end{array}$$

32 objects

Embedded Mathematical Practices

Encouraging Mathematical Mindsets

Developing proficiency in the **Mathematical Practices** is about becoming a mathematical thinker. Learn to ask why, and to reason and communicate with others as you learn. The labels shown in this guide are present in the Teaching Edition to engage mathematical discussion and are directly related to problems throughout the program.

1

One way to **Make Sense of Problems and Persevere in Solving Them** is to use the Problem-Solving Plan. Take time to analyze the given information and what the problem is asking to help you plan a solution pathway.

Look for labels such as:

- Find Entry Points
- Analyze a Problem
- Interpret a Solution
- Make a Plan
- Use a Similar Problem
- Check Your Work

There are 33 students on a bus. 10 more get on. How many students are on the bus now?

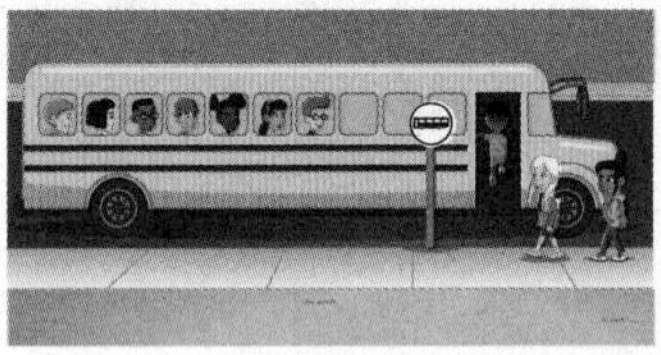

Addition equation:

MP **Check Your Work** When adding 10, should the digit in the tens place or the ones place change?

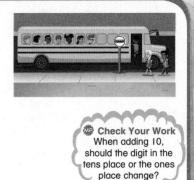

____ students

5. MP **Analyze a Problem** Use the numbers shown to write two addition equations.

8   10   2

____ + ____ = ____

____ + ____ = ____

2

Reason Abstractly when you explore an example using numbers and models to represent the problem. Other times, **Reason Quantitatively** when you see relationships in numbers or models and draw conclusions about the problem.

7. MP **Reasoning** The minute hand points to the 7. What number will it point to in 10 minutes?

Look for labels such as:

- Reasoning
- Number Sense
- Use Equations
- Use Expressions

3. MP **Number Sense** Which numbers can you subtract from 55 without regrouping?

15   49   33   24

Model 27 two ways.

7. MP **Logic** Complete.

37 + 4

37 + ◯ + ◯

40 + ◯

37 + 4 = _____

Tens	Ones

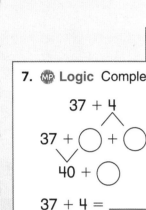

MP **Construct an Argument** Can you model 27 using only tens? Why or why not?

_____ tens and _____ ones is _____.

_____ tens and _____ ones is _____.

3

When you **Construct Viable Arguments and Critique the Reasoning of Others**, you make and justify conclusions and decide whether others' arguments are correct or flawed.

Look for labels such as:

- Construct an Argument
- You Be the Teacher
- Logic
- Make a Conjecture
- Justify a Result
- Compare Arguments

7. MP **Graph Data** Complete the weather chart to show an equal number of sunny days and rainy days. Write an equation to show how many sunny days and rainy days there are in all.

SUN	MON	TUE	WED	THU	FRI	SAT

___ + ___ = ___

Think and Grow: Modeling Real Life

Will the scissors fit inside a pencil case that is 7 color tiles long?

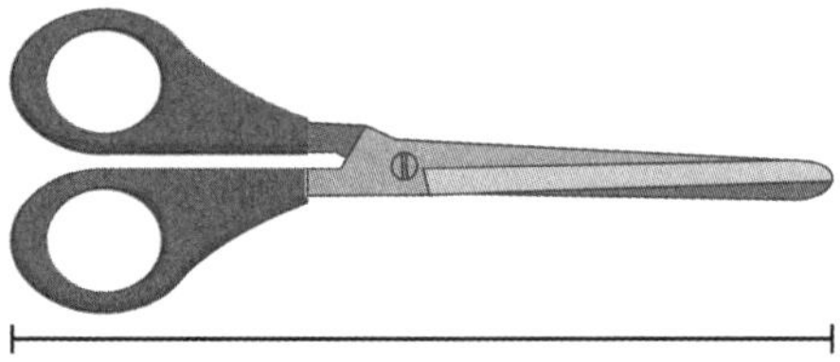

Circle: Yes No

Tell how you know:

MP **Does It Make Sense?** To fit inside, should the scissors be shorter or longer than the case?

4

To **Model with Mathematics**, apply the math you learned to a real-life problem and interpret mathematical results in the context of the situation.

Look for labels such as:

- Modeling Real Life
- Graph Data
- Analyze a Relationship
- Does It Make Sense?

BUILDING TO FULL UNDERSTANDING

Throughout each course, you have opportunities to demonstrate specific aspects of the mathematical practices. Labels throughout the book indicate gateways to those aspects. Collectively, these opportunities will lead to a full understanding of each mathematical practice. Developing these mindsets and habits will give meaning to the mathematics you learn.

5

To **Use Appropriate Tools Strategically**, you need to know what tools are available and think about how each tool might help you solve a mathematical problem. When you choose a tool to use, remember that it may have limitations.

Look for labels such as:

- Choose Tools
- Use Math Tools
- Use Technology

8. MP **Choose Tools** Would you measure the length of a bus with a centimeter ruler or a meter stick? Why?

MP Use Math Tools
How can you use a drawing to help organize the information given?

11. DIG DEEPER! There are 63 people in a theater, 21 people in the lobby, and 10 people in the parking lot. How many more people are in the theater than in both the lobby and the parking lot?

_____ more people

6

When you **Attend to Precision**, you are developing a habit of being careful in how you talk about concepts, label work, and write answers.

Look for labels such as:

- Precision
- Communicate Clearly
- Maintain Accuracy

7. DIG DEEPER! Complete the model and the equation to match.

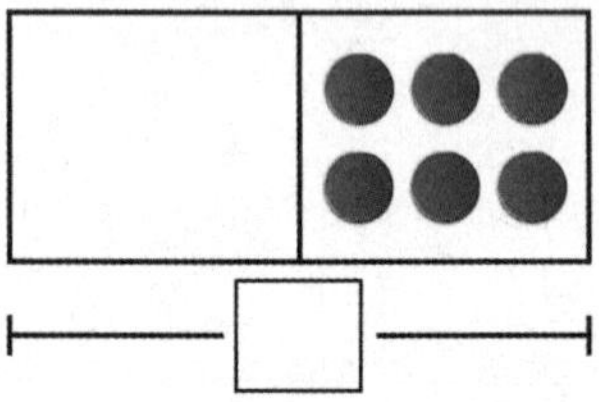

___ + ___ = 8

MP Communicate Clearly
In the model, what shows the addends? the sum?

5. MP **Precision** Which picture shows the correct way to measure the straw?

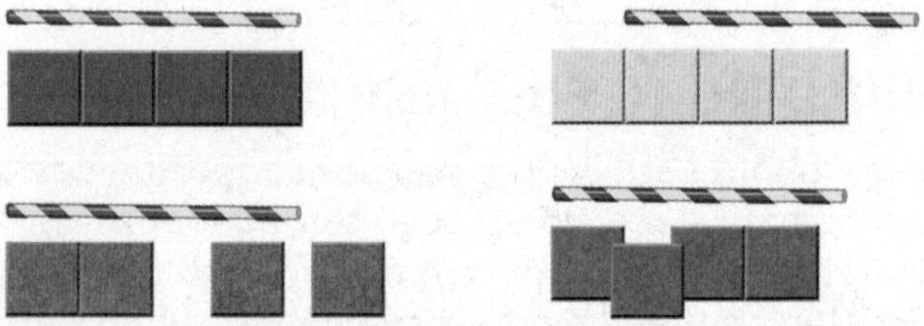

6. **MP Patterns** Find the sums. Think: What do you notice?

$4 + 5 =$ ____

$4 + 4 =$ ____

$5 + 5 =$ ____

	Tens	Ones
	☐	
	3	8
+	2	4

$38 + 24 =$ ____

MP Structure What step did you use to find 38 + 24 that you would not use to find 31 + 24? Why?

7

Look For and Make Use of Structure by looking closely to see structure within a mathematical statement, or stepping back for an overview to see how individual parts make one single object.

Look for labels such as:
- Structure
- Patterns

8. **MP Repeated Reasoning** What other shape has the same number of surfaces, vertices, and edges as a rectangular prism? How is that shape different from a rectangular prism?

$4 + 1 = 5$

$4 - 1 = 3$

MP Find a Rule When you add or subtract 1, what is true about the sum or difference?

8

When you **Look For and Express Regularity in Repeated Reasoning**, you can notice patterns and make generalizations. Remember to keep in mind the goal of a problem, which will help you evaluate reasonableness of answers along the way.

Look for labels such as:
- Repeated Reasoning
- Find a Rule

Visible Learning Through Learning Targets,

Making Learning Visible

Knowing the learning intention of a chapter or lesson helps you focus on the purpose of an activity, rather than simply completing it in isolation. This program supports visible learning through the consistent use of Learning Targets and Success Criteria to help you become successful.

Every chapter shows a **Learning Target** and four related **Success Criteria**. These are incorporated throughout the chapter content to help guide you in your learning.

Every lesson shows a **Learning Target** that is purposefully integrated into each carefully written lesson.

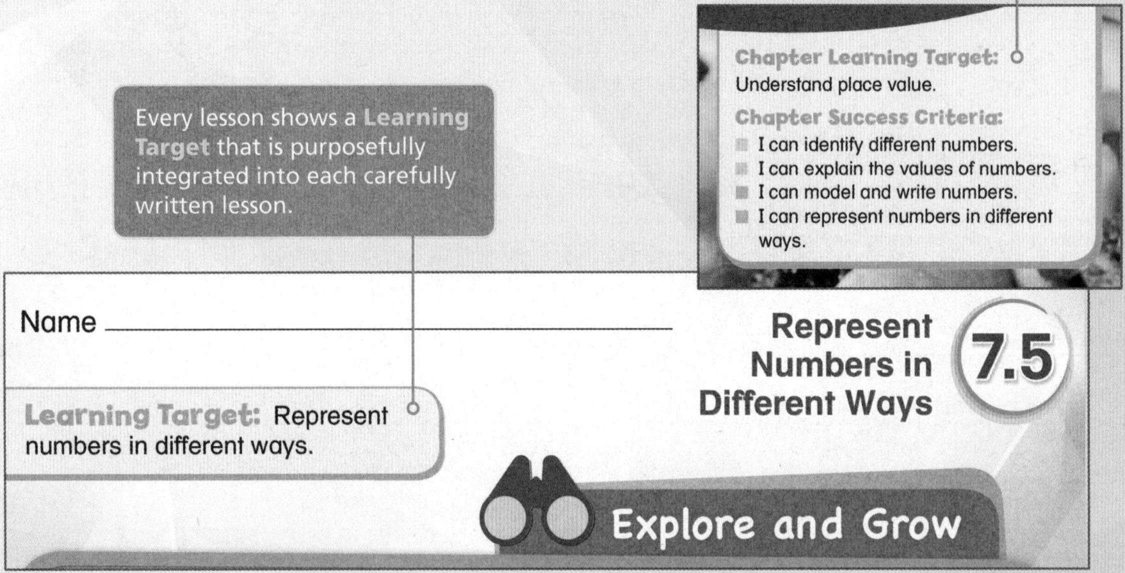

Chapter Learning Target:
Understand place value.
Chapter Success Criteria:
I can identify different numbers.
I can explain the values of numbers.
I can model and write numbers.
I can represent numbers in different ways.
Name
Learning Target: Represent numbers in different ways.
Represent Numbers in Different Ways
7.5
Explore and Grow

Access the **Learning Target** and **Success Criteria** on every page of the Dynamic Student Edition.

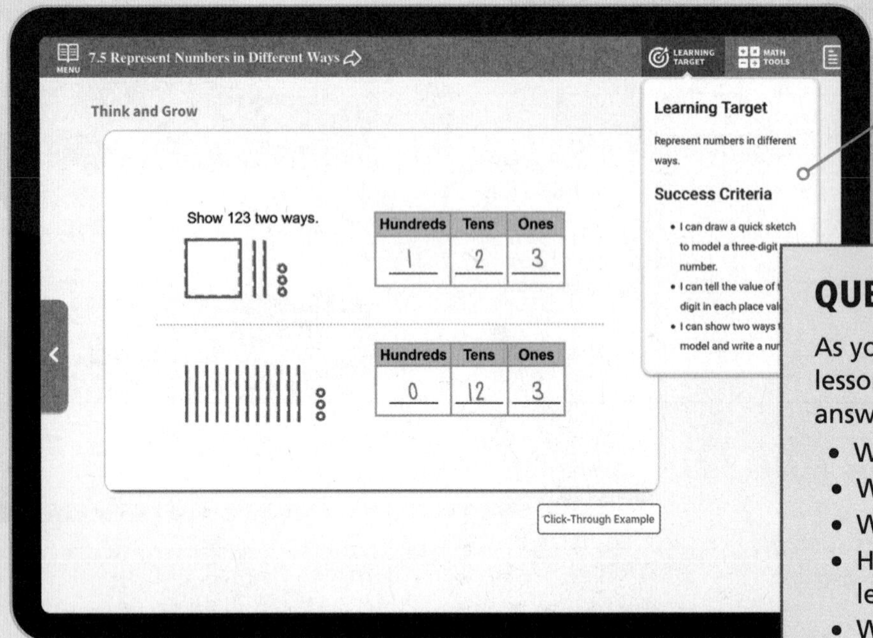

QUESTIONS FOR LEARNING

As you progress through a lesson, you should be able to answer the following questions.

- What am I learning?
- Why am I learning this?
- Where am I in my learning?
- How will I know when I have learned it?
- Where am I going next?

Success Criteria, and Self-Assessment

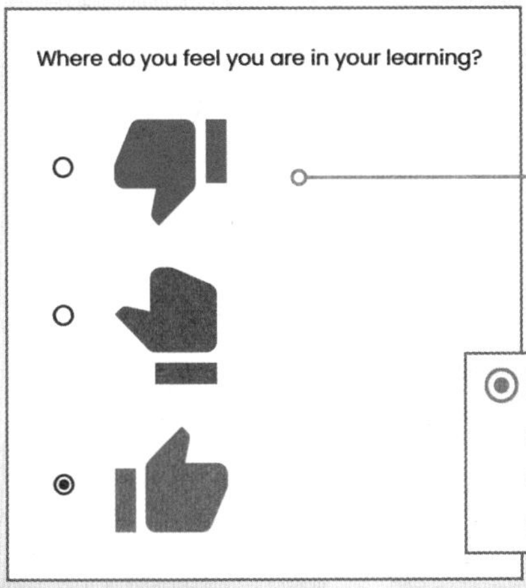

Where do you feel you are in your learning?

Use your thumb signals to rate your understanding of each success criterion. Your teacher will prompt you to self-assess throughout each lesson, and you can keep track of your learning online.

Have students indicate with their thumb signals how well they can find the sum in a word problem and write an addition equation. Have students turn and talk with a partner to explain all of the math vocabulary in an addition equation.

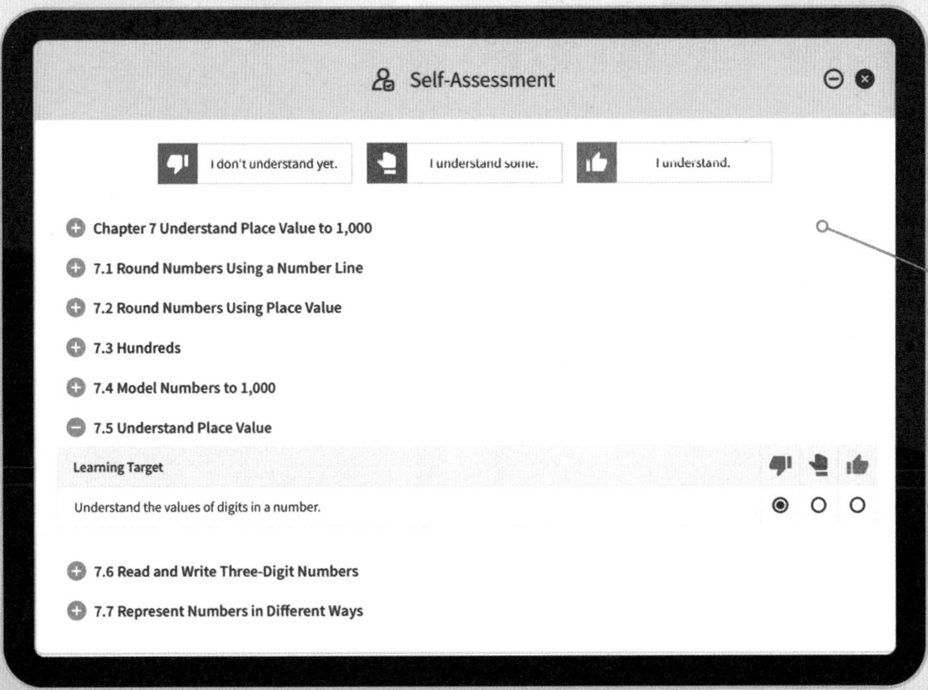

Self-Assessments are included throughout every lesson, and in the **Chapter Review**, to help you take ownership of your learning and think about where to go next.

Ensuring Positive Outcomes

John Hattie's *Visible Learning* research consistently shows that using Learning Targets and Success Criteria can result in two years' growth in one year, ensuring positive outcomes for your learning and achievement.

Sophie Murphy, M.Ed., wrote the chapter-level Learning Targets and Success Criteria for this program. Sophie is currently completing her Ph.D. at the University of Melbourne in Australia with Professor John Hattie as her leading supervisor. Sophie completed her Master's thesis with Professor John Hattie in 2015. Sophie has over 20 years of experience as a teacher and school leader in private and public school settings in Australia.

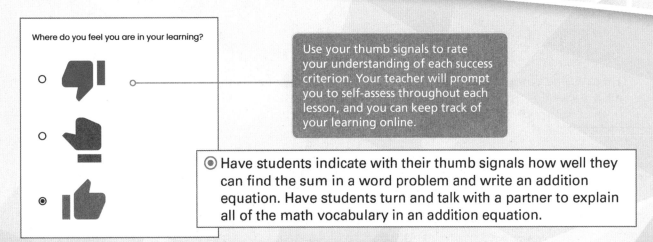

Strategic Support for Online Learning

Get the Support You Need, When You Need It

There will be times throughout this course when you may need help. Whether you missed a lesson, did not understand the content, or just want to review, take advantage of the resources provided in the *Dynamic Student Edition*.

Use the **Self-Assessment** tool to keep track of your understanding of the lesson's Learning Target and Success Criteria.

Choose **Math Tools** to engage with pattern blocks, digital number lines, linking cubes, and other tools to explore and understand math concepts.

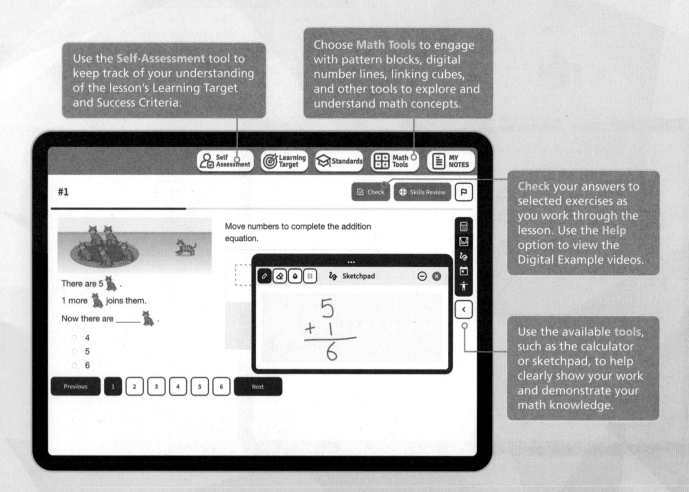

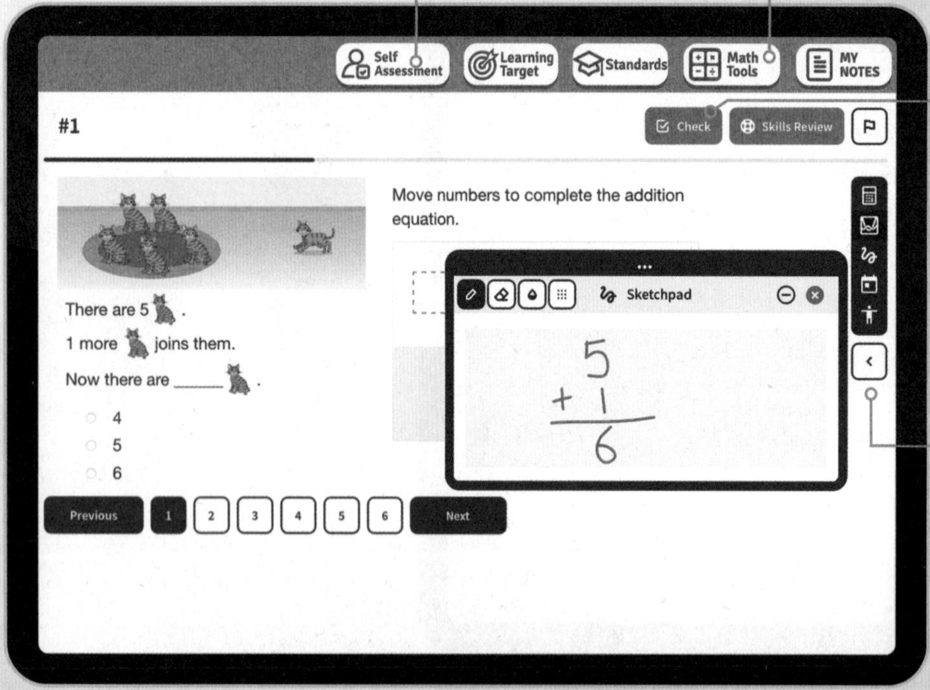

Check your answers to selected exercises as you work through the lesson. Use the **Help** option to view the Digital Example videos.

Use the available **tools**, such as the calculator or sketchpad, to help clearly show your work and demonstrate your math knowledge.

USE THESE QR CODES TO EXPLORE ADDITIONAL RESOURCES

Multi-Language Glossary
View definitions and examples of vocabulary words

Skills Trainer
Practice previously learned skills

Interactive Tools
Visualize mathematical concepts

Skills Review Handbook
A collection of review topics

Learning with Newton and Descartes

Who are Newton and Descartes?

Newton and Descartes are helpful math assistants who appear throughout your math book! They encourage you to think deeply about concepts and develop strong mathematical mindsets with Mathematical Practice questions.

MP Check Your Work
How can you use the addition facts to check that the differences are correct?
MP Precision
Which unit of measure did you use in your answer? Why?

Newton & Descartes's Math Musicals

Math Musicals offer an engaging connection between math, literature, and music! Newton and Descartes team up in these educational stories and songs to bring mathematics to life!

Math Musicals animation and story

Sheet Music

1

Count and Write Numbers 0 to 5

Vocabulary 2
1.1 Model and Count 1 and 2 3
1.2 Understand and Write 1 and 2 9
1.3 Model and Count 3 and 4 15
1.4 Understand and Write 3 and 4 21
1.5 Model and Count 5 27
1.6 Understand and Write 5 33
1.7 The Concept of Zero 39
1.8 Count and Order Numbers to 5 45
Performance Task: Farm Animals 51
Game: Number Land 52
Chapter Practice 53

2

Compare Numbers 0 to 5

Vocabulary 58
2.1 Equal Groups 59
2.2 Greater Than 65
2.3 Less Than 71
2.4 Compare Groups to 5 by Counting 77
2.5 Compare Numbers to 5 83
Performance Task: Games 89
Game: Toss and Compare 90
Chapter Practice 91

- Major Topic
- Supporting Topic
- Additional Topic

3 Count and Write Numbers 6 to 10

Vocabulary 96

3.1 Model and Count 6 97

3.2 Understand and Write 6 103

3.3 Model and Count 7 109

3.4 Understand and Write 7 115

3.5 Model and Count 8 121

3.6 Understand and Write 8 127

3.7 Model and Count 9 133

3.8 Understand and Write 9 139

3.9 Model and Count 10 145

3.10 Understand and Write 10 151

3.11 Count and Order Numbers to 10 157

Performance Task: Safari Animals 163

Game: Number Land 164

Chapter Practice 165

Think and Grow: Modeling Real Life

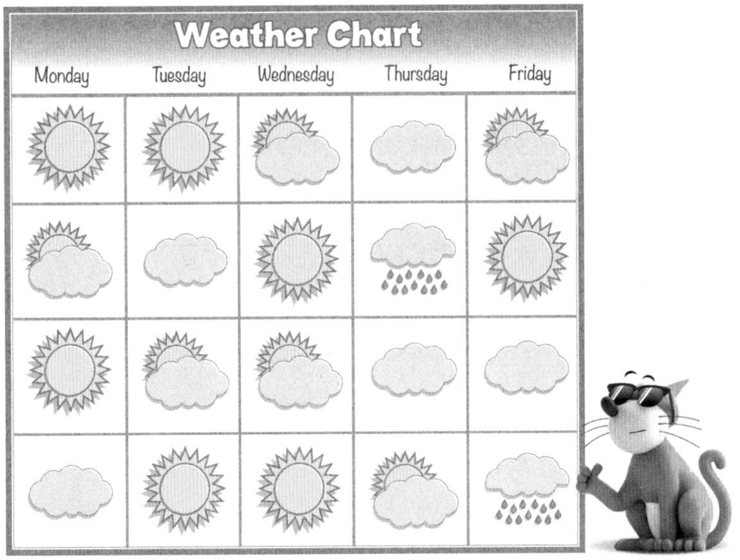

4 Compare Numbers to 10

	Vocabulary	170
■ 4.1	Compare Groups to 10 by Matching	171
■ 4.2	Compare Groups to 10 by Counting	177
■ 4.3	Compare Numbers to 10	183
■ 4.4	Classify Objects into Categories	189
■ 4.5	Classify and Compare by Counting	195
	Performance Task: Toys	201
	Game: Toss and Compare	202
	Chapter Practice	203
	Cumulative Practice	207

5 Compose and Decompose Numbers to 10

	Vocabulary	212
■ 5.1	Partner Numbers to 5	213
■ 5.2	Use Number Bonds to Represent Numbers to 5	219
■ 5.3	Compose and Decompose 6	225
■ 5.4	Compose and Decompose 7	231
■ 5.5	Compose and Decompose 8	237
■ 5.6	Compose and Decompose 9	243
■ 5.7	Compose and Decompose 10	249
■ 5.8	Compose and Decompose Using a Group of 5	255
	Performance Task: Insects	261
	Game: Number Bond Spin and Cover	262
	Chapter Practice	263

■ Major Topic
■ Supporting Topic
■ Additional Topic

6 Add Numbers Within 10

Vocabulary 268
6.1 Understand Addition 269
6.2 Addition: Add To 275
6.3 Addition: Put Together 281
6.4 Addition: Partner Numbers 287
6.5 Addition Number Patterns 293
6.6 Practice Addition 299
6.7 Use a Group of 5 to Add 305
6.8 Add to Make 10 311
Performance Task: Fish 317
Game: Add and Cover 318
Chapter Practice 319

7 Subtract Numbers Within 10

Vocabulary 324
7.1 Understand Subtraction 325
7.2 Subtraction: Take From 331
7.3 Subtraction: Take Apart 337
7.4 Subtraction Number Patterns 343
7.5 Practice Subtraction 349
7.6 Use a Group of 5 to Subtract 355
7.7 Related Facts 361
Performance Task: Bubbles 367
Game: Losing Teeth 368
Chapter Practice 369
Cumulative Practice 373

Let's learn how to subtract numbers within 10!

8 Represent Numbers 11 to 19

Vocabulary 378
8.1 Identify Groups of 10 379
8.2 Count and Write 11 and 12 385
8.3 Understand 11 and 12 391
8.4 Count and Write 13 and 14 397
8.5 Understand 13 and 14 403
8.6 Count and Write 15 409
8.7 Understand 15 415
8.8 Count and Write 16 and 17 421
8.9 Understand 16 and 17 427
8.10 Count and Write 18 and 19 433
8.11 Understand 18 and 19 439
Performance Task: Stars 445
Game: Number Flip and Find 446
Chapter Practice 447

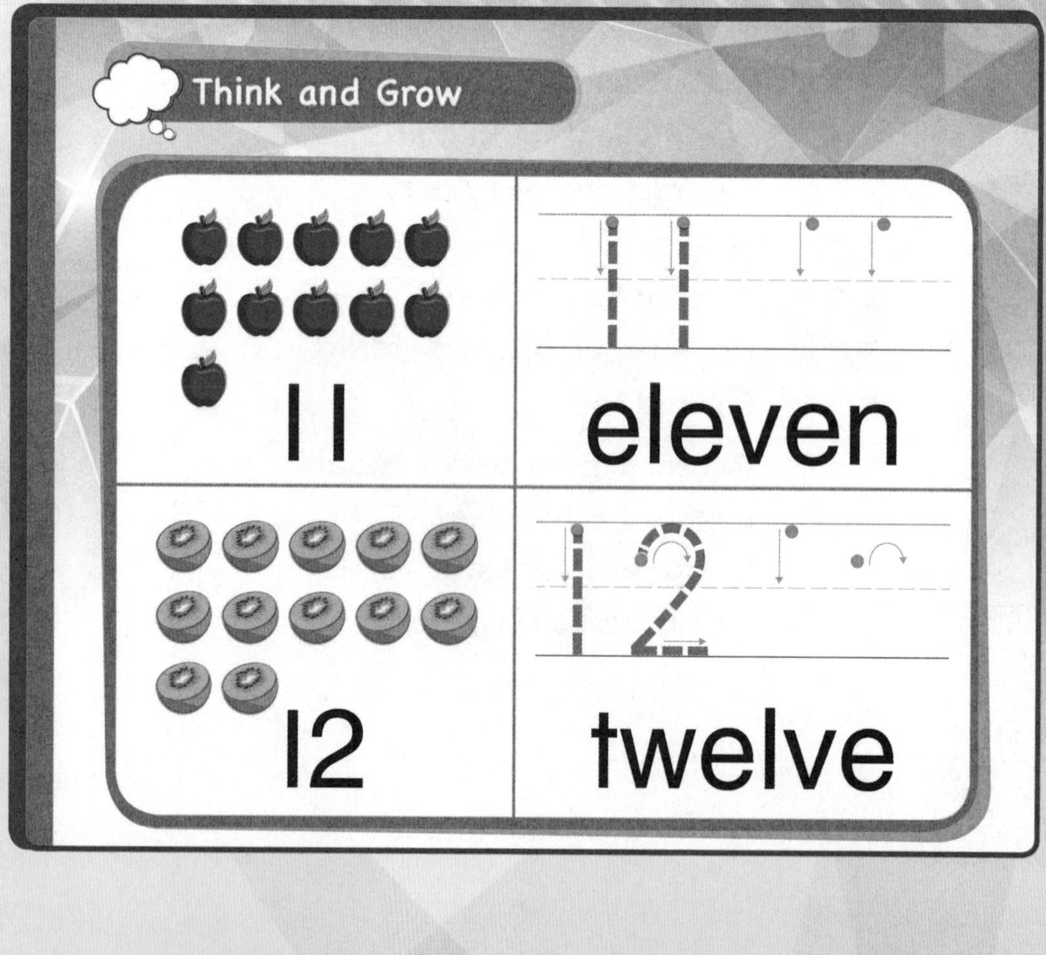

9 Count and Compare Numbers to 20

Vocabulary 454
9.1 Model and Count 20 455
9.2 Count and Write 20 461
9.3 Count to Find How Many 467
9.4 Count Forward from Any Number to 20 473
9.5 Order Numbers to 20 479
9.6 Compare Numbers to 20 485
Performance Task: Fruit 491
Game: Number Boss 492
Chapter Practice 493

10 Count to 100

Vocabulary 498
10.1 Count to 30 by Ones 499
10.2 Count to 50 by Ones 505
10.3 Count to 100 by Ones 511
10.4 Count to 100 by Tens 517
10.5 Count by Tens and Ones 523
10.6 Count by Tens from a Number 529
Performance Task: Party Supplies 535
Game: Hundred Chart Puzzle 536
Chapter Practice 537
Cumulative Practice 541

11 Identify Two-Dimensional Shapes

		Vocabulary	546
■	11.1	Describe Two-Dimensional Shapes	547
■	11.2	Triangles	553
■	11.3	Rectangles	559
■	11.4	Squares	565
■	11.5	Hexagons and Circles	571
■	11.6	Join Two-Dimensional Shapes	577
■	11.7	Build Two-Dimensional Shapes	583
		Performance Task: Pets	589
		Game: Shape Flip and Find	590
		Chapter Practice	591

12 Identify Three-Dimensional Shapes and Positions

		Vocabulary	596
■	12.1	Two- and Three-Dimensional Shapes	597
■	12.2	Describe Three-Dimensional Shapes	603
■	12.3	Cubes and Spheres	609
■	12.4	Cones and Cylinders	615
■	12.5	Build Three-Dimensional Shapes	621
■	12.6	Positions of Solid Shapes	627
		Performance Task: Recycling	633
		Game: Solid Shapes: Spin and Cover	634
		Chapter Practice	635

■ Major Topic
■ Supporting Topic
■ Additional Topic

13 Measure and Compare Objects

Vocabulary 640
13.1 Compare Heights 641
13.2 Compare Lengths 647
13.3 Use Numbers to Compare Lengths 653
13.4 Compare Weights 659
13.5 Use Numbers to Compare Weights 665
13.6 Compare Capacities 671
13.7 Describe Objects by Attributes 677
Performance Task: Rainwater 683
Game: Measurement Boss 684
Chapter Practice 685
Cumulative Practice 689

Glossary A1
Index A15

Think and Grow

1 Count and Write Numbers 0 to 5

- What kinds of animals live on a farm?
- How many legs does each animal have?

Chapter Learning Target:
Understand counting.

Chapter Success Criteria:
- I can identify numbers.
- I can name numbers.
- I can order numbers.
- I can write numbers.

Name ____________________

I

Vocabulary

Review Word
color

Directions: Trace and color the ducks.

Chapter 1 Vocabulary Cards

count	five
five frame	four
number	one
order	three

5

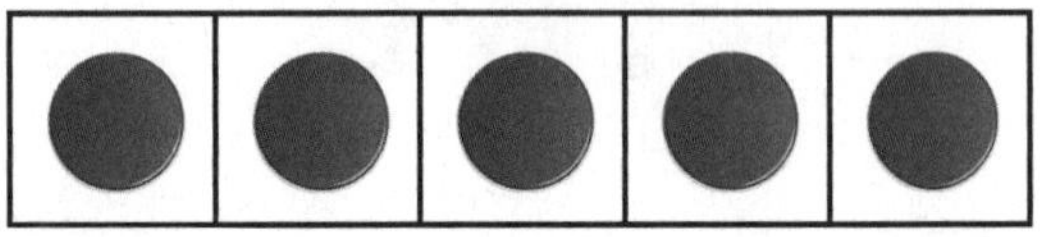

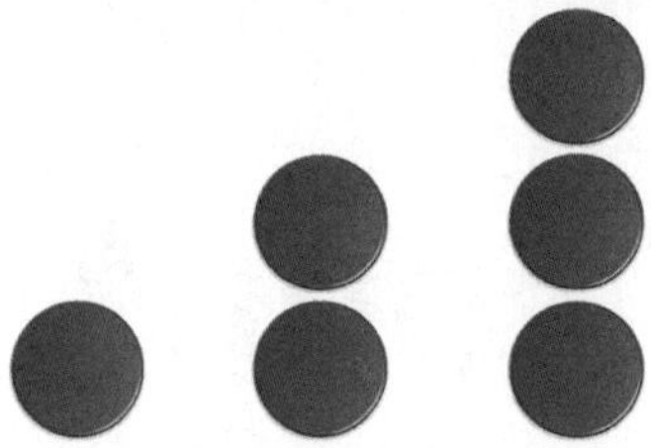

1 2 3

4

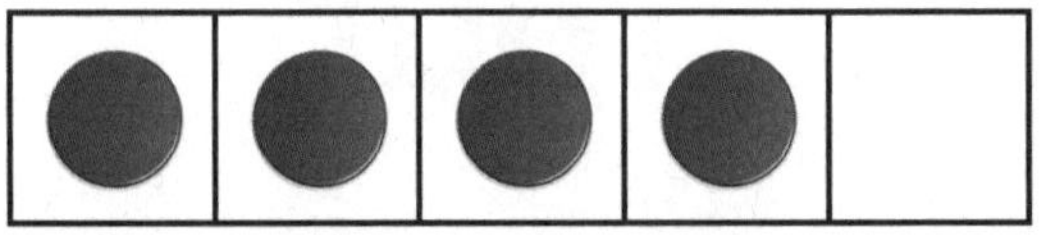

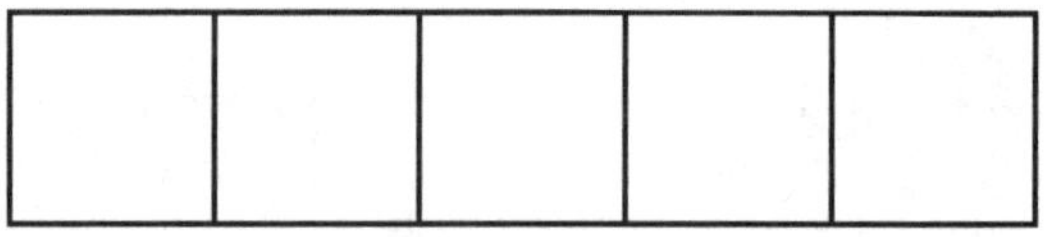

1

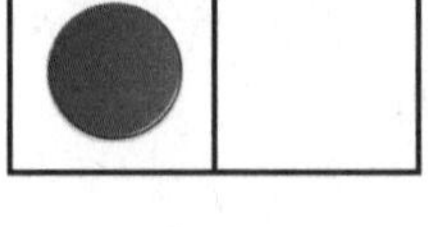

1 2 3 4 5

3

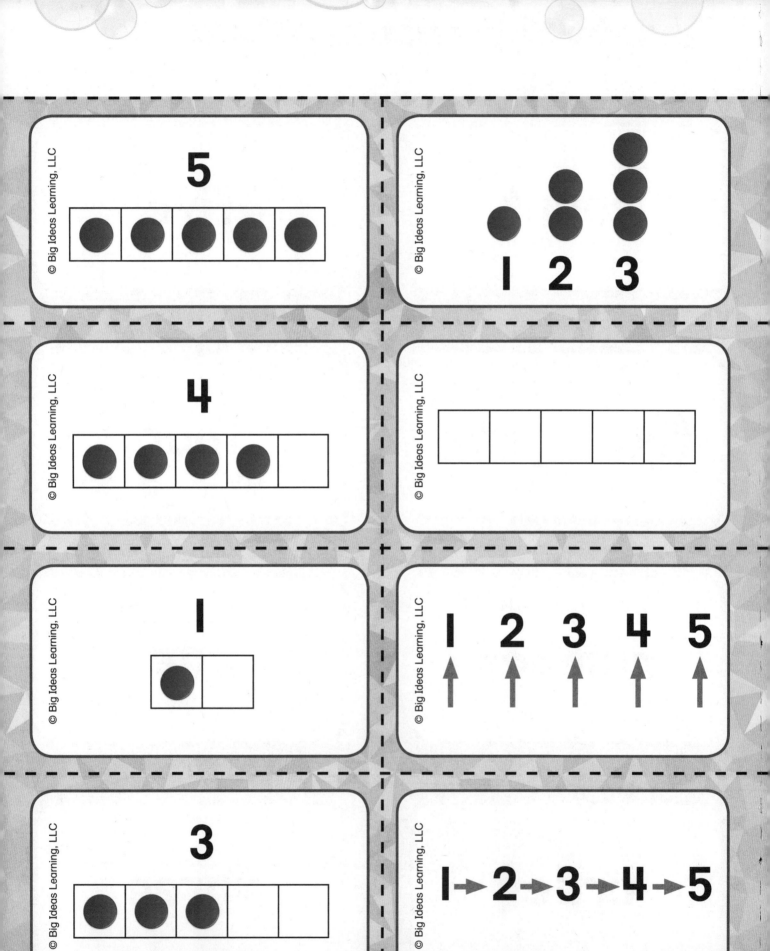

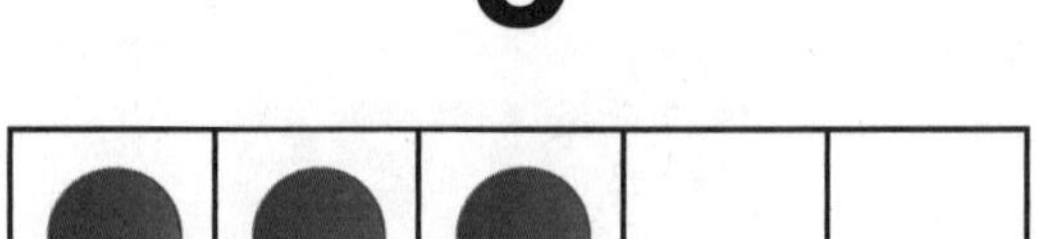

1 → 2 → 3 → 4 → 5

Chapter 1 Vocabulary Cards

two

zero

0

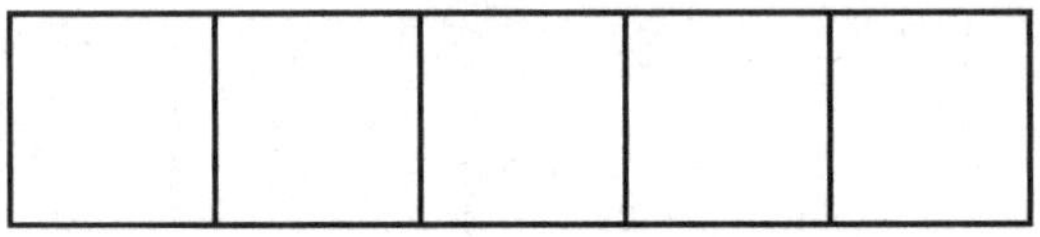

2

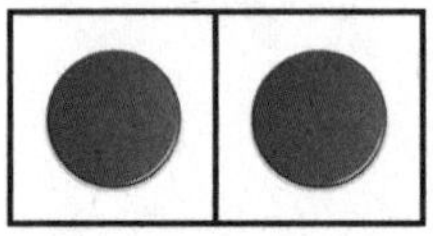

© Big Ideas Learning, LLC

© Big Ideas Learning, LLC

© Big Ideas Learning, LLC

© Big Ideas Learning, LLC

© Big Ideas Learning, LLC

© Big Ideas Learning, LLC

Name ____________________

Model and Count 1 and 2

Learning Target: Show and count the numbers 1 and 2.

Explore and Grow

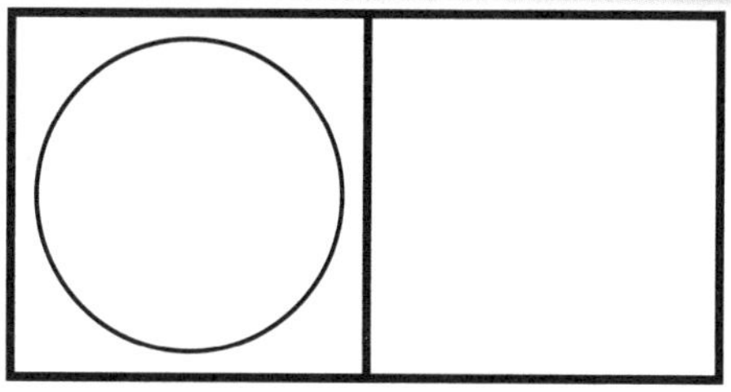

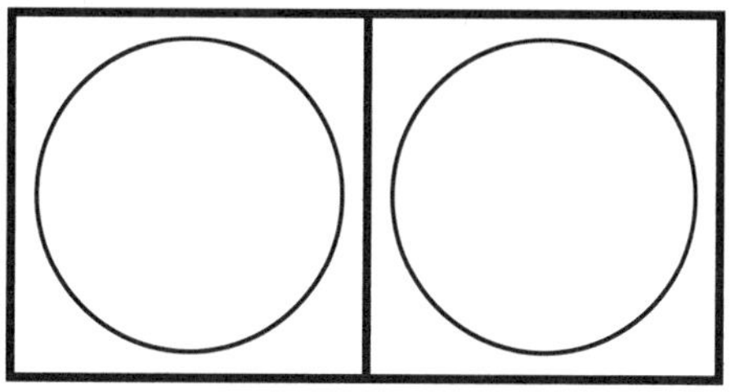

Directions:

- Place 1 counter on the blue sky. Decide which frame shows 1. Slide the counter to the frame.
- Place 2 counters on the green grass. Decide which frame shows 2. Slide the counters to the frame.

Think and Grow

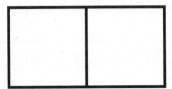

Directions: Count the objects. Color the boxes to show how many.

Name ______________________________

Apply and Grow: Practice

1

2

3

4

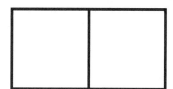

Directions: 1–4 Count the objects. Color the boxes to show how many.

Think and Grow: Modeling Real Life

Directions: Count the objects in the picture. Color the boxes to show how many.

Name ______________________

Practice 1.1

Learning Target: Show and count the numbers 1 and 2.

Directions: Count the pinecones. Color the boxes to show how many.

1

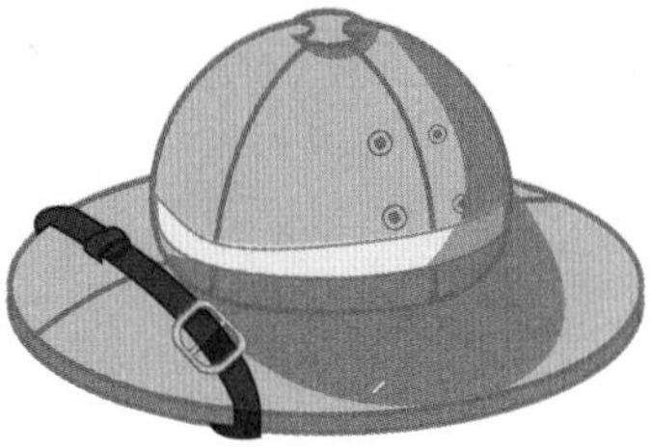

2

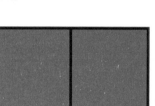

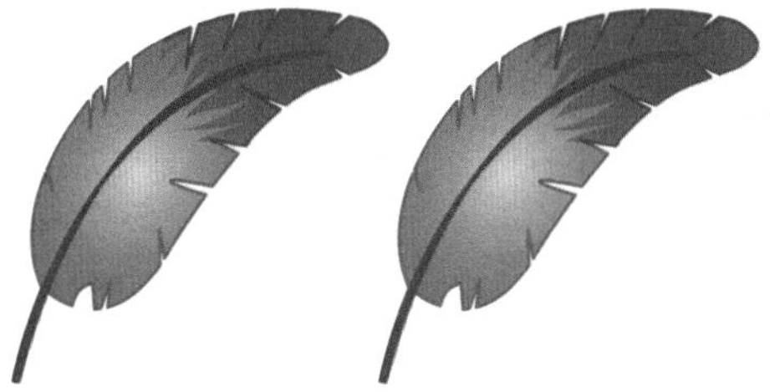

Directions: 1 and 2 Count the objects. Color the boxes to show how many.

3

4

5

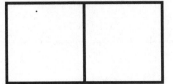

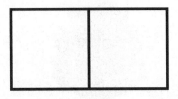

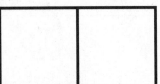

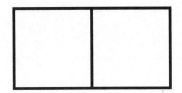

Directions: 3 and 4 Count the objects. Color the boxes to show how many.
5 Count the objects in the picture. Color the boxes to show how many.

Name ______________________________

Understand and Write 1 and 2

1.2

Learning Target: Understand and write the numbers 1 and 2.

Explore and Grow

Directions: Use counters to show how many dogs and how many fish are in the story *My Pets*. Write how many dogs and how many fish are in the story.

Think and Grow

1	1	one

2	2	two

Directions: Count the objects. Say the number. Trace and write the number.

Name ______________________________

Apply and Grow: Practice

1

2

3

4

5

6

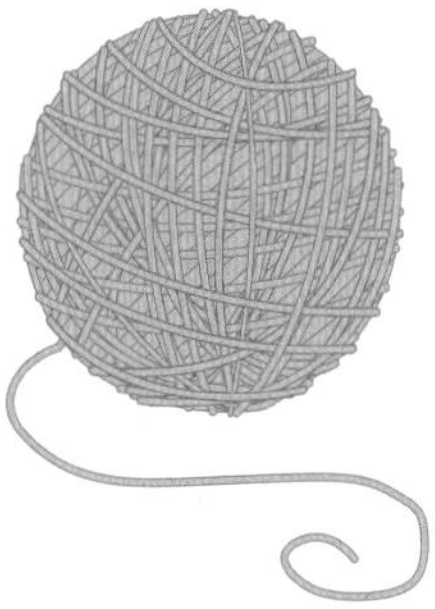

7

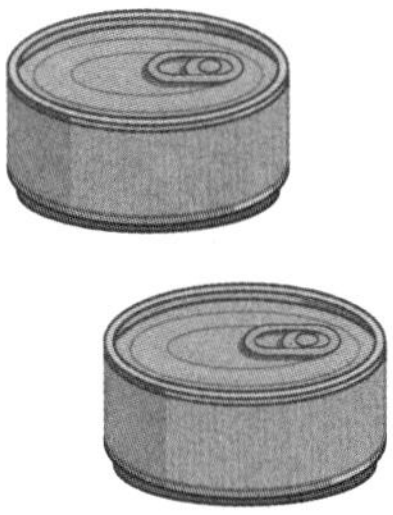

8

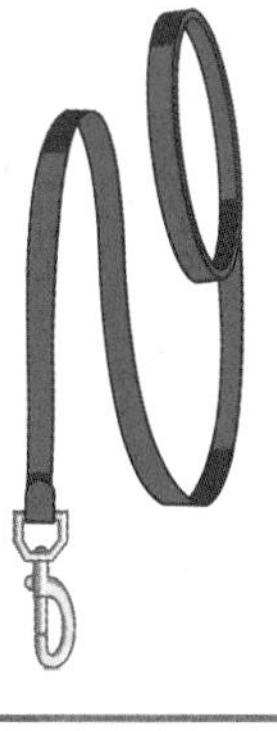

Directions: 1–8 Count the objects. Say the number. Write the number.

Think and Grow: Modeling Real Life

Directions: Count the objects in the picture. Say the number. Write the number.

Name ____________________

Practice 1.2

Learning Target: Understand and write the numbers 1 and 2.

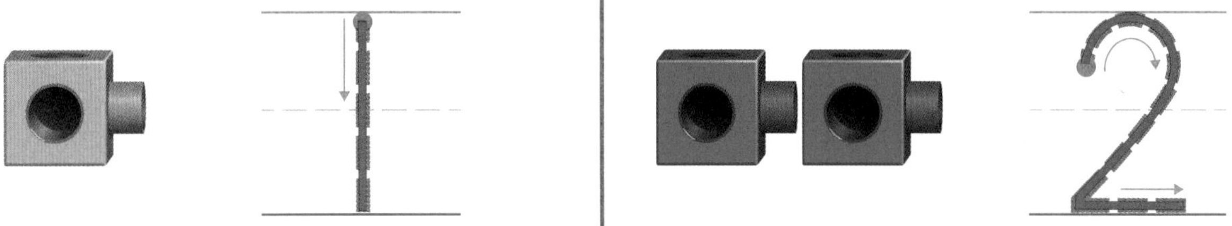

Directions: Count the linking cubes. Say the number. Write the number.

1

2

3

4

Directions: 1–4 Count the objects. Say the number. Write the number.

5

6

7

8

9

Directions: 5 – 8 Count the objects. Say the number. Write the number.
9 Count the objects in the picture. Say the number. Write the number.

Name ______________________

1.3 Model and Count 3 and 4

Learning Target: Show and count the numbers 3 and 4.

Explore and Grow

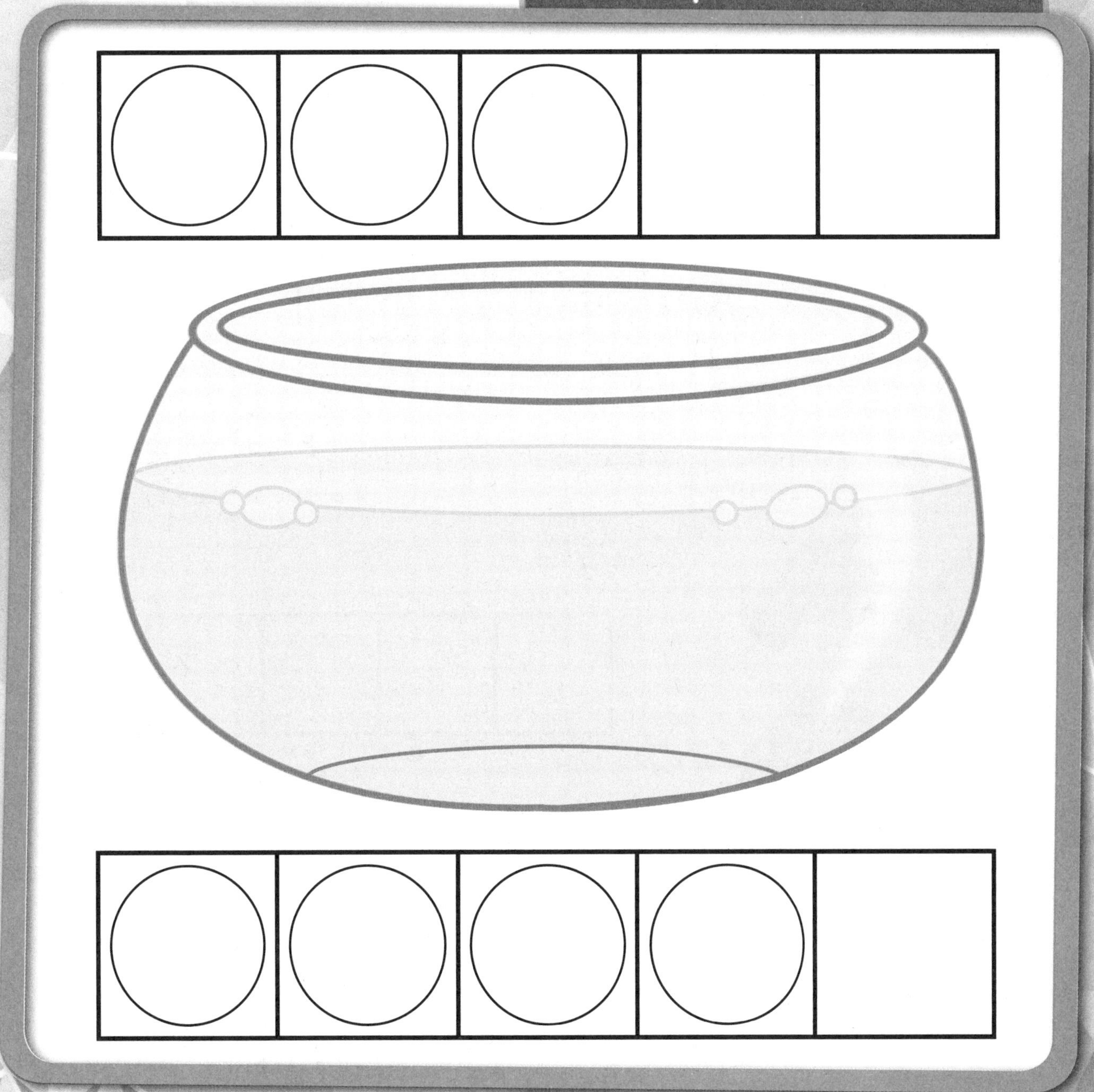

Directions:

- Place 4 counters on top of the water. Decide which frame shows 4. Slide the counters to the frame.
- Place 3 counters at the bottom of the bowl. Decide which frame shows 3. Slide the counters to the frame.

Think and Grow

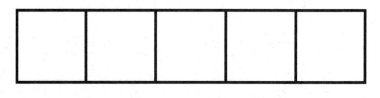

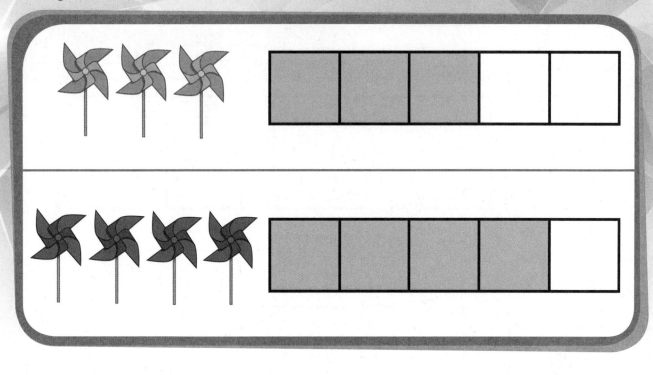

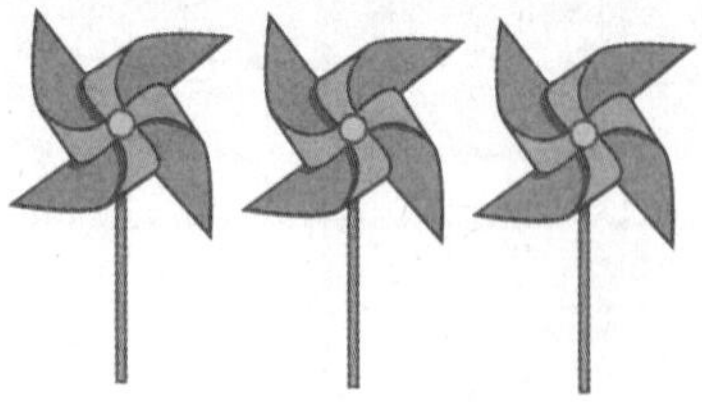

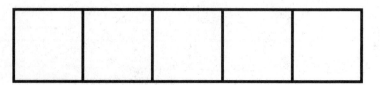

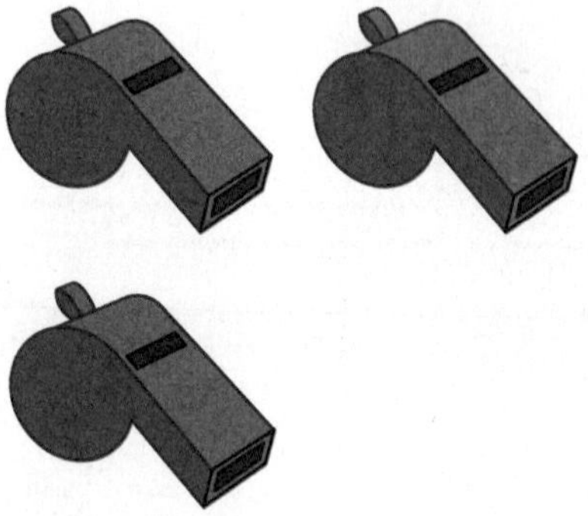

Directions: Count the objects. Color the boxes to show how many.

Name ______________________________

Apply and Grow: Practice

1

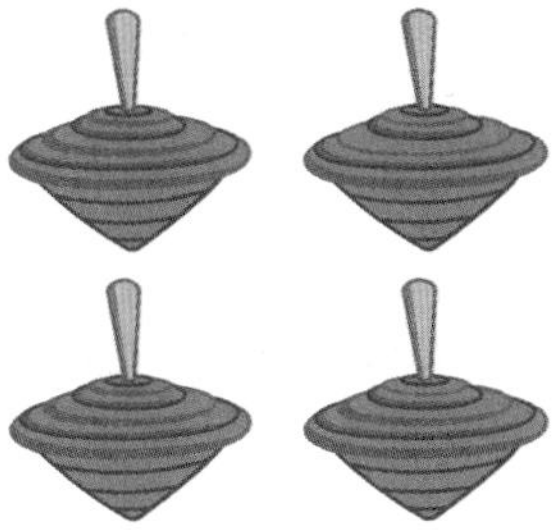

2

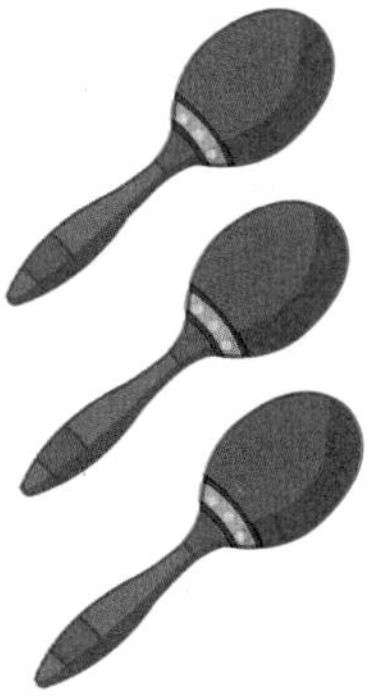

3

4

Directions: 1–4 Count the objects. Color the boxes to show how many.

Think and Grow: Modeling Real Life

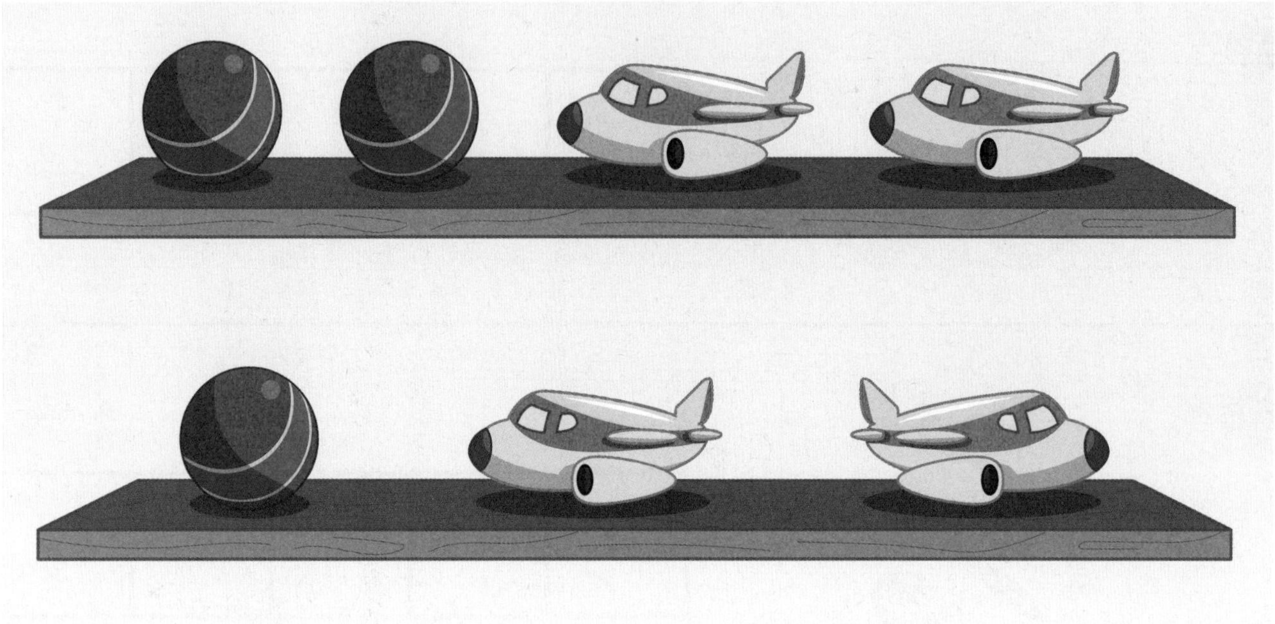

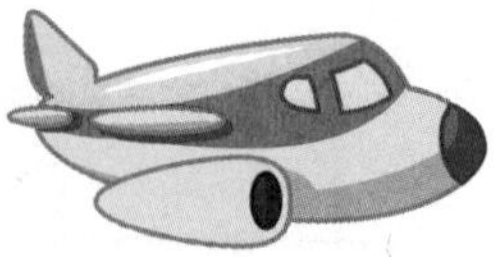

Directions: Count the objects in the picture. Color the boxes to show how many.

Name ________________________________

Learning Target: Show and count the numbers 3 and 4.

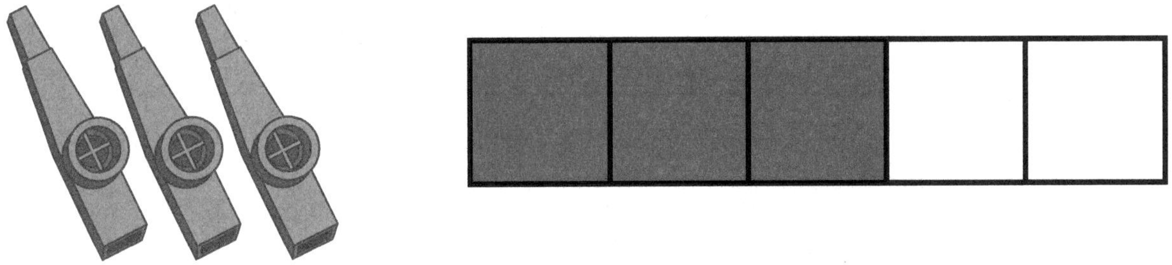

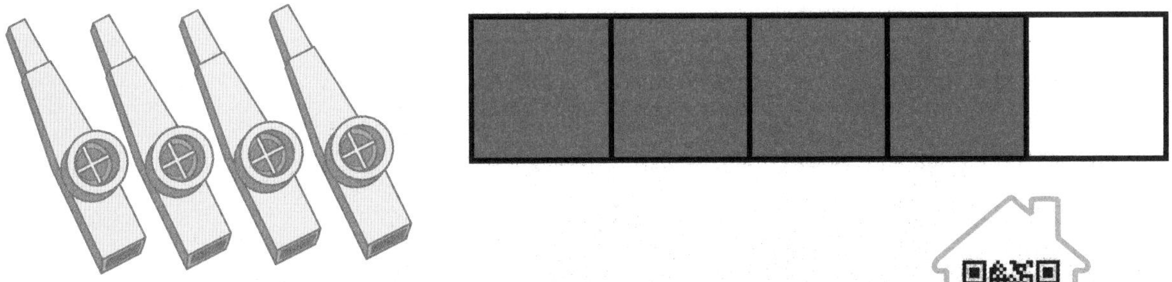

Directions: Count the kazoos. Color the boxes to show how many.

1

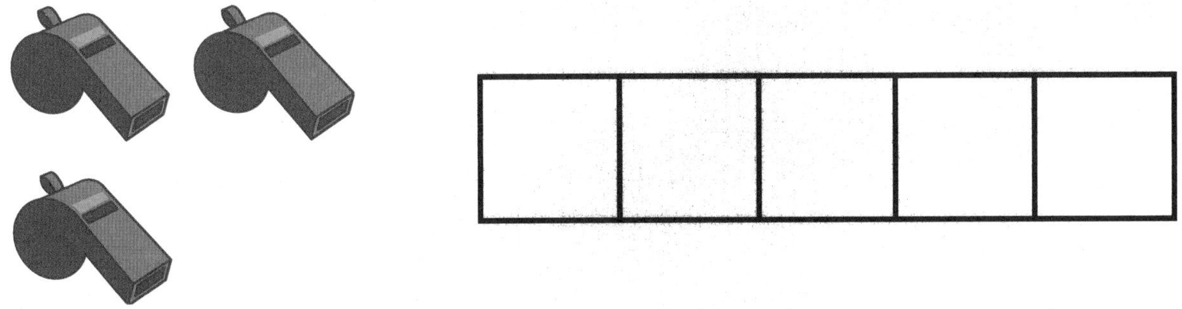

2

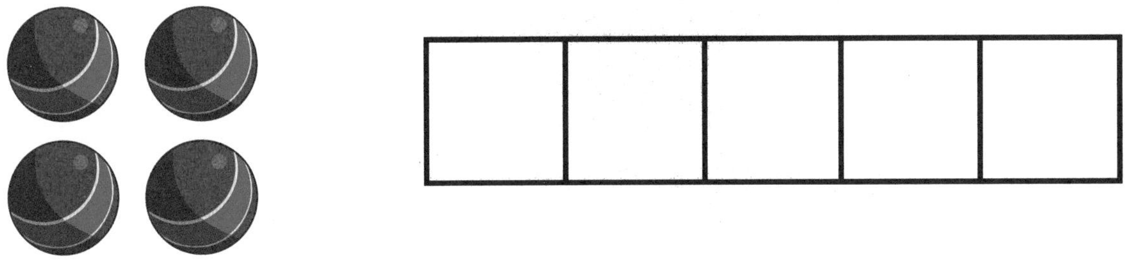

Directions: 1 and 2 Count the objects. Color the boxes to show how many.

3

4

5

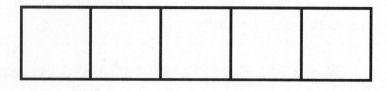

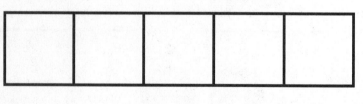

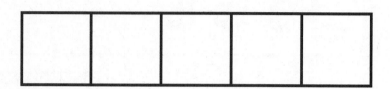

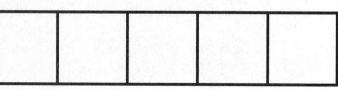

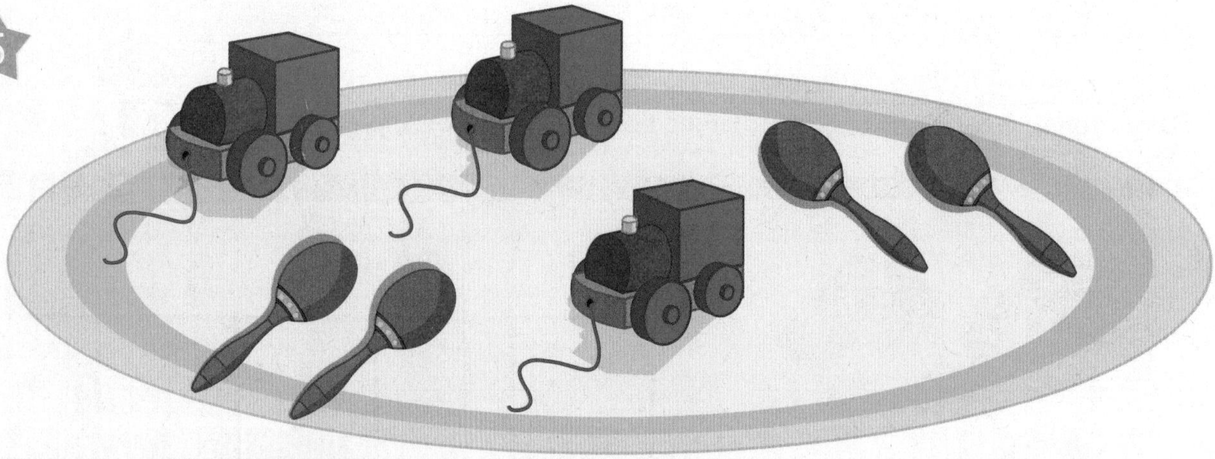

Directions: 3 and 4 Count the objects. Color the boxes to show how many.
5 Count the objects in the picture. Color the boxes to show how many.

Name ___________________________

Learning Target: Understand and write the numbers 3 and 4.

Explore and Grow

Directions: Use counters to show how many trees and how many birds are in the story *We Go Camping*. Write how many trees and how many birds are in the story.

Think and Grow

	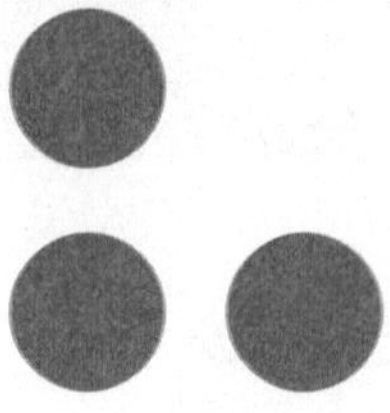	3
3	3	three

3 3

	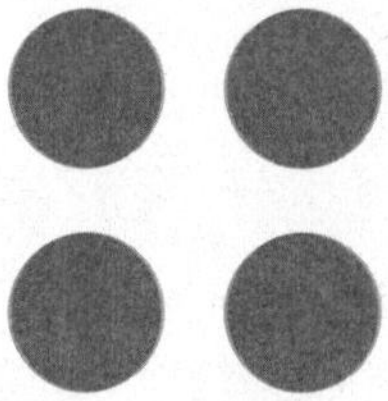	4
4	4	four

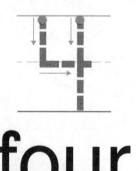

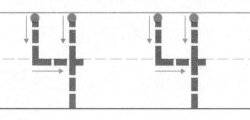

4 4

Directions: Count the objects. Say the number. Trace and write the number.

Name ____________________

Apply and Grow: Practice

1

2

3

4

5

6

Directions: 1–6 Count the objects. Say the number. Write the number.

Think and Grow: Modeling Real Life

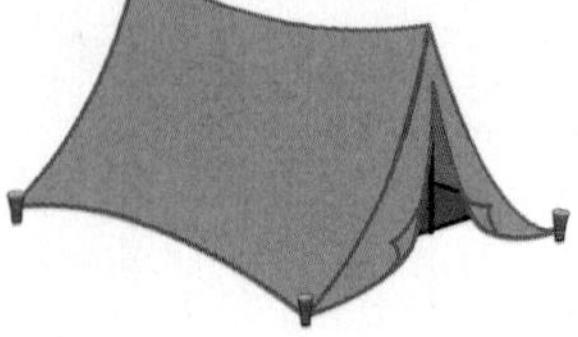

Directions: Count the objects in the picture. Say the number. Write the number.

Name ______________________

Practice 1.4

Learning Target: Understand and write the numbers 3 and 4.

three

3

four

4

Directions: Count the linking cubes. Say the number. Write the number.

1

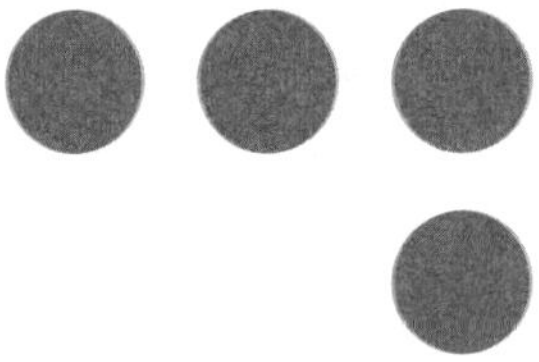

2

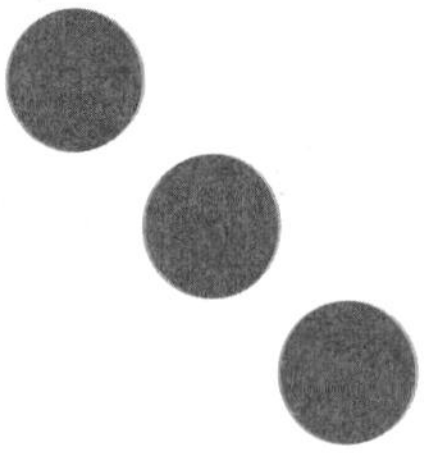

3

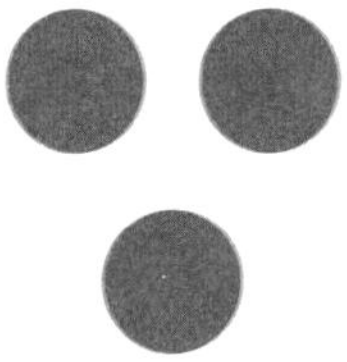

4

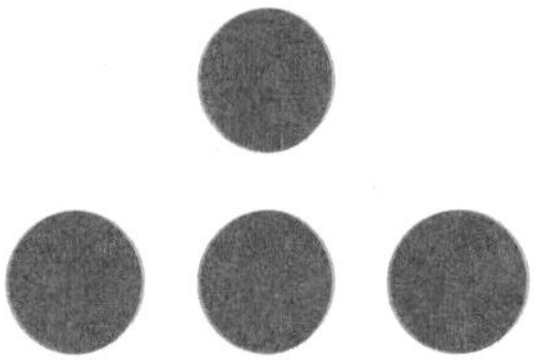

Directions: 1–4 Count the dots. Say the number. Write the number.

5

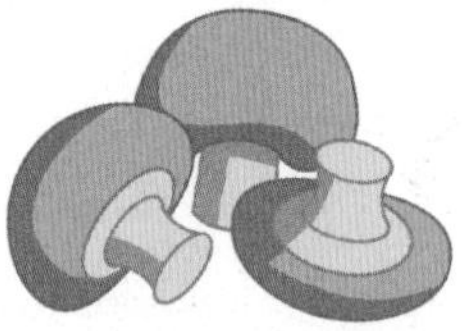

6

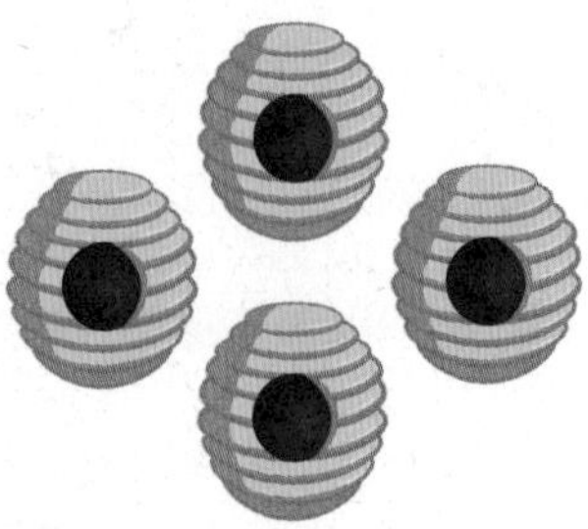

7

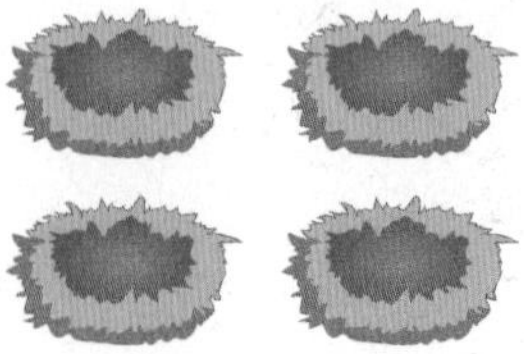

8

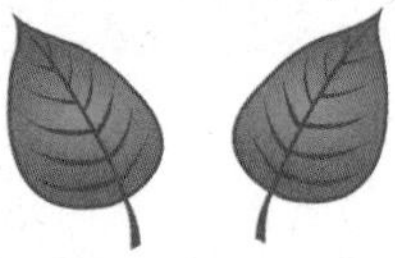

9

Directions: 5 – 8 Count the objects. Say the number. Write the number.
9 Count the objects in the picture. Say the number. Write the number.

Name ______________________________

Model and Count 5

1.5

Learning Target: Show and count the number 5.

Explore and Grow

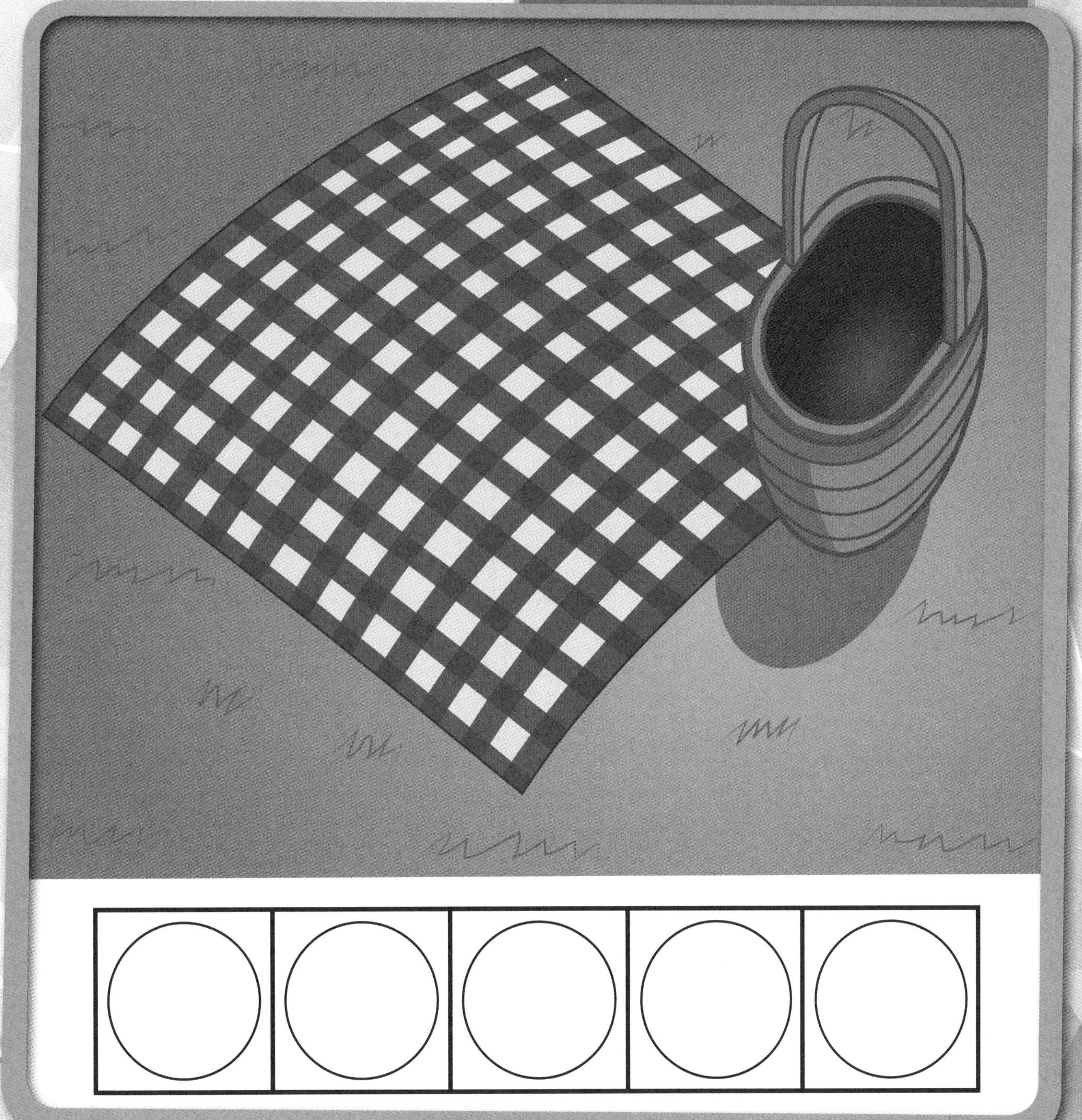

Directions: Place 5 counters on the blanket. Slide the counters to the frame.

Think and Grow

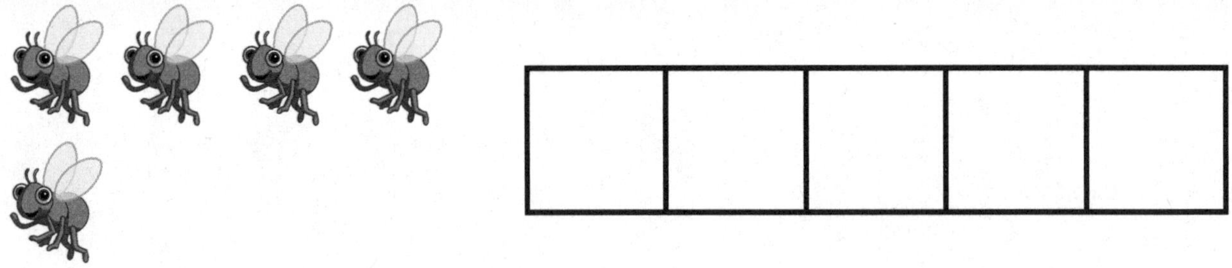

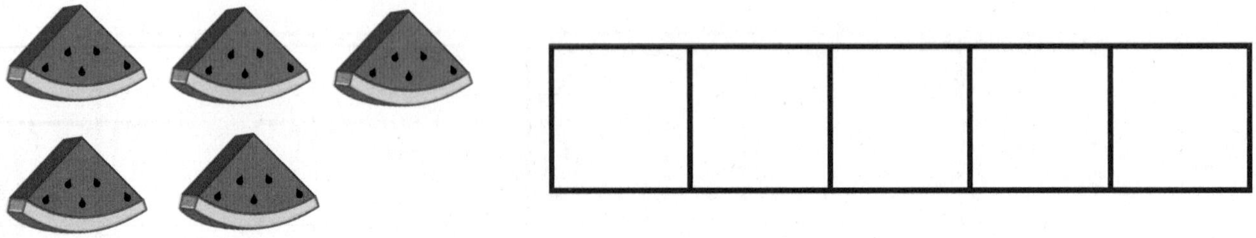

Directions: Count the objects. Color the boxes to show how many.

Name ______________________________

Apply and Grow: Practice

1

2

3

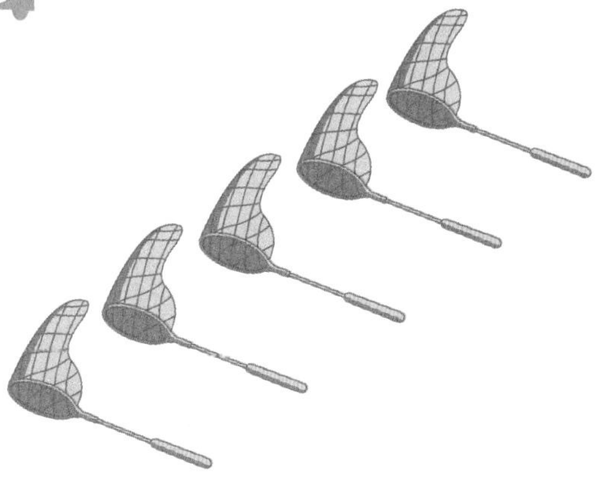

Directions: 1–3 Count the objects. Color the boxes to show how many.

Think and Grow: Modeling Real Life

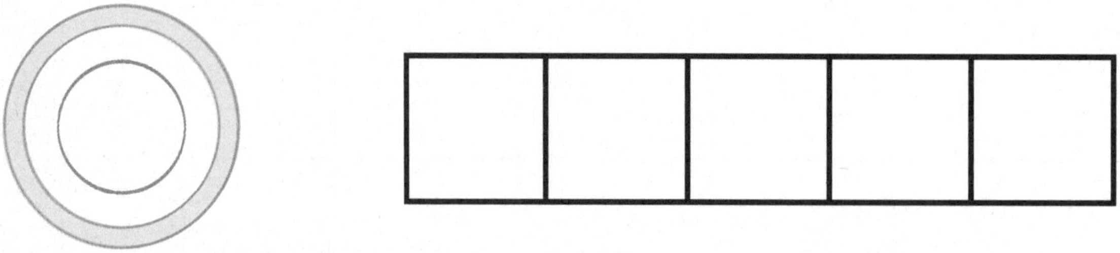

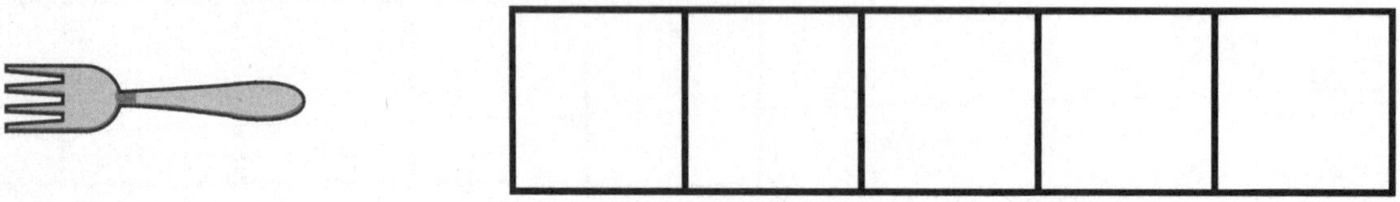

Directions: Count the objects in the picture. Color the boxes to show how many.

Name ______________________________

Practice **1.5**

Learning Target: Show and count the number 5.

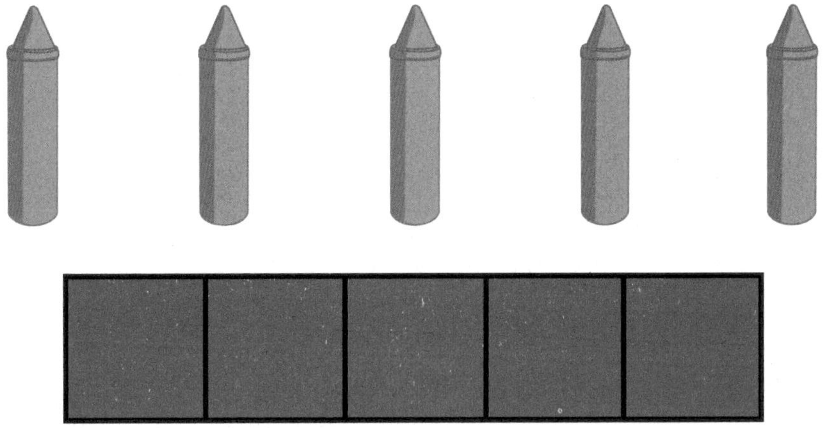

Directions: Count the pieces of chalk. Color the boxes to show how many.

1

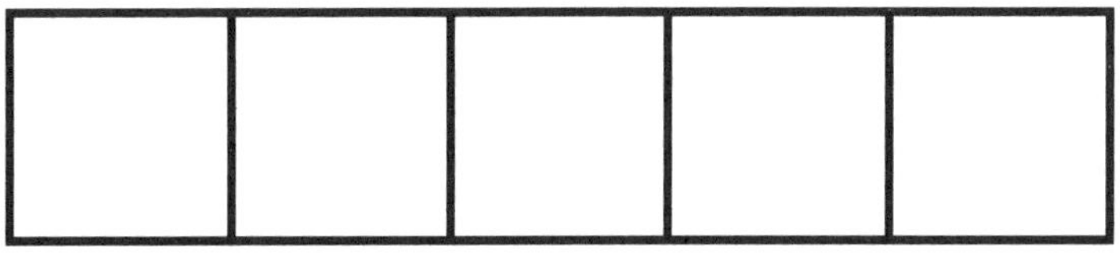

2

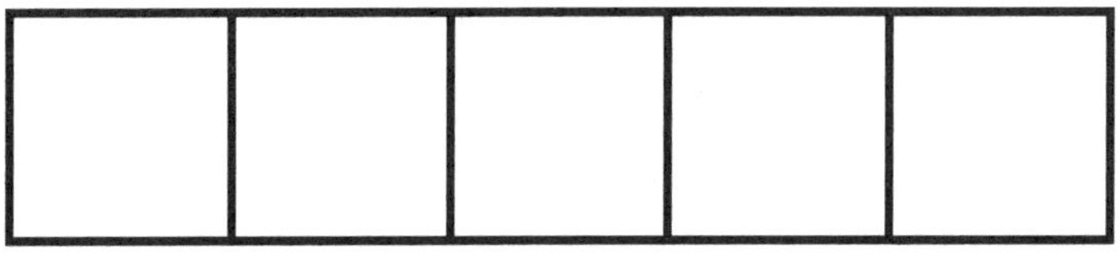

Directions: 1 and 2 Count the objects. Color the boxes to show how many.

3

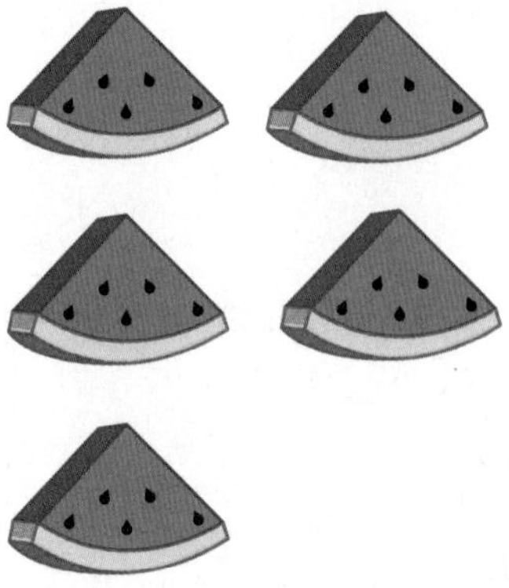

4

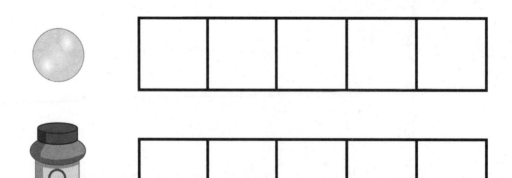

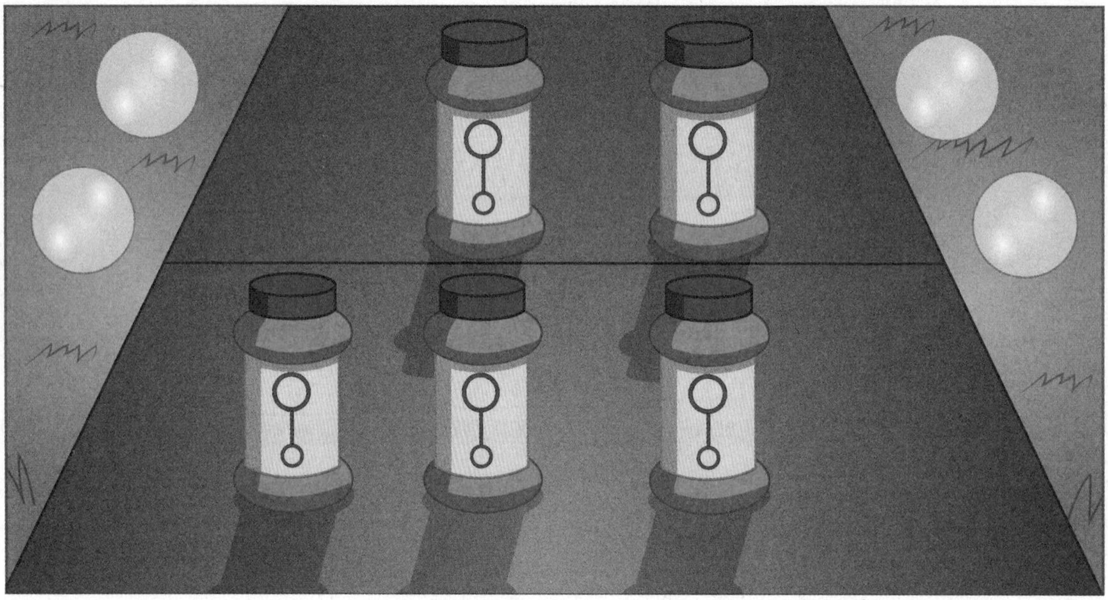

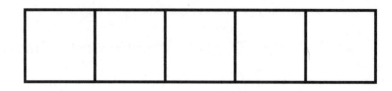

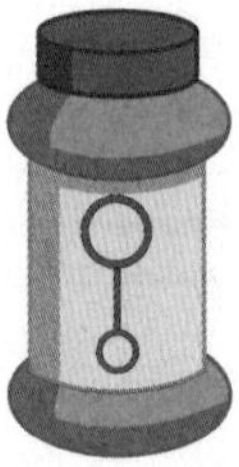

Directions: 3 Count the watermelon slices. Color the boxes to show how many.
4 Count the objects in the picture. Color the boxes to show how many.

Name ______________________________

Understand and Write 5 1.6

Learning Target: Understand and write the number 5.

Explore and Grow

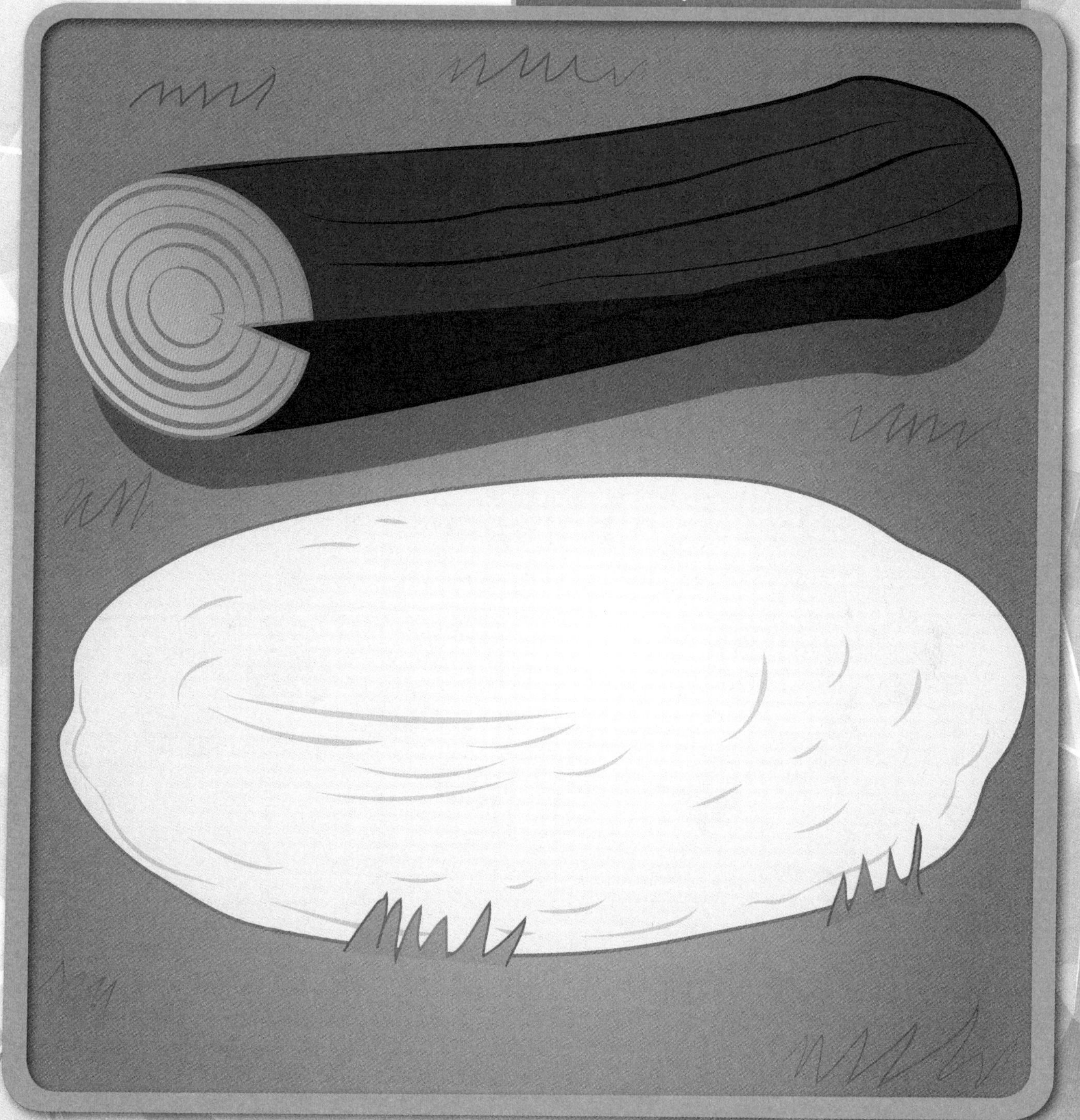

Directions: Use counters to show how many turtles are in the story *At the Pond*. Write how many turtles are in the story.

Think and Grow

	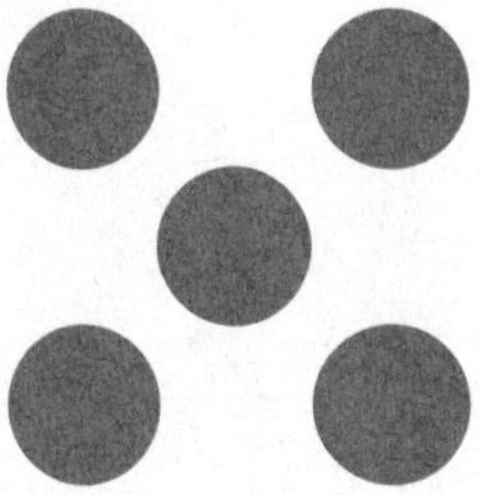	
5	5	five

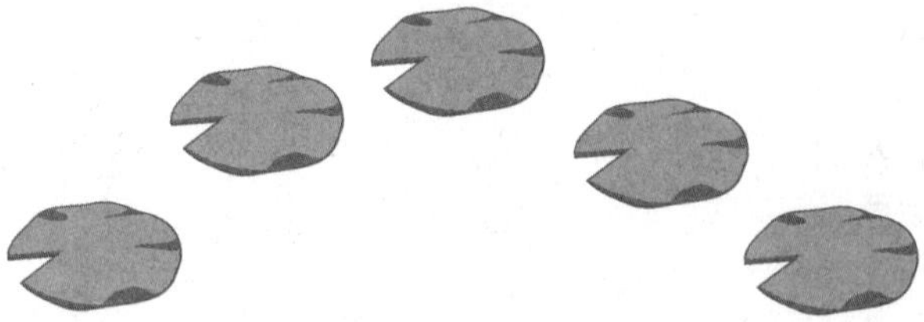

Directions:

- Count the objects. Say the number. Trace and write the number.
- Count the objects. Say the number. Write the number.

Name ______________________________

Apply and Grow: Practice

1

2

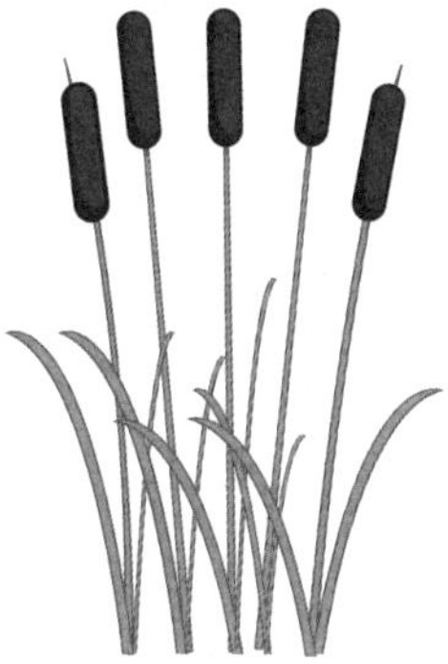

3

4

Directions: 1–4 Count the objects. Say the number. Write the number.

Think and Grow: Modeling Real Life

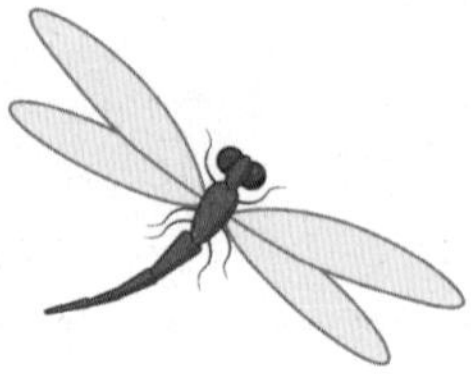

Directions: Count the objects in the picture. Say the number. Write the number.

Name ______________________

Practice 1.6

Learning Target: Understand and write the number 5.

five

5

Directions: Count the linking cubes. Say the number. Write the number.

1

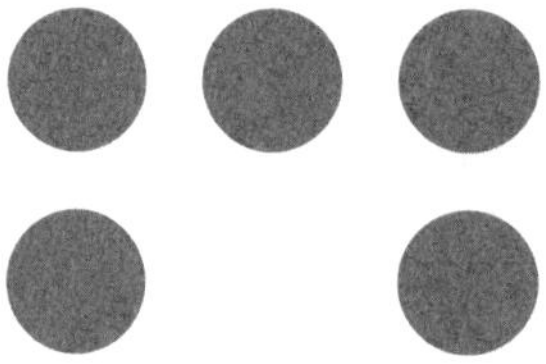

2

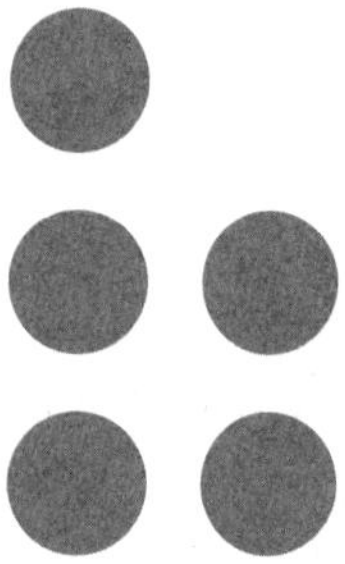

3

4

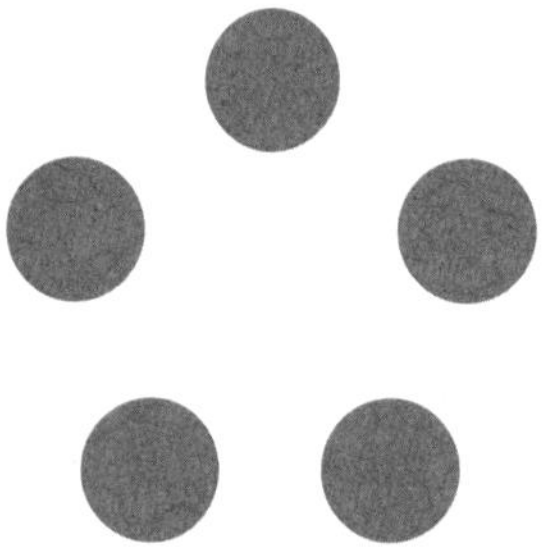

Directions: 1–4 Count the dots. Say the number. Write the number.

5

6

7

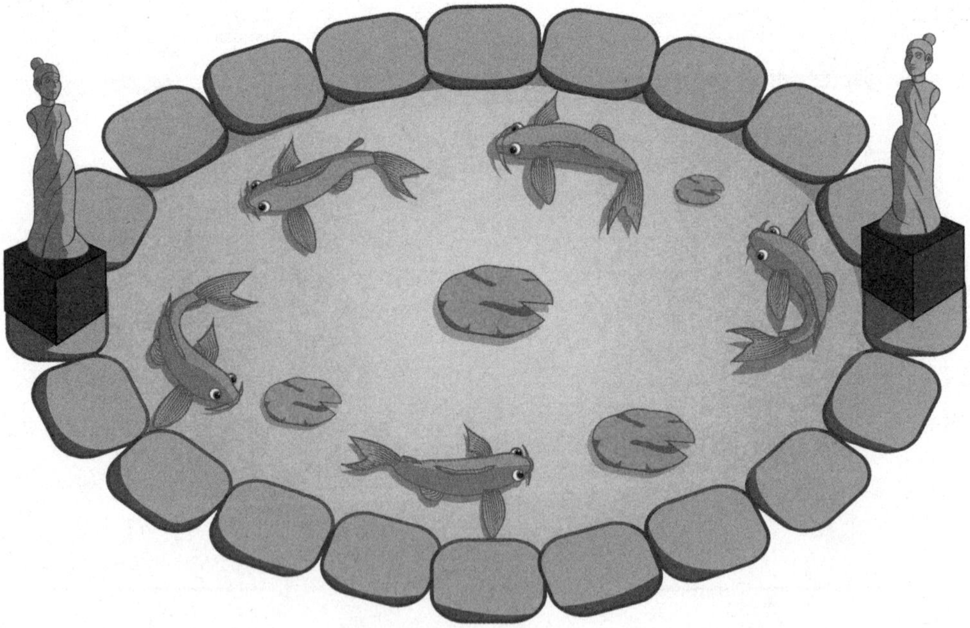

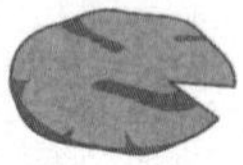

Directions: 5 and 6 Count the objects. Say the number. Write the number.
7 Count the objects in the picture. Say the number. Write the number.

Name ________________________________

The Concept of Zero 1.7

Learning Target: Understand, name, and write the number 0.

Explore and Grow

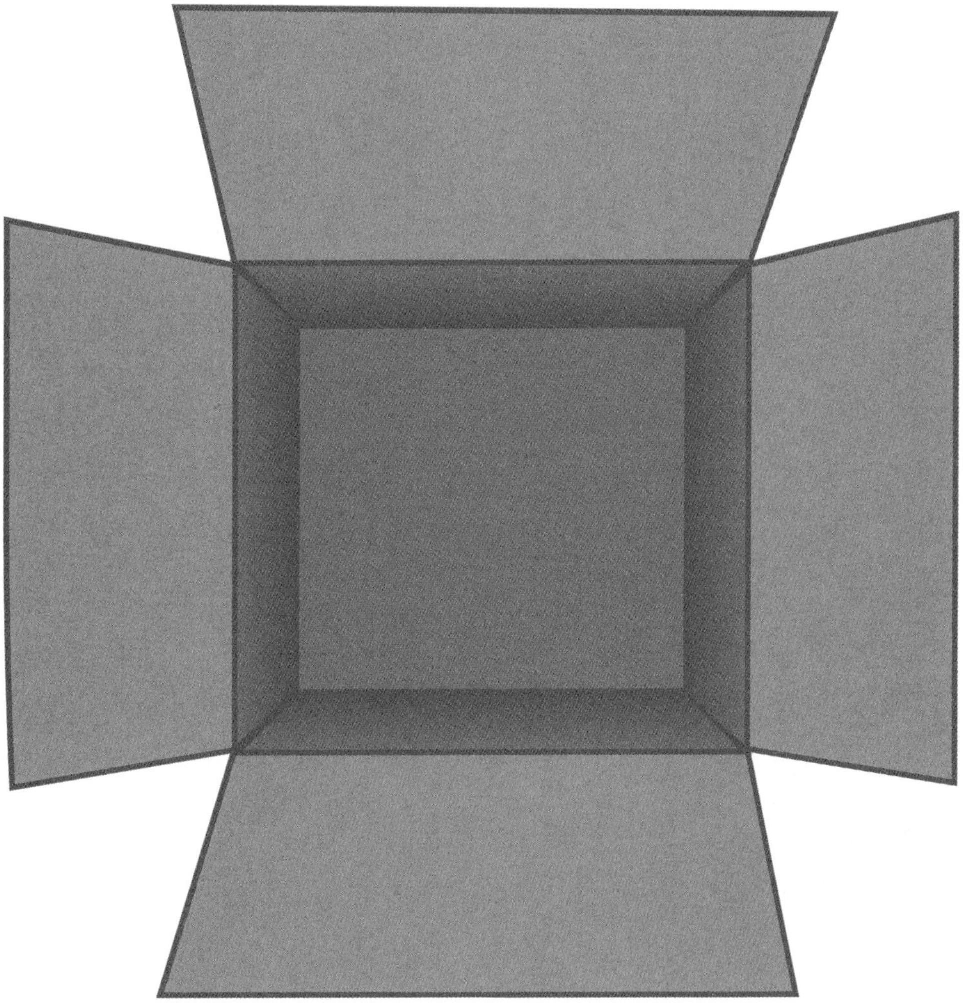

Directions: The box is empty. Show the number of toys in the box. Write the number on a box flap.

Think and Grow

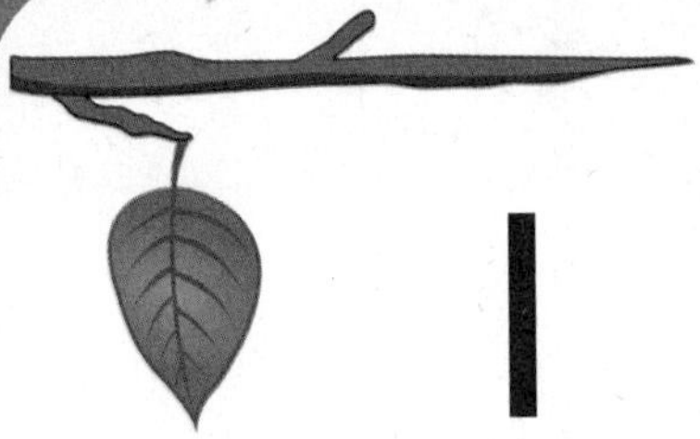

1

0

0

zero

0 0

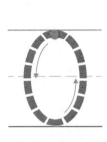

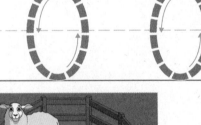

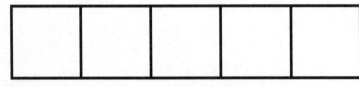

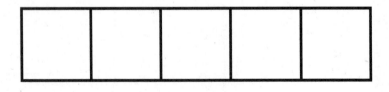

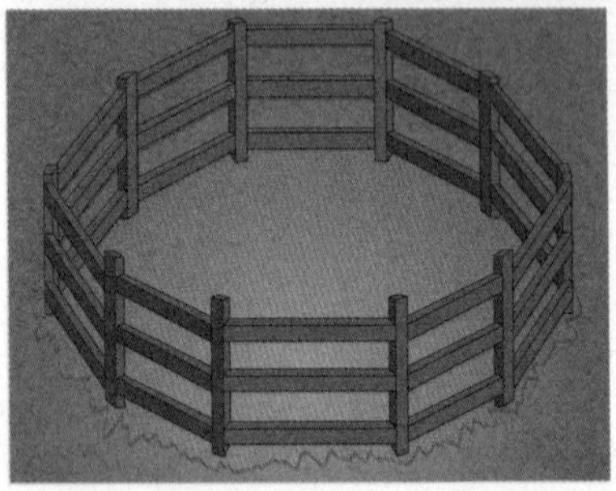

Directions:

- Count the leaves on the bottom branch. Say the number. Trace and write the number.
- Count the sheep in each pen. Color the boxes to show how many.

Name ____________________

Apply and Grow: Practice

1

2

3

4

Directions: 1–4 Count the fireflies. Say the number. Write the number.

Think and Grow: Modeling Real Life

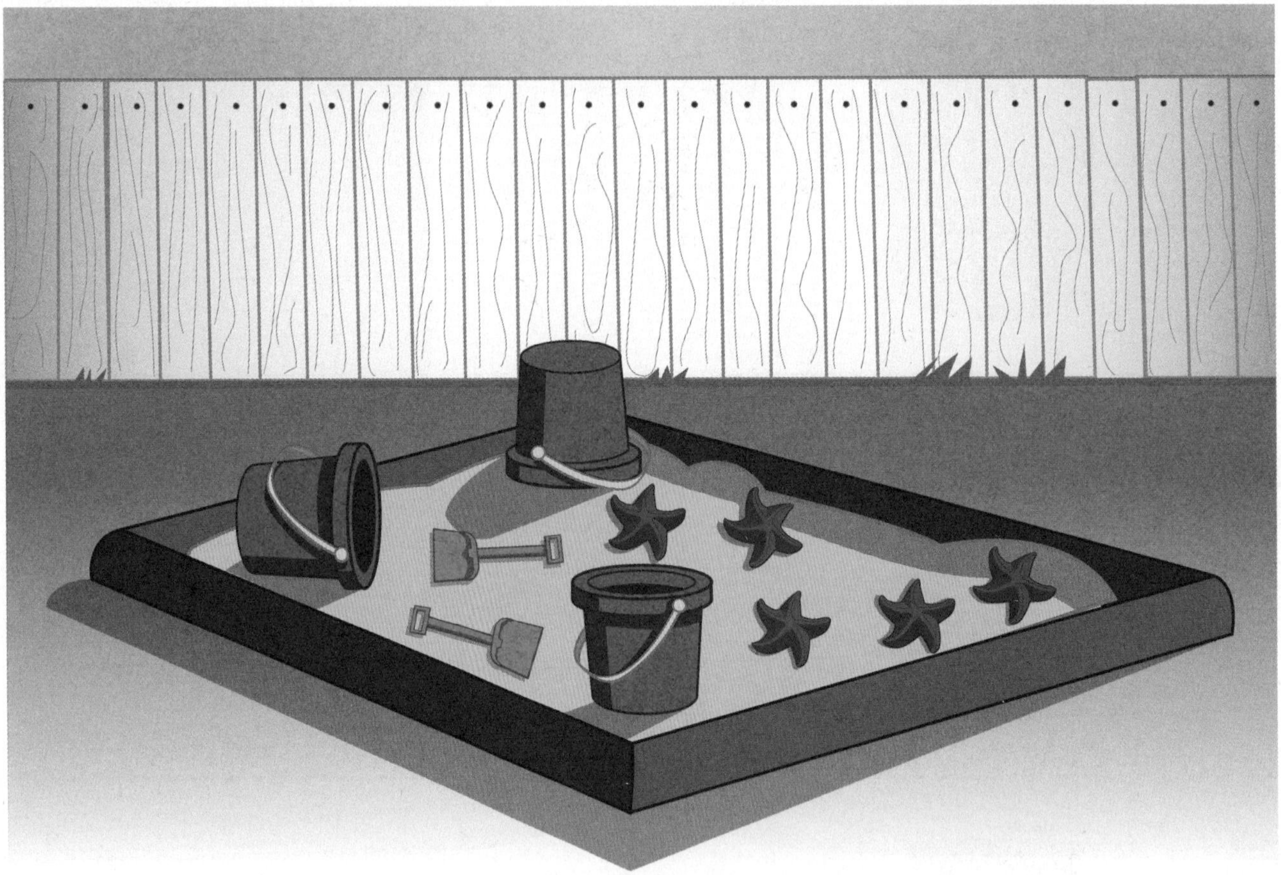

Directions: Count the objects in the picture. Say the number. Write the number.

Name ______________________________

Practice 1.7

Learning Target: Understand, name, and write the number 0.

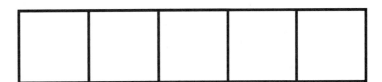

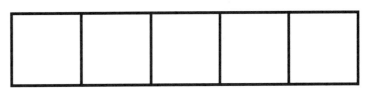

zero

0

Directions: Count the flowers. Say the number. Write the number. Color the boxes to show how many.

1

2

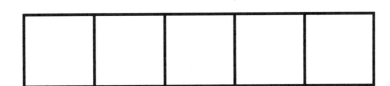

Directions: 1 and 2 Count the flowers. Color the boxes to show how many.

3

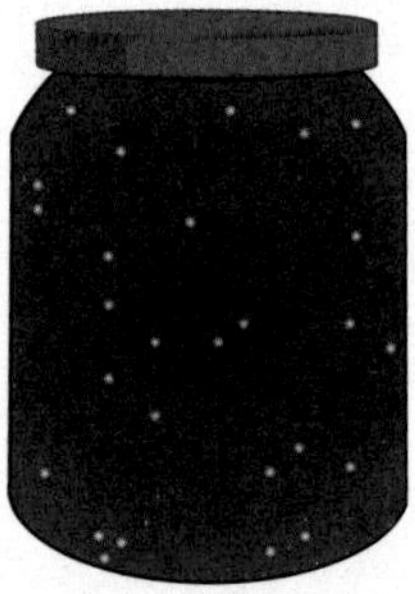

4

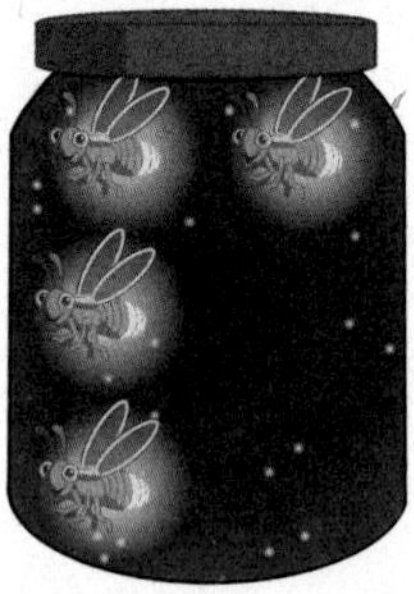

5

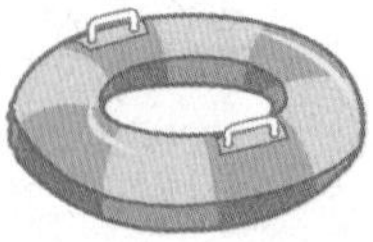

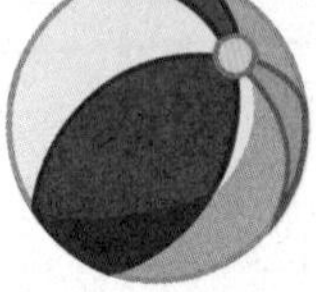

Directions: 3 and 4 Count the fireflies. Say the number. Write the number.
5 Count the objects in the picture. Say the number. Write the number.

Name ____________________

Count and Order Numbers to 5

1.8

Learning Target: Count and order numbers to 5.

Explore and Grow

0

1 

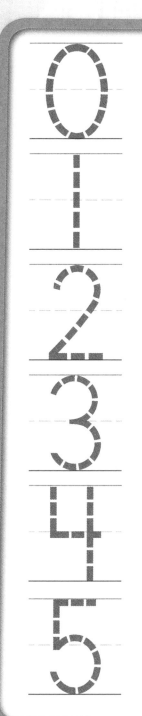

2

3

4

5

Directions: Trace the numbers. Then make linking cube trains that are 0 to 5 cubes long. Order the trains to match the numbers 0 to 5.

Think and Grow

2

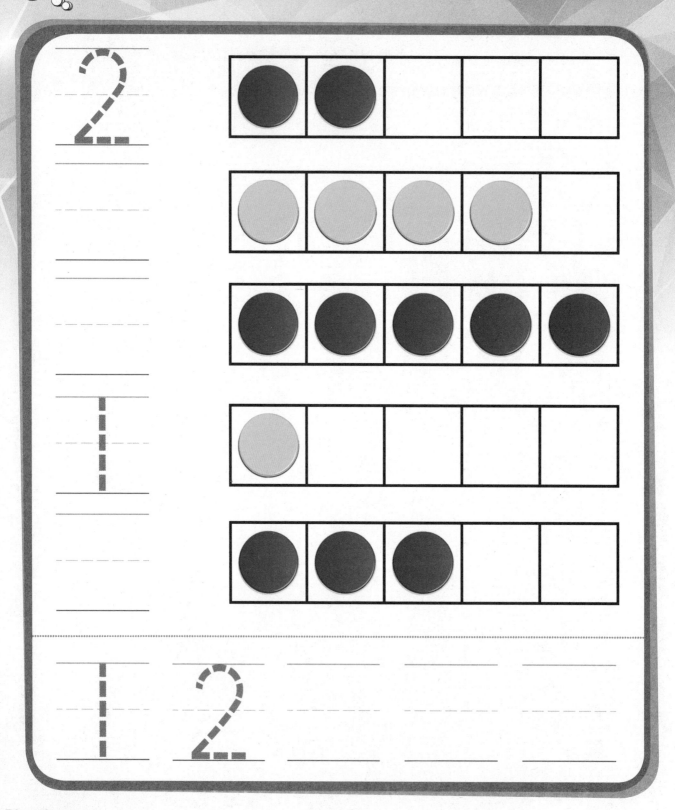

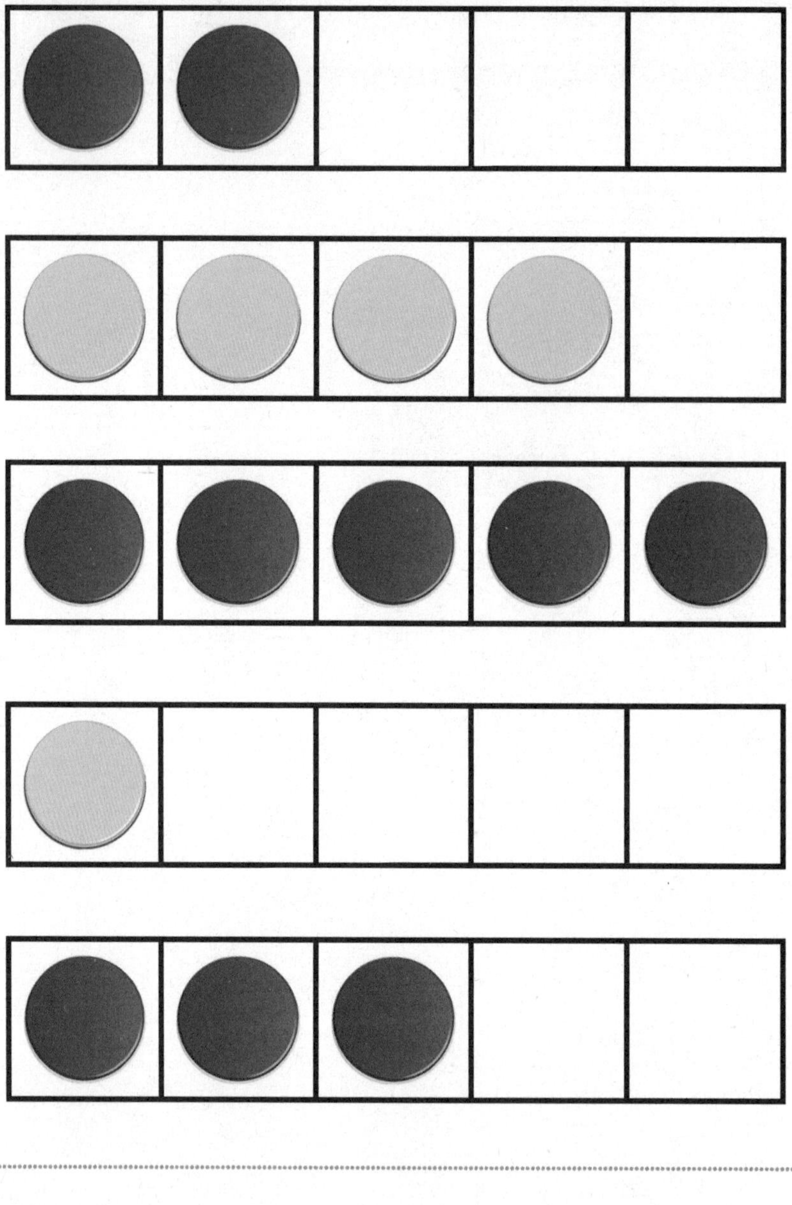

1

1 2

Directions:

- Count the objects in each five frame. Say the number. Write the number.
- Write the numbers in order. Start with the number 1.

Name ______

Apply and Grow: Practice

1 

2 

3 

4 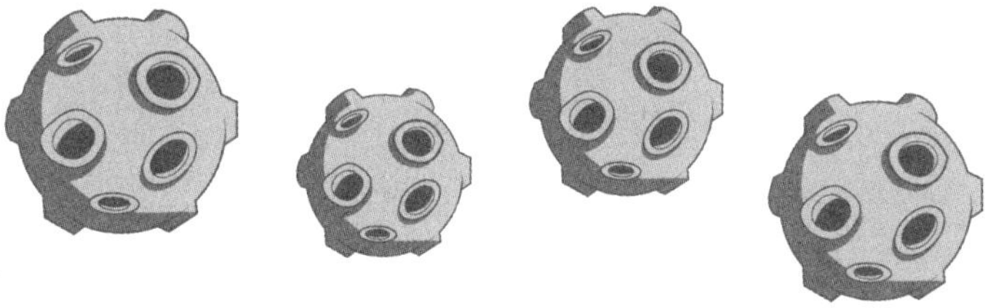

5 

6 1

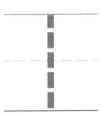

Directions: 1–5 Count the objects. Say the number. Write the number.
6 Write the numbers in order. Start with the number 1.

Think and Grow: Modeling Real Life

Directions:

- Count the stars in the picture. Say the number. Write the number.
- Write the numbers in reverse order. Start with the number 5.

Name ______________________

Practice 1.8

Learning Target: Count and order numbers to 5.

3
1
2

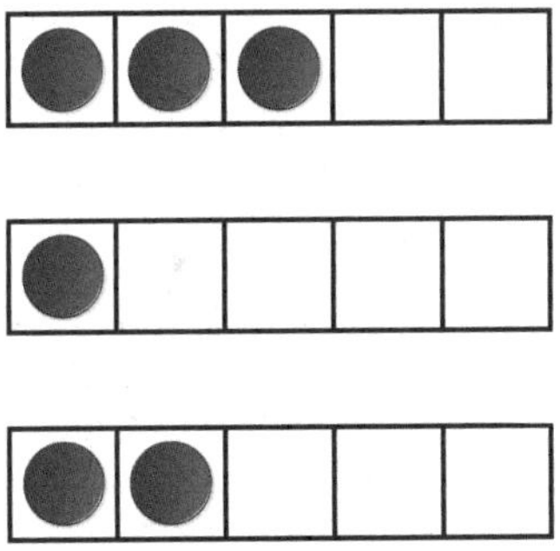

1 2 3

Directions: Count the objects in each five frame. Say the number. Write the number. Then write the numbers in order. Start with the number 1.

1

2

3

4 ____ ____ ____

Directions: 1–3 Count the birds. Say the number. Write the number. 4 Write the numbers in order. Start with the number 1.

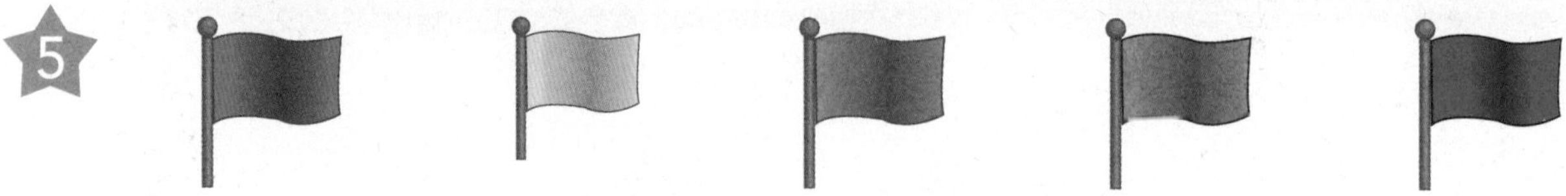

Directions: 5 Count the flags in the picture. Say the number. Write the number.

6 Write the numbers in order. Start with the number 1.

7 Write the numbers in reverse order. Start with the number 5.

Name ______________________________

Performance Task 1

1

2

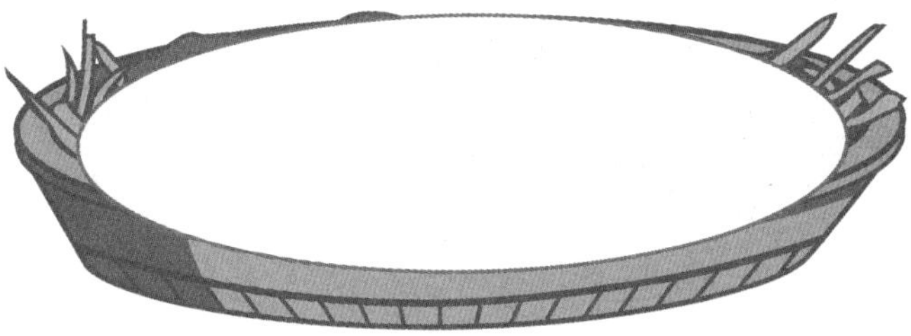

3

Directions: 1 Count the objects in the picture. Say the number. Write the number. Write the numbers in order. Start with the number 0. 2 A chicken lays five eggs. Draw to show how many eggs. 3 Show how many eggs in another way.

Number Land

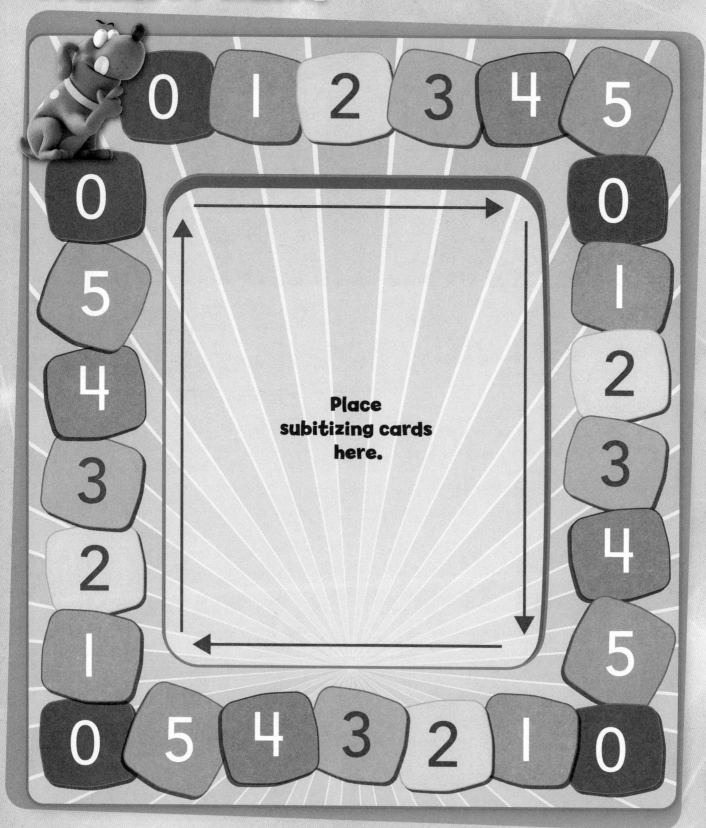

Directions: Put the Subitizing Cards 0–5 into a pile. Start at Newton. Take turns drawing a card and moving your piece to the matching number. Repeat this process until you have gone around the board and back to Newton.

Name ________________________________

Chapter Practice 1

1.1 Model and Count 1 and 2

1
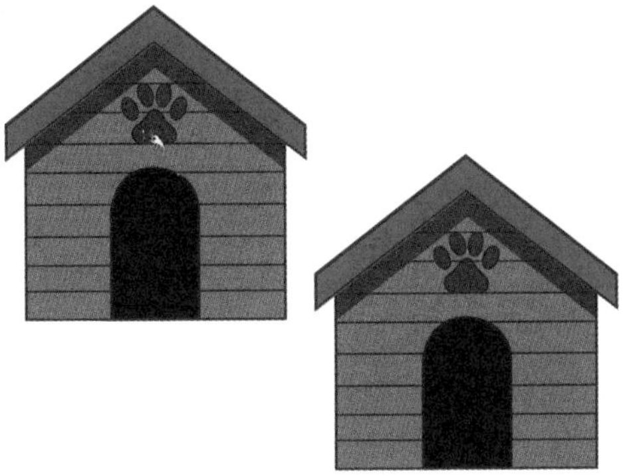

2

1.2 Understand and Write 1 and 2

3

4

Directions: 1 and 2 Count the objects. Color the boxes to show how many.
3 and 4 Count the objects. Say the number. Write the number.

1.3 Model and Count 3 and 4

5

6

1.4 Understand and Write 3 and 4

7

8

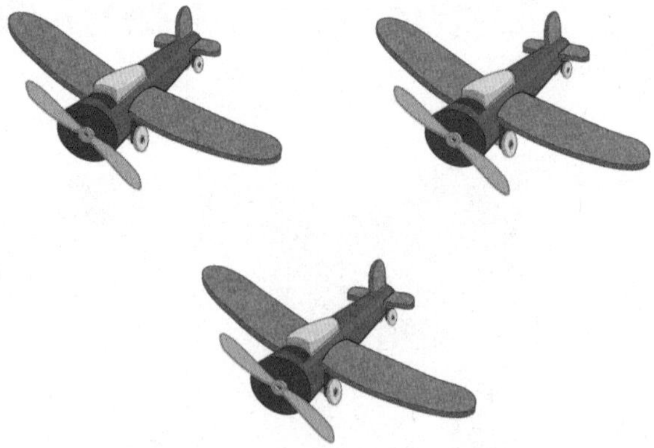

Directions: 5 and 6 Count the objects. Color the boxes to show how many.
7 and 8 Count the objects. Say the number. Write the number.

1.5 Model and Count 5

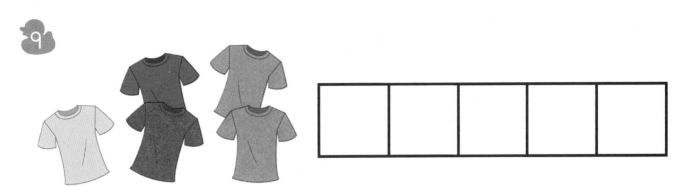

9

1.6 Understand and Write 5

10

1.7 The Concept of Zero

11

12

Directions: 9 Count the shirts. Color the boxes to show how many.
10 Count the beavers. Say the number. Write the number.
11 and 12 Count the owls. Say the number. Write the number.

1.8 Count and Order Numbers to 5

13

14

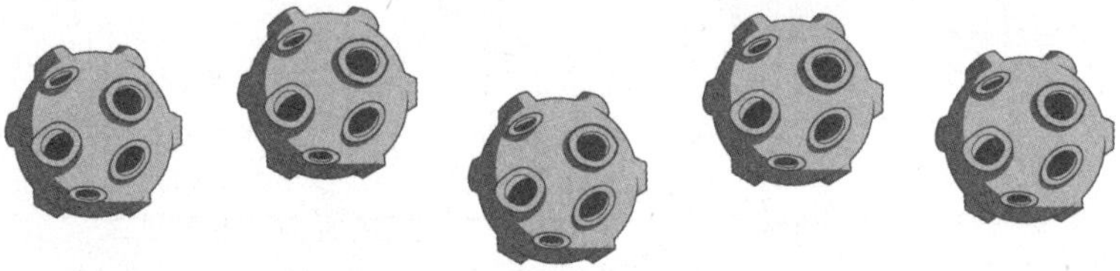

15

16

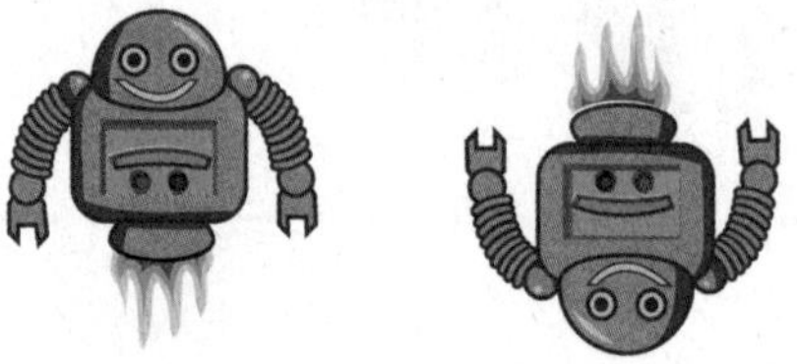

17

18

1 ____ ____ ____ ____

Directions: 13–17 Count the objects. Say the number. Write the number.
18 Write the numbers in order. Start with the number 1.

2 Compare Numbers 0 to 5

- What does it mean to follow the rules of a game?
- Are there more blue game pieces or green game pieces shown here?

Chapter Learning Target:
Understand grouping.

Chapter Success Criteria:
- I can identify groups of objects.
- I can match objects.
- I can compare groups.
- I can draw groups of objects.

Name ____________________

2 Vocabulary

Review Words
count
number

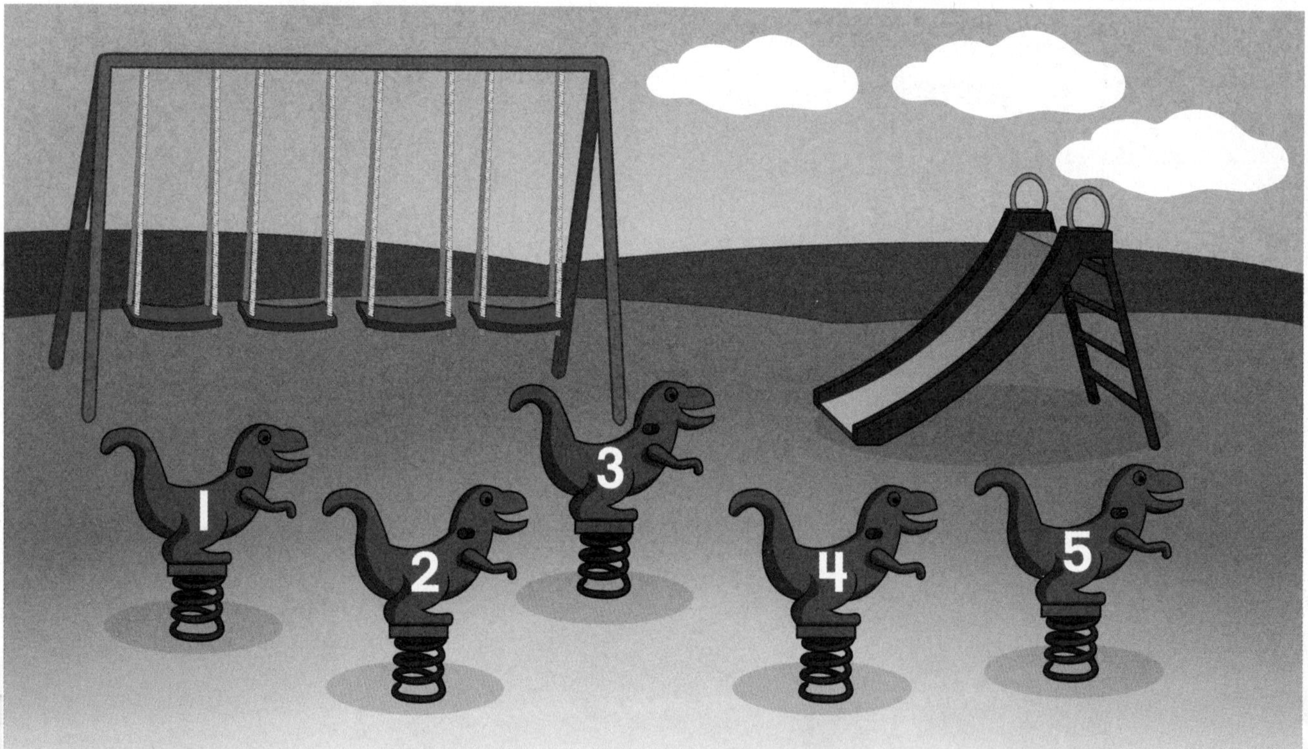

 ______

 ______

 ______

 ______

Directions: Count the objects. Say the number. Write the number.

Chapter 2 Vocabulary Cards

compare	equal
fewer	greater than
less than	more
same as	

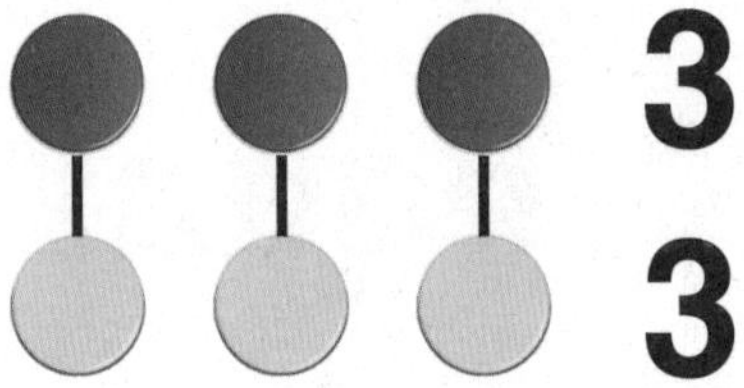
3
3

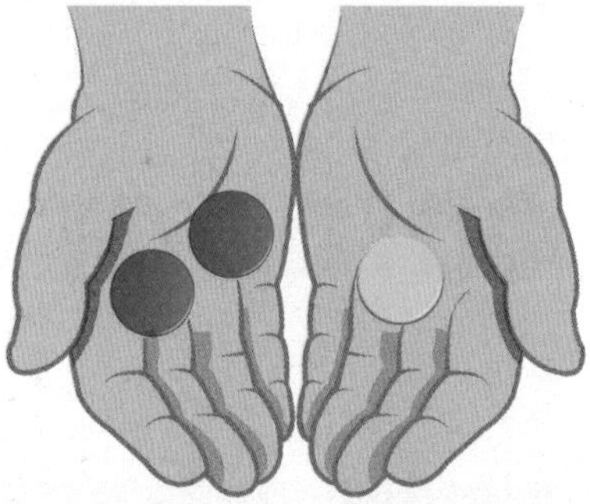

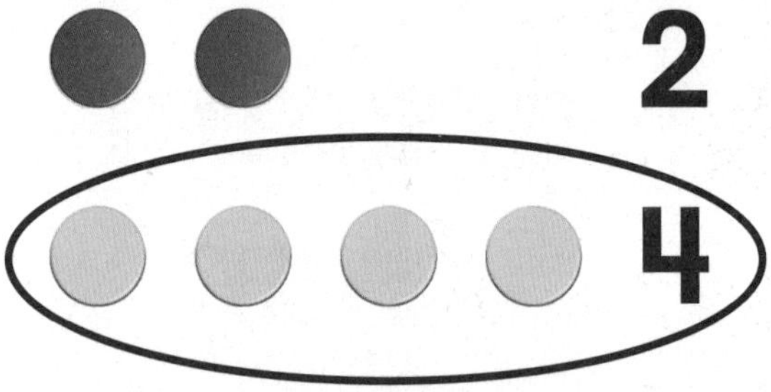
2
4

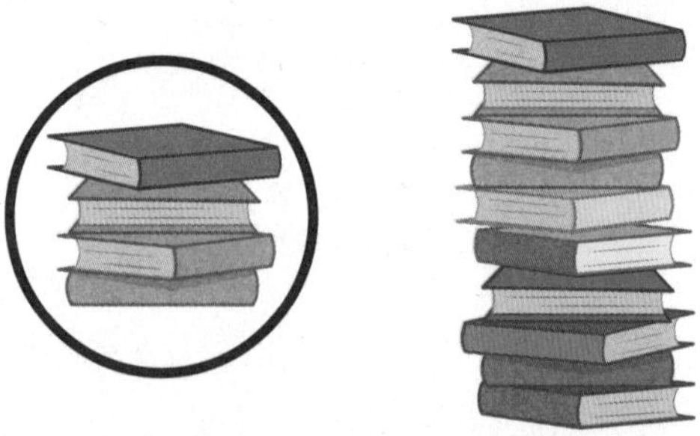

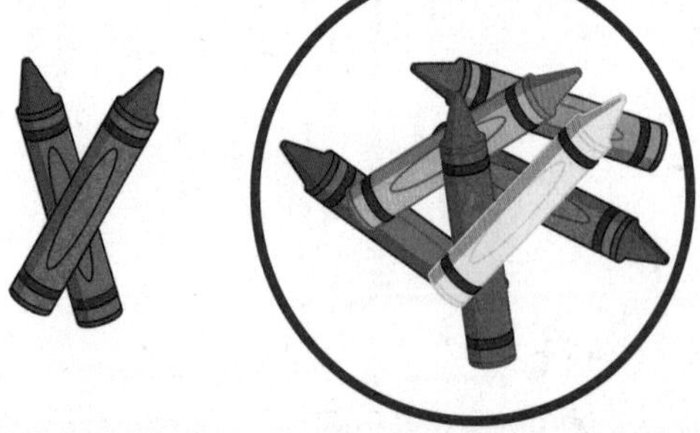

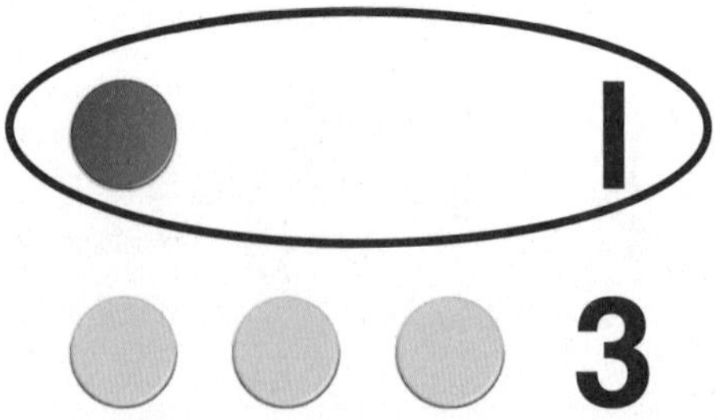
1
3

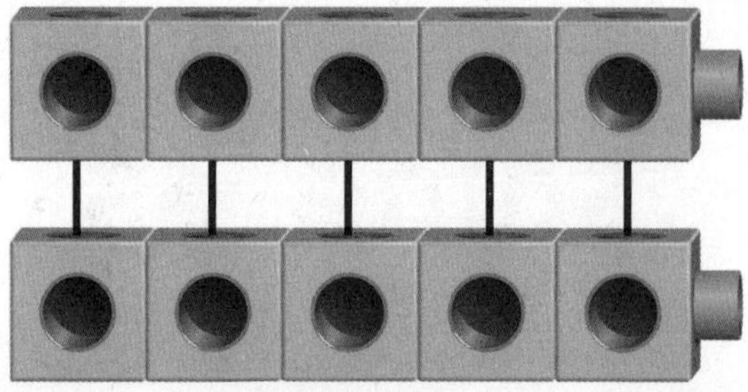

Name ______________________________

Learning Target: Show and tell whether two groups are equal in number.

Explore and Grow

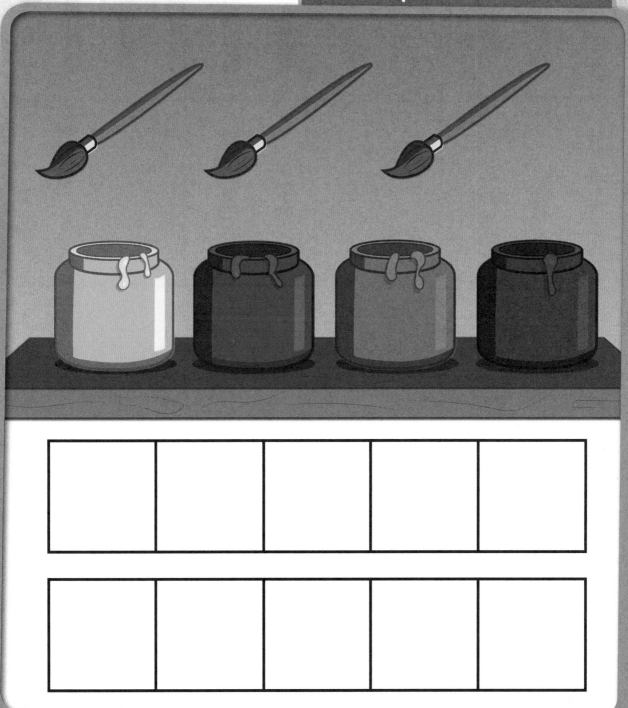

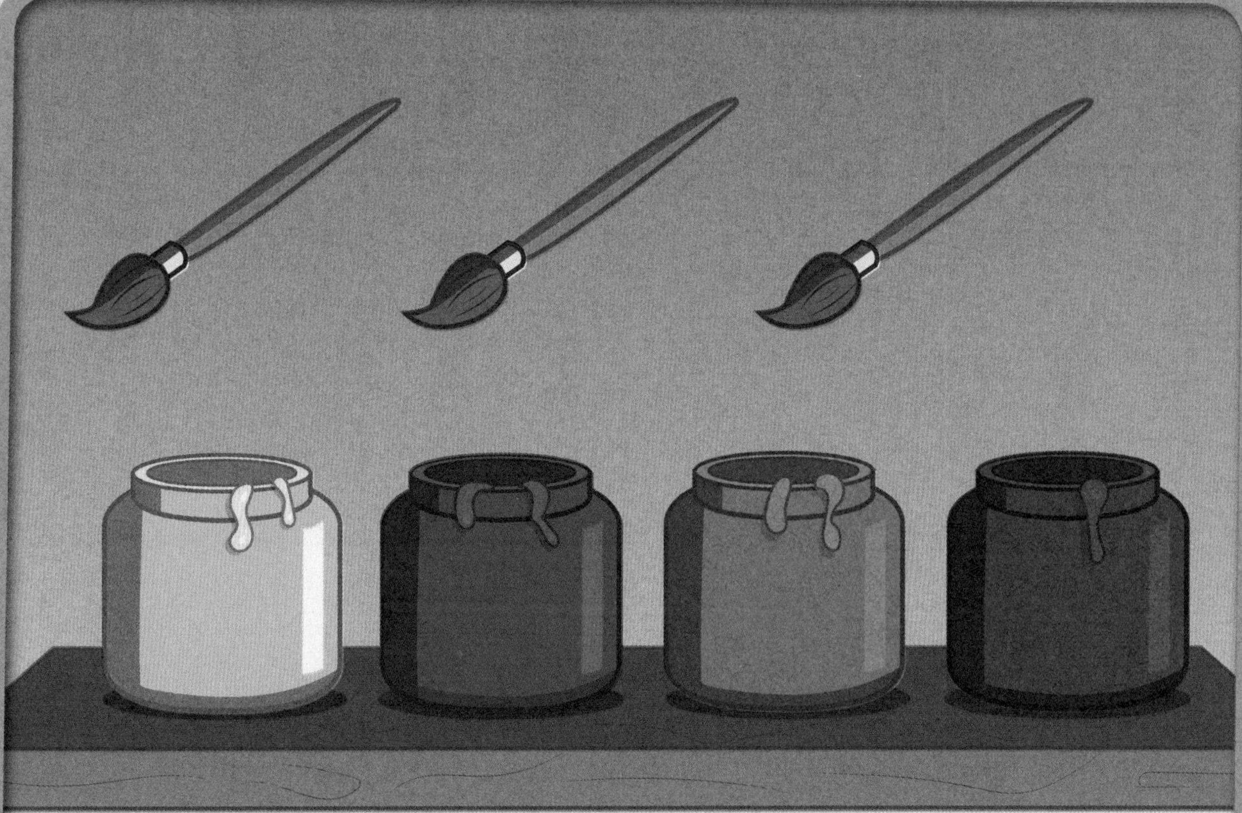

Directions: Use counters to show the number of paintbrushes. Use counters to show the number of paint jars. Is there a paintbrush for each paint jar?

Think and Grow

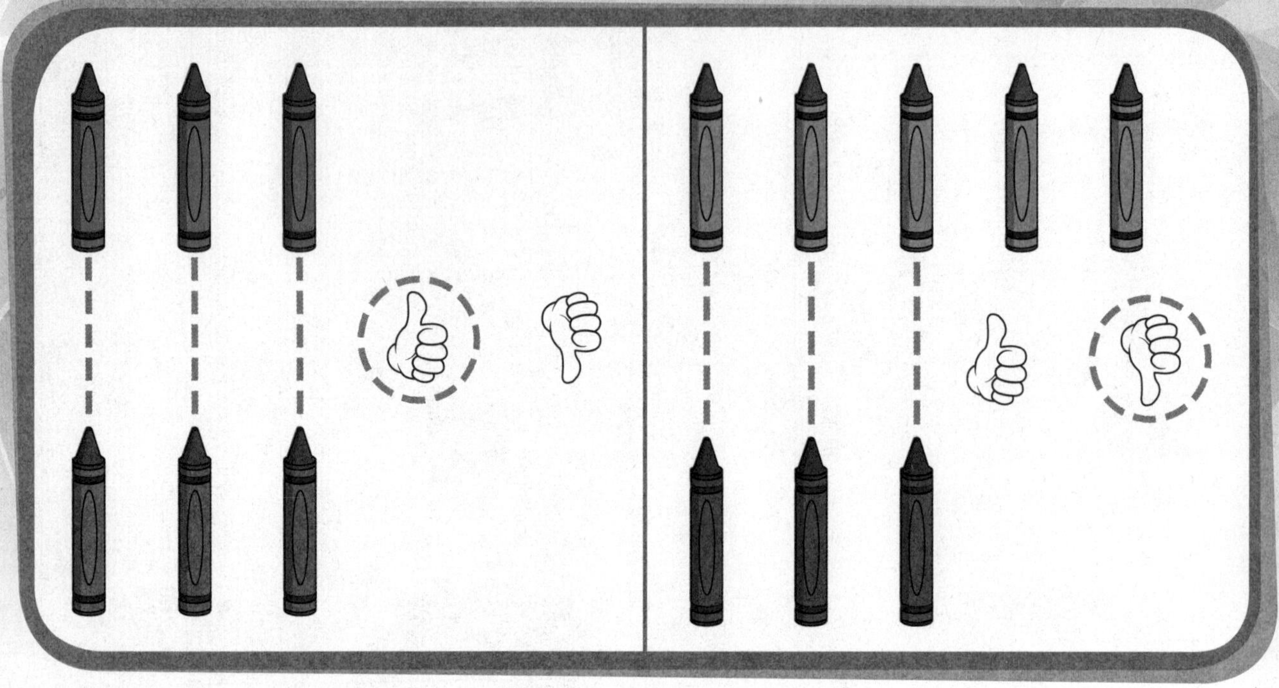

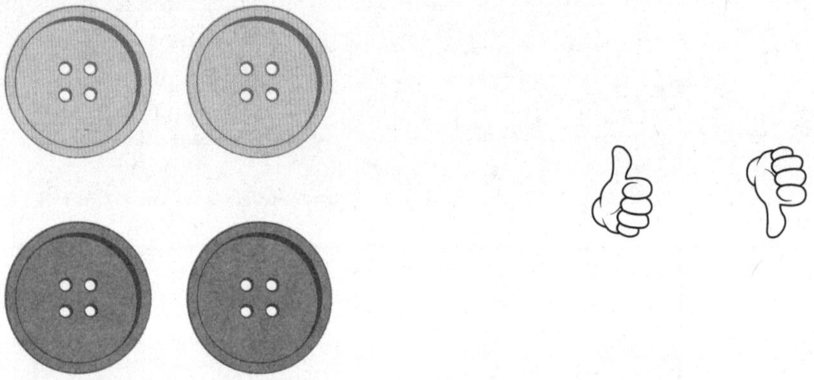

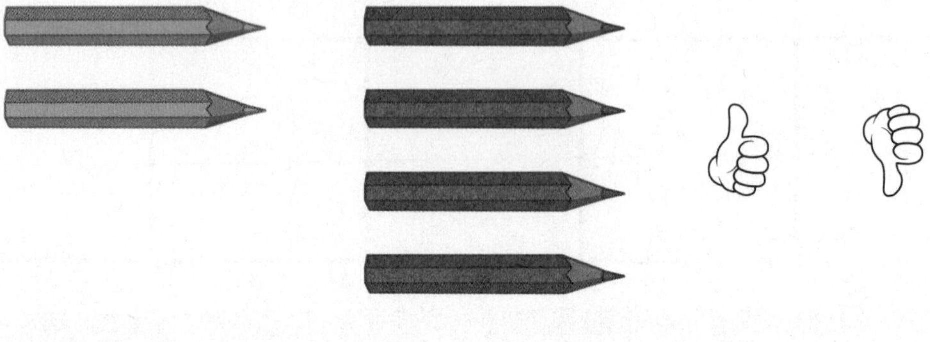

Directions: Draw lines between the objects in each group. Are the numbers of objects equal? Circle the thumbs up for *yes* or the thumbs down for *no*.

Name ____________________

Apply and Grow: Practice

1

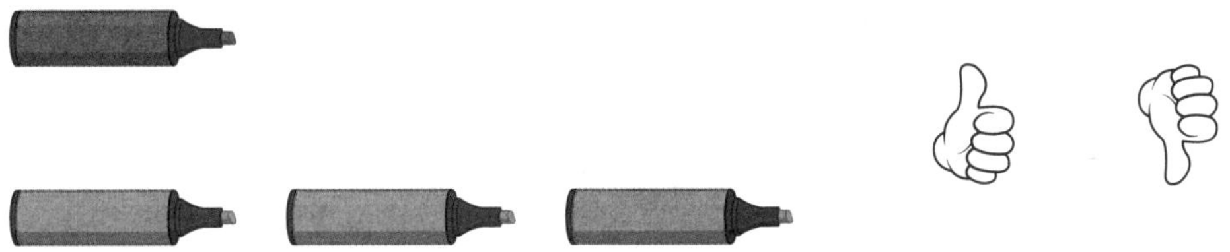

2

3

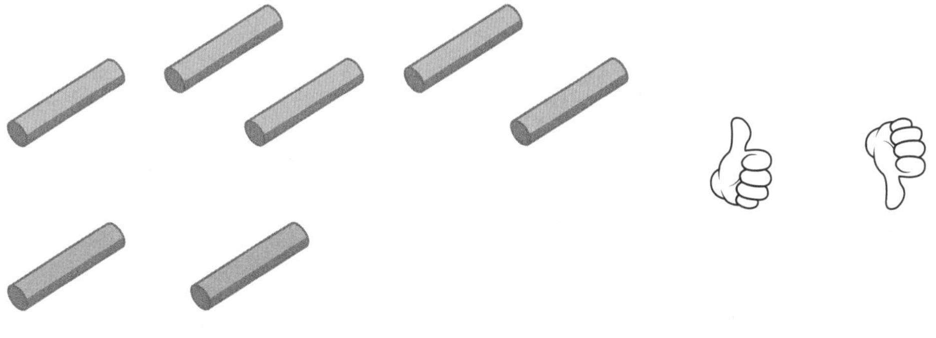

4

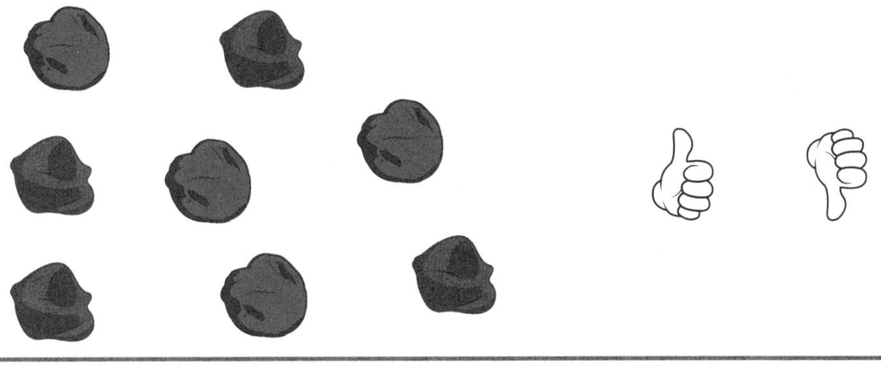

Directions: 1–4 Draw lines between the objects in each group. Are the numbers of objects equal? Circle the thumbs up for *yes* or the thumbs down for *no*.

Think and Grow: Modeling Real Life

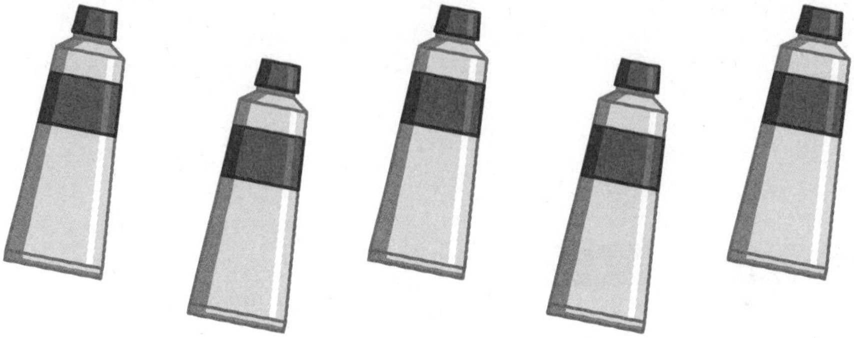

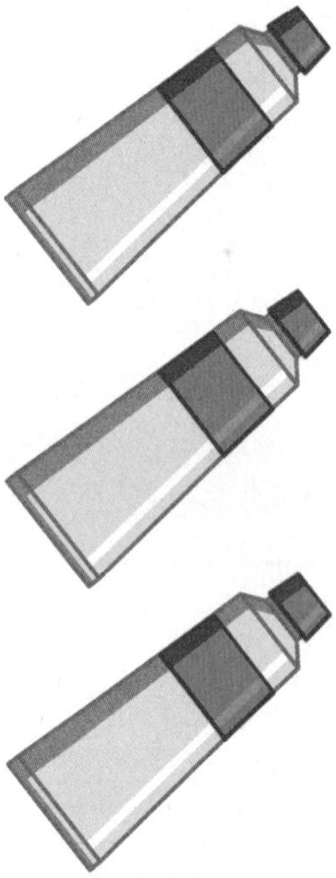

Directions:

- Draw paint spots so that the numbers of paint tubes and paint spots are equal. Draw lines between the objects in each group to show that you are correct.
- Draw paint spots so that the numbers of paint tubes and paint spots are not equal. Draw lines between the objects in each group to show that you are correct.

Name ______________________________

Practice 2.1

Learning Target: Show and tell whether two groups are equal in number.

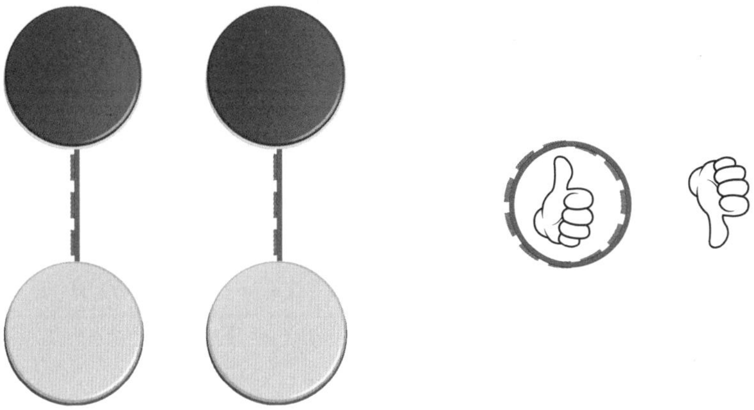

Directions: Draw lines between the counters in each group. Are the numbers of counters equal? Circle the thumbs up for *yes* or the thumbs down for *no*.

1

2

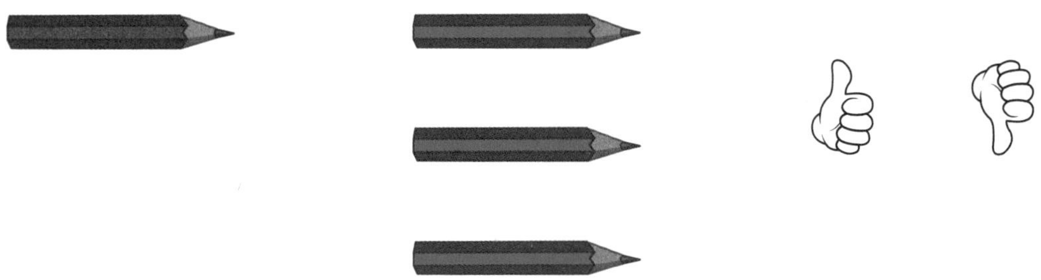

Directions: 1 and 2 Draw lines between the objects in each group. Are the numbers of objects equal? Circle the thumbs up for *yes* or the thumbs down for *no*.

3

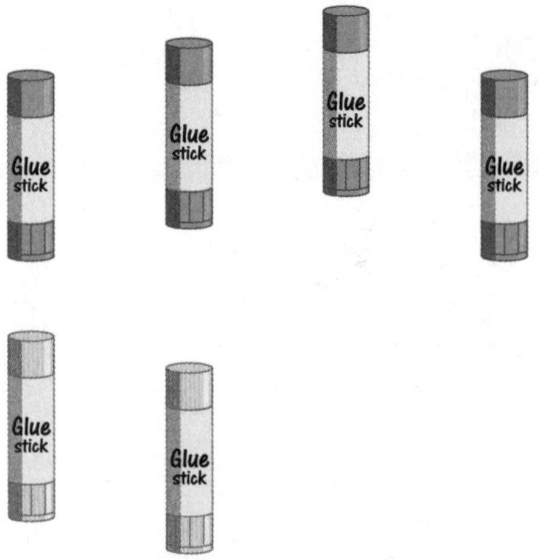

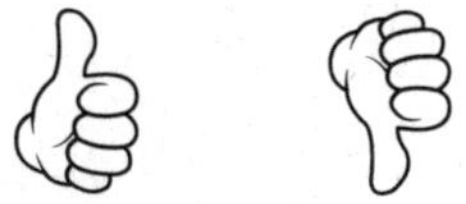

4

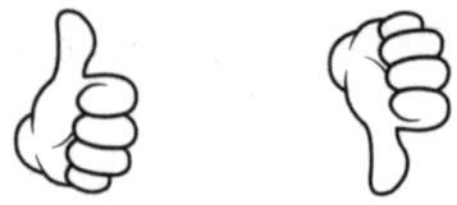

5

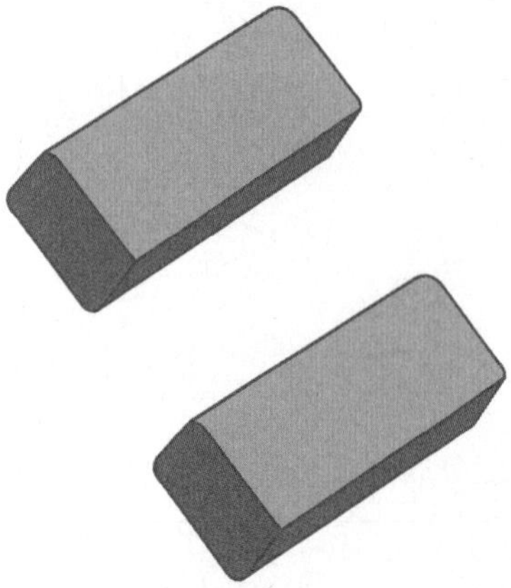

Directions: 3 and 4 Draw lines between the objects in each group. Are the numbers of objects equal? Circle the thumbs up for *yes* or the thumbs down for *no.* 5 Draw pencils so that the numbers of erasers and pencils are equal. Draw lines between the objects in each group to show that you are correct.

Name ______________________________

Learning Target: Show and tell whether one group has a greater number of objects than another group.

Explore and Grow

Directions: Use counters to show the number of suitcases. Use counters to show the number of stuffed animals. Are there more suitcases or more stuffed animals?

Think and Grow

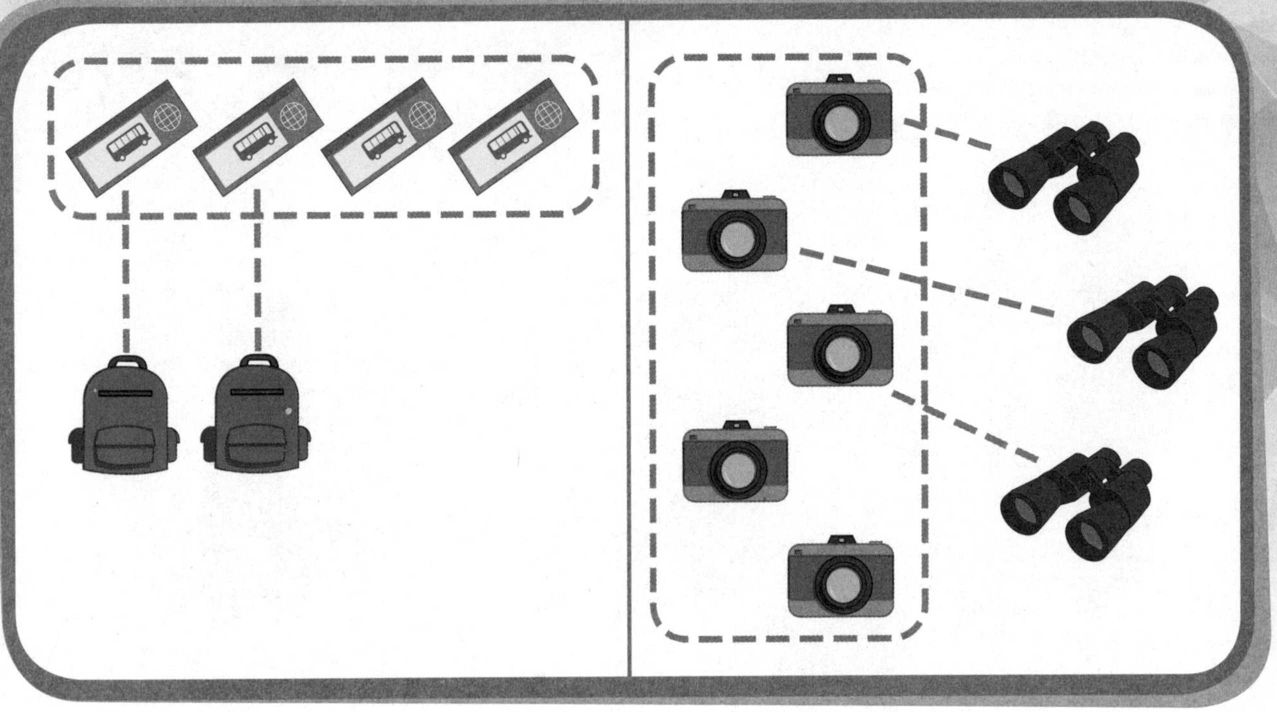

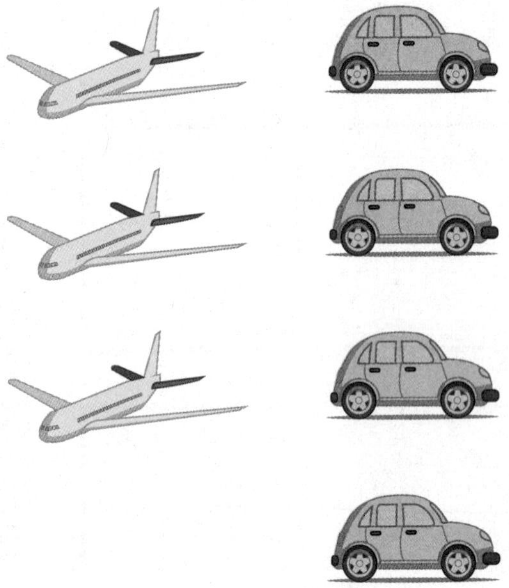

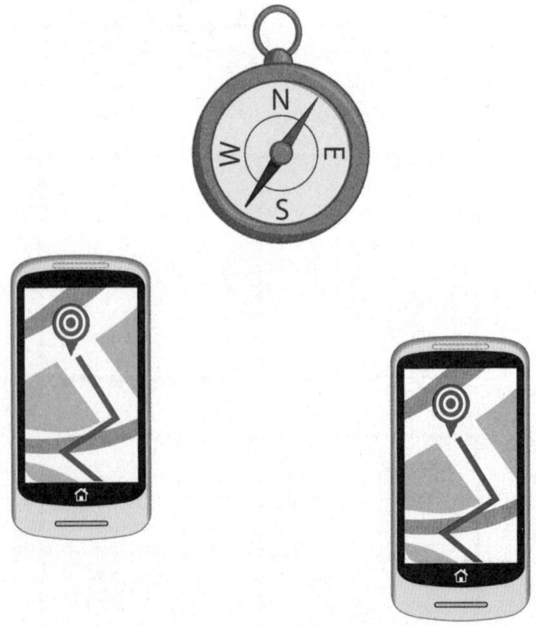

Directions: Draw lines between the objects in each group. Circle the group that is greater in number than the other group.

Name ________________________________

Apply and Grow: Practice

1

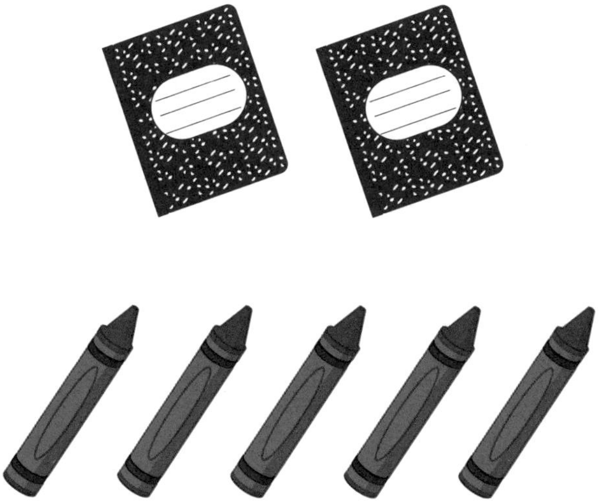

2

3

4

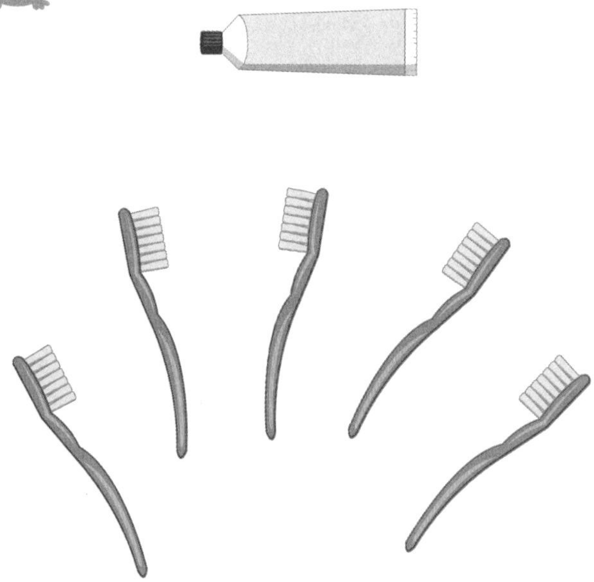

Directions: 1 – 4 Draw lines between the objects in each group. Circle the group that is greater in number than the other group.

Think and Grow: Modeling Real Life

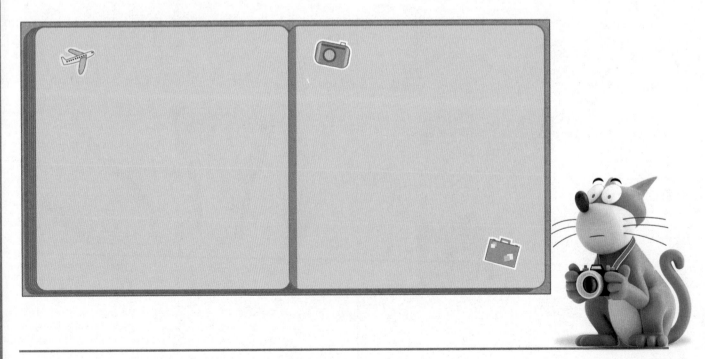

Directions: Draw photos on the scrapbook so that the number of photos is greater than the number of stickers. Draw lines between the objects in each group to show that you are correct.

Name ______________________________

Practice 2.2

Learning Target: Show and tell whether one group has a greater number of objects than another group.

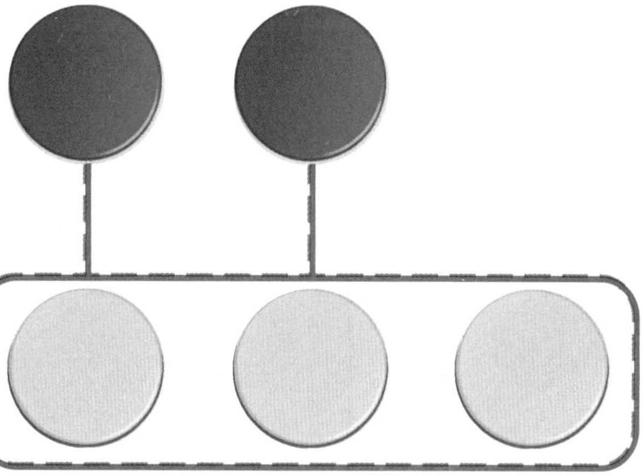

Directions: Draw lines between the counters in each group. Circle the group that is greater in number than the other group.

1

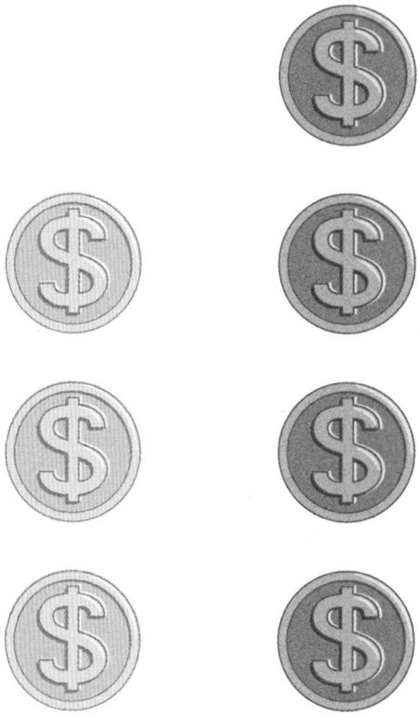

2

Directions: 1 and 2 Draw lines between the objects in each group. Circle the group that is greater in number than the other group.

3

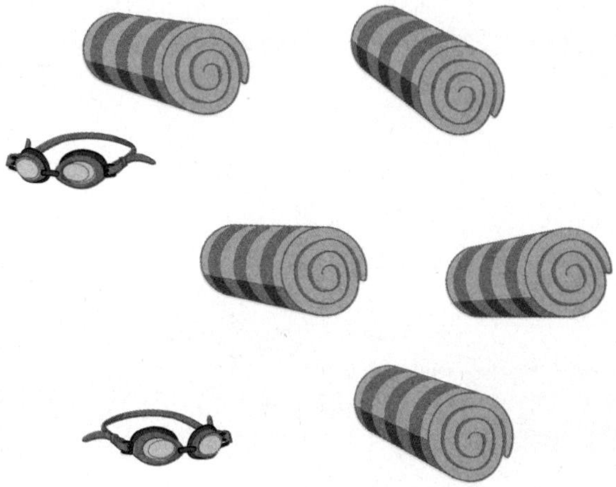

4

5

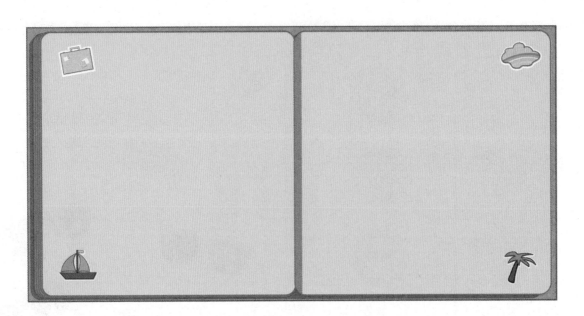

Directions: 3 and 4 Draw lines between the objects in each group. Circle the group that is greater in number than the other group. 5 Draw photos on the scrapbook so that the number of photos is greater than the number of stickers. Draw lines between the objects in each group to show that you are correct.

Name ______________________________

Less Than 2.3

Learning Target: Show and tell whether one group has a lesser number of objects than another group.

Explore and Grow

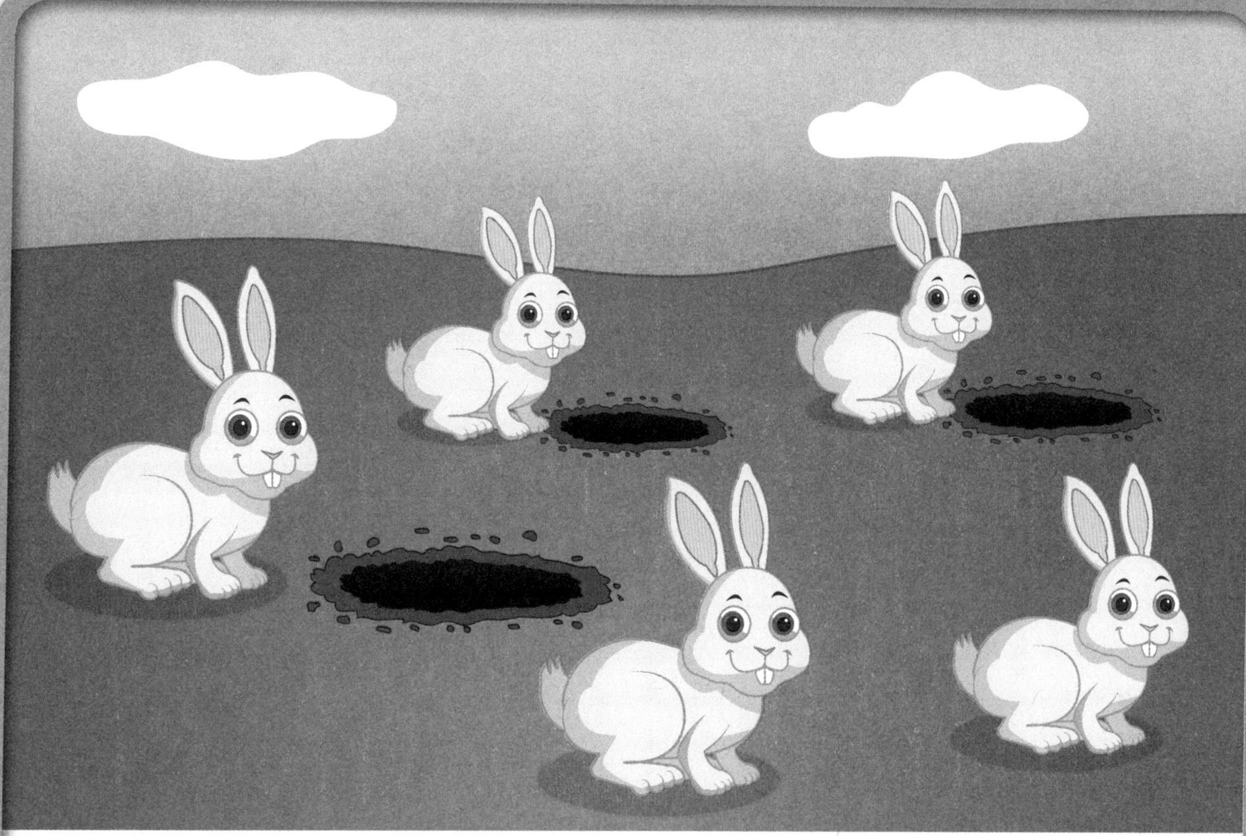

Directions: Use counters to show the number of rabbits. Use counters to show the number of holes. Are there fewer rabbits or fewer holes?

Think and Grow

Directions: Draw lines between the objects in each group. Draw a line through the group that is less in number than the other group.

Name ______________________________

Apply and Grow: Practice

1

2

3

4

Directions: 1 – 4 Draw lines between the objects in each group. Draw a line through the group that is less in number than the other group.

Think and Grow: Modeling Real Life

Directions:
- Draw flowers on the bush so that the number of hummingbirds is less than the number of flowers. Draw lines between the objects in each group to show that you are correct.
- Draw flowers on the bush so that the number of flowers is less than the number of hummingbirds. Draw lines between the objects in each group to show that you are correct.

Name ______________________________

Practice 2.3

Learning Target: Show and tell whether one group has a lesser number of objects than another group.

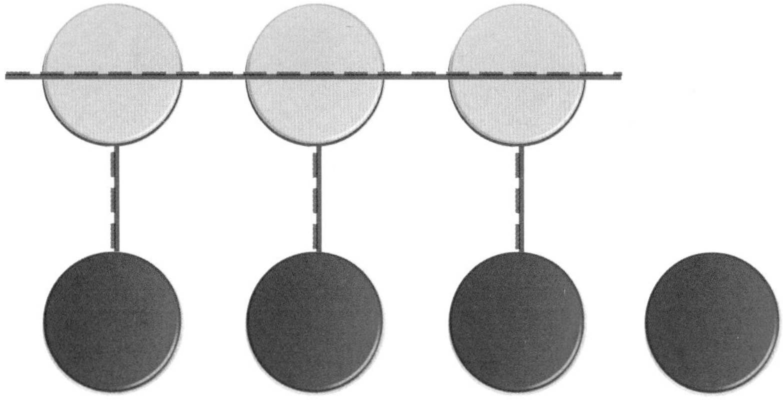

Directions: Draw lines between the counters in each group. Draw a line through the group that is less in number than the other group.

1

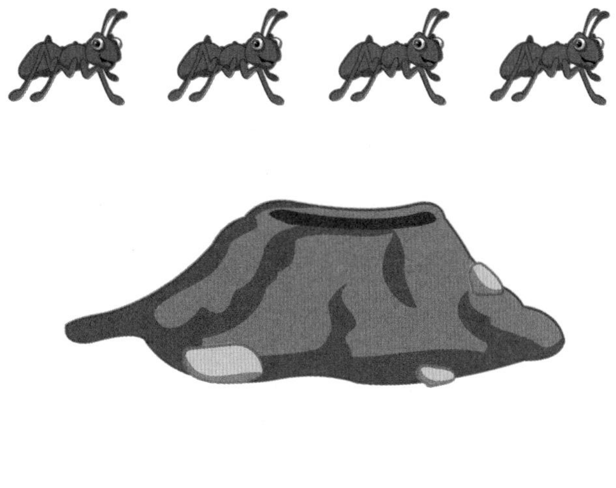

2

Directions: 1 and 2 Draw lines between the objects in each group. Draw a line through the group that is less in number than the other group.

3

4

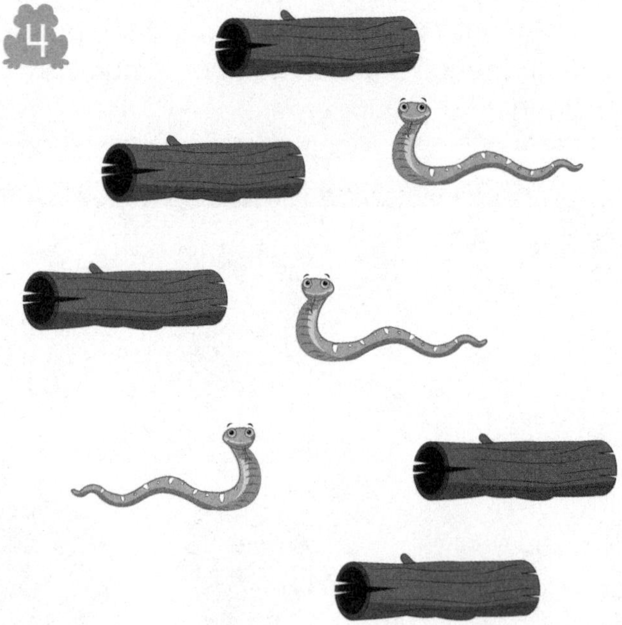

5

Directions: 3 and 4 Draw lines between the objects in each group. Draw a line through the group that is less in number than the other group.
5 Draw berries on the bush so that the number of berries is less than the number of bears. Draw lines between the objects in each group to show that you are correct.

Name ___________________________

Compare Groups to 5 by Counting

2.4

Learning Target: Use counting to compare the number of objects in two groups.

Explore and Grow

Directions: Use counters to show the number of yellow jerseys. Use counters to show the number of red jerseys. Tell which group has more and which group has less.

Think and Grow

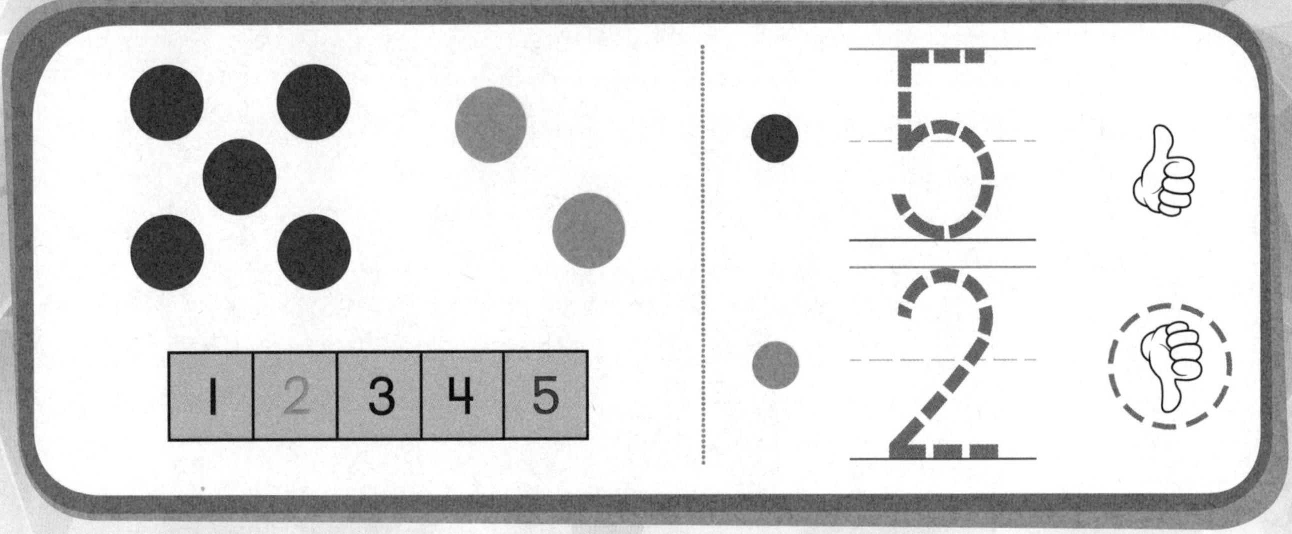

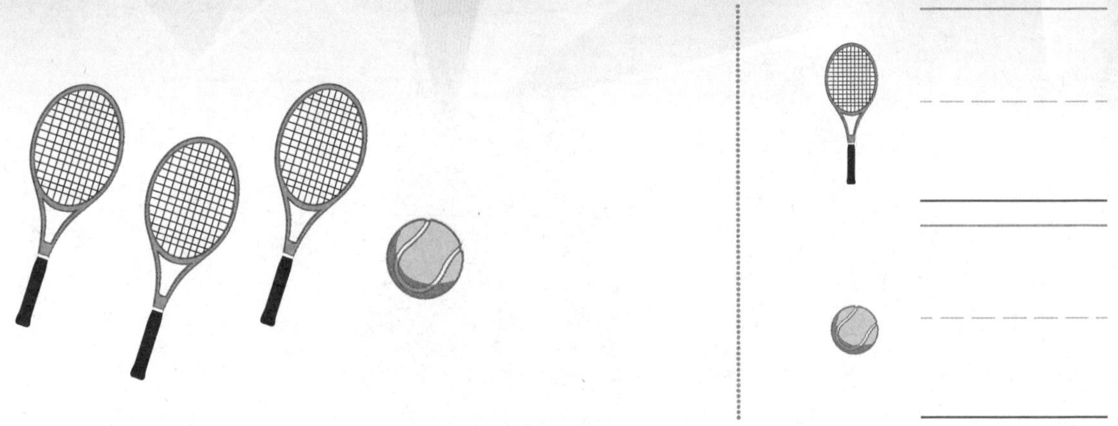

Directions: Count the objects in each group. Write each number.

- Is the number of purple dots equal to the number of green dots? Circle the thumbs up for *yes* or the thumbs down for *no*.
- Compare the numbers of tennis rackets and tennis balls. Circle the number that is greater than the other number.
- Compare the numbers of hockey sticks and hockey pucks. Draw a line through the number that is less than the other number.

Name ______________________________

Apply and Grow: Practice

1

2

3

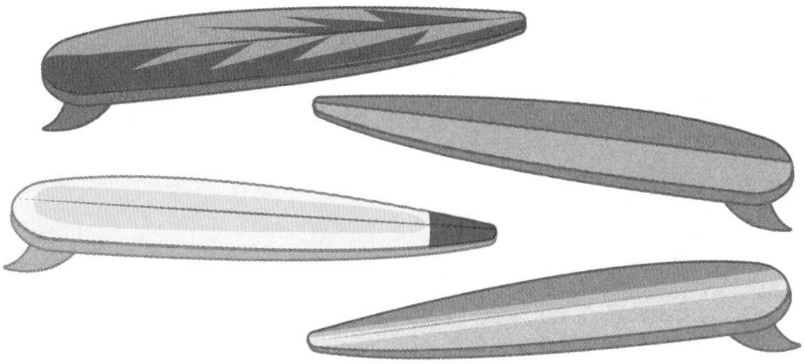

Directions: Count the objects in each group. Write each number. 1 Is the number of soccer balls equal to the number of soccer goals? Circle the thumbs up for *yes* or the thumbs down for *no*. 2 Circle the number that is greater than the other number. 3 Draw a line through the number that is less than the other number.

Think and Grow: Modeling Real Life

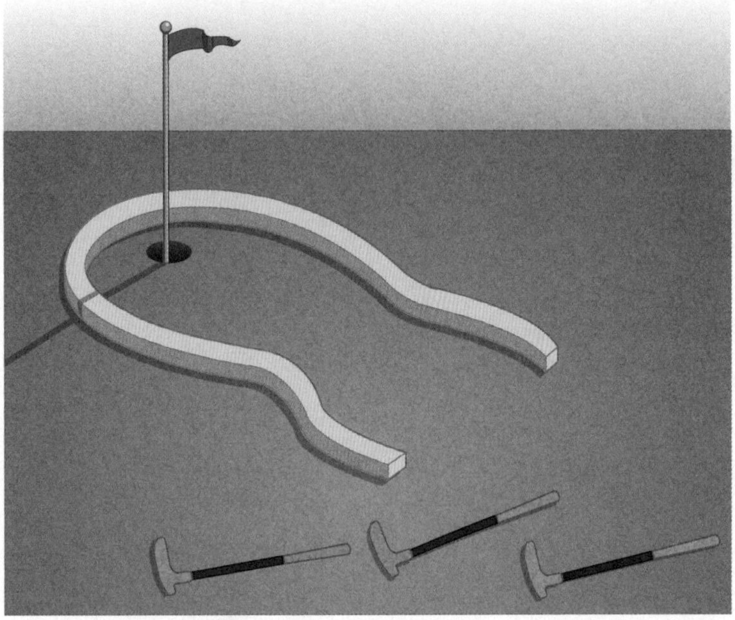

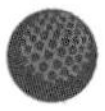

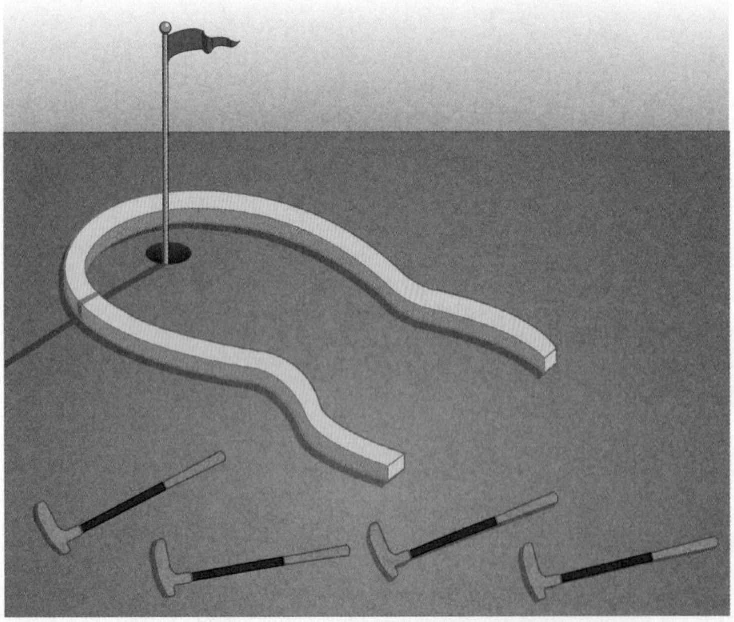

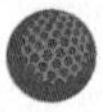

Directions:

- Draw golf balls on the ground so that the number of golf balls is greater than the number of golf clubs. Write the number of each object. Circle the number that is greater than the other number.
- Draw golf balls on the ground so that the number of golf balls is less than the number of golf clubs. Write the number of each object. Draw a line through the number that is less than the other number.

Name ________________________________

Learning Target: Use counting to compare the numbers of objects in two groups.

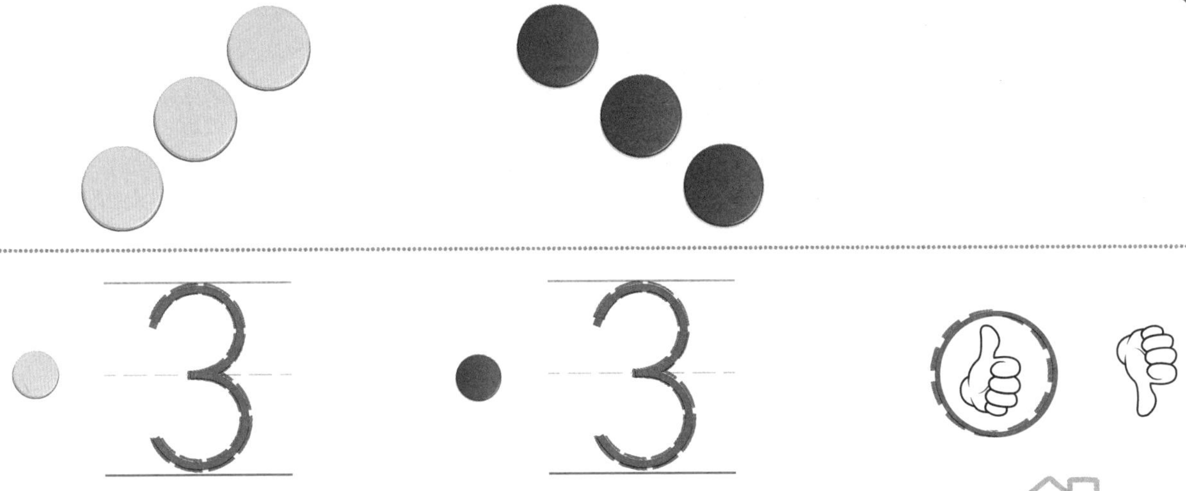

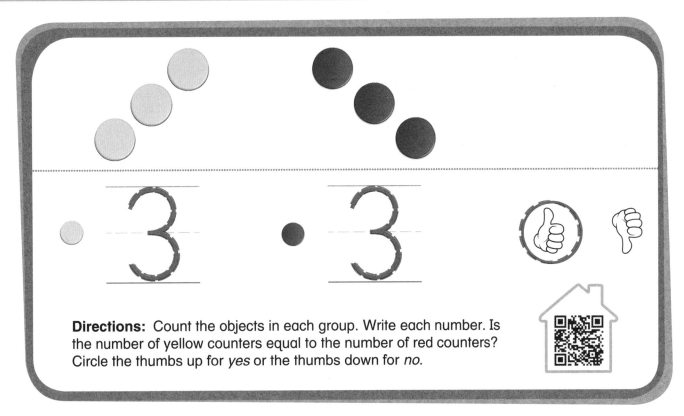

Directions: Count the objects in each group. Write each number. Is the number of yellow counters equal to the number of red counters? Circle the thumbs up for *yes* or the thumbs down for *no*.

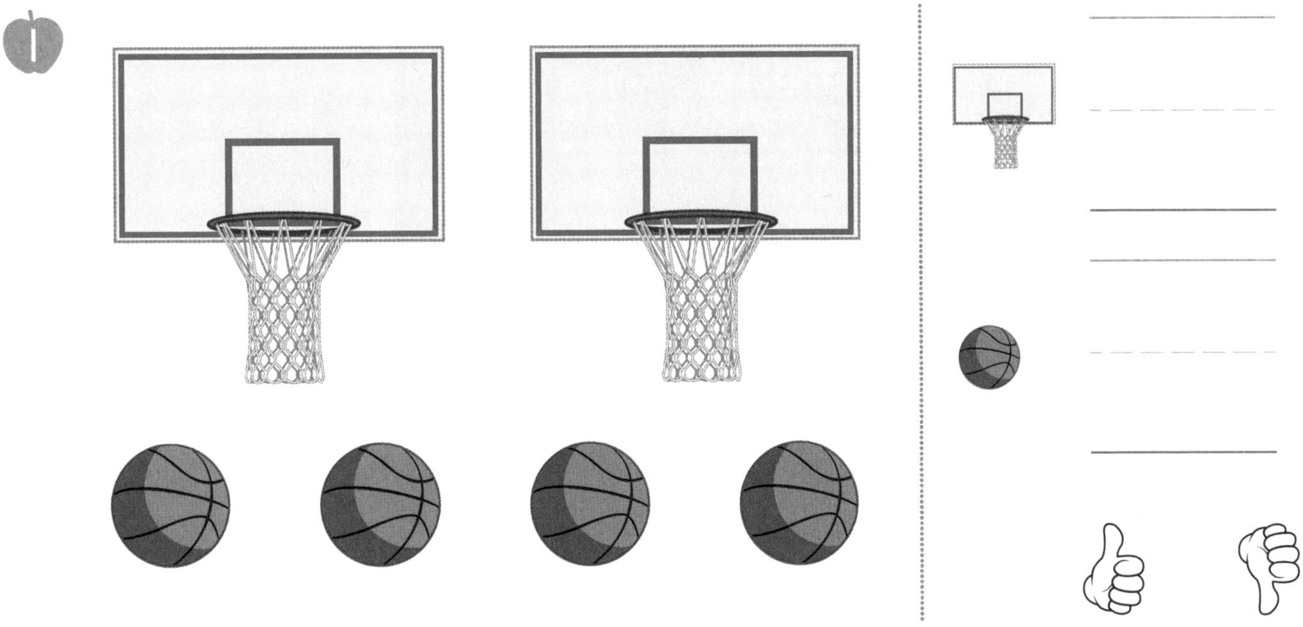

Directions: 1 Count the objects in each group. Write each number. Is the number of basketball hoops equal to the number of basketballs? Circle the thumbs up for *yes* or the thumbs down for *no*.

2

3

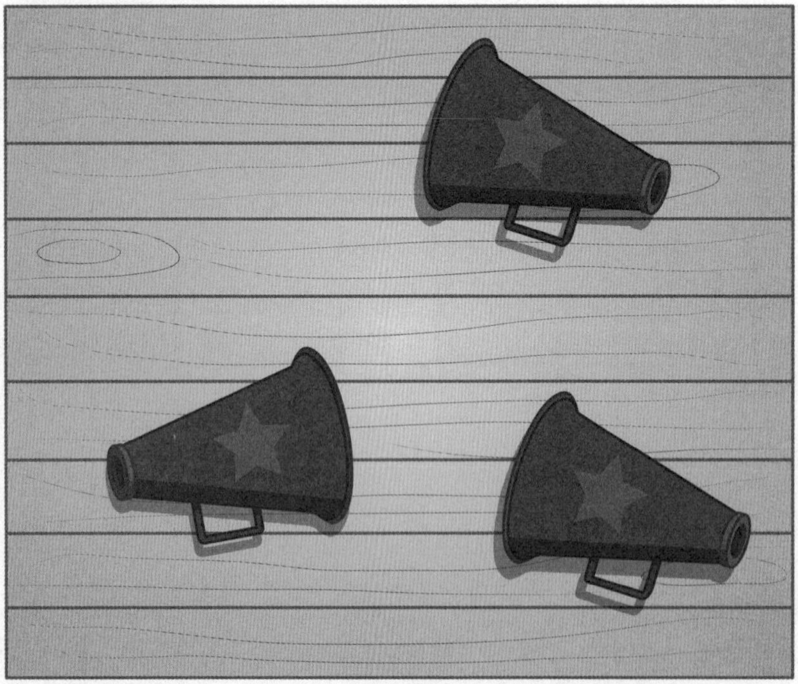

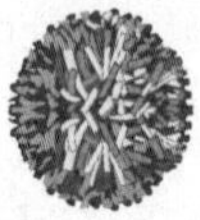

Directions: 2 Count the objects in each group. Write each number. Circle the number that is greater than the other number. 3 Draw pom-poms on the floor in the picture so that the number of pom-poms is less than the number of megaphones. Write the number of each object. Draw a line through the number that is less than the other number.

Name ______________________________

Learning Target: Compare two numbers.

Explore and Grow

5

3

Directions: Which number is greater than the other number? Which number is less than the other number? Use counters to show how you know.

Think and Grow

2

2

1

5

4

3

Directions: Compare the numbers.

- Are the numbers equal? Circle the thumbs up for *yes* or the thumbs down for *no*. Draw to show how you know.
- Circle the number that is greater than the other number. Draw to show how you know.
- Draw a line through the number that is less than the other number. Draw to show how you know.

Name ____________________

Apply and Grow: Practice

1

2

3

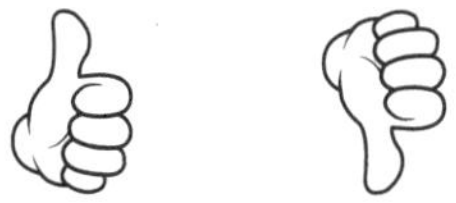

2

1

2

3

5

4

Directions: Compare the numbers.

1 Are the numbers equal? Circle the thumbs up for *yes* or the thumbs down for *no*. Draw to show how you know. 2 Circle the number that is greater than the other number. Draw to show how you know. 3 Draw a line through the number that is less than the other number. Draw to show how you know.

Think and Grow: Modeling Real Life

Directions:

- Write the number that is equal to the number on the car. Draw to show how you know your number is correct.
- Write a number that is greater than the number on the car. Draw to show how you know your number is correct.
- Write a number that is less than the number on the car. Draw to show how you know your number is correct.

Name ______________________________

Learning Target: Compare two numbers.

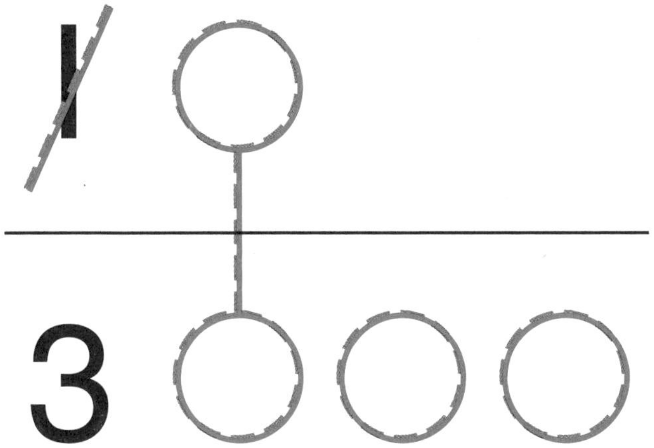

Directions: Compare the numbers. Draw a line through the number that is less than the other number. Draw to show how you know.

1

1

1

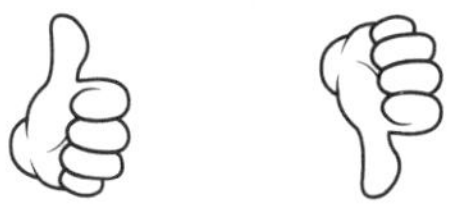

Directions: 1 Compare the numbers. Are the numbers equal? Circle the thumbs up for *yes* or the thumbs down for *no.* Draw to show how you know.

2

4

2

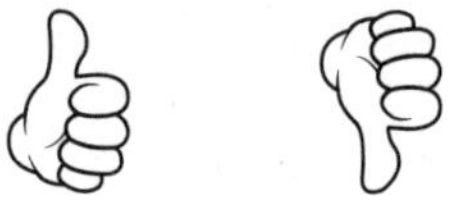

3

2

5

4

Directions: 2 Compare the numbers. Are the numbers equal? Circle the thumbs up for *yes* or the thumbs down for *no*. Draw to show how you know. 3 Compare the numbers. Draw a line through the number that is less than the other number. Draw to show how you know. 4 Write a number that is greater than the number on the jersey. Draw to show how you know your number is correct.

Name ______________________

Performance Task 2

1

2
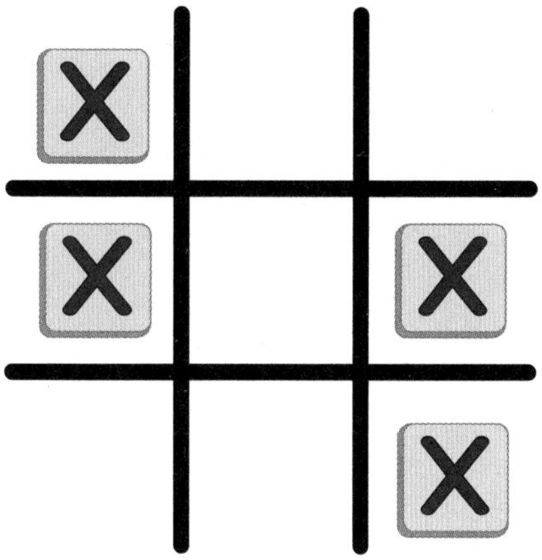

3

Directions: 1 Count the dots on each side of the domino. Write the 2 numbers. Draw a line through the number that is less than the other number. 2 Draw O's on the game board so that the number of O's is greater than the number of X's. Write each number. Circle the number that is greater than the other number. 3 Write each number. Circle the numbers that are equal.

Toss and Compare

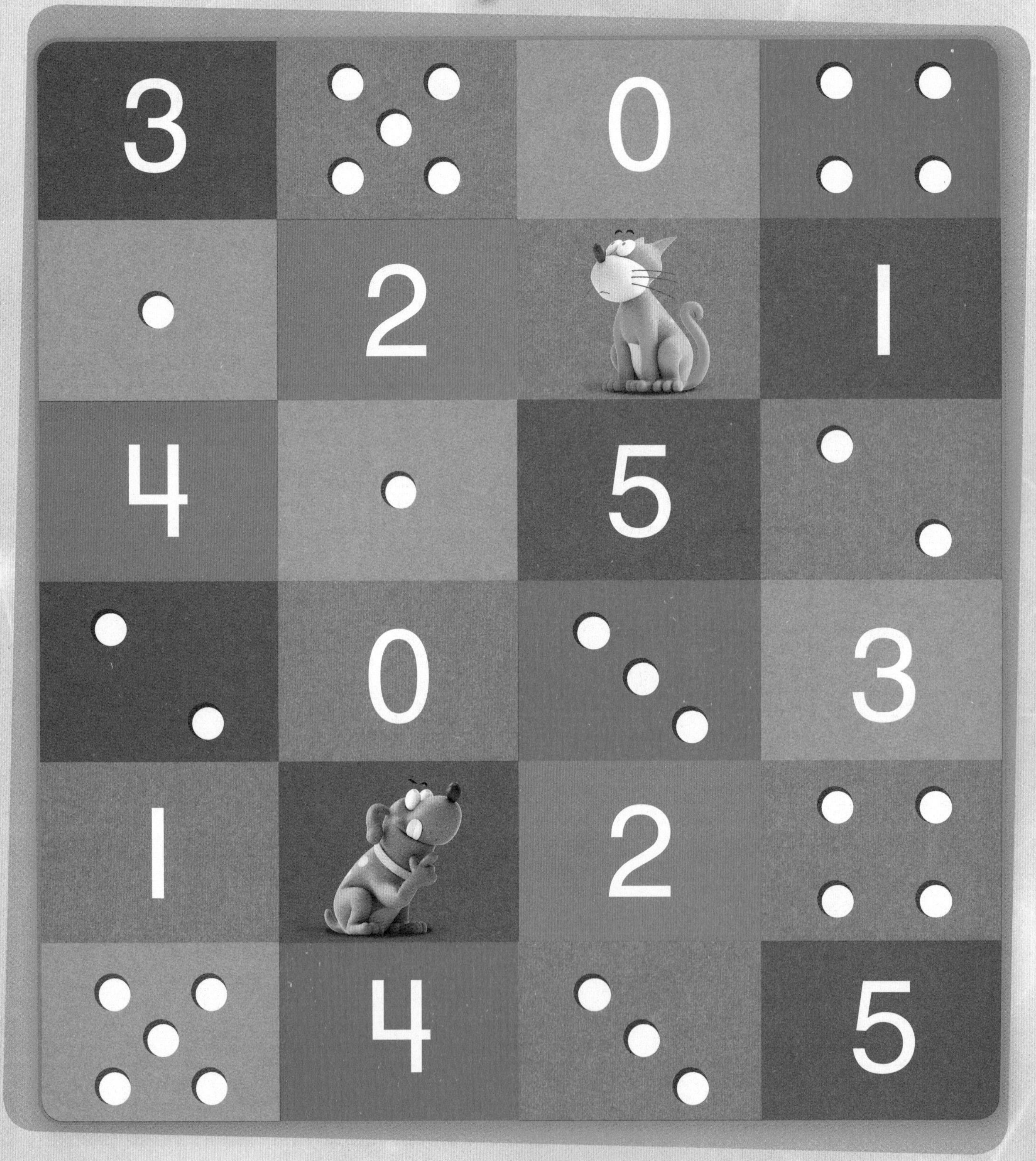

Directions: Take turns tossing a counter onto the board. If the counter lands on Newton or Descartes, choose any number from 0 to 5. Write the numbers on your Toss and Compare Numbers from 0 to 5 Recording Sheet. Circle the number that is greater than the other number. Circle both numbers if they are equal. Repeat this process until you fill your sheet.

Name ______________________________

Chapter 2 Practice

2.1 Equal Groups

1

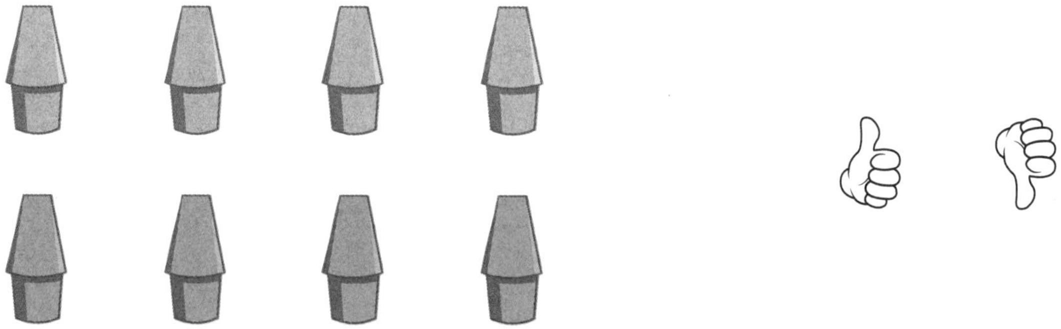

2

3

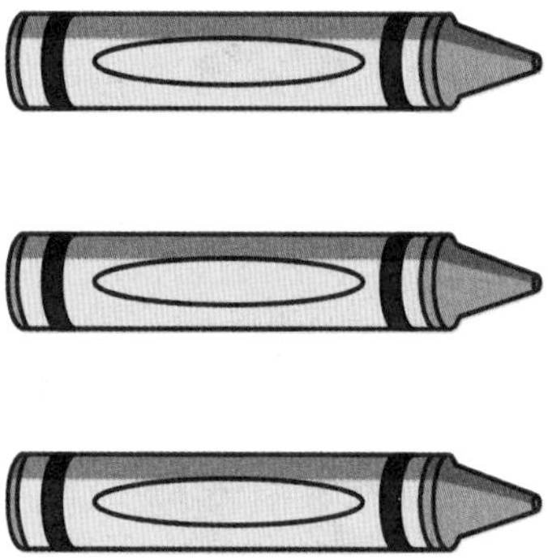

Directions: 1 and 2 Draw lines between the objects in each group. Are the numbers of objects equal? Circle the thumbs up for *yes* or the thumbs down for *no*. 3 Draw pencils so that the numbers of crayons and pencils are equal. Draw lines between the objects in each group to show that you are correct.

2.2 Greater Than

4

2.3 Less Than

5

Directions: Draw lines between the objects in each group.
4 Circle the group that is greater in number than the other group.
5 Draw a line through the group that is less in number than the other group.

2.4 Compare Groups to 5 by Counting

6

7

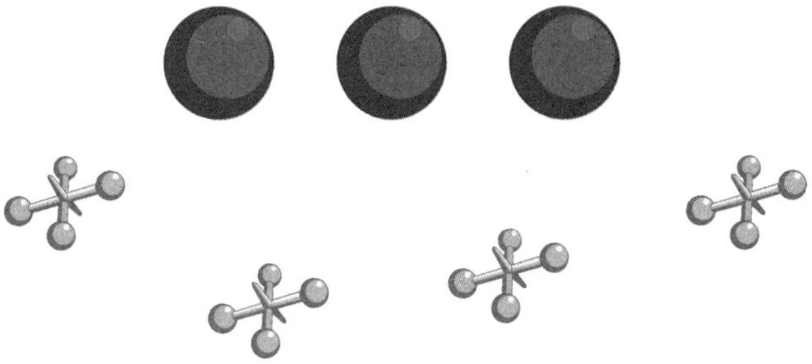

8

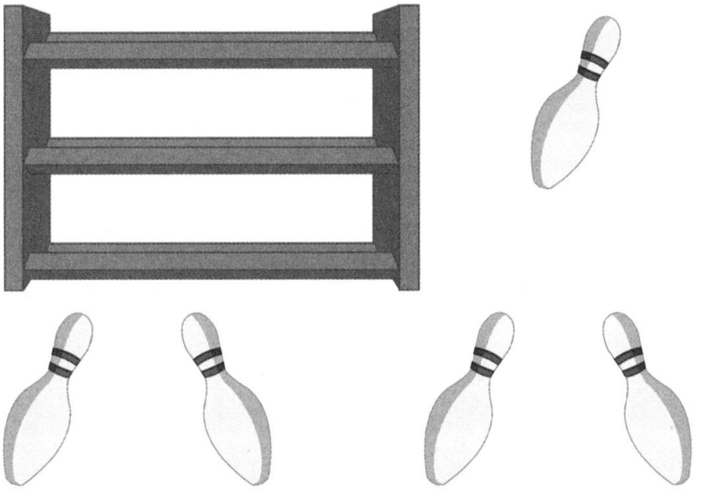

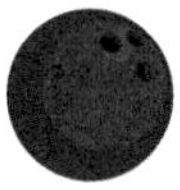

Directions: Count the objects in each group. Write each number.
6 Is the number of helmets equal to the number of bikes? Circle the thumbs up for *yes* or the thumbs down for *no*. 7 Circle the number that is greater than the other number. 8 Draw a line through the number that is less than the other number.

2.5 Compare Numbers to 5

9

5

5

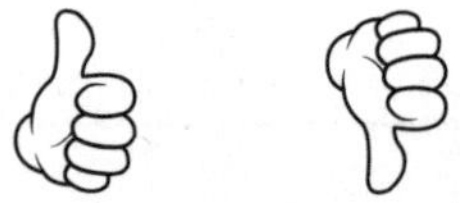

10

3

4

11

2

4

Directions: Compare the numbers.
9 Are the numbers equal? Circle the thumbs up for *yes* or the thumbs down for *no.* Draw to show how you know. 10 Circle the number that is greater than the other number. Draw to show how you know. 11 Draw a line through the number that is less than the other number. Draw to show how you know.

3 Count and Write Numbers 6 to 10

- What kinds of animals do you see here?
- How many animals are there?

Chapter Learning Target:
Understand numbers.

Chapter Success Criteria:
- I can identify numbers.
- I can name numbers.
- I can order numbers.
- I can write numbers.

Name ____________________

3 Vocabulary

Review Word
compare

Directions:
- Count the objects. Say the number. Write the number.
- Compare the number of lions to the number of cars. Circle the number that is greater than the other number.

Chapter 3 Vocabulary Cards

eight

nine

seven

six

ten

ten frame

9

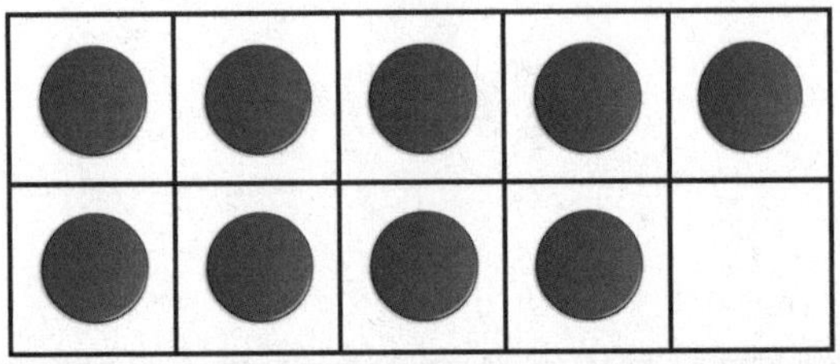

8

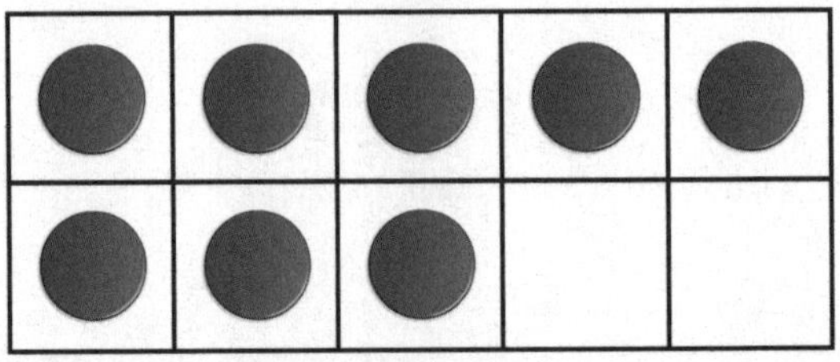

6

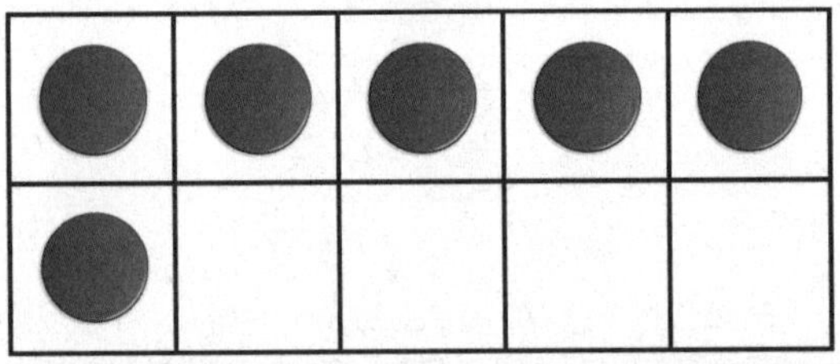

7

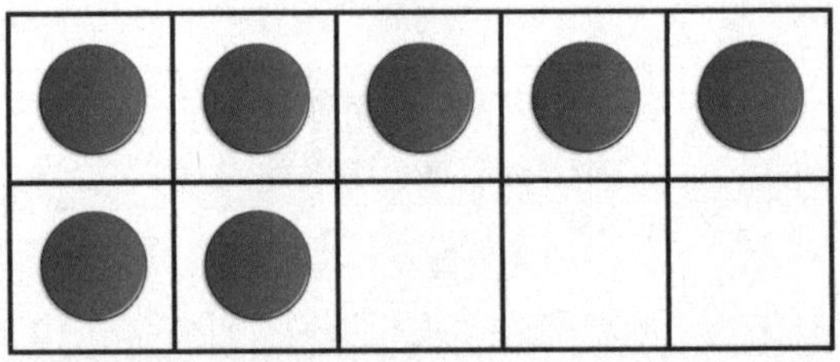

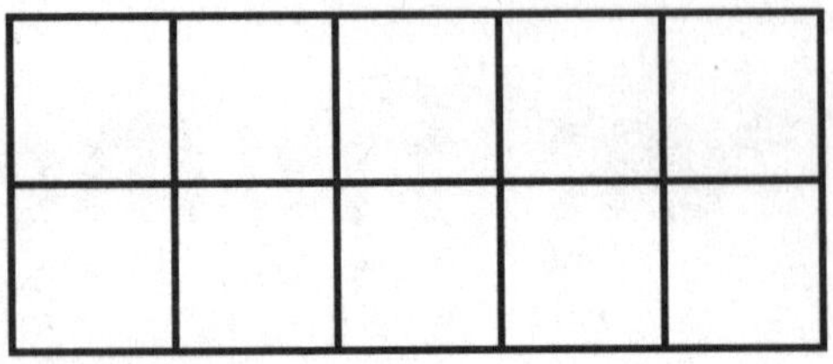

10

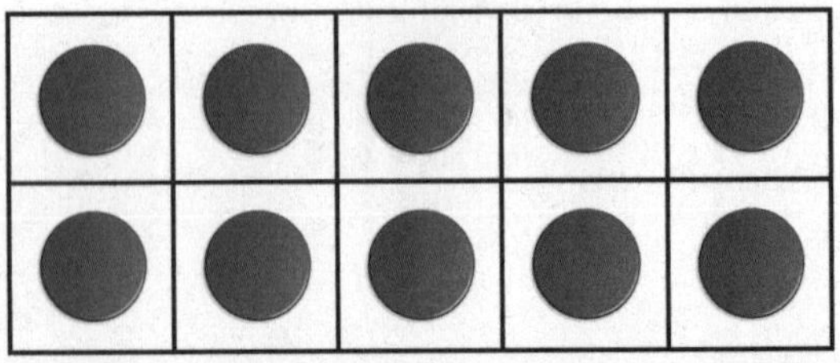

Name ______________________________

Model and Count 6 3.1

Learning Target: Show and count the number 6.

Explore and Grow

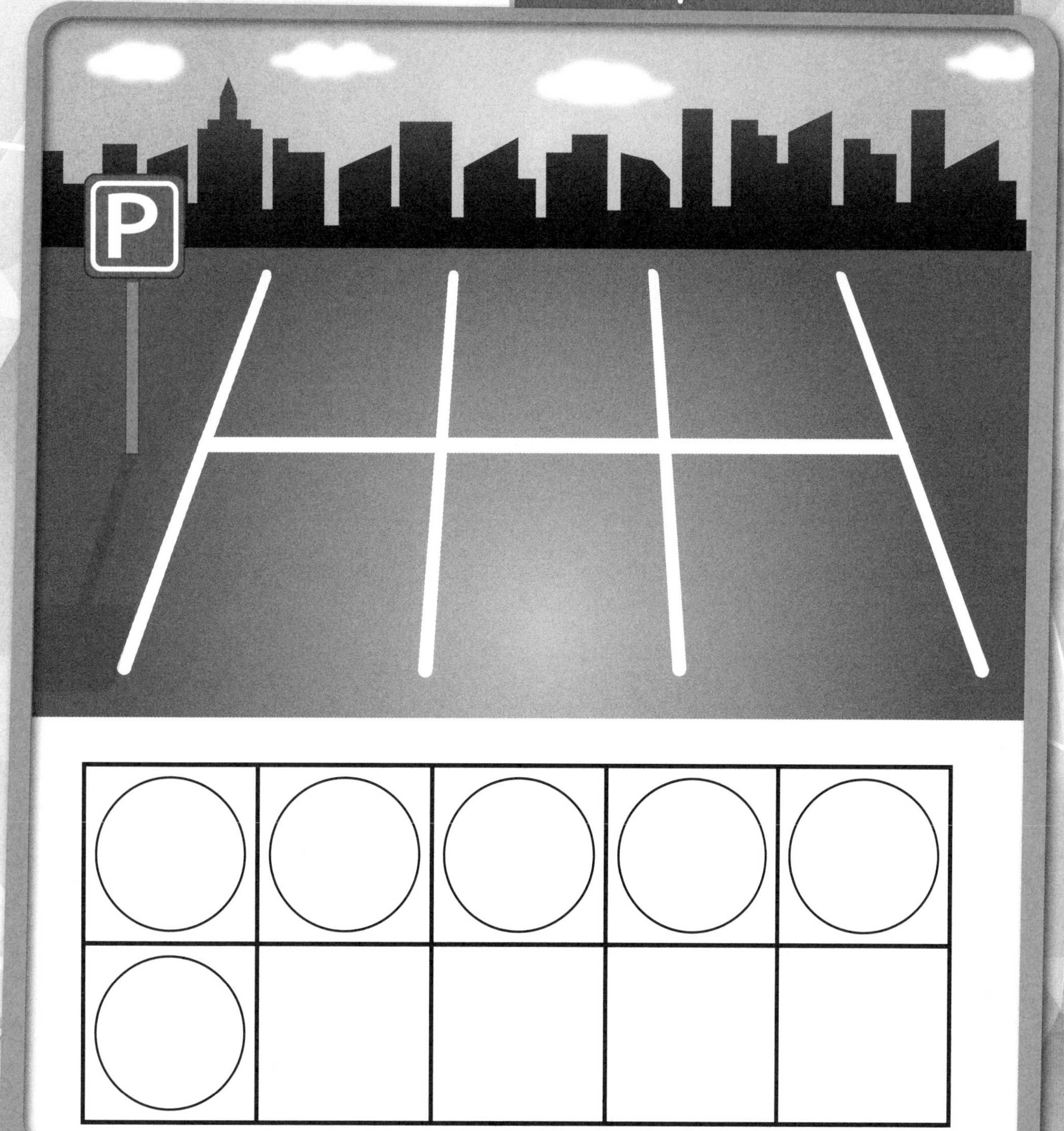

Directions: Place 6 counters on the parking lot. Slide the counters to the frame.

Think and Grow

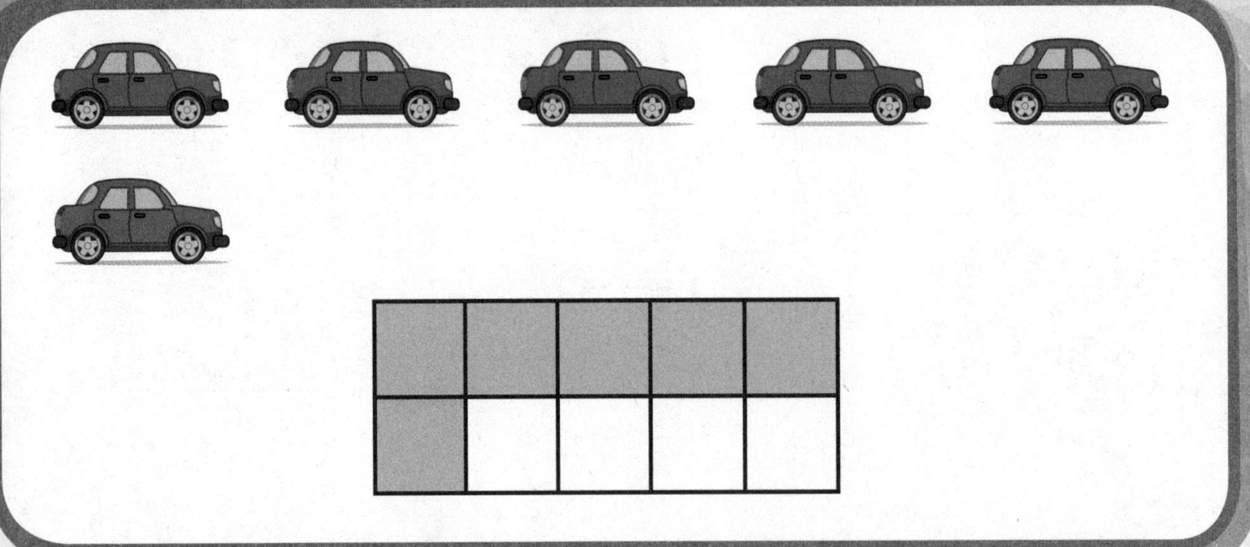

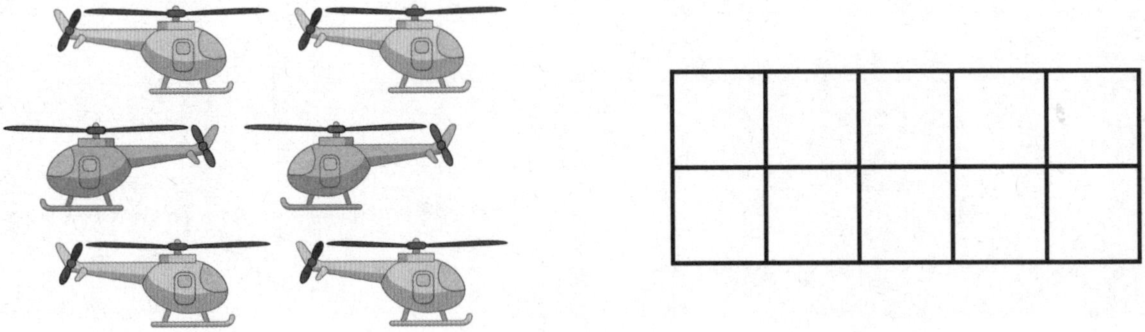

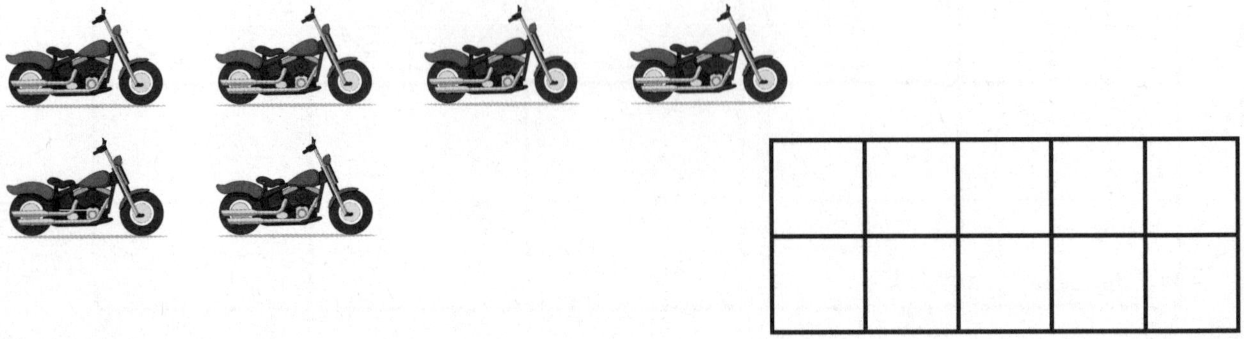

Directions: Count the objects. Color the boxes to show how many.

Name ______________________________

Apply and Grow: Practice

1

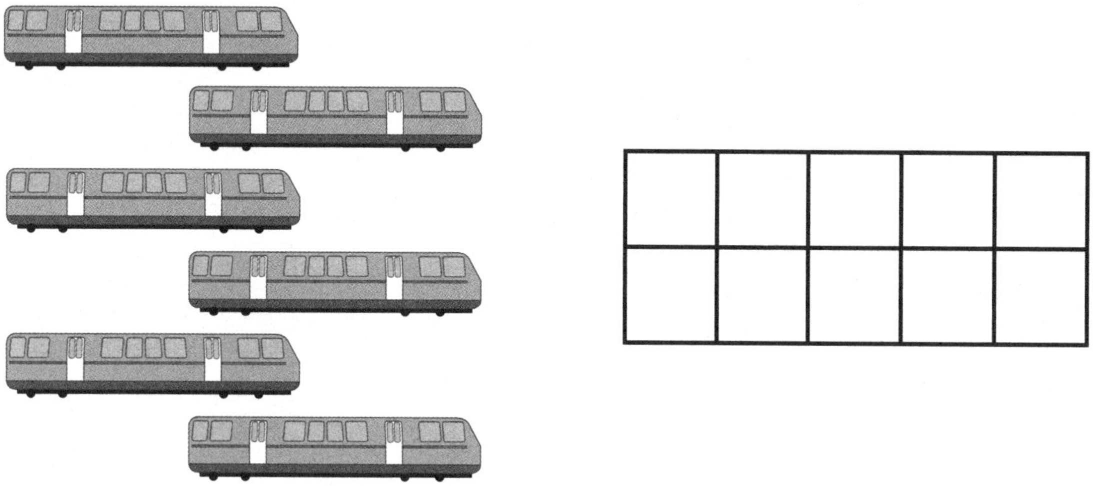

2

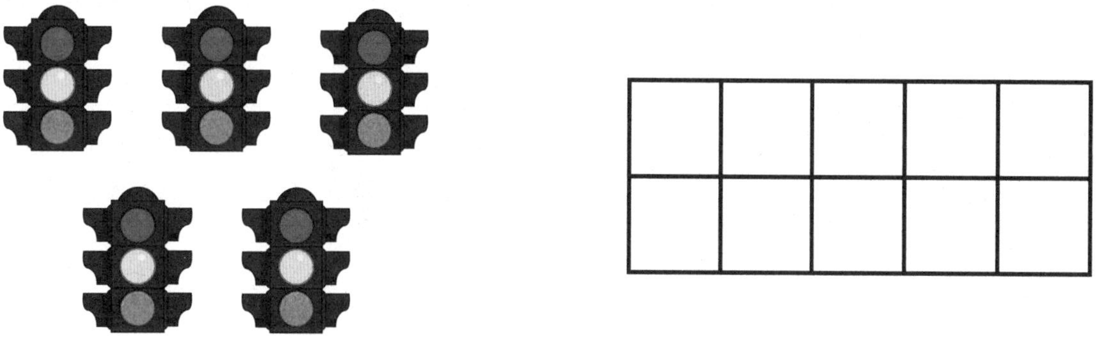

3

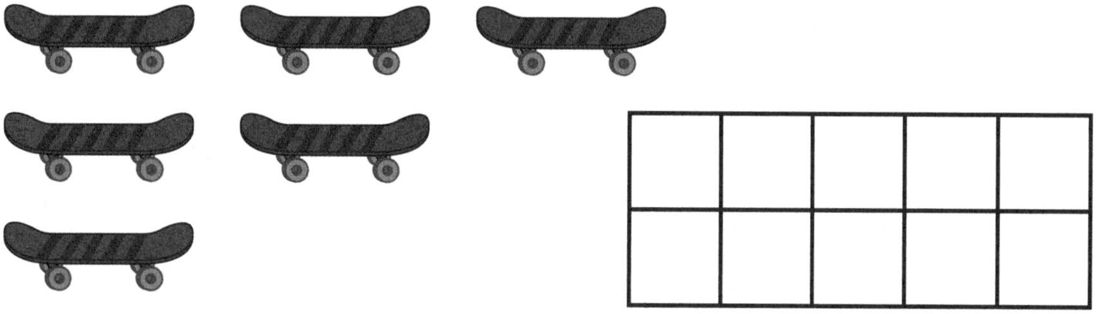

Directions: 1 – 3 Count the objects. Color the boxes to show how many.

Think and Grow: Modeling Real Life

Directions: Count the objects in the picture. Color the boxes to show how many.

Name ______________________________

Practice 3.1

Learning Target: Show and count the number 6.

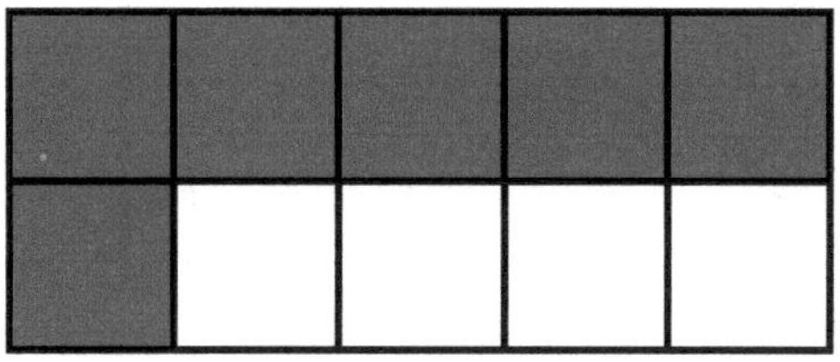

Directions: Count the trucks. Color the boxes to show how many.

1

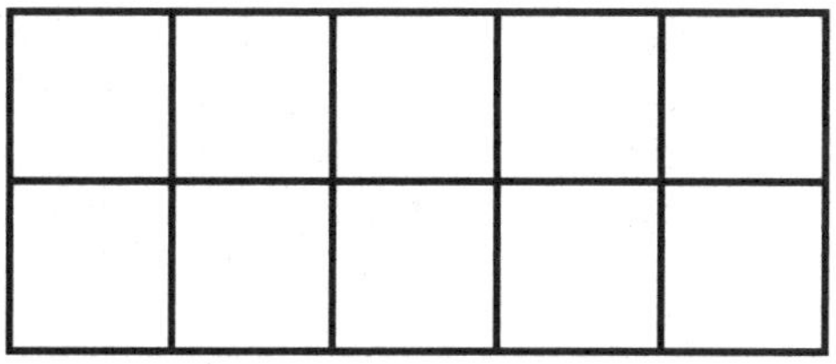

2

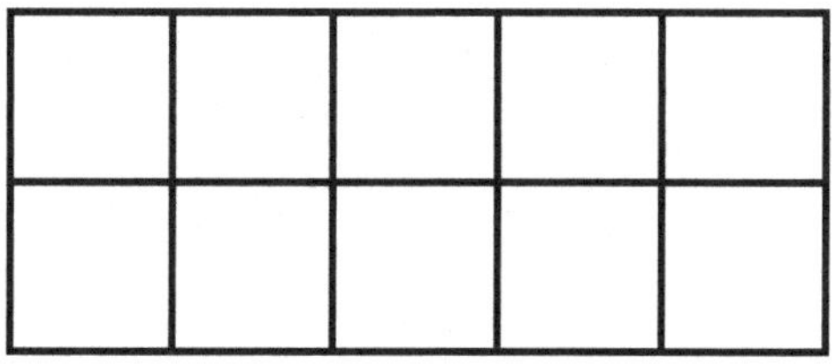

Directions: 1 and 2 Count the objects. Color the boxes to show how many.

3

4

5

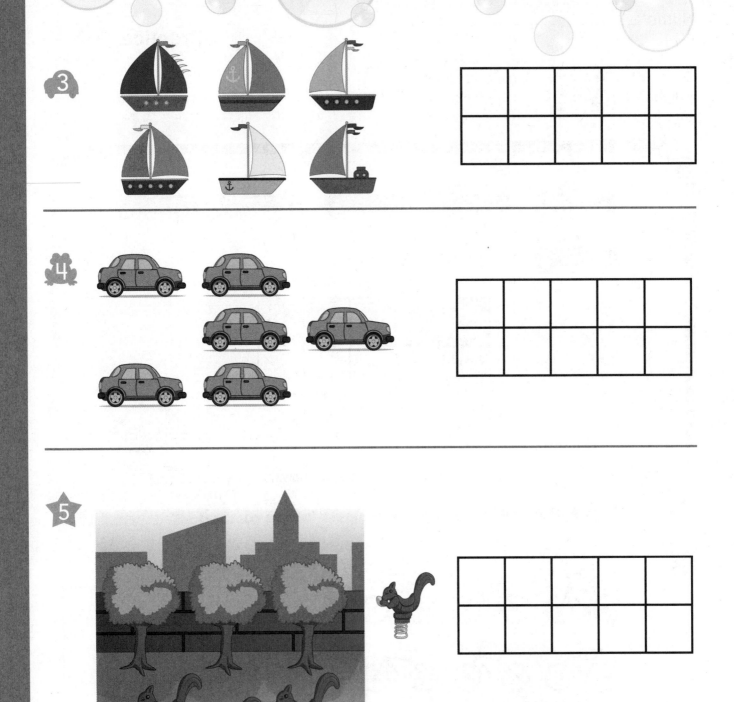

Directions: 3 and 4 Count the objects. Color the boxes to show how many.
5 Count the objects in the picture. Color the boxes to show how many.

Name ____________________

Learning Target: Understand and write the number 6.

Explore and Grow

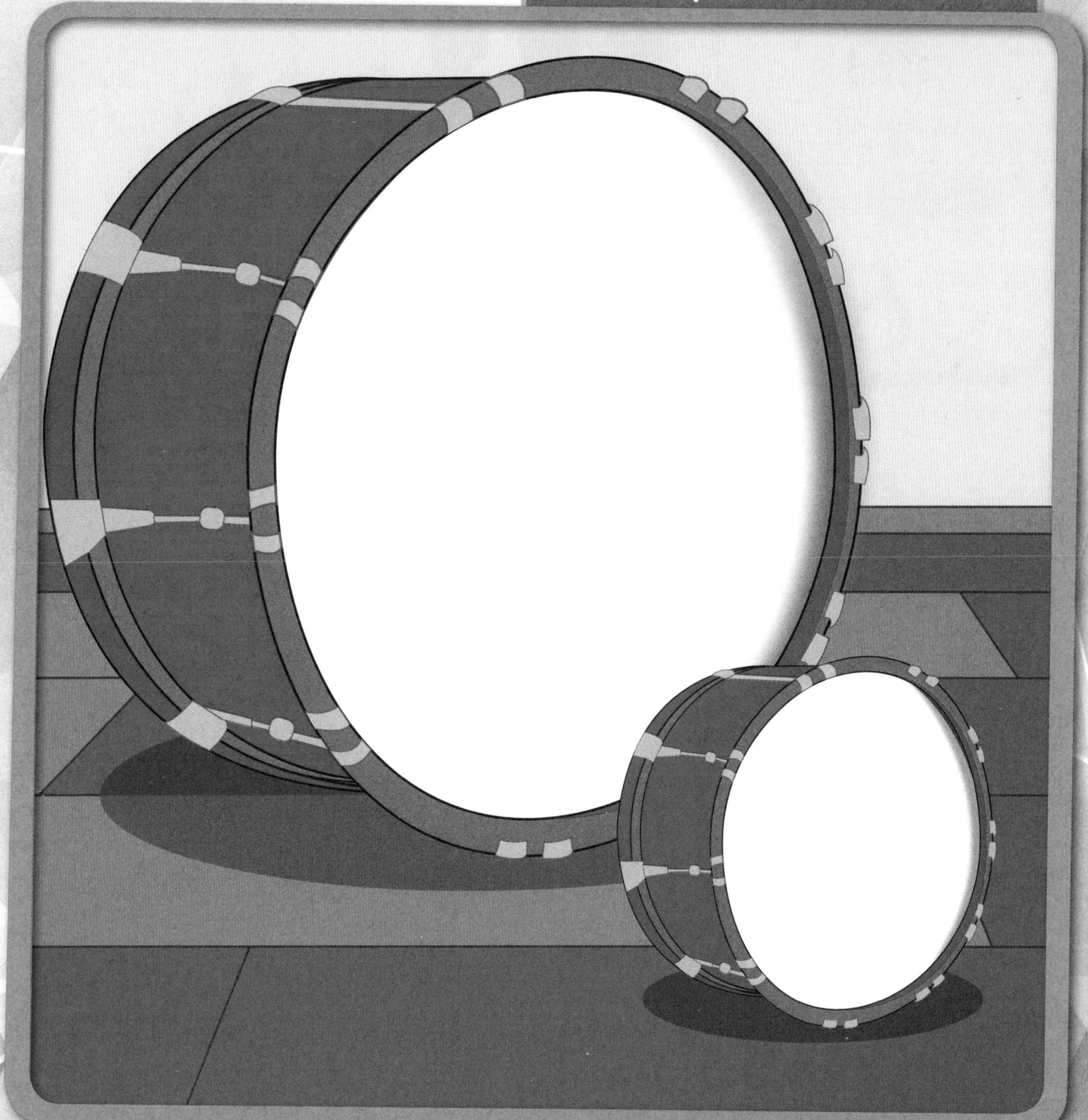

Directions: Use counters to show how many drums are in the story *Music Class*. Write how many drums are in the story.

Think and Grow

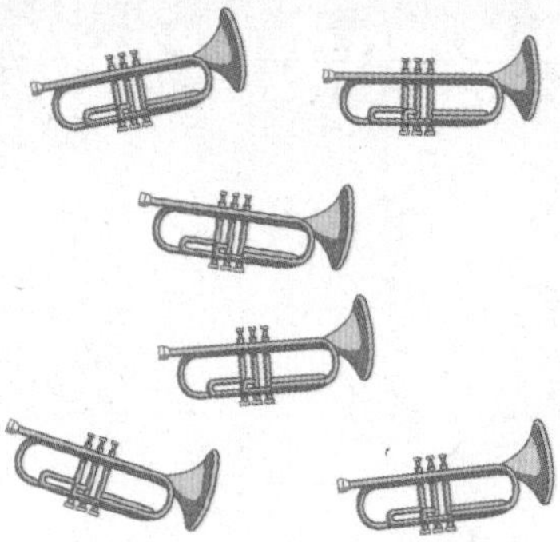

6

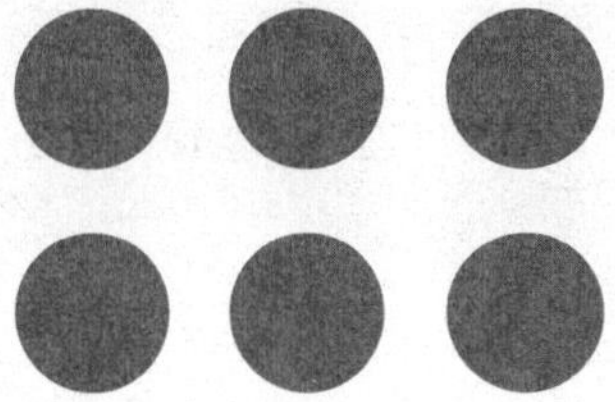

6

six

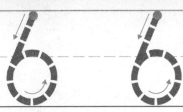

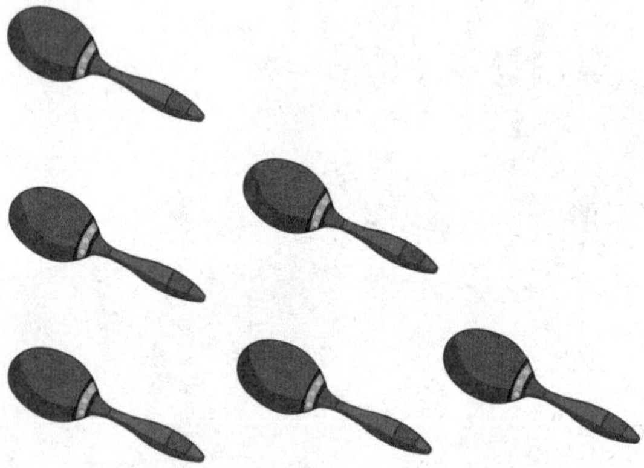

Directions:
- Count the objects. Say the number. Trace and write the number.
- Count the instruments. Say the number. Write the number.

Name ________________

Apply and Grow: Practice

1

2

3

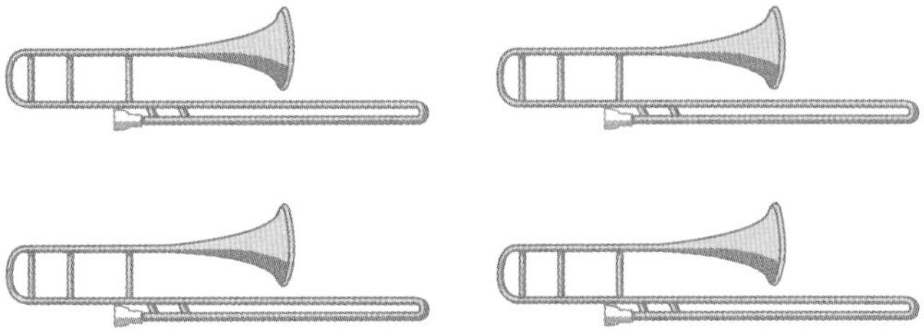

4

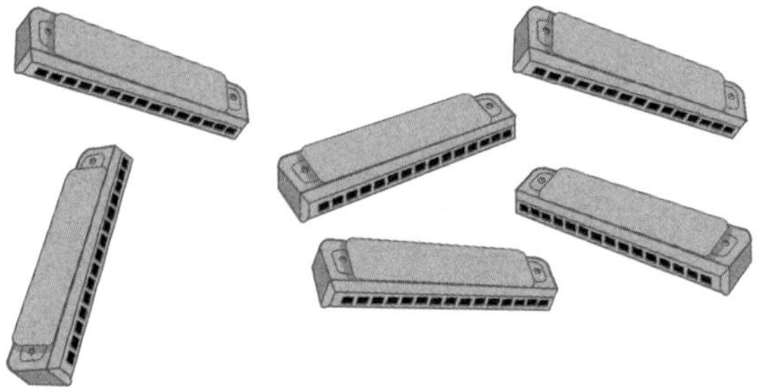

Directions: 1–4 Count the objects. Say the number. Write the number.

Think and Grow: Modeling Real Life

Directions: Count the instruments in the picture. Say the number. Write the number.

Name ____________________

Practice 3.2

Learning Target: Understand and write the number 6.

six

Directions: Count the linking cubes. Say the number. Write the number.

1

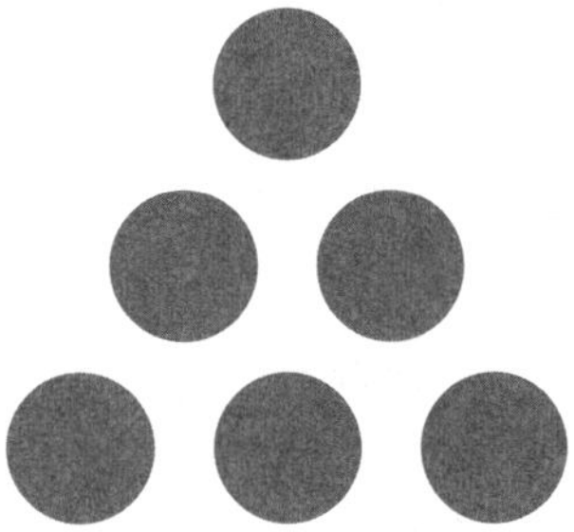

2

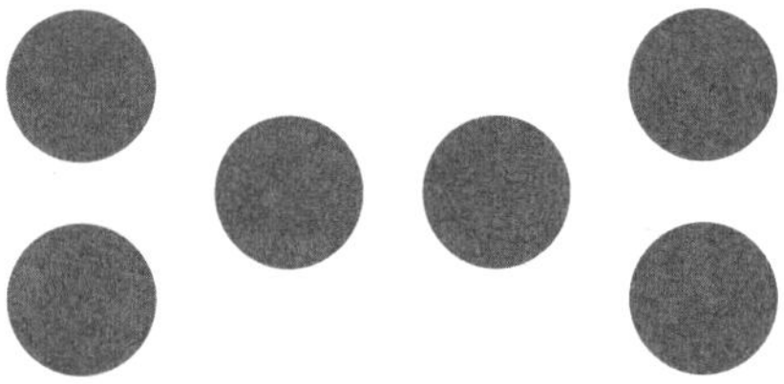

Directions: 1 and 2 Count the dots. Say the number. Write the number.

3

4

5

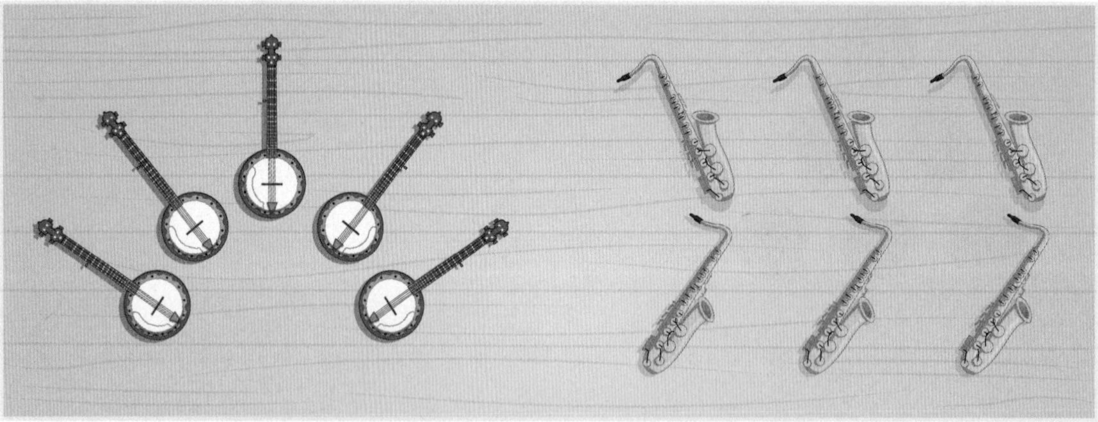

Directions: 3 and 4 Count the objects. Say the number. Write the number.
5 Count the instruments in the picture. Say the number. Write the number.

Name ________________________________

Model and Count 7

3.3

Learning Target: Show and count the number 7.

Explore and Grow

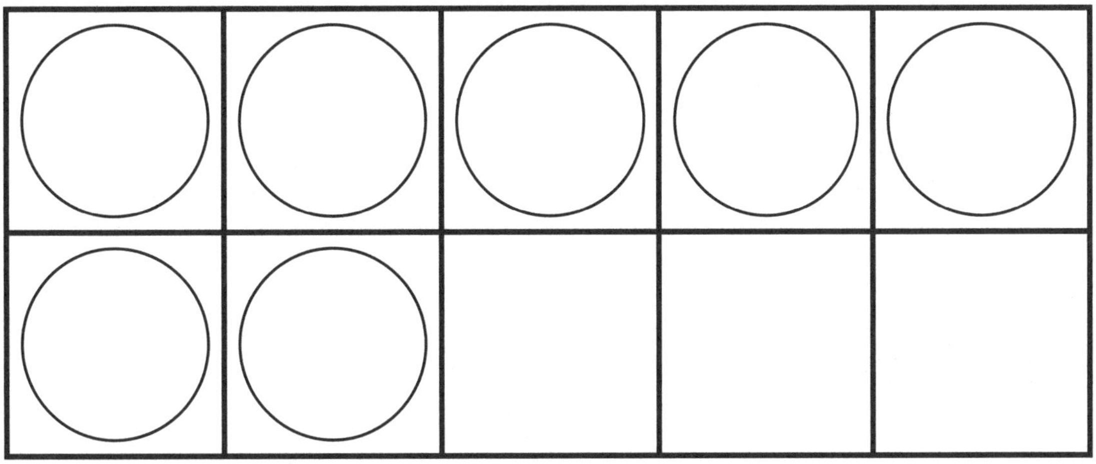

Directions: Place 7 counters in the forest. Slide the counters to the frame.

Think and Grow

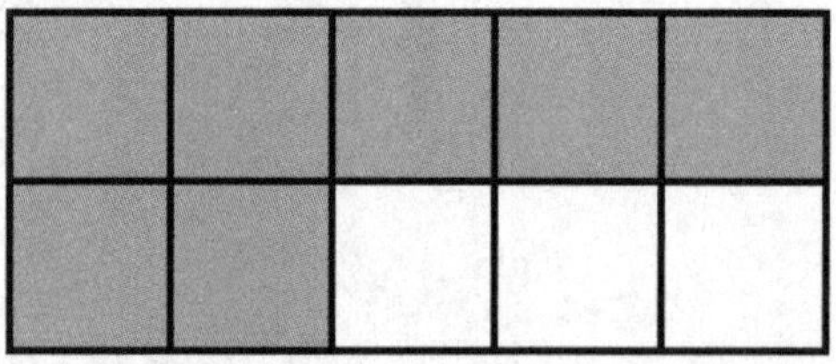

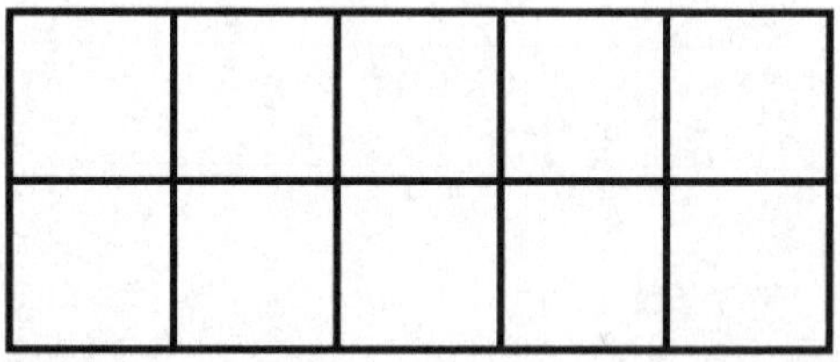

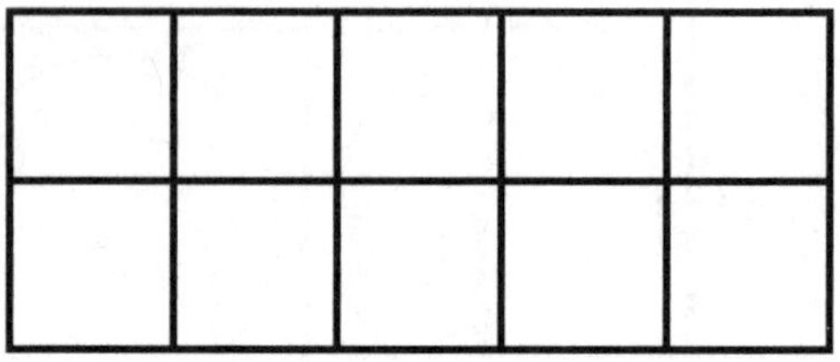

Directions: Count the objects. Color the boxes to show how many.

Name ____________________

Apply and Grow: Practice

1

2

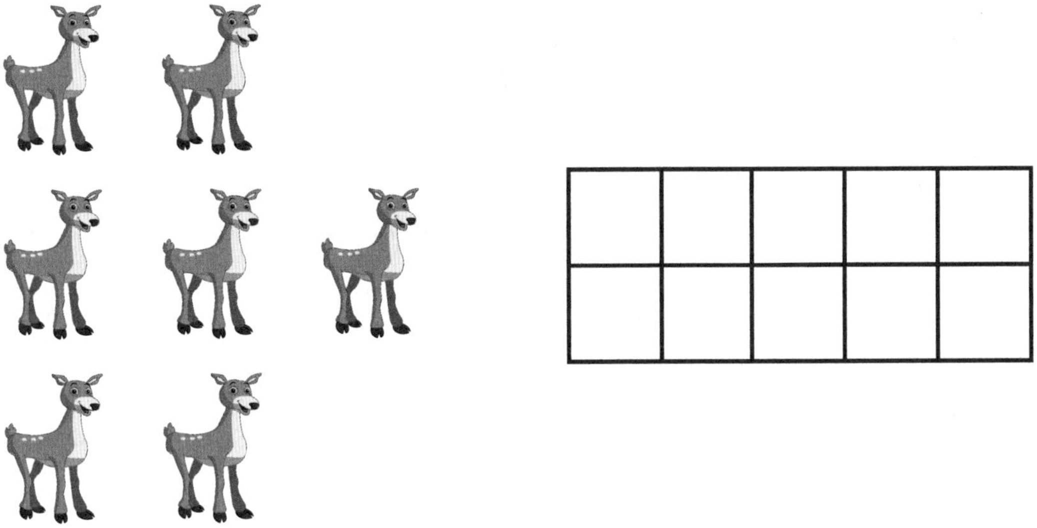

3

Directions: 1 – 3 Count the animals. Color the boxes to show how many.

Think and Grow: Modeling Real Life

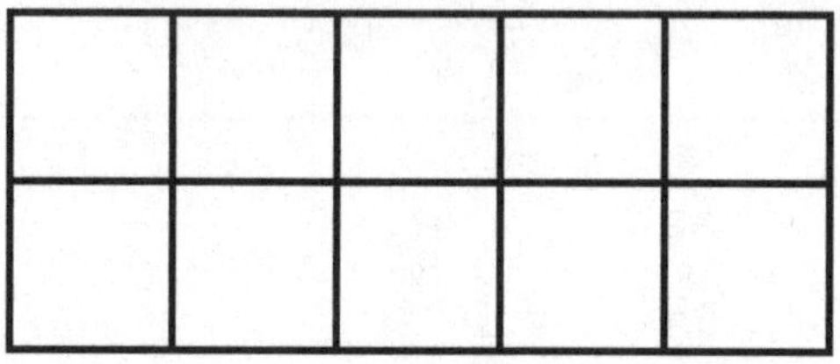

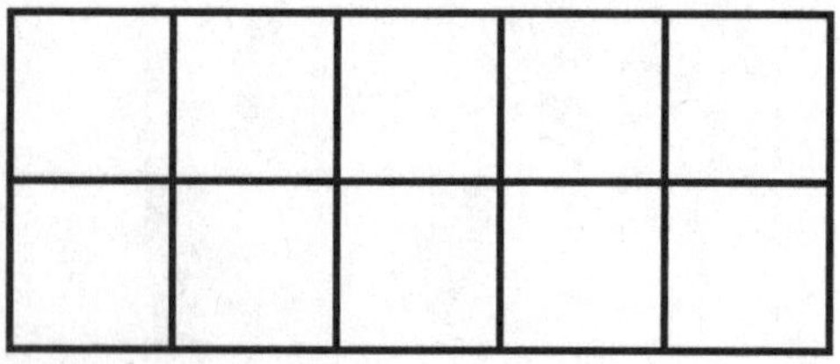

Directions: Count the animals in the picture. Color the boxes to show how many.

Name ____________________

Learning Target: Show and count the number 7.

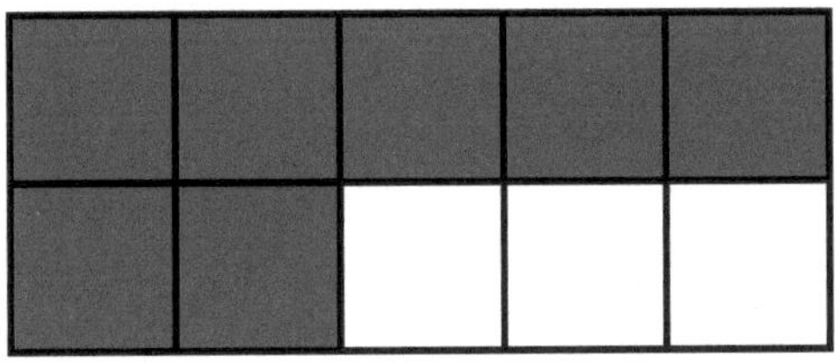

Directions: Count the badgers. Color the boxes to show how many.

1

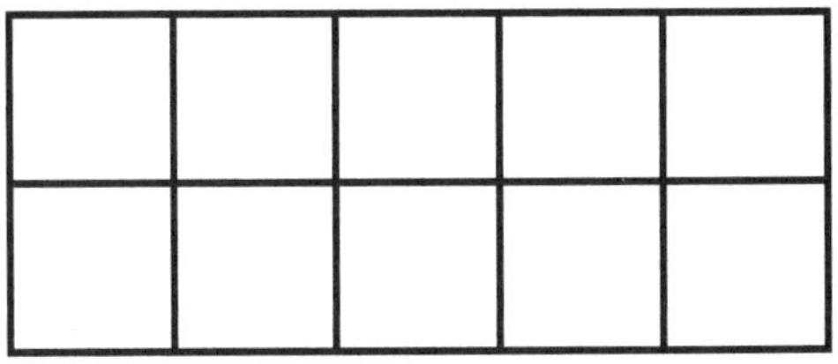

2

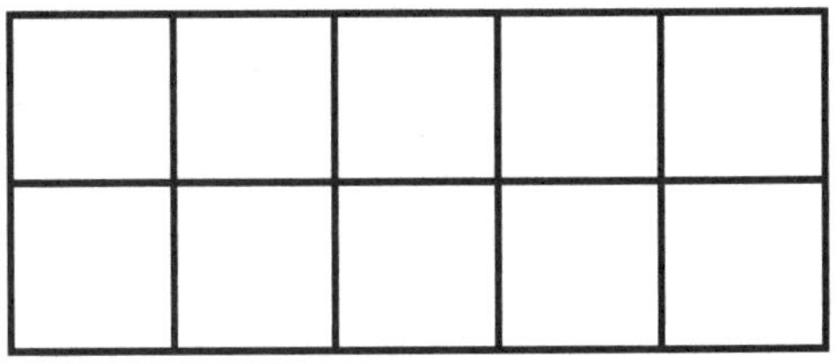

Directions: 1 and 2 Count the animals. Color the boxes to show how many.

3

4

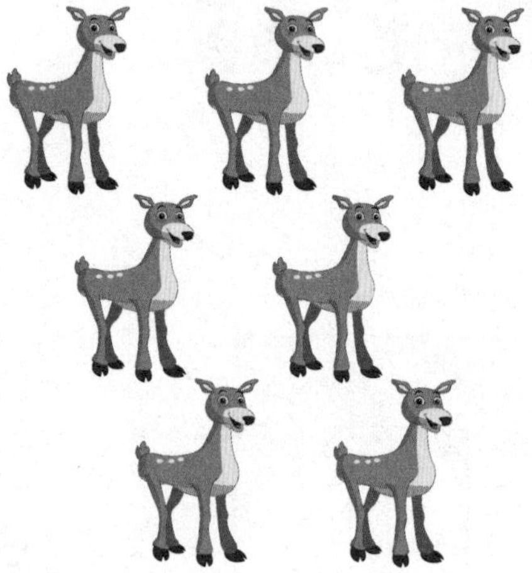

5

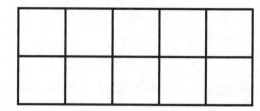

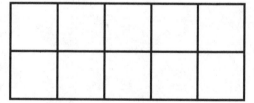

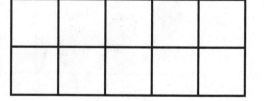

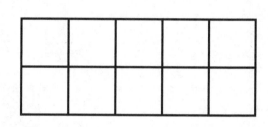

Directions: 3 and 4 Count the animals. Color the boxes to show how many.
5 Count the animals in the picture. Color the boxes to show how many.

Name ______________________________

Understand and Write 7 3.4

Learning Target: Understand and write the number 7.

Explore and Grow

Directions: Use counters to show how many raindrops are in the story *Rainy Day*. Write how many raindrops are in the story.

Think and Grow

7

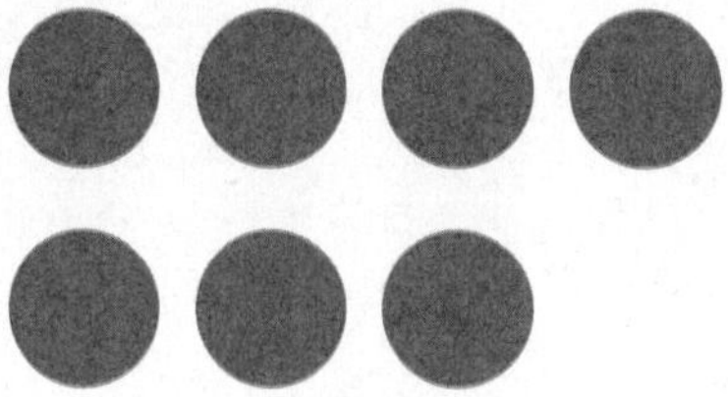

7

seven

Directions:

- Count the objects. Say the number. Trace and write the number.
- Count the objects. Say the number. Write the number.

Name ______________________

Apply and Grow: Practice

1

2
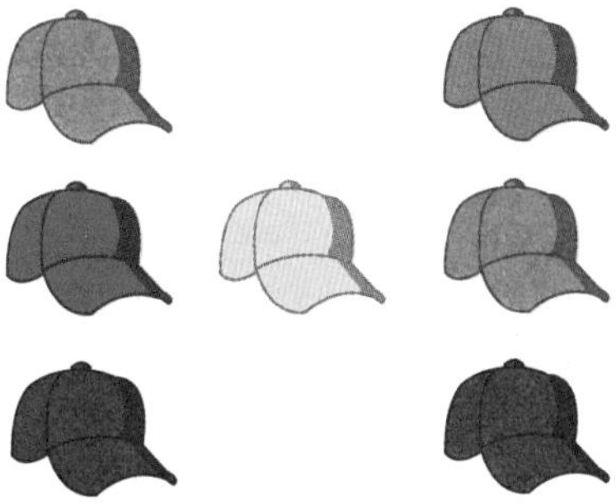

3
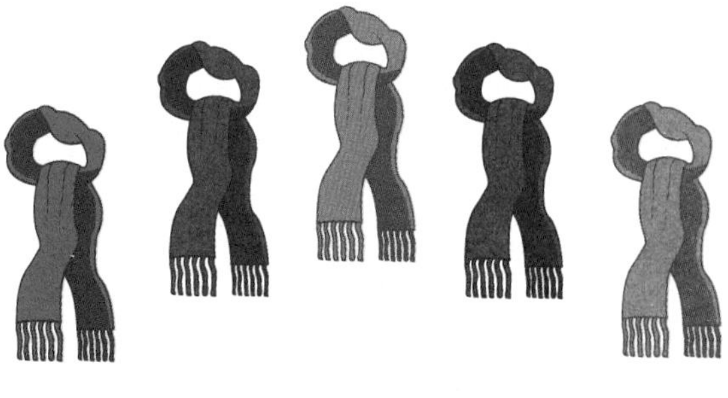

4

Directions: 1–4 Count the objects. Say the number. Write the number.

Think and Grow: Modeling Real Life

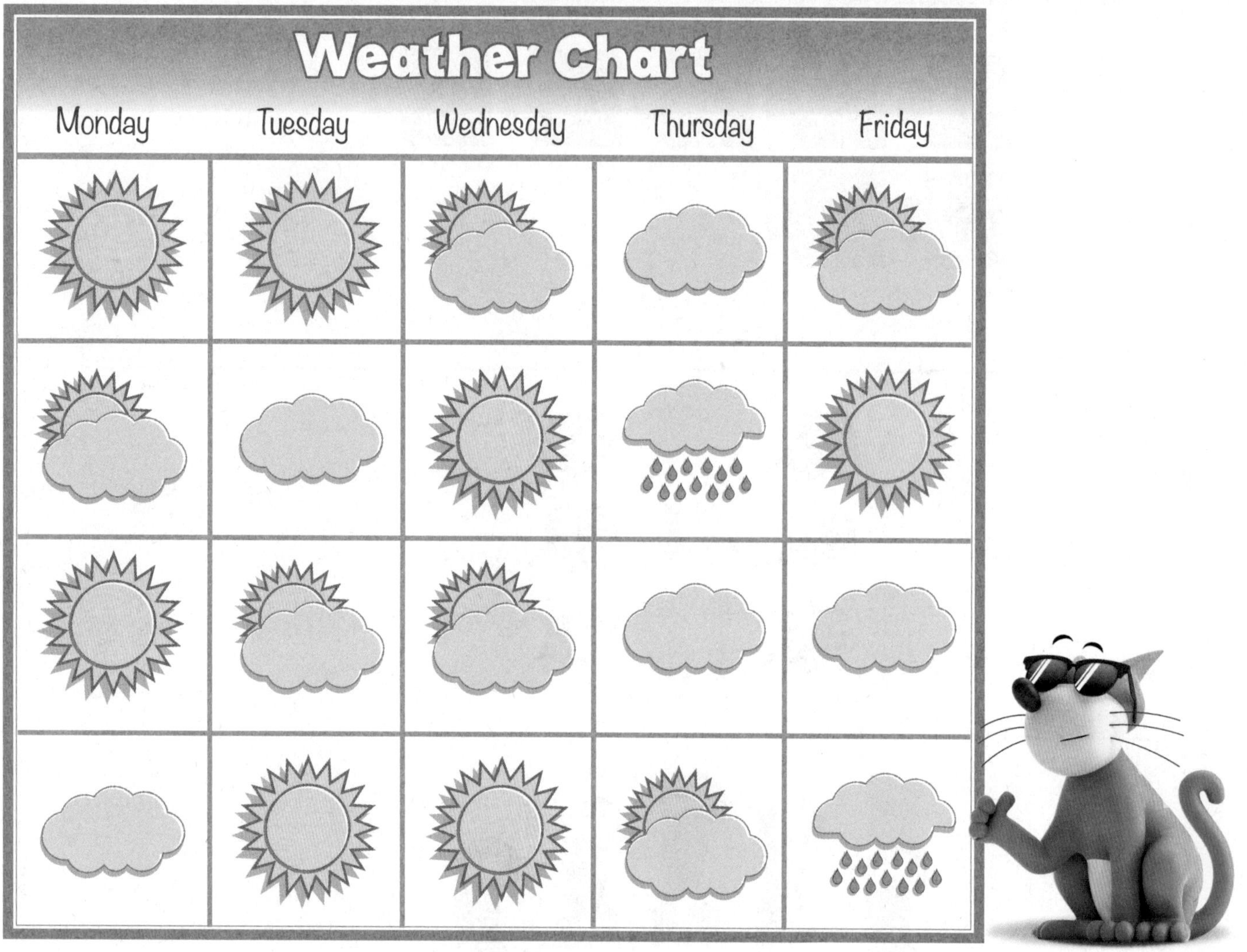

Directions: Count the objects in the picture. Say the number. Write the number.

Name ______________________________

Practice 3.4

Learning Target: Understand and write the number 7.

seven

7

Directions: Count the linking cubes. Say the number. Write the number.

1

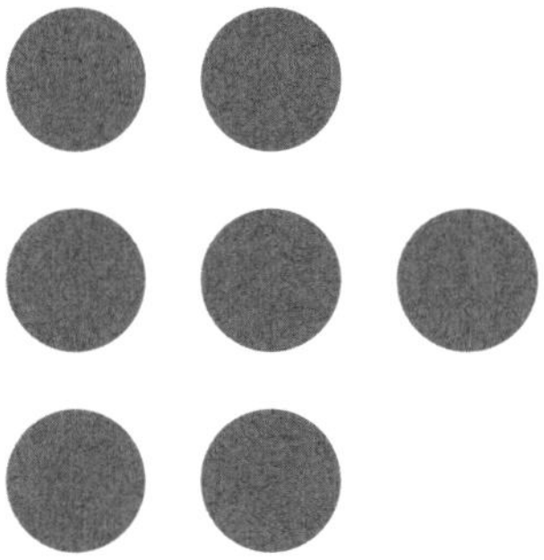

2

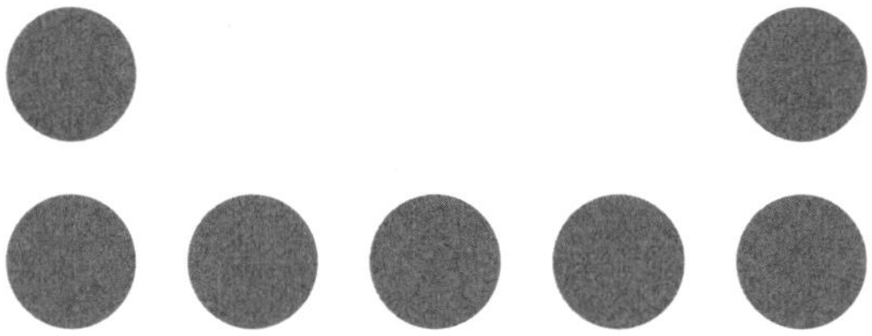

Directions: 1 and 2 Count the dots. Say the number. Write the number.

3

4

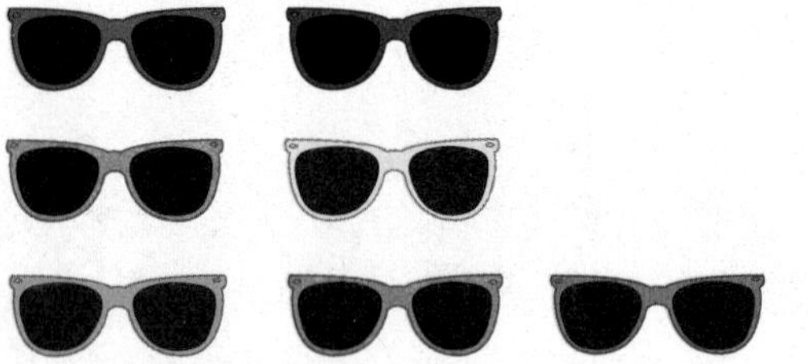

5

Directions: 3 and 4 Count the objects. Say the number. Write the number.
5 Count the objects in the picture. Say the number. Write the number.

Name ______________________

Model and Count 8 3.5

Learning Target: Show and count the number 8.

Explore and Grow

Directions: Place 8 counters in the desert. Slide the counters to the frame.

Think and Grow

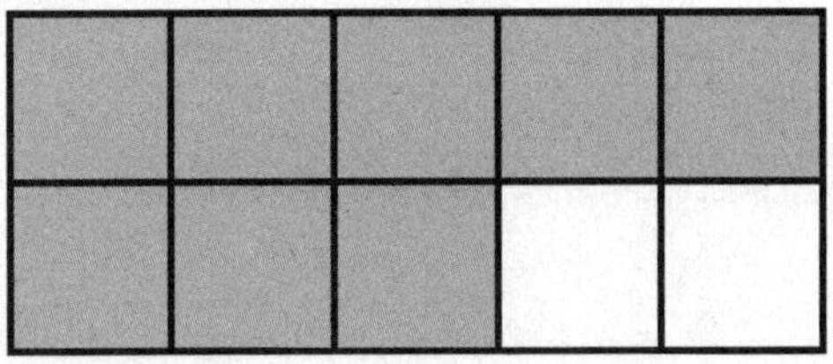

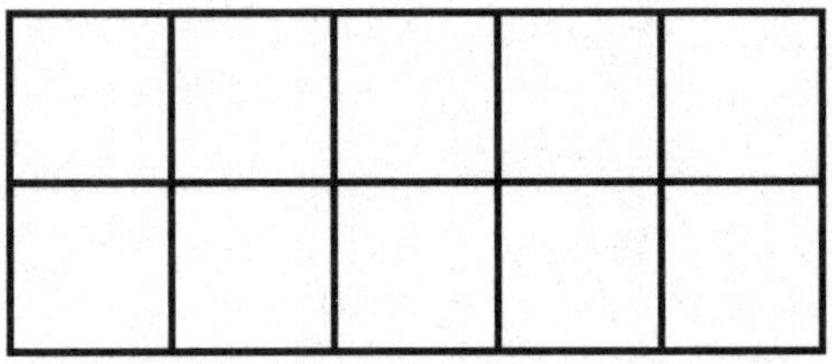

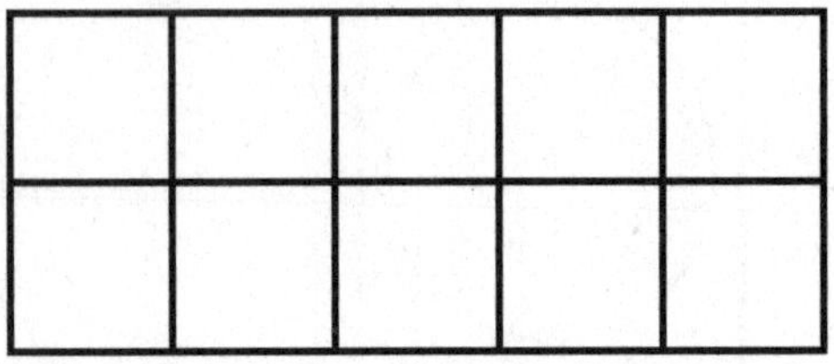

Directions: Count the objects. Color the boxes to show how many.

Name ________________________________

Apply and Grow: Practice

1

2

3

Directions: 1 – 3 Count the objects. Color the boxes to show how many.

Think and Grow: Modeling Real Life

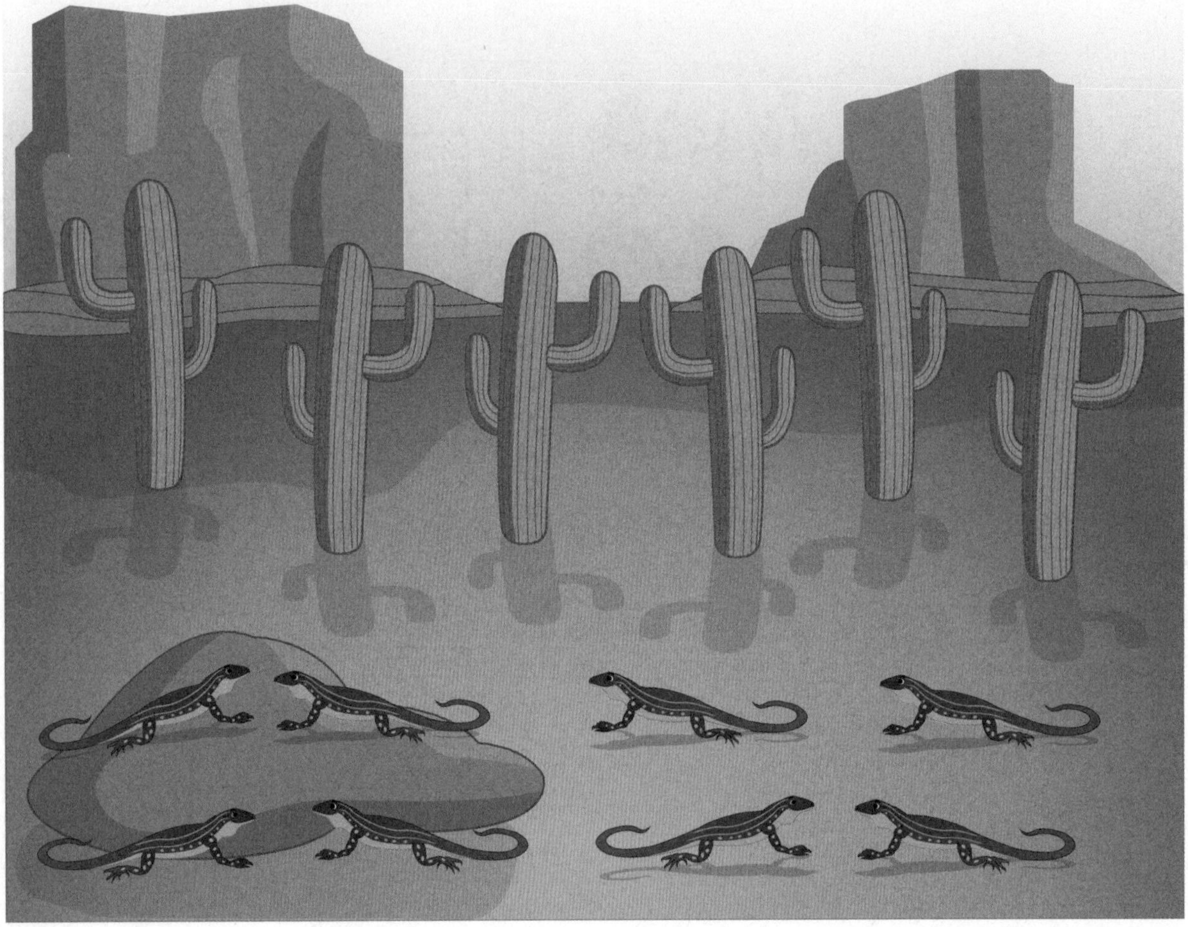

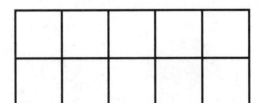

Directions: Count the objects in the picture. Color the boxes to show how many.

Name ______________________________

Practice 3.5

Learning Target: Show and count the number 8.

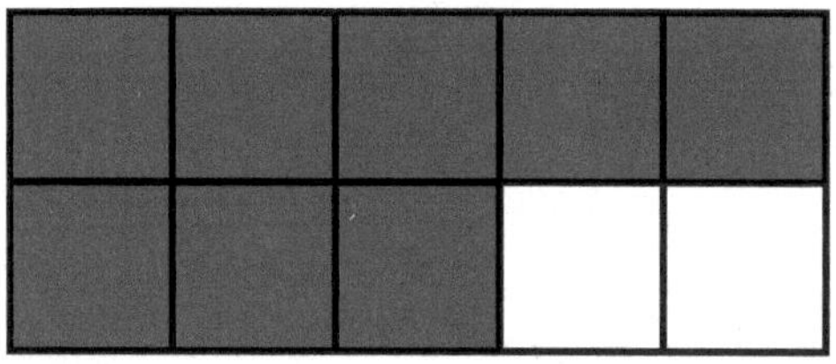

Directions: Count the lizards. Color the boxes to show how many.

1

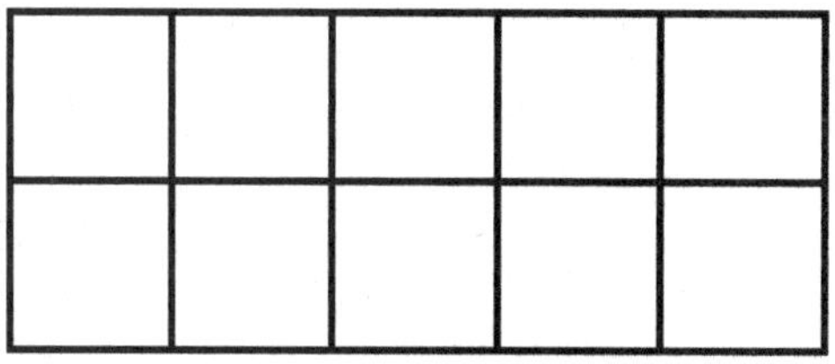

2

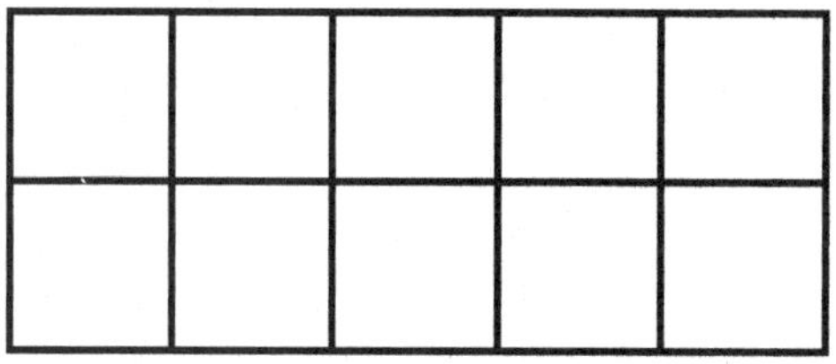

Directions: 1 and 2 Count the objects. Color the boxes to show how many.

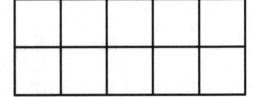

3

4

5

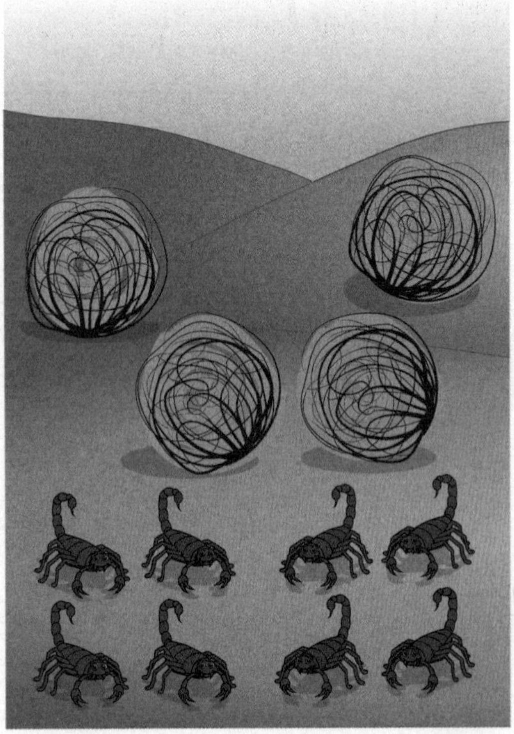

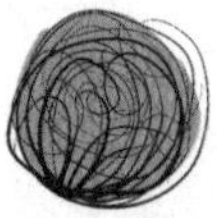

Directions: 3 and 4 Count the objects. Color the boxes to show how many.
5 Count the objects in the picture. Color the boxes to show how many.

Name ______________________

Learning Target: Understand and write the number 8.

Explore and Grow

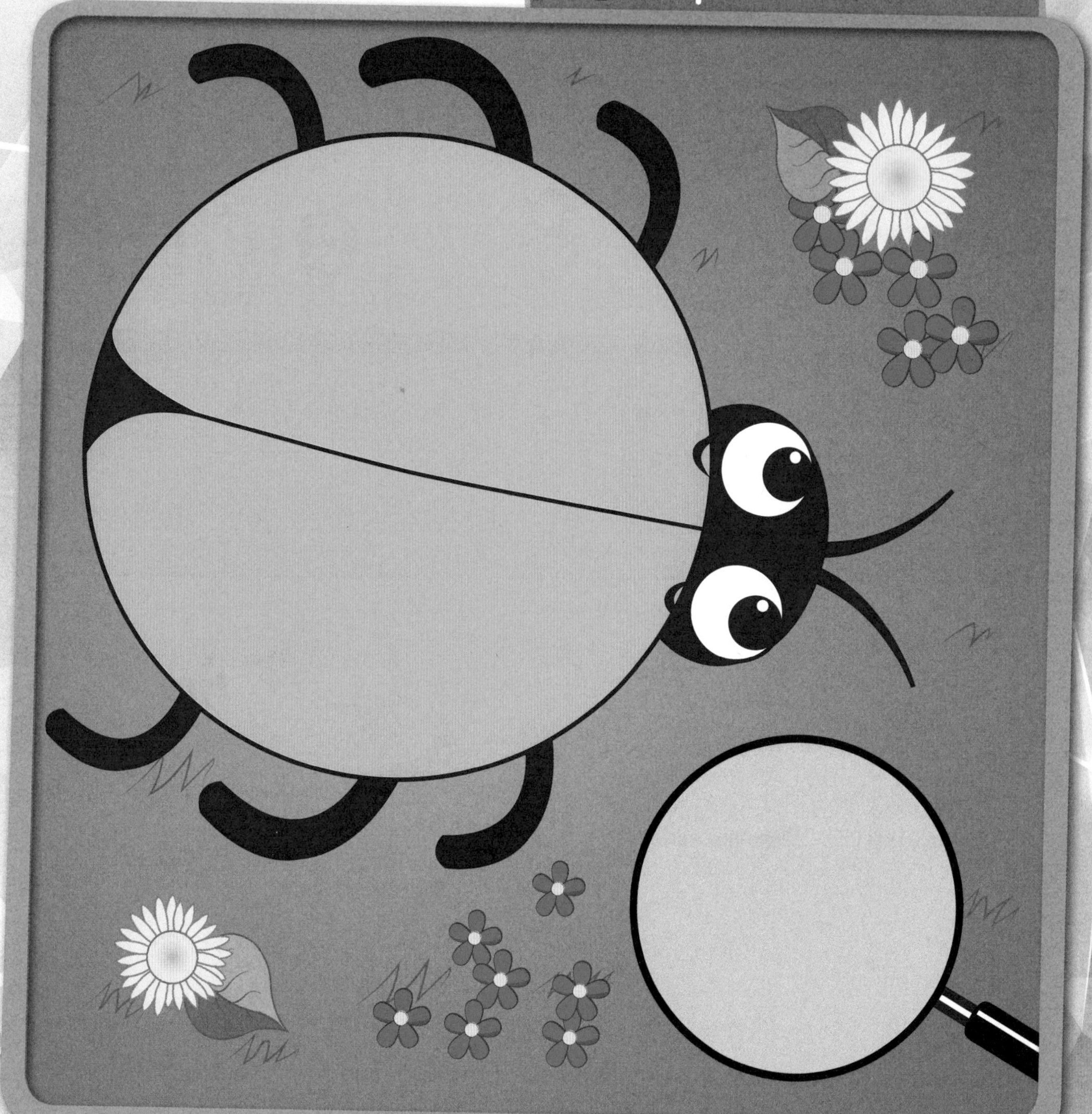

Directions: Use counters to show how many spots are on the ladybug in the story *Bugs, Bugs, Bugs*. Write how many spots are on the ladybug.

Think and Grow

8

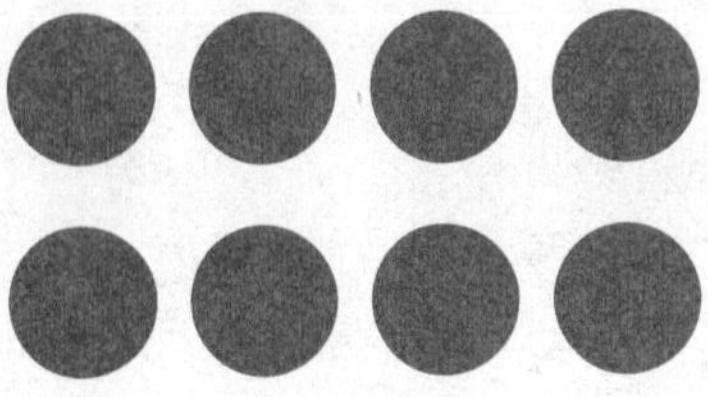

8

eight

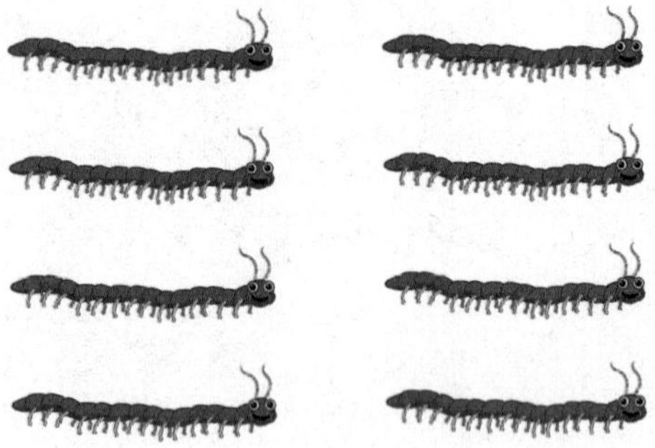

Directions:

- Count the objects. Say the number. Trace and write the number.
- Count the bugs. Say the number. Write the number.

Name ______________________________

Apply and Grow: Practice

1

2

3

4

Directions: 1–4 Count the objects. Say the number. Write the number.

Think and Grow: Modeling Real Life

Directions: Count the objects in the picture. Say the number. Write the number.

Name ______________________

Practice 3.6

Learning Target: Understand and write the number 8.

eight

8

Directions: Count the linking cubes. Say the number. Write the number.

1

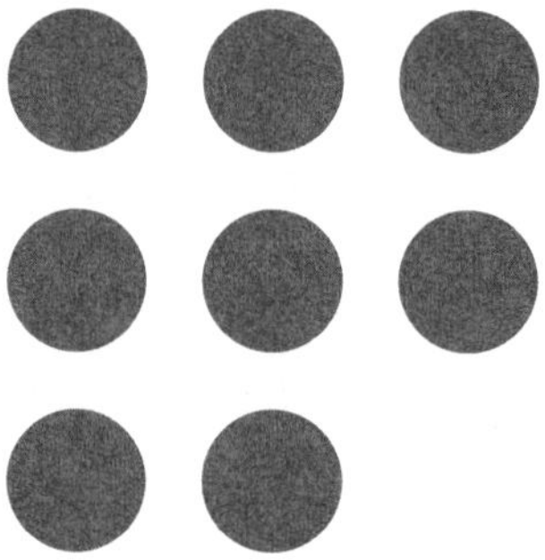

______

2

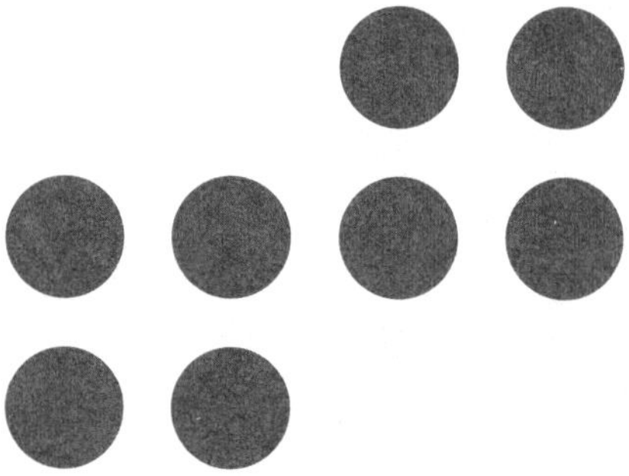

______

Directions: 1 and 2 Count the dots. Say the number. Write the number.

3

4

5

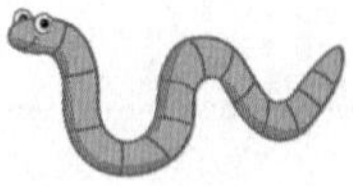

Directions: 3 and 4 Count the objects. Say the number. Write the number.
5 Count the objects in the picture. Say the number. Write the number.

Name ______________________________

Learning Target: Show and count the number 9.

Explore and Grow

Directions: Place 9 counters on the beach. Slide the counters to the frame.

Think and Grow

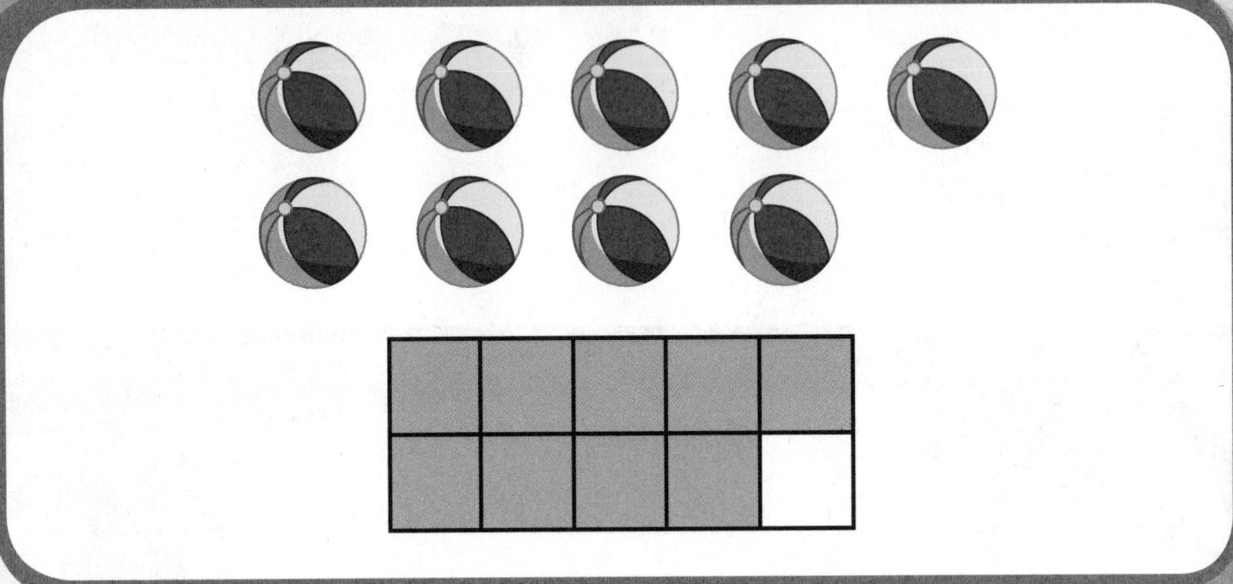

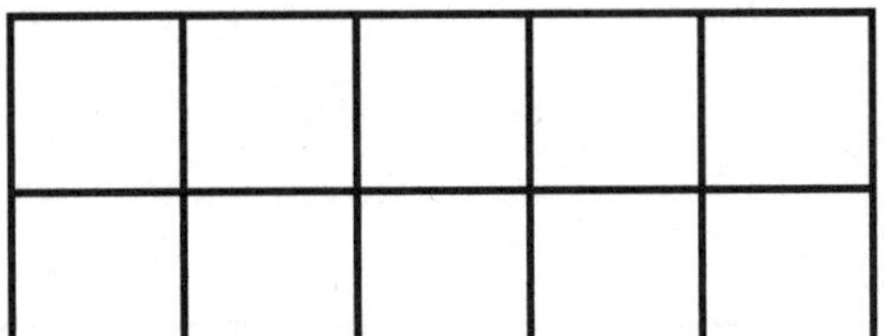

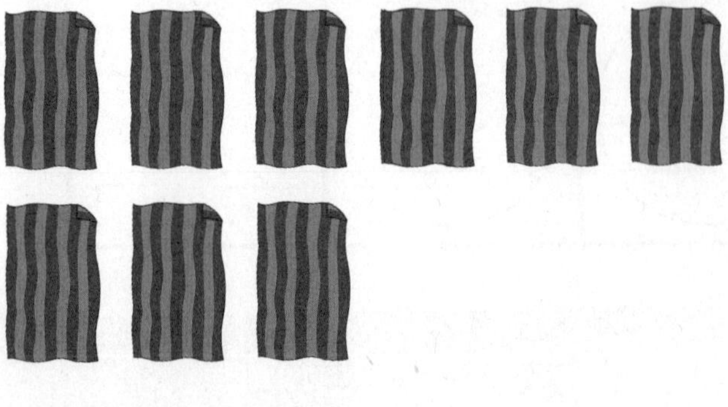

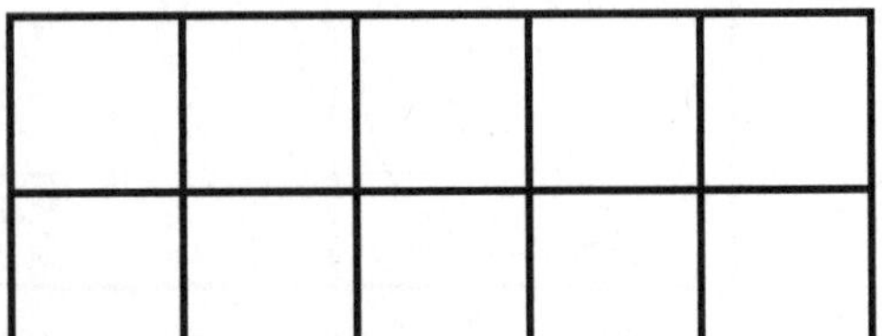

Directions: Count the objects. Color the boxes to show how many.

Name ______________________________

Apply and Grow: Practice

1

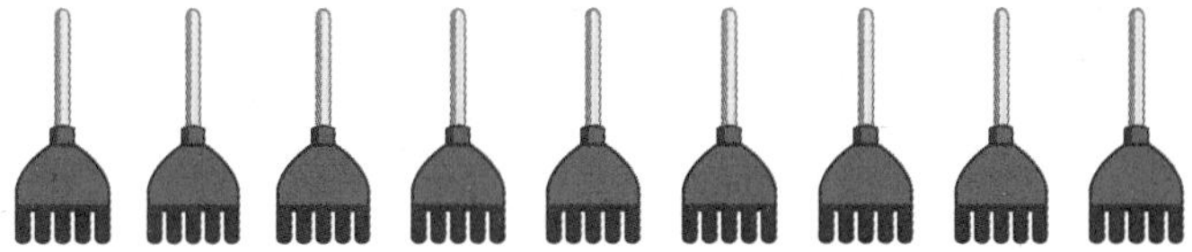

2

3

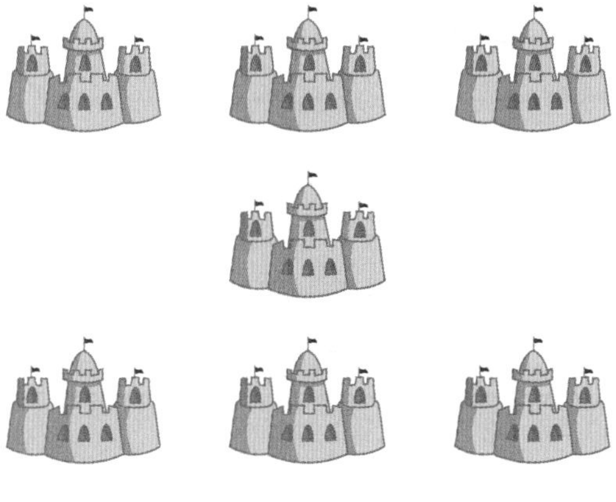

Directions: 1–3 Count the objects. Color the boxes to show how many.

Think and Grow: Modeling Real Life

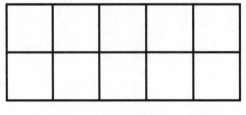

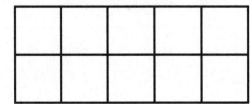

Directions: Count the objects in the picture. Color the boxes to show how many.

Name ____________________

Practice 3.7

Learning Target: Show and count the number 9.

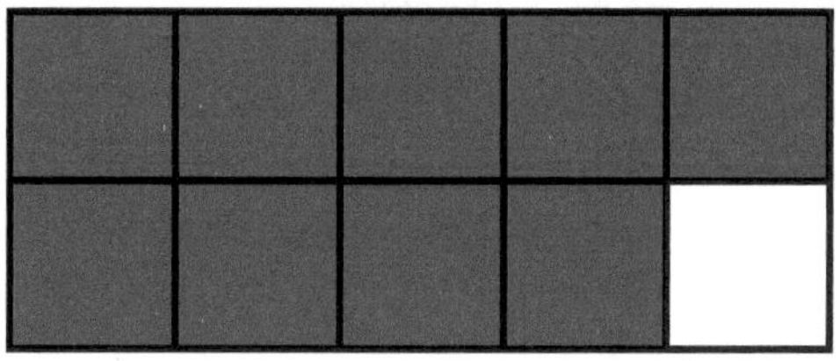

Directions: Count the shells. Color the boxes to show how many.

1

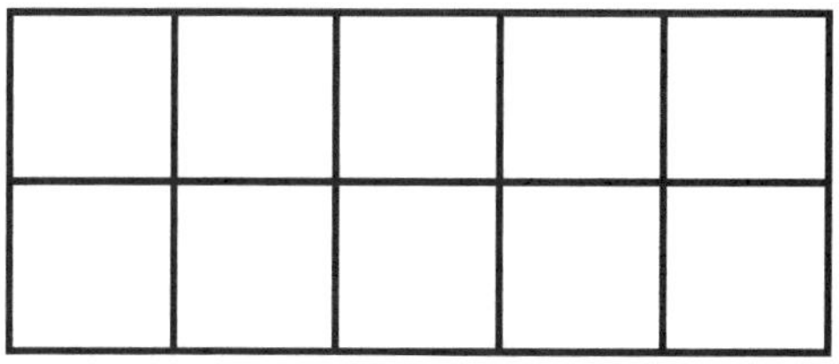

2

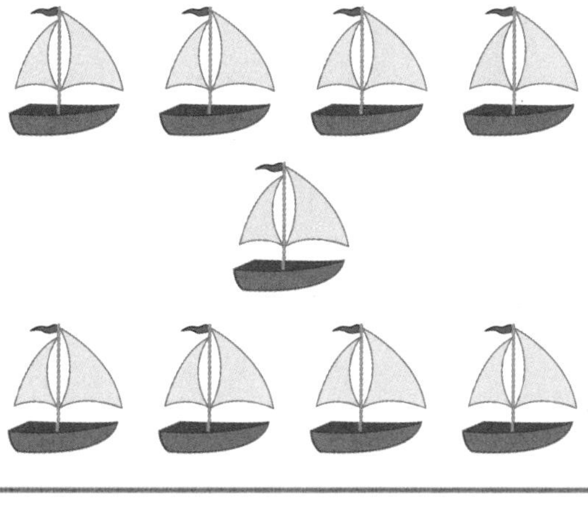

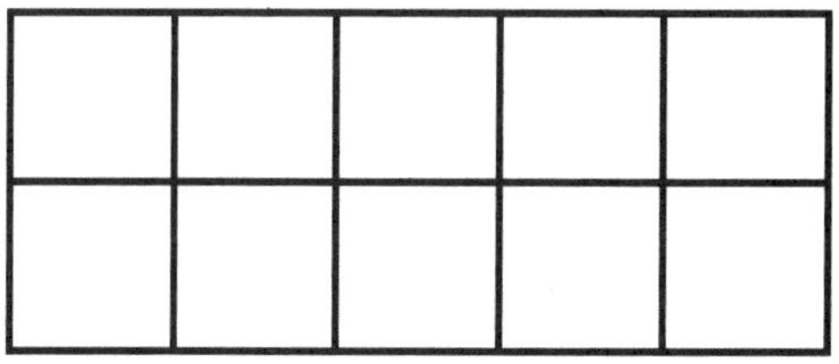

Directions: 1 and 2 Count the objects. Color the boxes to show how many.

3

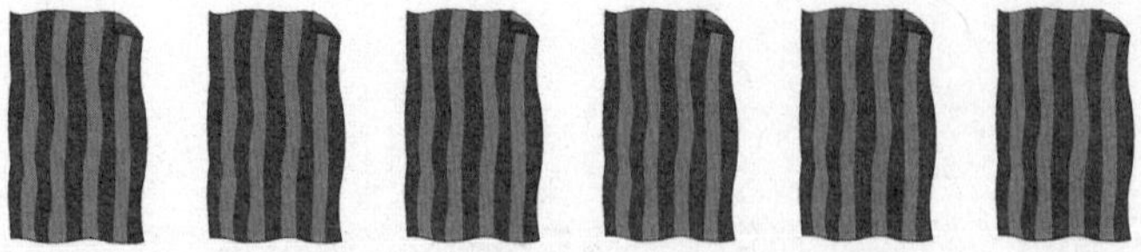

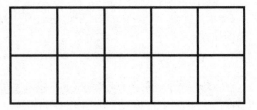

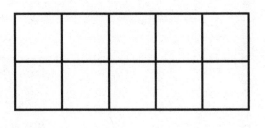

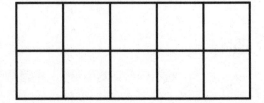

4

5

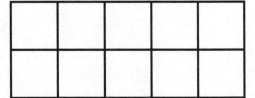

Directions: 3 and 4 Count the objects. Color the boxes to show how many.
5 Count the animals in the picture. Color the boxes to show how many.

Name ______________________

Learning Target: Understand and write the number 9.

Explore and Grow

Directions: Use counters to show how many baseballs are in the story *My Baseball Game.* Write how many baseballs are in the story.

Think and Grow

9

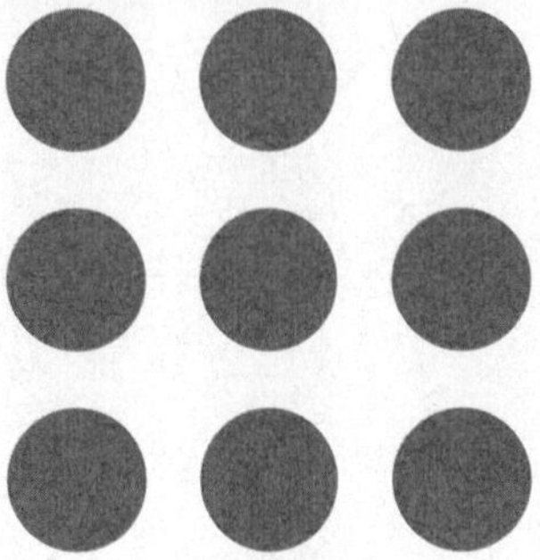

9

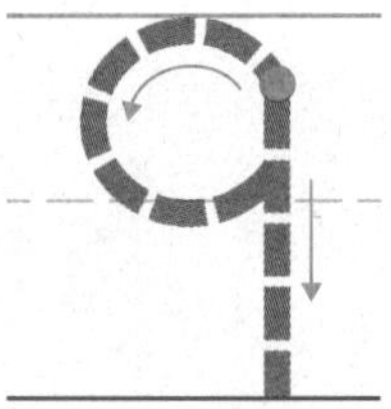

nine

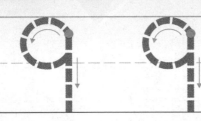

Directions:

- Count the objects. Say the number. Trace and write the number.
- Count the objects. Say the number. Write the number.

Name ______________________________

✓ Apply and Grow: Practice

1

______

2
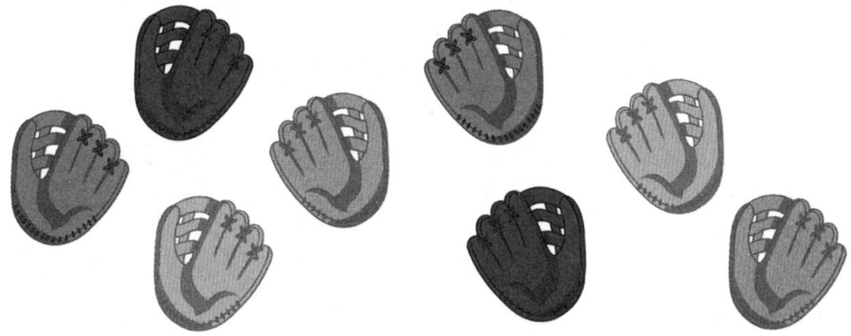

______

3
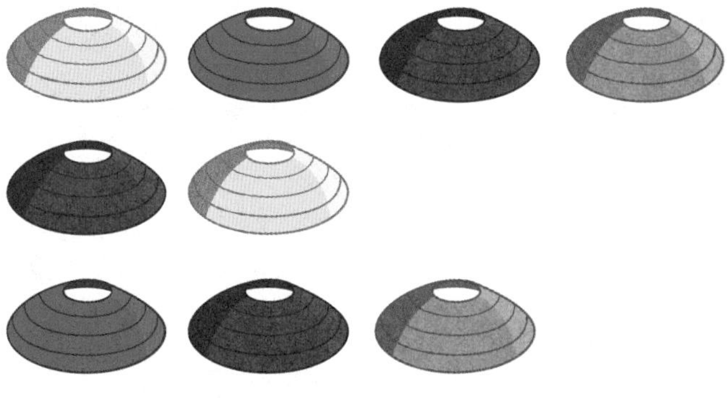

______

4

______

Directions: 1–4 Count the objects. Say the number. Write the number.

Think and Grow: Modeling Real Life

Directions: Count the balls in the picture. Say the number. Write the number.

Name ________________

Learning Target: Understand and write the number 9.

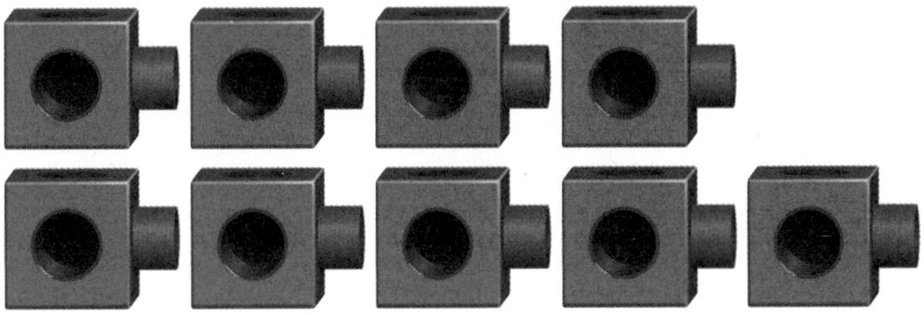

nine

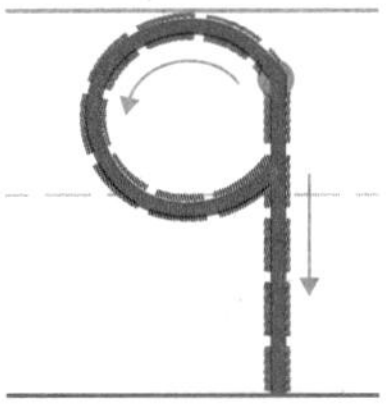

Directions: Count the linking cubes. Say the number. Write the number.

1

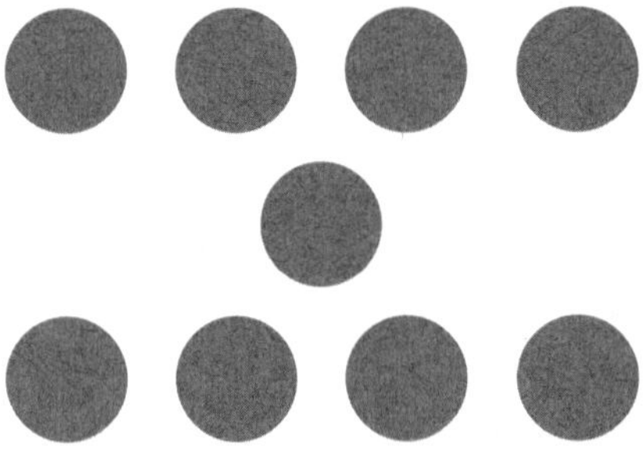

2

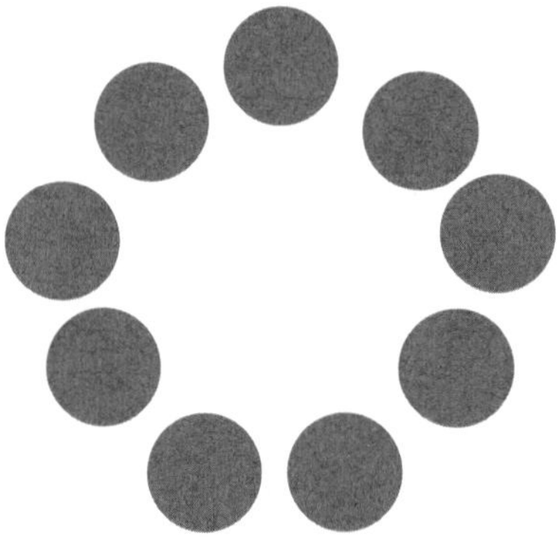

Directions: 1 and 2 Count the dots. Say the number. Write the number.

3

4

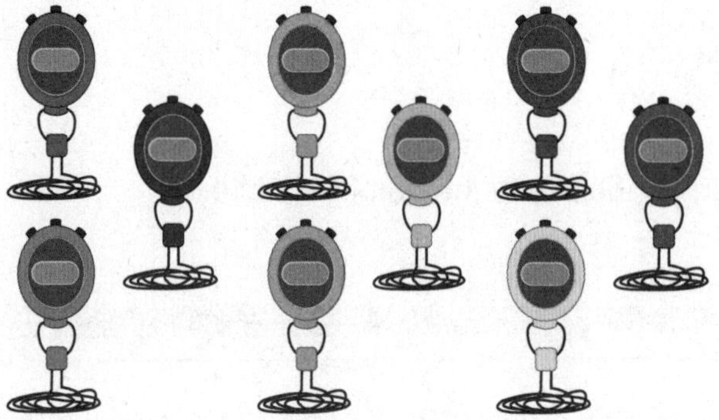

5

Directions: 3 and 4 Count the objects. Say the number. Write the number.
5 Count the bowling balls in the picture. Say the number. Write the number.

Name ______________________

Model and Count 10 3.9

Learning Target: Show and count the number 10.

Explore and Grow

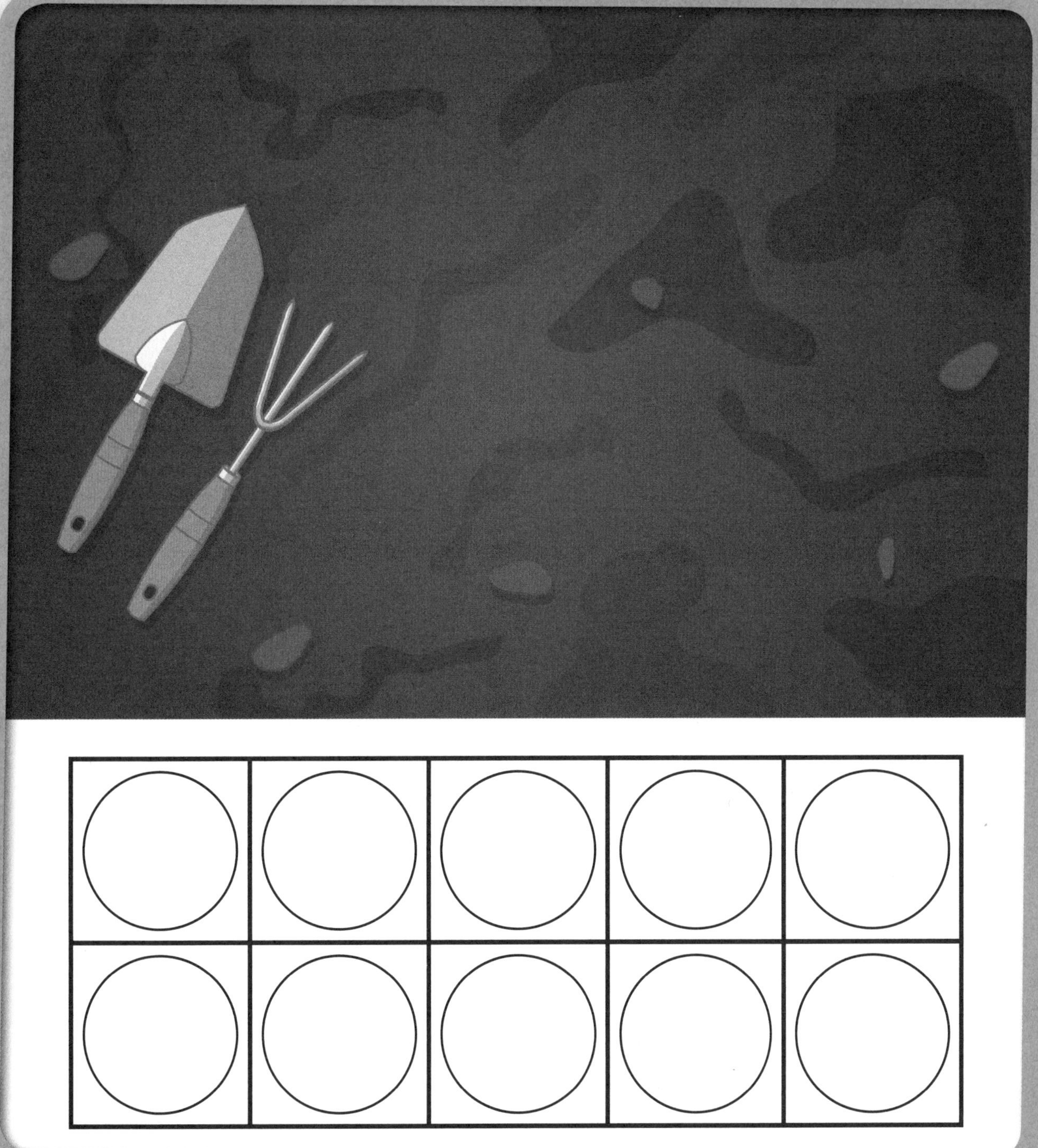

Directions: Place 10 counters in the soil. Slide the counters to the frame.

Think and Grow

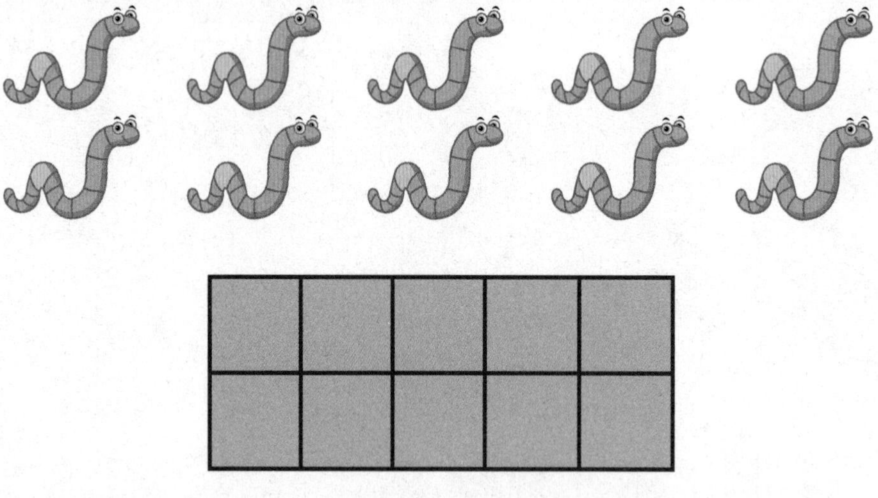

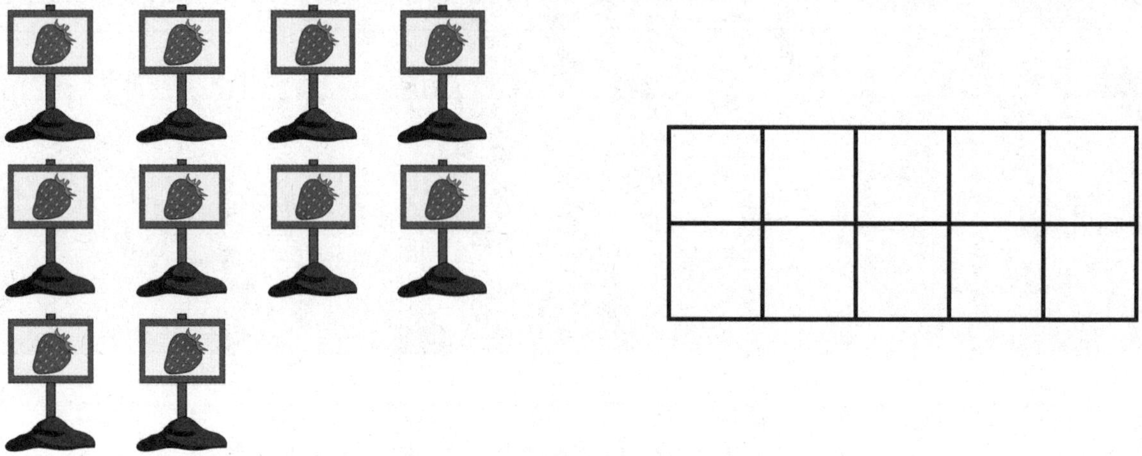

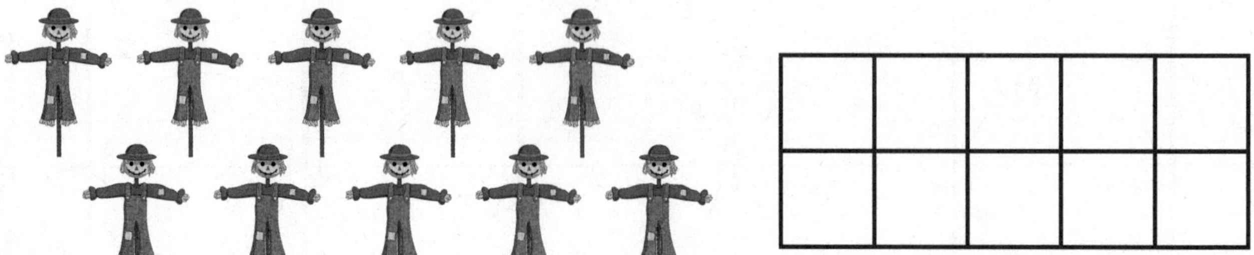

Directions: Count the objects. Color the boxes to show how many.

Name ____________________

Apply and Grow: Practice

1

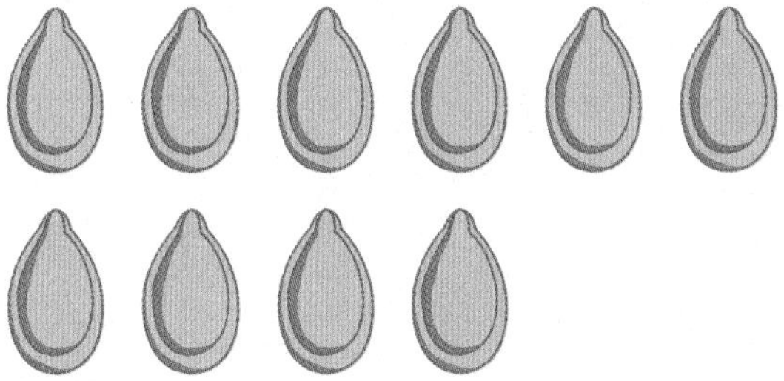

2

3

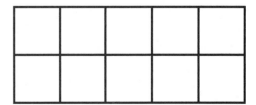

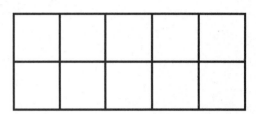

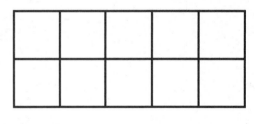

Directions: 1–3 Count the objects. Color the boxes to show how many.

Think and Grow: Modeling Real Life

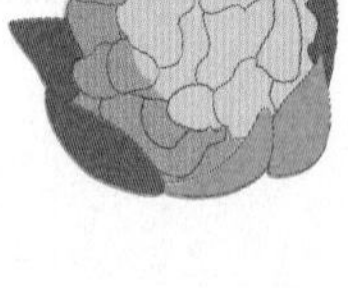

Directions: Count the objects in the picture. Color the boxes to show how many.

Name ____________________________

Learning Target: Show and count the number 10.

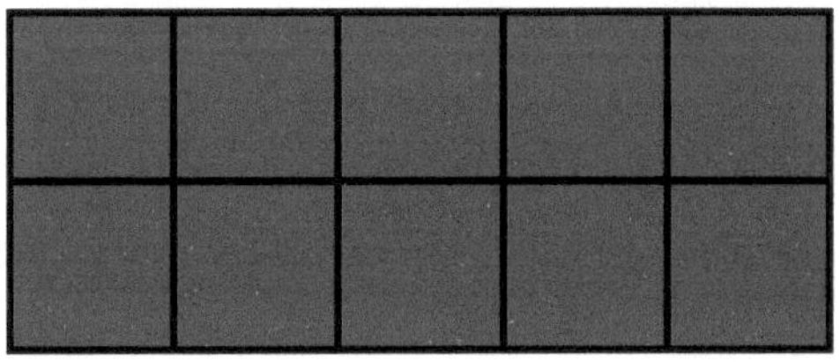

Directions: Count the peppers. Color the boxes to show how many.

1

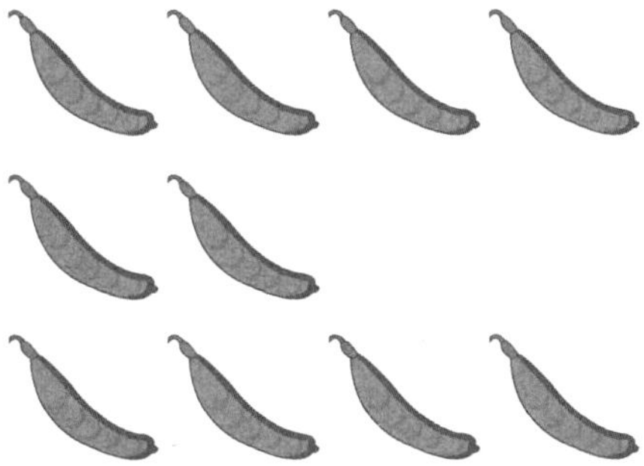

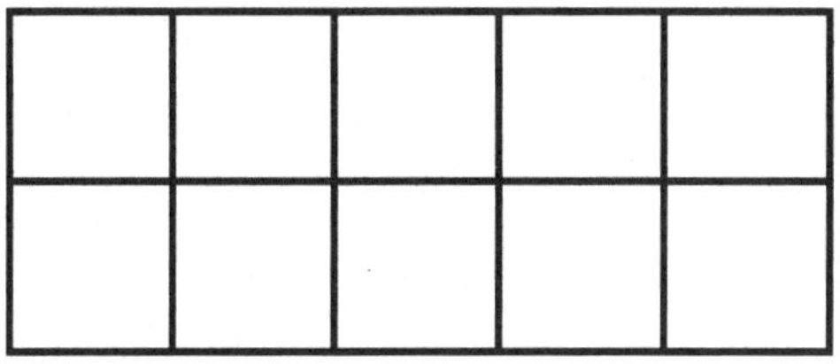

2

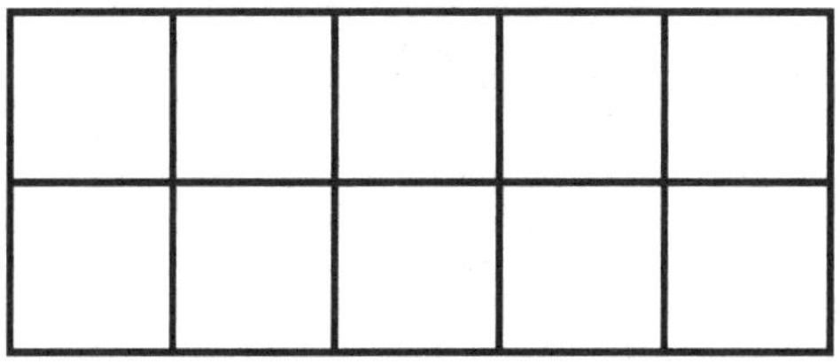

Directions: 1 and 2 Count the objects. Color the boxes to show how many.

3

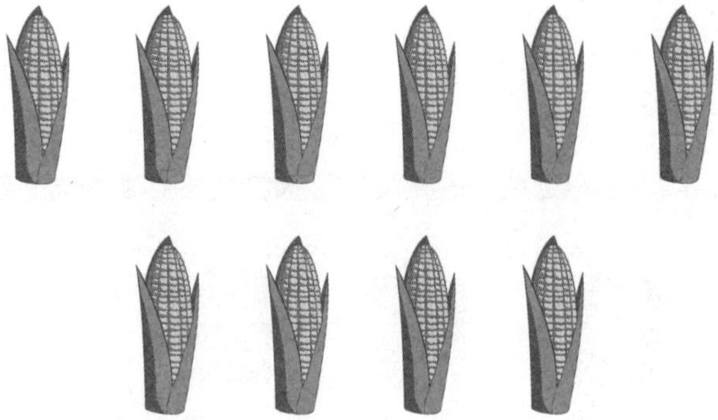

4

5

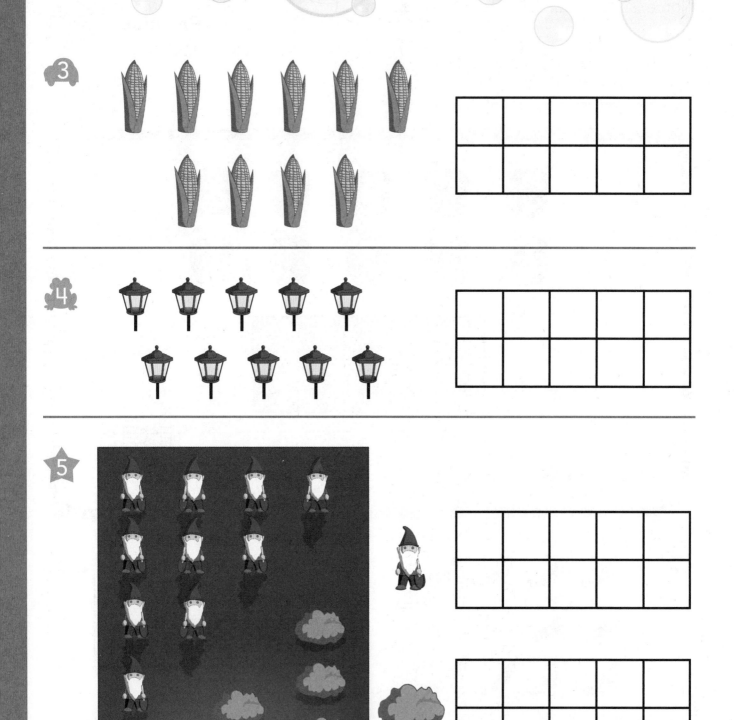

Directions: 3 and 4 Count the objects. Color the boxes to show how many.
5 Count the objects in the picture. Color the boxes to show how many.

Name ______________________________

Understand and Write 10

3.10

Learning Target: Understand and write the number 10.

Explore and Grow

Directions: Use counters to show how many starfish are in the story *In the Water*. Write how many starfish are in the story.

Think and Grow

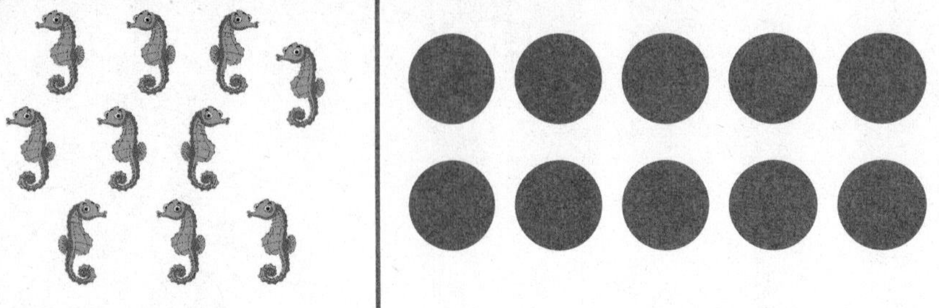

10	10	ten

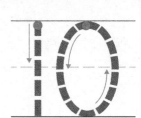

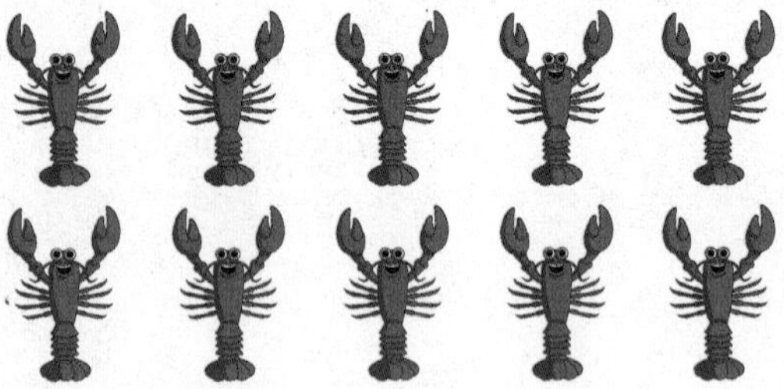

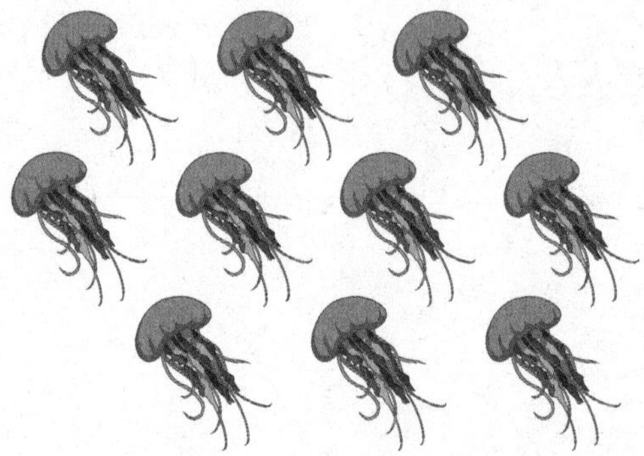

Directions:

- Count the objects. Say the number. Trace and write the number.
- Count the sea creatures. Say the number. Write the number.

Name ______________________________

Apply and Grow: Practice

1

______

2

______

3

______

4

______

Directions: 1–4 Count the objects. Say the number. Write the number.

Think and Grow: Modeling Real Life

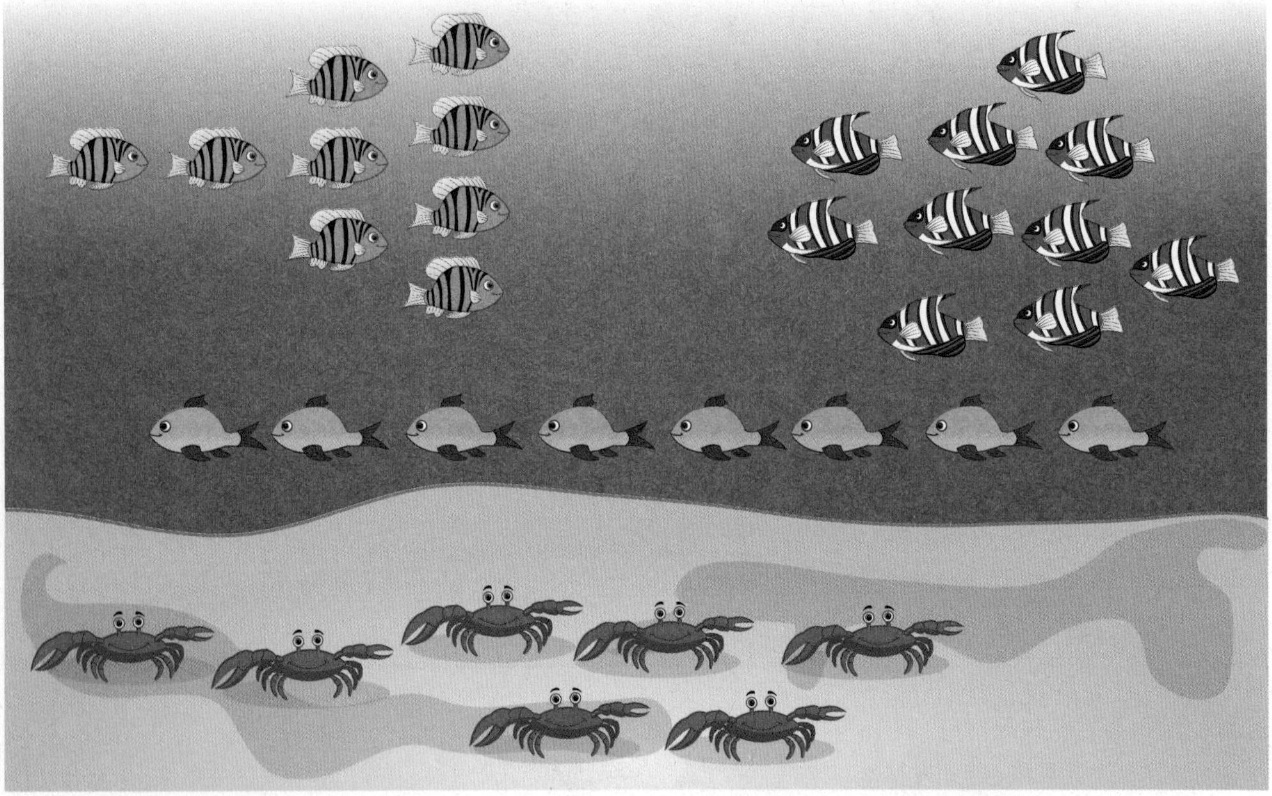

Directions: Count the sea creatures in the picture. Say the number. Write the number.

Name ______________________

Practice 3.10

Learning Target: Understand and write the number 10.

ten

10

Directions: Count the linking cubes. Say the number. Write the number.

1

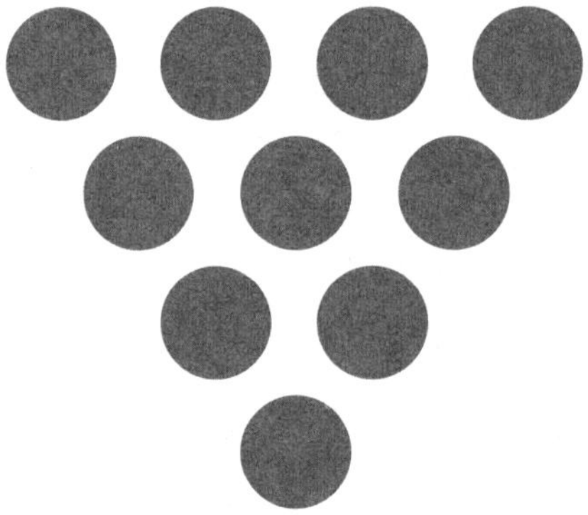

2

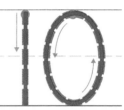

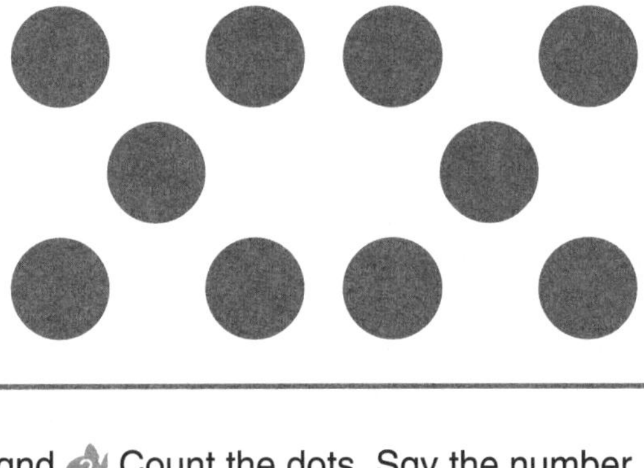

Directions: 1 and 2 Count the dots. Say the number. Write the number.

3

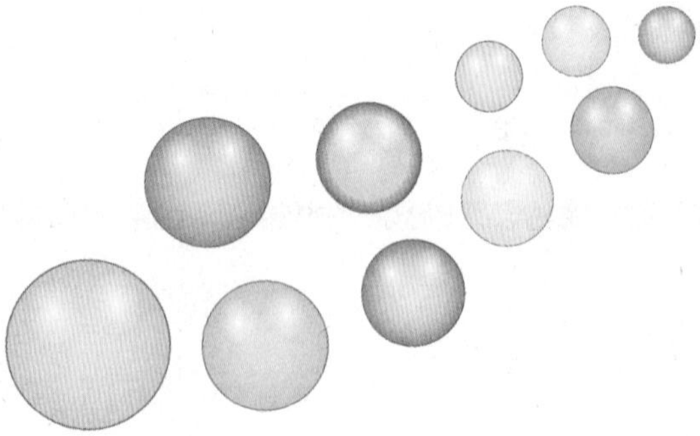

4

5

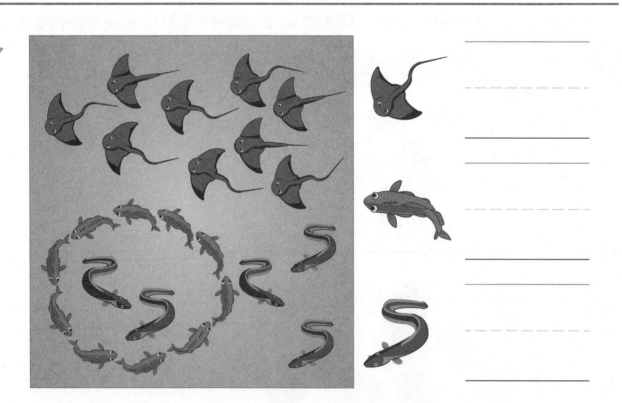

Directions: 3 and 4 Count the objects. Say the number. Write the number.
5 Count the sea creatures in the picture. Say the number. Write the number.

Name ______________________

Count and Order Numbers to 10

3.11

Learning Target: Count and order numbers to 10.

Explore and Grow

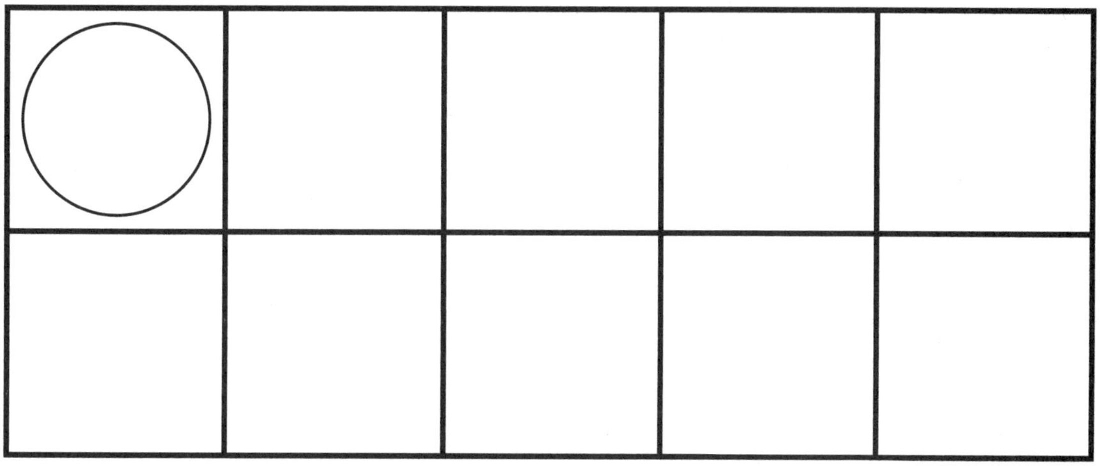

1 2 3 4 5 6 7 8 9 10

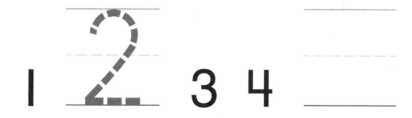

1 2 3 4 ____

6 7 8 ____ 10

Directions: Place counters in the ten frame as you count forward to 10. Trace and write the missing numbers.

Think and Grow

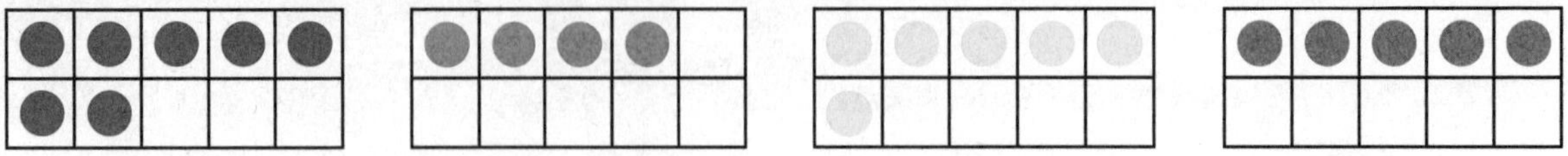

7 4 6 5

4 5 6 7

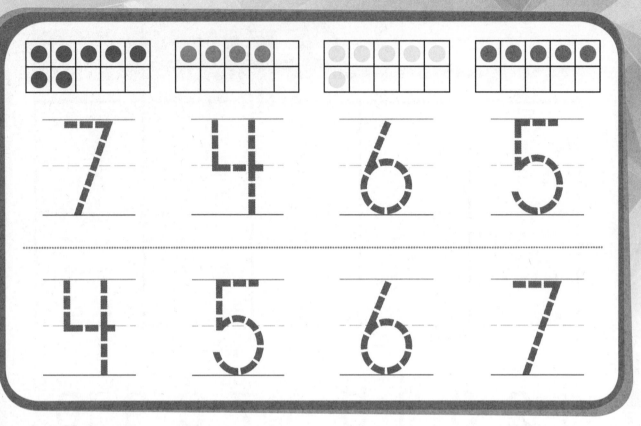

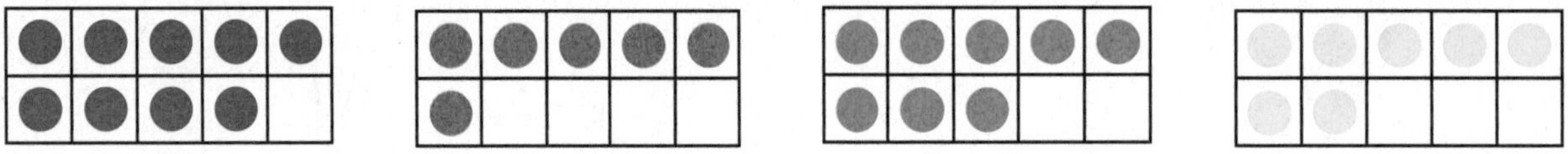

6

6

Directions: Count the dots in each ten frame. Say the number. Write the number. Write the numbers in order. Start with the given number.

Name ____________________

Apply and Grow: Practice

1

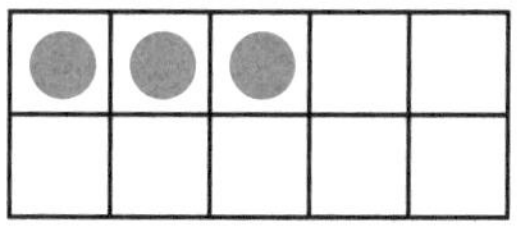
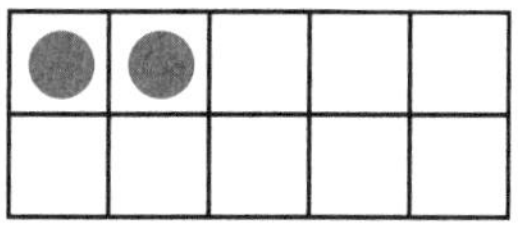
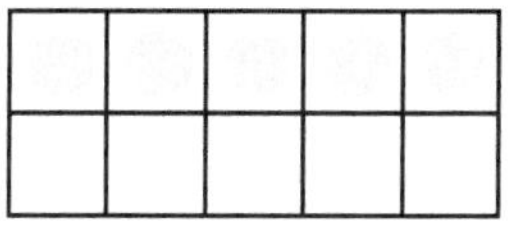
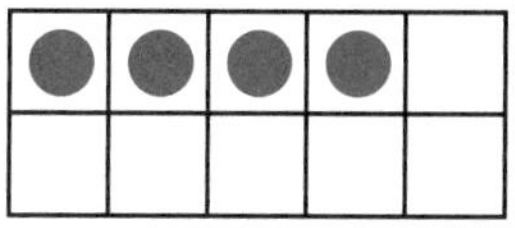

2

2

2

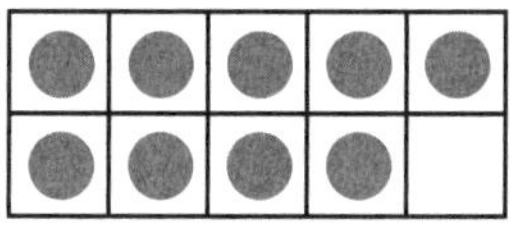
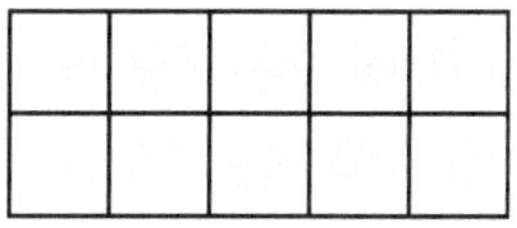
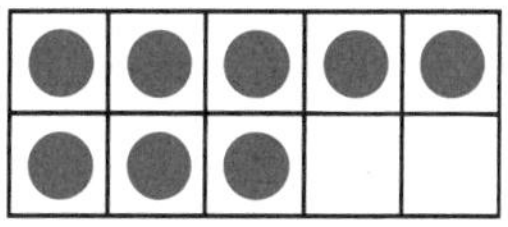
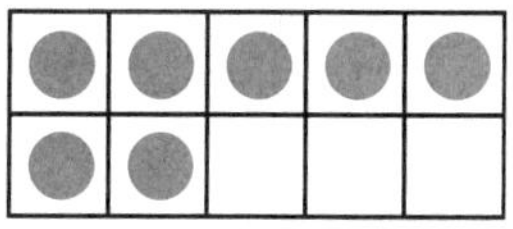

Directions: 1 and 2 Count the dots in each ten frame. Say the number. Write the number. Then write the numbers in order.

Think and Grow: Modeling Real Life

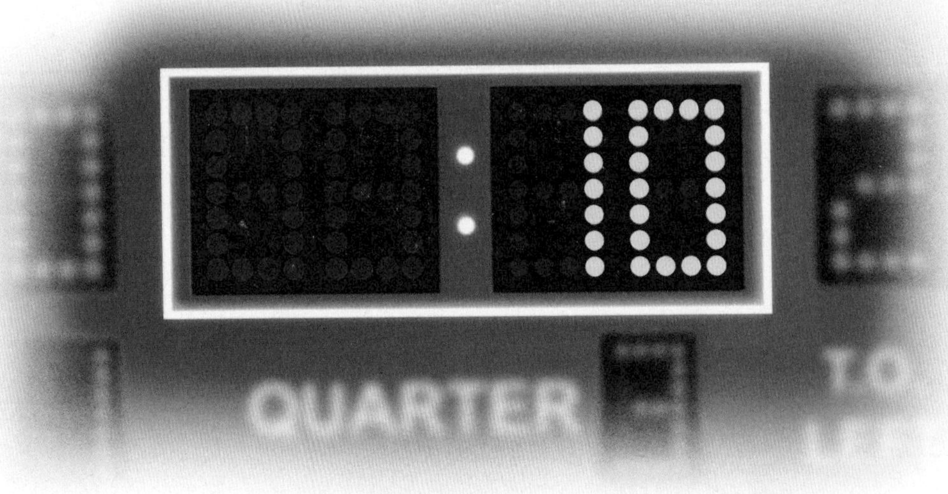

10

Directions: Count backward from the number on the timer. Write the numbers.

Name ______________________

Practice **3.11**

Learning Target: Count and order numbers to 10.

8	5	7	6
5	6	7	8

Directions: Count the dots. Say the number. Write the number. Then write the numbers in order. Start with the given number.

1

		3	
3			

Directions: 1 Count the dots. Say the number. Write the number. Then write the numbers in order.

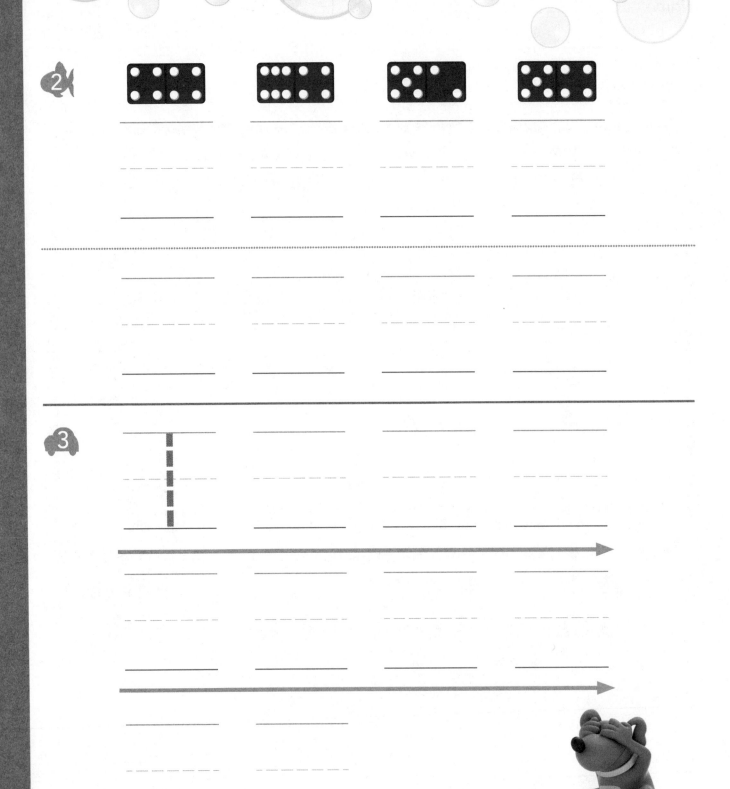

2

3

1

Directions:

2 Count the dots on each domino. Say the number. Write the number. Write the numbers in order. Start with the number 7. 3 You are playing hide-and-seek. Count forward from 1. Write the numbers.

Name ______________________________

Performance Task 3

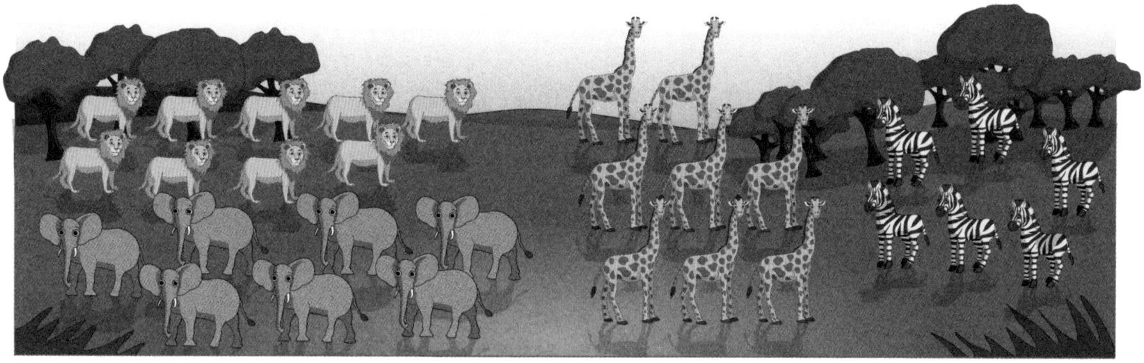

1

2

3

Directions:

1 Count the animals in the picture. Say the number. Write the number. Then write the numbers in order. 2 Draw dots to show 10 birds in the tree. 3 Show how many birds in another way.

Number Land

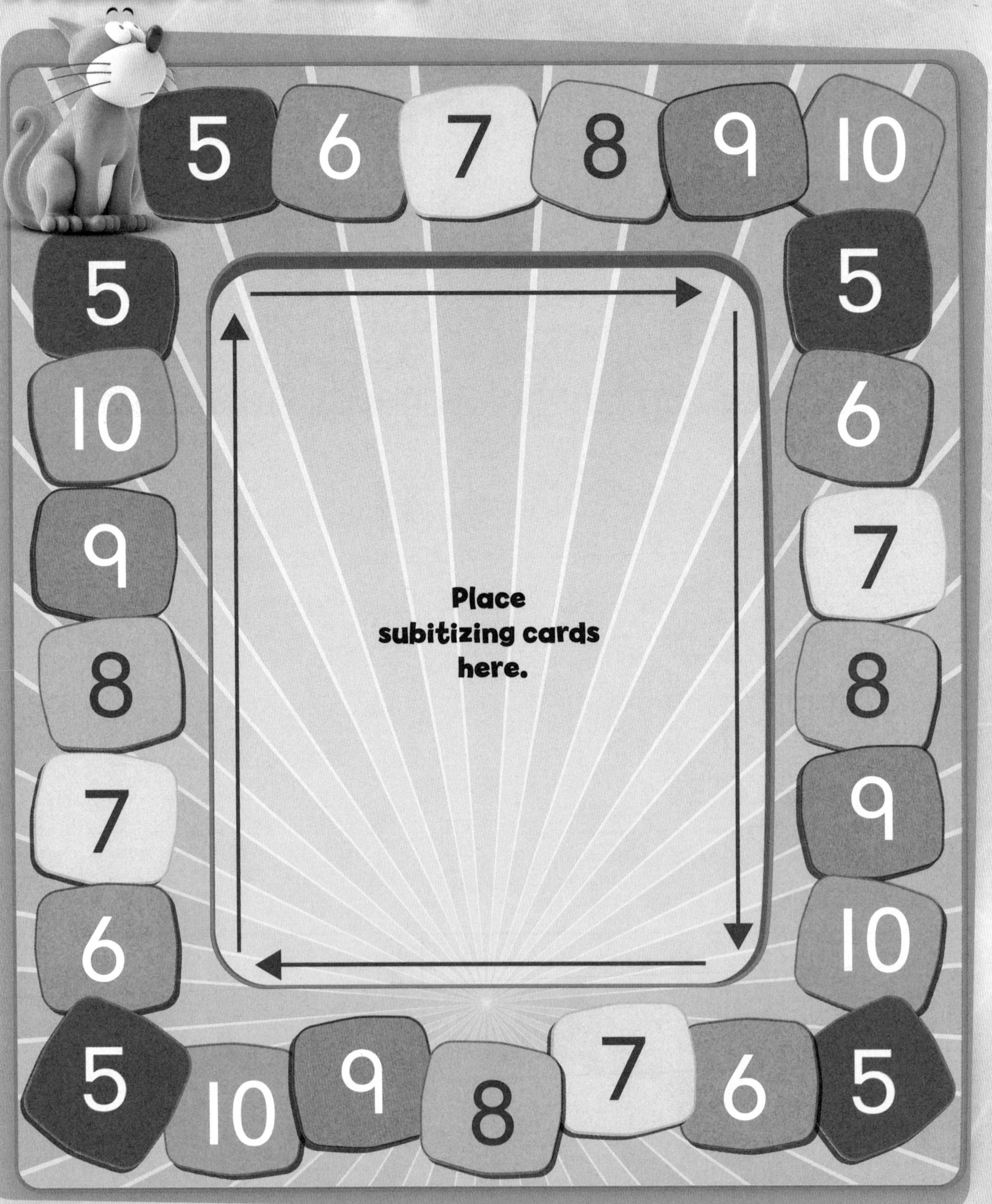

Directions: Put the Subitizing Cards 5–10 into a pile. Start at Descartes. Take turns drawing a card and moving your piece to that matching number. Repeat this process until you have gone around the board and back to Descartes.

Name ______________________________

Chapter Practice 3

3.1 Model and Count 6

1

3.2 Understand and Write 6

2

3.3 Model and Count 7

3

Directions: 1 Count the train engines. Color the boxes to show how many. 2 Count the music notes. Say the number. Write the number. 3 Count the foxes. Color the boxes to show how many.

3.4 Understand and Write 7

4

3.5 Model and Count 8

5

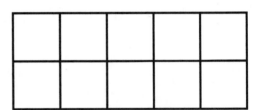

3.6 Understand and Write 8

6

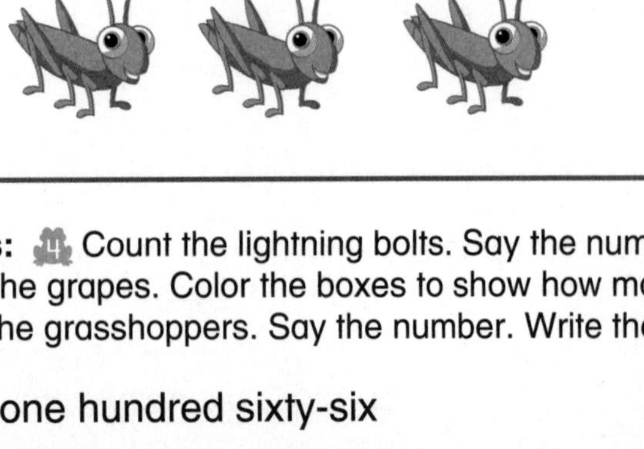

Directions: 4 Count the lightning bolts. Say the number. Write the number.
5 Count the grapes. Color the boxes to show how many.
6 Count the grasshoppers. Say the number. Write the number.

3.7 Model and Count 9

7

3.8 Understand and Write 9

8

3.9 Model and Count 10

9

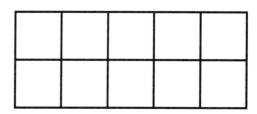

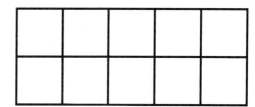

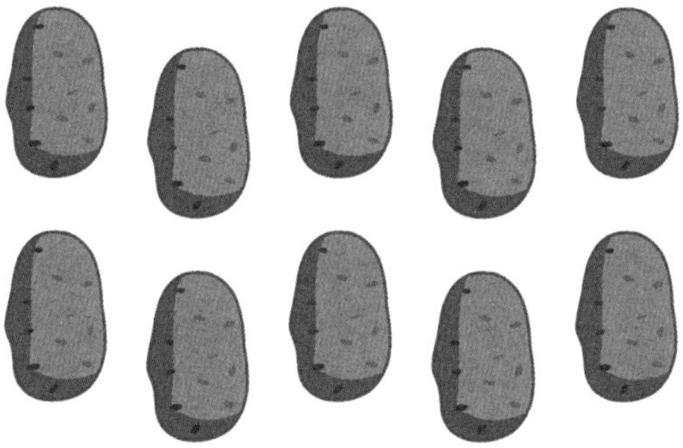

Directions: 7 Count the shovels. Color the boxes to show how many.
8 Count the softballs. Say the number. Write the number.
9 Count the potatoes. Color the boxes to show how many.

3.10 Understand and Write 10

3.11 Count and Order Numbers to 10

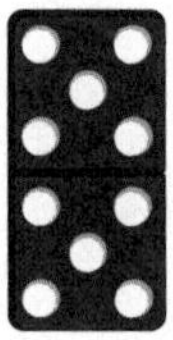

Directions: Count the shells. Say the number. Write the number. Count the dots on each domino. Say the number. Write the number. Then write the numbers in order.

4 Compare Numbers to 10

- Have you ever played with one of these toys?
- What colors do you see in the picture?

Chapter Learning Target:
Understand categories.

Chapter Success Criteria:
- I can match objects.
- I can explain how to compare numbers of objects.
- I can classify objects into categories.
- I can tell how many objects are in a category.

Name ______________________________

4 Vocabulary

Review Word
greater than

Directions: Count the number of dog toys in front of each dog. Write each number. Circle the number that is greater than the other number.

Chapter 4 Vocabulary Cards

category	chart
classify	mark

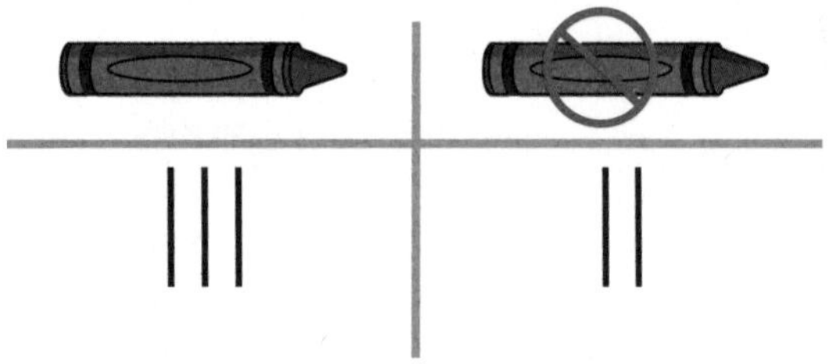

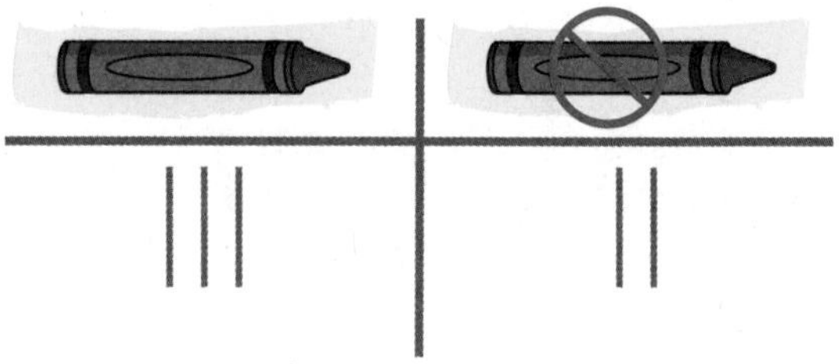

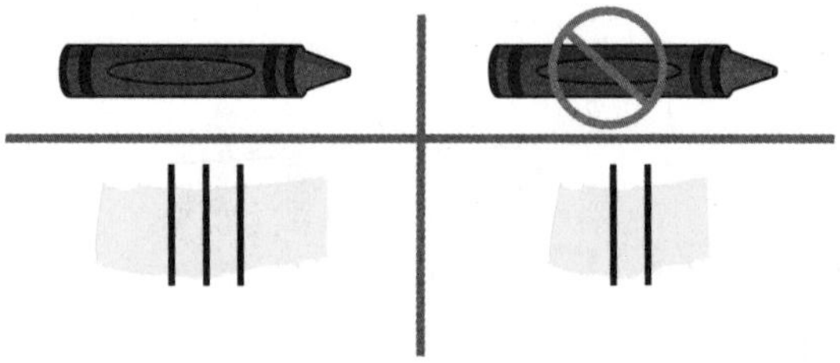

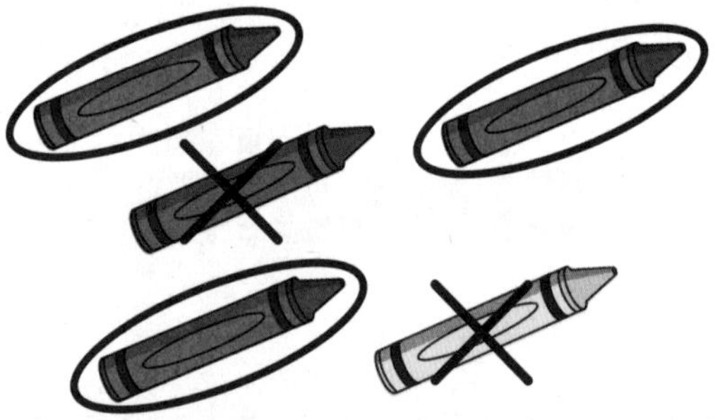

Name ________________________________

Compare Groups to 10 by Matching

4.1

Learning Target: Use matching to compare the numbers of objects in two groups.

Explore and Grow

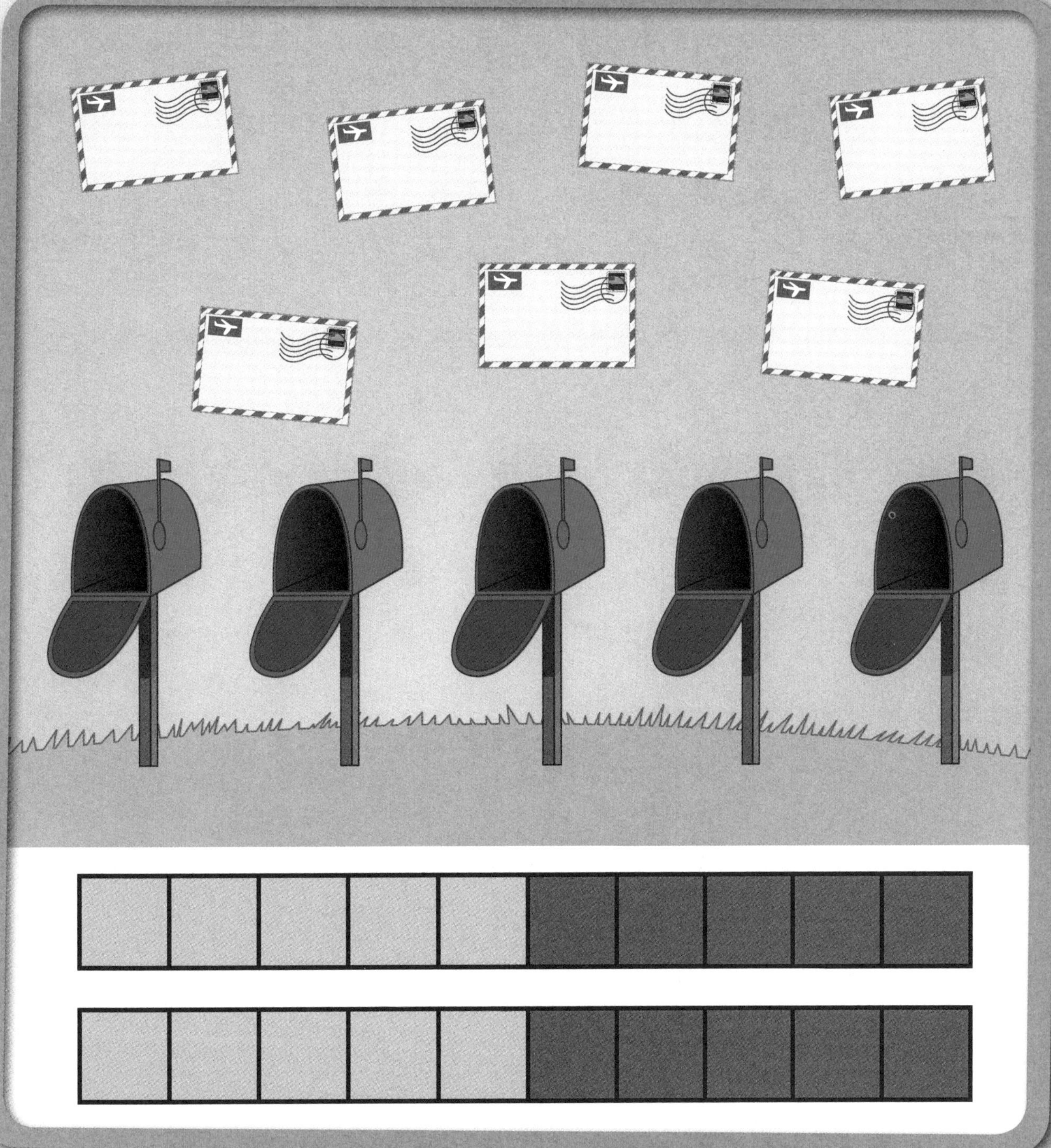

Directions: Use cubes to show the number of letters. Use cubes to show the number of mailboxes. Tell which group has more and which group has less.

Think and Grow

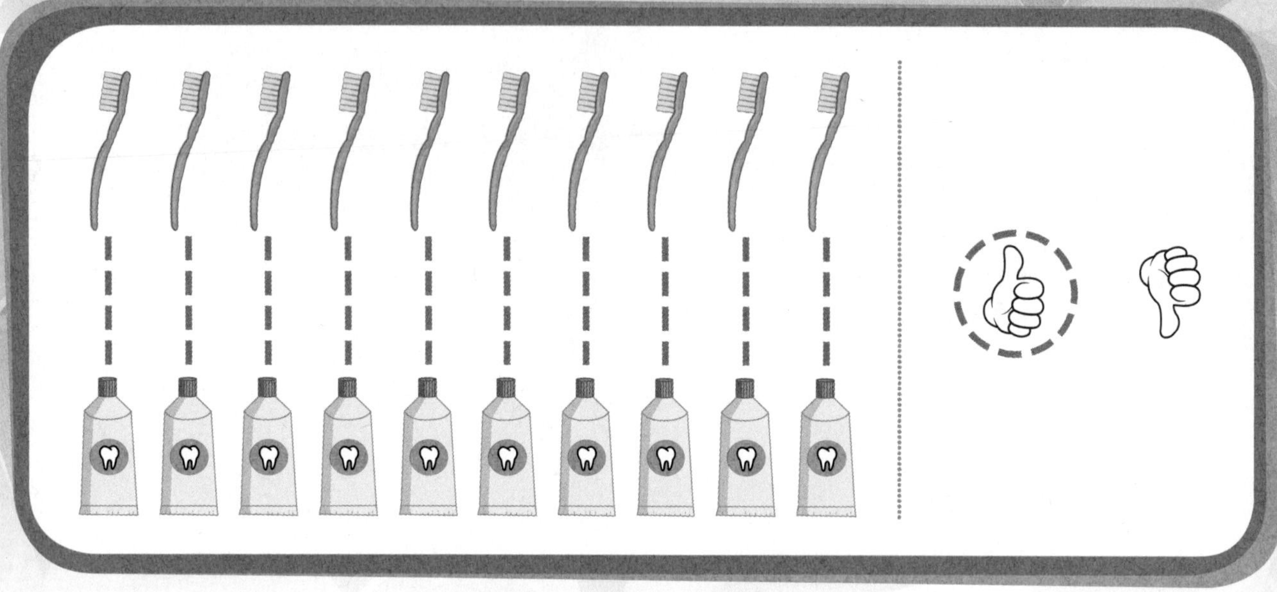

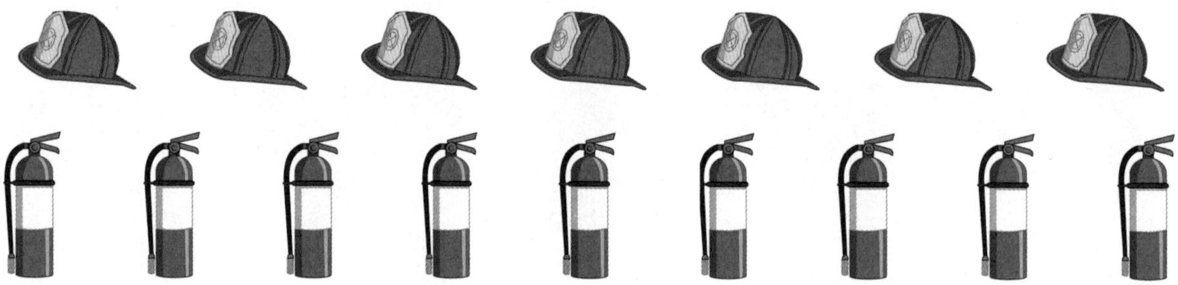

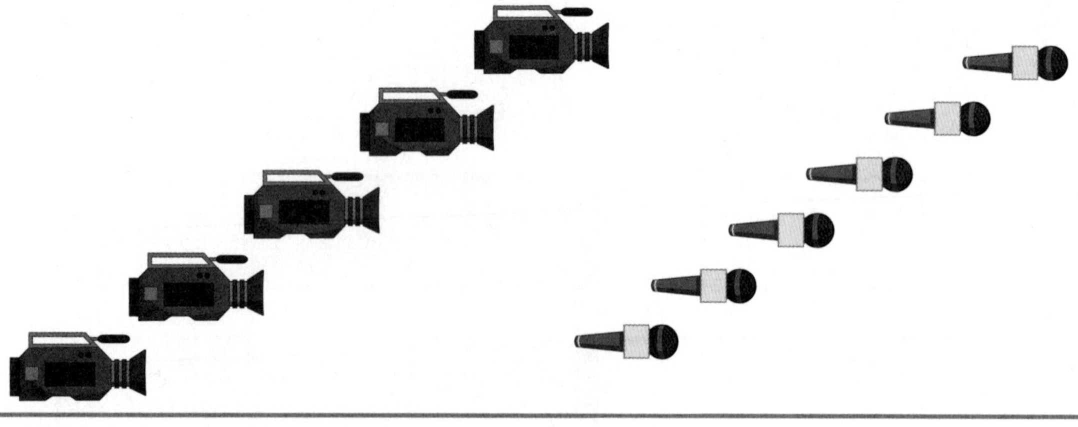

Directions: Draw lines between the objects in each group.

- Is the number of toothbrushes equal to the number of toothpaste tubes? Circle the thumbs up for *yes* or the thumbs down for *no*.
- Circle the group that is greater in number than the other group.
- Draw a line through the group that is less in number than the other group.

Name ____

Apply and Grow: Practice

1

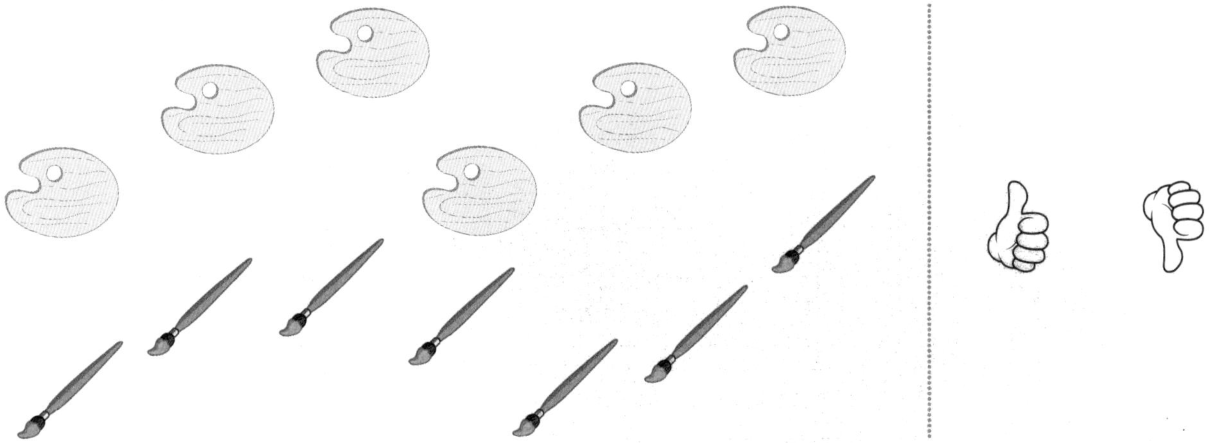

2

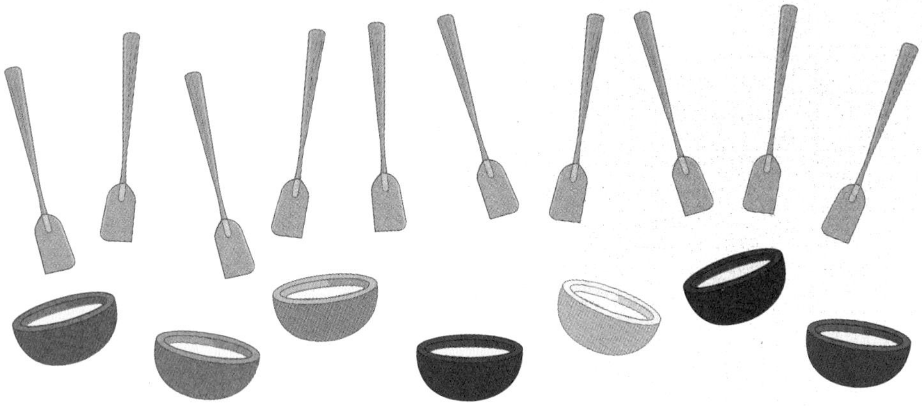

3

Directions: Draw lines between the objects in each group.
1 Is the number of paint palettes equal to the number of paintbrushes? Circle the thumbs up for *yes* or the thumbs down for *no*. 2 Circle the group that is greater in number than the other group. 3 Draw a line through the group that is less in number than the other group.

Think and Grow: Modeling Real Life

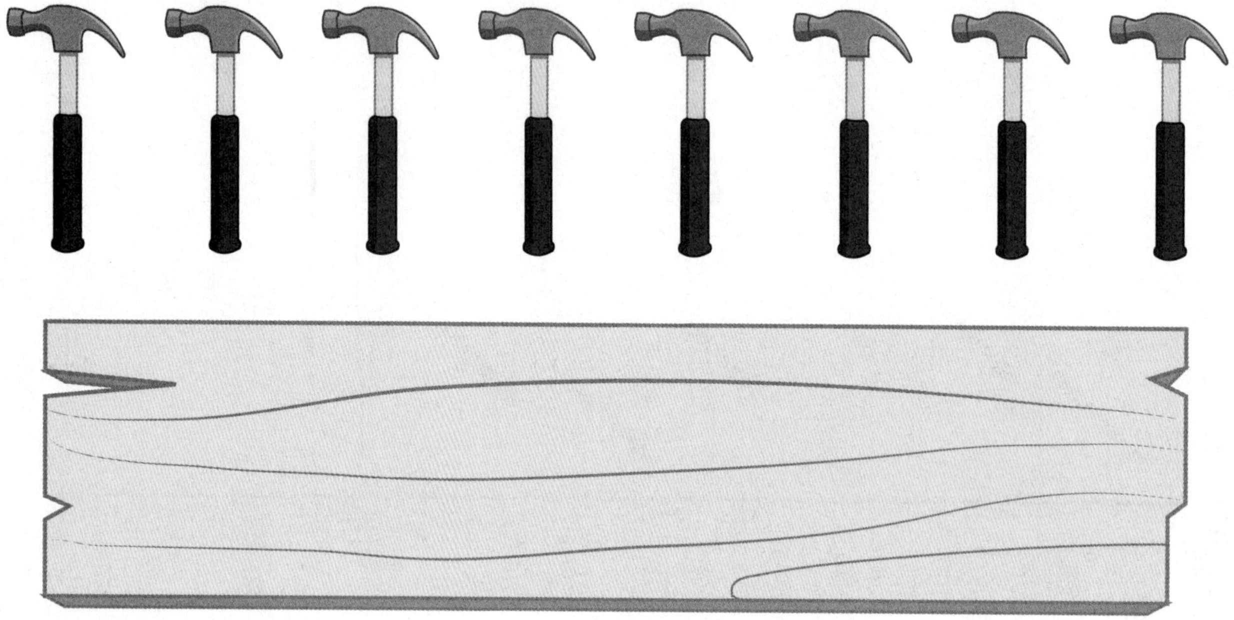

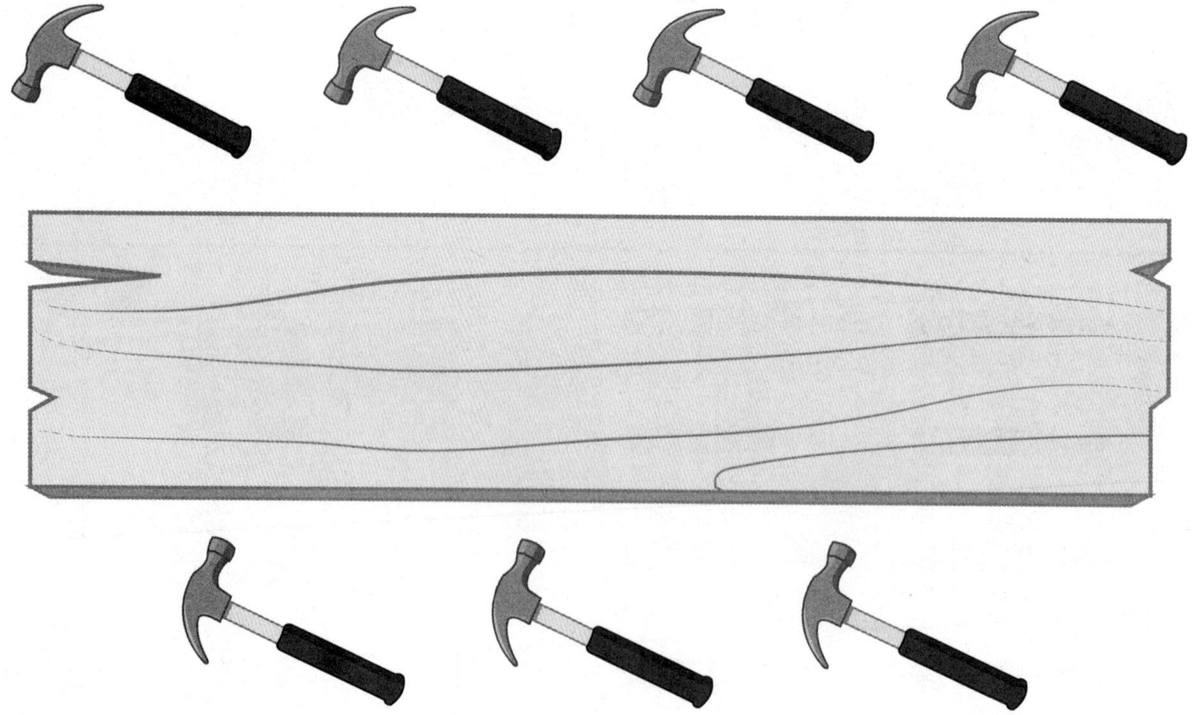

Directions:

- Draw nails on the board so that the number of nails is greater than the number of hammers. Draw lines between the objects in each group to show that you are correct.
- Draw nails on the board so that the number of nails is less than the number of hammers. Draw lines between the objects in each group to show that you are correct.

Name ______________________

Practice **4.1**

Learning Target: Use matching to compare the numbers of objects in two groups.

Directions: Draw lines between the objects in each group. Is the number of police hats equal to the number of badges? Circle the thumbs up for *yes* or the thumbs down for *no*.

1

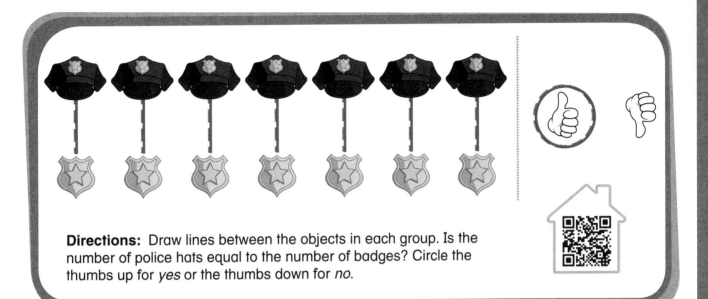

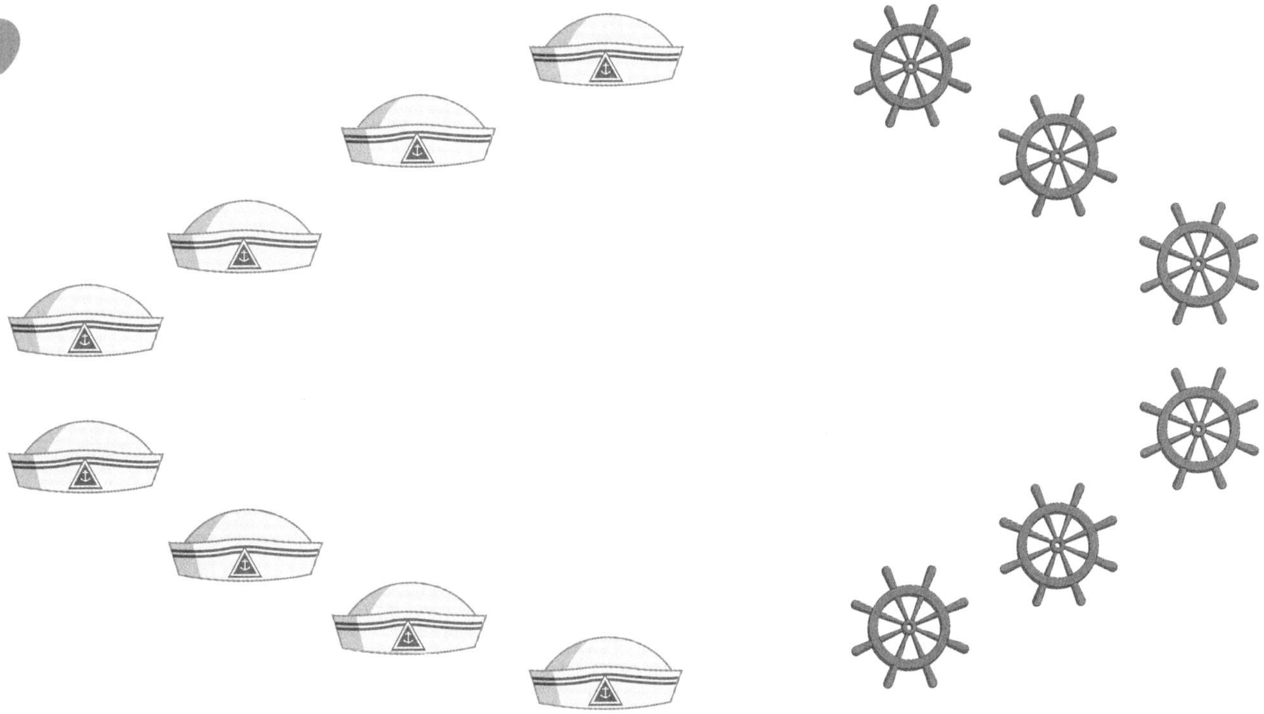

Directions: 1 Draw lines between the objects in each group. Circle the group that is greater in number than the other group.

2

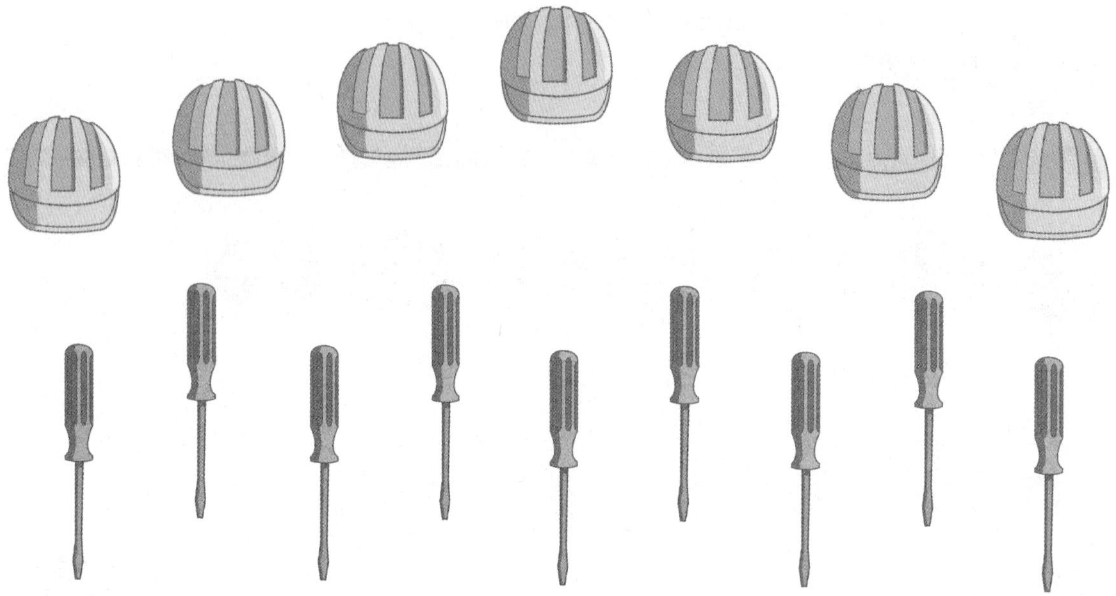

3

Directions: 2 Draw lines between the objects in each group. Draw a line through the group that is less in number than the other group. 3 Draw wands on the cloth so that the number of wands is equal to the number of magician hats. Draw lines between the objects in each group to show that you are correct.

Name ______________________________

Compare Groups to 10 by Counting 4.2

Learning Target: Use counting to compare the numbers of objects in two groups.

Explore and Grow

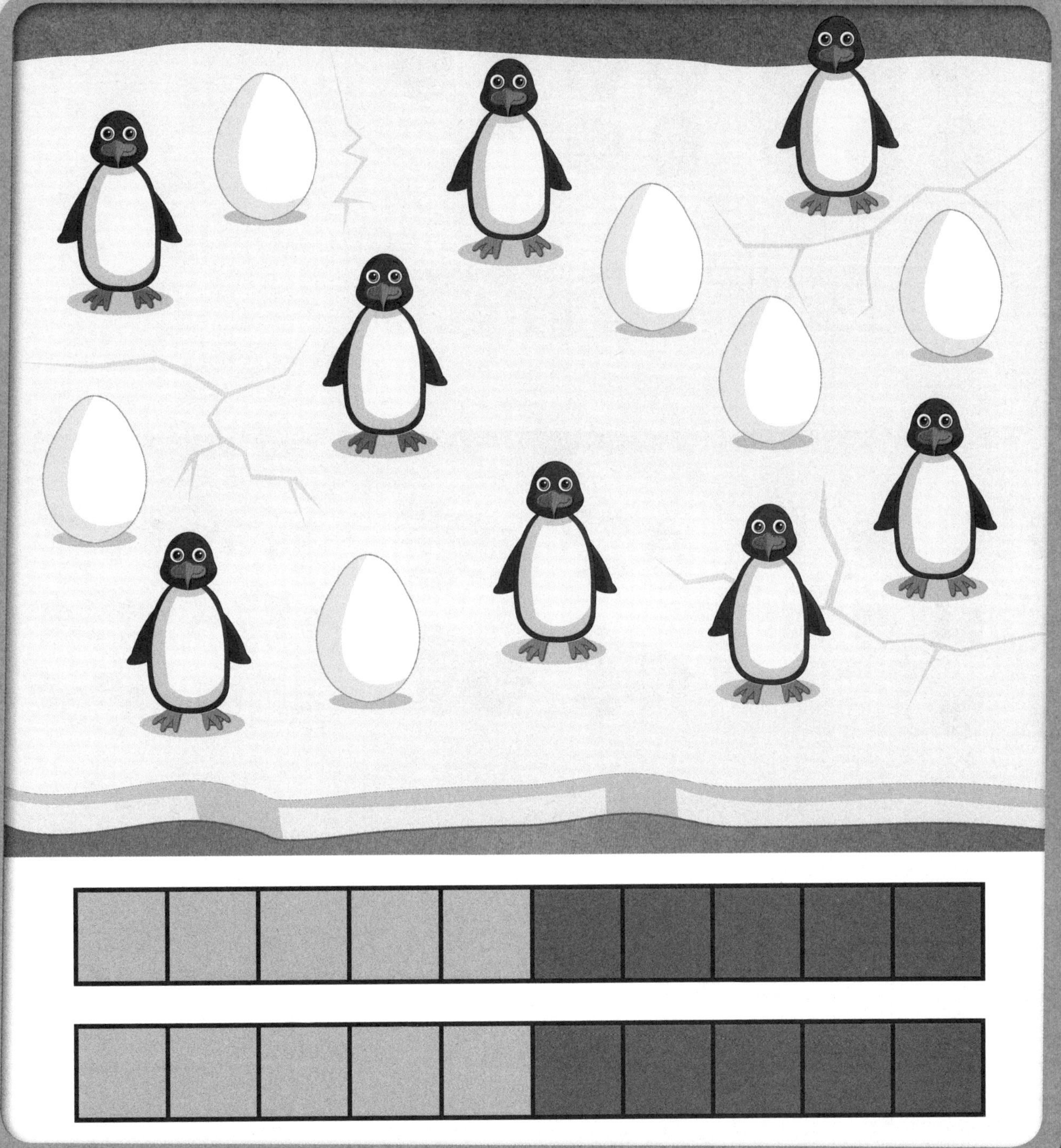

Directions: Use cubes to show the number of penguins. Use cubes to show the number of eggs. Tell which group has more and which group has less.

Think and Grow

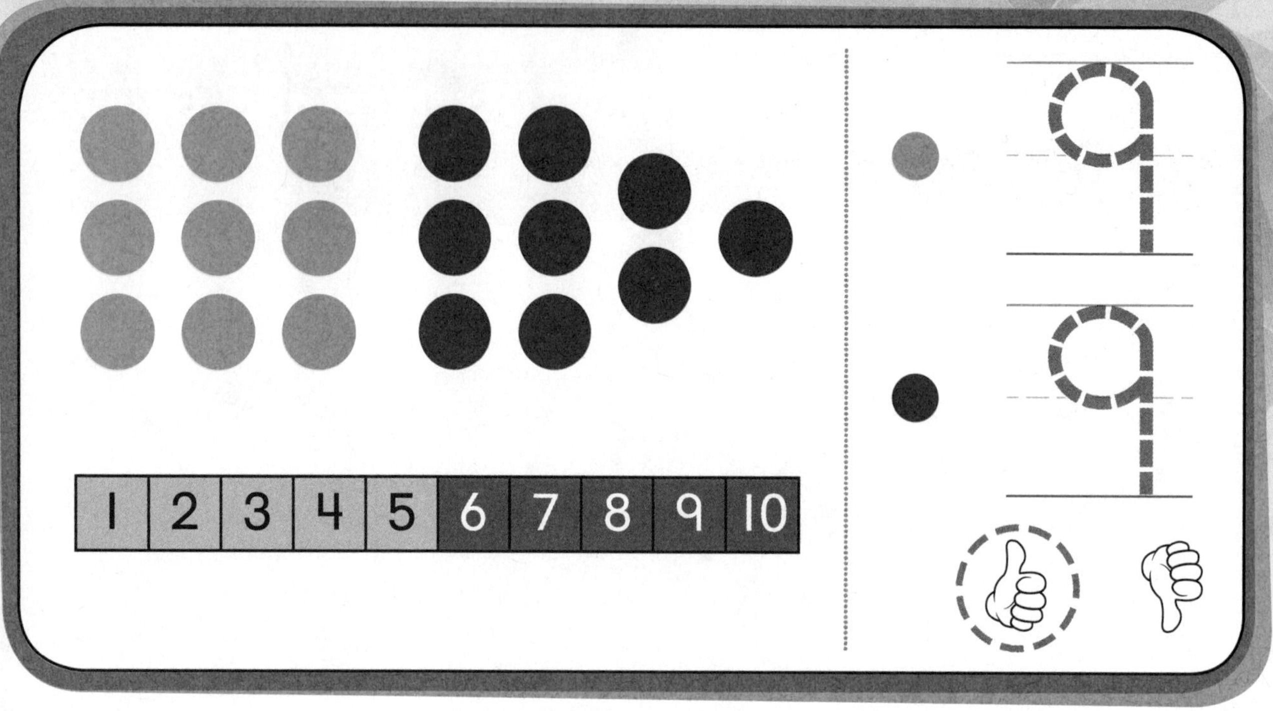

Directions: Count the objects in each group. Write each number.

- Is the number of green dots equal to the number of purple dots? Circle the thumbs up for *yes* or the thumbs down for *no*.
- Compare the numbers of blackberries and bears. Circle the number that is greater than the other number.
- Compare the numbers of bears and fish. Draw a line through the number that is less than the other number.

Name

Apply and Grow: Practice

1

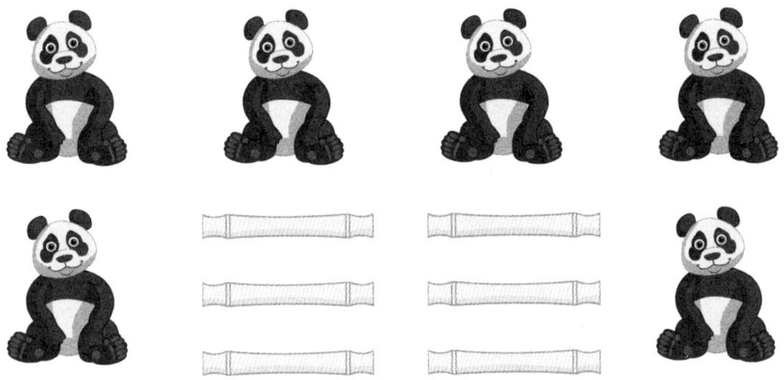

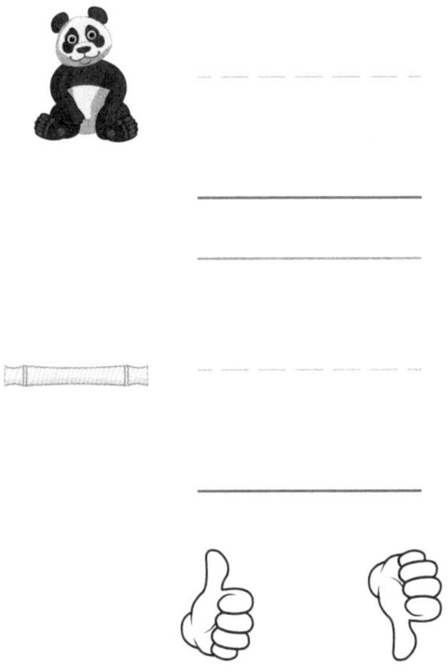

2

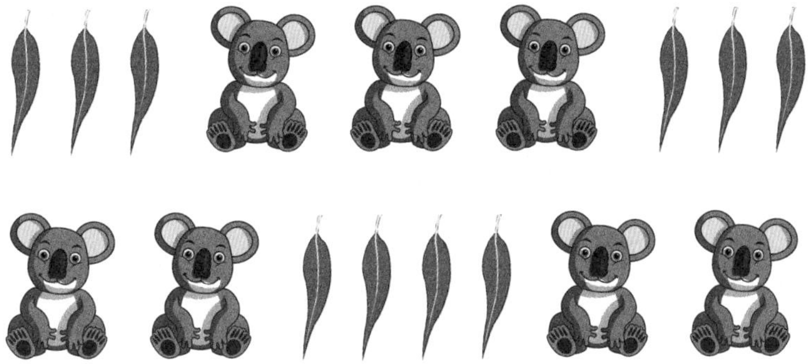

3

Directions: Count the objects in each group. Write each number. 1 Is the number of panda bears equal to the number of bamboo sticks? Circle the thumbs up for *yes* or the thumbs down for *no*. 2 Circle the number that is greater than the other number. 3 Draw a line through the number that is less than the other number.

Think and Grow: Modeling Real Life

Directions:

- Draw bananas hanging from the tree so that the number of bananas is greater than the number of monkeys. Write the number of each object. Circle the number that is greater than the other number.
- Draw bananas hanging from the tree so that the number of bananas is less than the number of monkeys. Write the number of each object. Draw a line through the number that is less than the other number.

Name ______________________

Practice 4.2

Learning Target: Use counting to compare the numbers of objects in two groups.

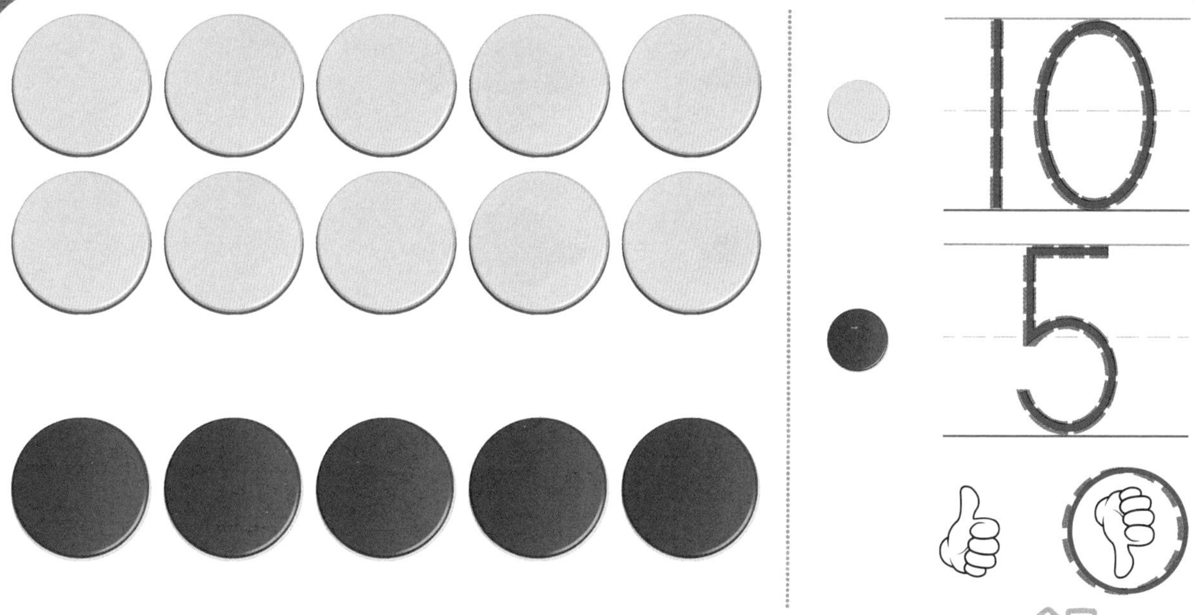

Directions: Count the objects in each group. Write each number. Is the number of yellow counters equal to the number of red counters? Circle the thumbs up for *yes* or the thumbs down for *no*.

1

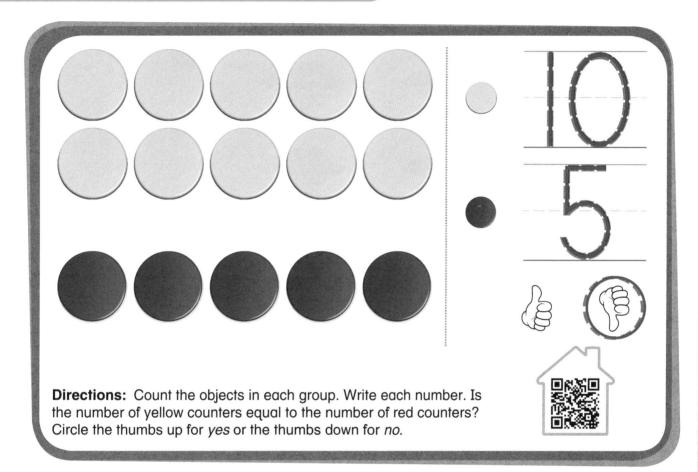

Directions: 1 Count the objects in each group. Write each number. Is the number of rabbits equal to the number of carrots? Circle the thumbs up for *yes* or the thumbs down for *no*.

2

3

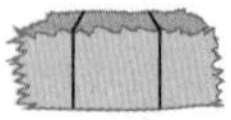

Directions: 2 Count the objects in each group. Write each number. Circle the number that is greater than the other number. 3 Draw hay bales in the pen so that the number of hay bales is less than the number of donkeys. Write the number of each object. Draw a line through the number that is less than the other number.

Name ______________________________

Compare Numbers to 10 4.3

Learning Target: Compare two numbers.

Explore and Grow

6

9

Directions: Which number is greater than the other number? Which number is less than the other number? Use counters to show how you know.

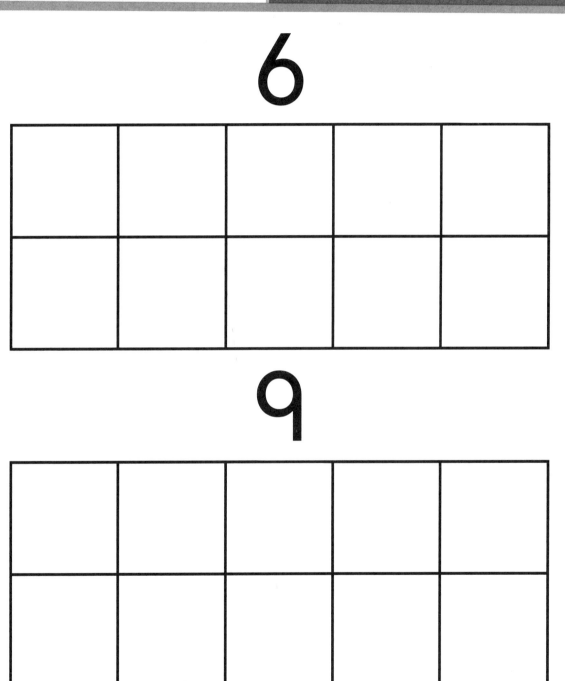

Think and Grow

8

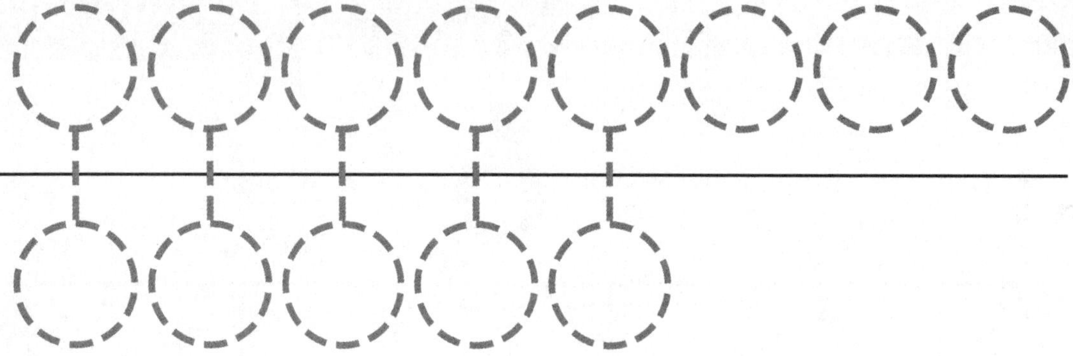

5

10

7

1

6

Directions: Compare the numbers.

- Are the numbers equal? Circle the thumbs up for *yes* or the thumbs down for *no*. Draw to show how you know.
- Circle the number that is greater than the other number. Draw to show how you know.
- Draw a line through the number that is less than the other number. Draw to show how you know.

Name ______________________________

Apply and Grow: Practice

1

5

9

2

8

6

3

9

8

Directions: Compare the numbers. 1 Are the numbers equal? Circle the thumbs up for *yes* or the thumbs down for *no*. Draw to show how you know. 2 Circle the number that is greater than the other number. Draw to show how you know. 3 Draw a line through the number that is less than the other number. Draw to show how you know.

Think and Grow: Modeling Real Life

You

Friend

You

Friend

Directions:

- You have a number of flowers that is greater than 6 and less than 8. Your friend has a number of flowers that is one more than 5. Write and draw how many flowers you each have. Circle the number that is greater than the other number.
- You have a number of flowers that is one more than 9. Your friend has a number of flowers that is one less than 10. Write and draw how many flowers you each have. Draw a line through the number that is less than the other number.

Name ____________________

Practice 4.3

Learning Target: Compare two numbers.

8

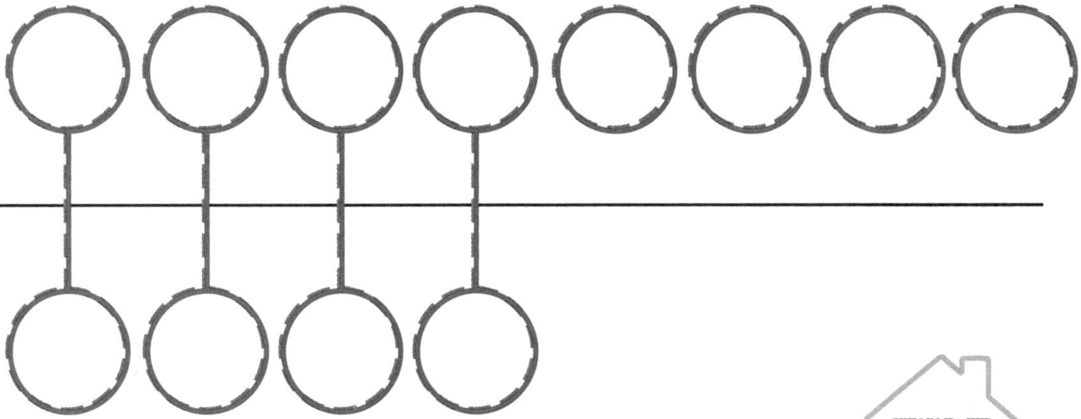

~~4~~

Directions: Compare the numbers. Draw a line through the number that is less than the other number. Draw to show how you know.

1

10

5

Directions: 1 Compare the numbers. Draw a line through the number that is less than the other number. Draw to show how you know.

2

9

7

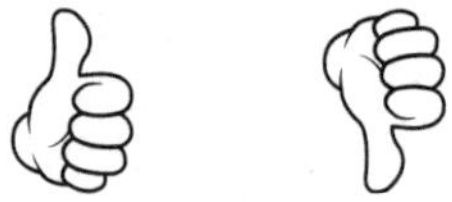

3

You

Friend

Directions: 2 Compare the numbers. Are the numbers equal? Circle the thumbs up for *yes* or the thumbs down for *no*. Draw to show how you know. 3 You have a number of marbles that is greater than 5 and less than 7. Your friend has a number of marbles that is one more than 4. Write and draw how many marbles you each have. Circle the number that is greater than the other number.

Name ___________________________

Classify Objects into Categories 4.4

Learning Target: Tell whether objects belong or do not belong in a category.

Explore and Grow

Directions: Place a yellow counter on each tree that is yellow. Place a red counter on each tree that is *not* yellow.

Think and Grow

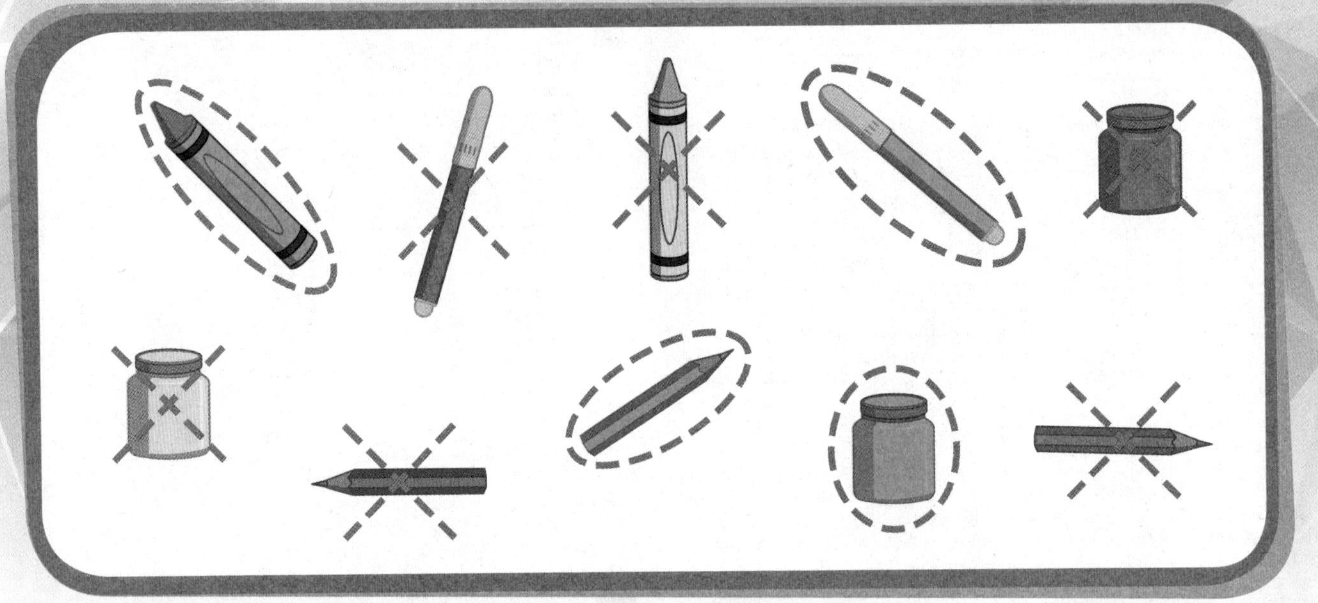

Directions:

- Circle the objects that are green. Cross out the objects that are *not* green.
- Circle the animals that are brown. Cross out the animals that are *not* brown.
- Circle the animals that have wings. Cross out the animals that do *not* have wings.

Name ______________________________

Apply and Grow: Practice

1

2

3

Directions: 1 Circle the pigs that have spots. Cross out the pigs that do *not* have spots. 2 Circle the blocks that have letters. Cross out the blocks that do *not* have letters. 3 Circle the animals that have tails. Cross out the animals that do *not* have tails.

Think and Grow: Modeling Real Life

Directions:

- Circle the dogs that are black. Cross out the dogs that are *not* black.
- Classify the dogs another way. Circle the dogs that belong in the new category. Cross out the dogs that do *not* belong in the new category. Tell how you classified the dogs.

Name ______________________________

Practice 4.4

Learning Target: Tell whether objects belong or do not belong in a category.

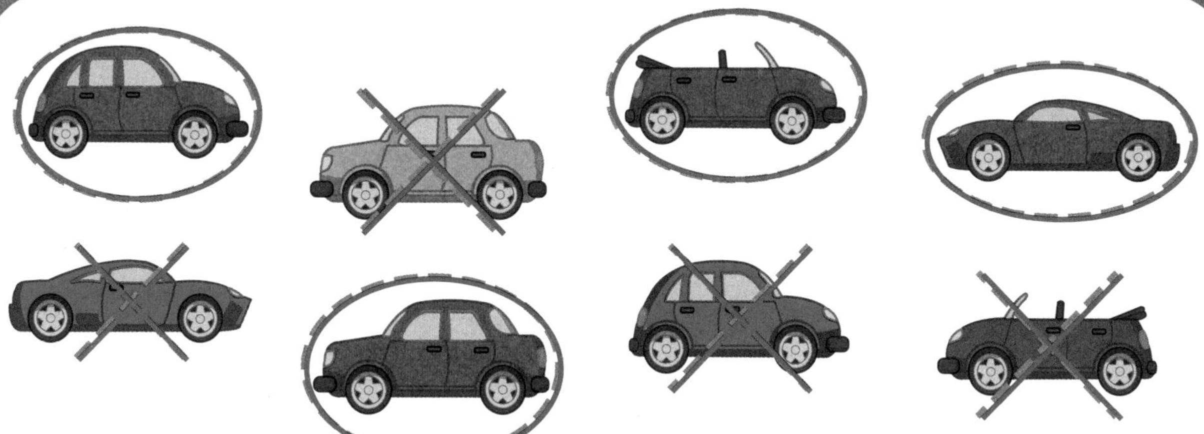

Directions: Circle the cars that are blue. Cross out the cars that are *not* blue.

1

2

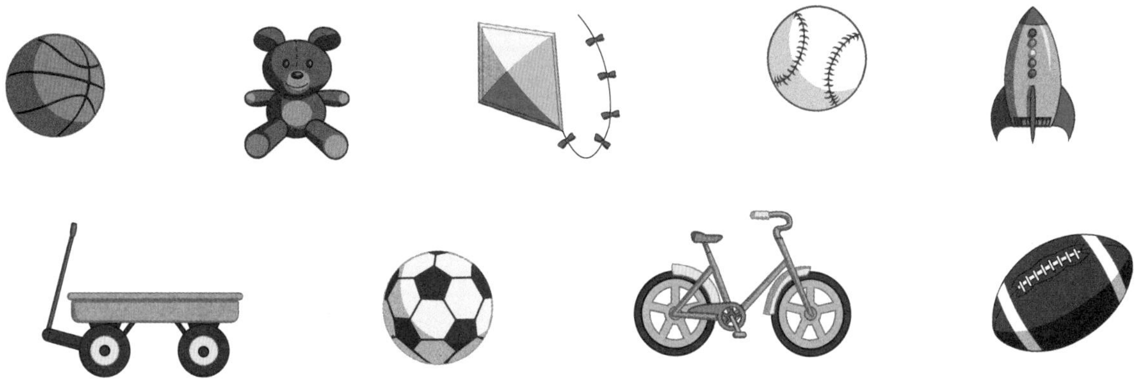

Directions: 1 Circle the scooters that are red. Cross out the scooters that are *not* red. 2 Circle the toys that are balls. Cross out the toys that are *not* balls.

3

4

5

Directions: 3 Circle the animals that have stripes. Cross out the animals that do *not* have stripes. 4 Circle the animals that have 2 legs. Cross out the animals that do *not* have 2 legs. 5 Classify the books into 2 categories. Circle the books in one category. Cross out the books in the other category. Tell how you classified the books.

Name ______________________________

Classify and Compare by Counting

4.5

Learning Target: Compare the numbers of objects in two categories.

Explore and Grow

in water	not in water

Directions: Show the number of vehicles in the water and the number of vehicles *not* in the water. Circle the category with the greater number of vehicles.

Think and Grow

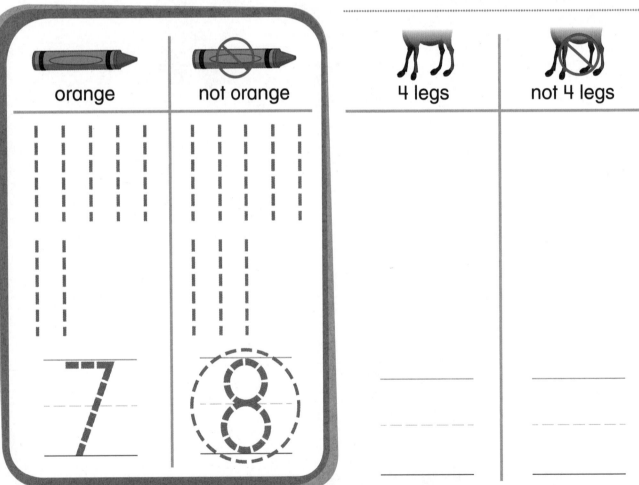

orange	not orange	4 legs	not 4 legs
7	8		

Directions: Classify the animals into the categories shown. Write the marks in the chart. Count the marks and write the numbers to tell how many animals are in each category. Circle the number that is greater than the other number.

Name ______________________________

Apply and Grow: Practice

1

4 legs	not 4 legs
____	____

2

beak	no beak
____	____

Directions: 1 and 2 Classify the animals into the categories shown. Write the marks in the chart. Count the marks and write the numbers to tell how many animals are in each category. Draw a line through the number that is less than the other number.

Think and Grow: Modeling Real Life

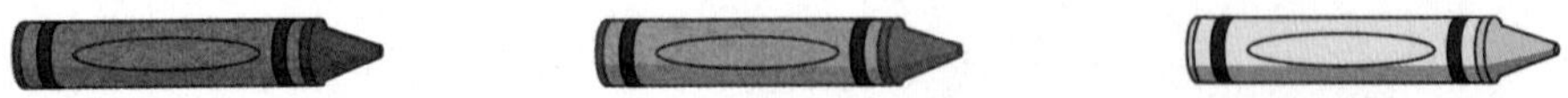

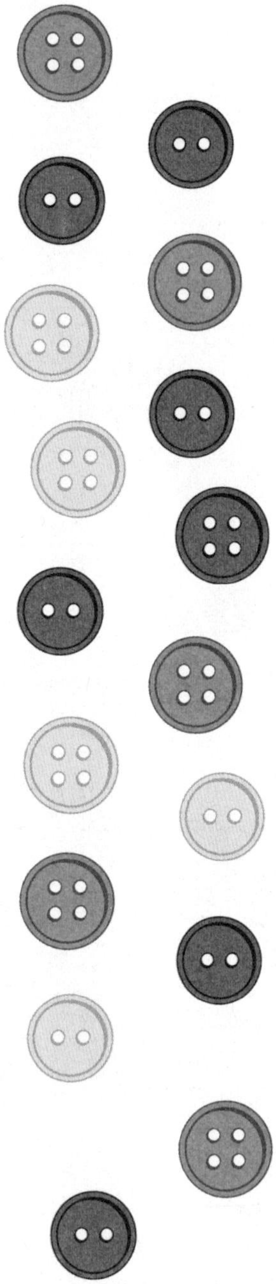

Directions:

- Classify the buttons into the categories shown. Write the marks in the chart. Count the marks and write the numbers to tell how many buttons are in each category. Circle the number that is greater than the other number.
- Classify the buttons by color. Count the number of buttons in each category. Write each number. Circle the numbers that are equal.

Name ______________________

Practice 4.5

Learning Target: Compare the numbers of objects in two categories.

 blue	 not blue
||||	||
4	2

Directions: Classify the animals into the categories shown. Write the marks in the chart. Count the marks and write the numbers to tell how many animals are in each category. Draw a line through the number that is less than the other number.

1

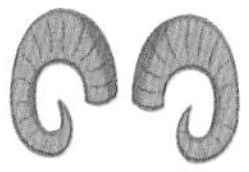 horns	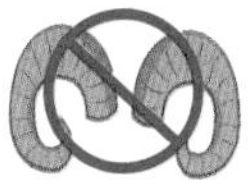 no horns
______	______
______	______

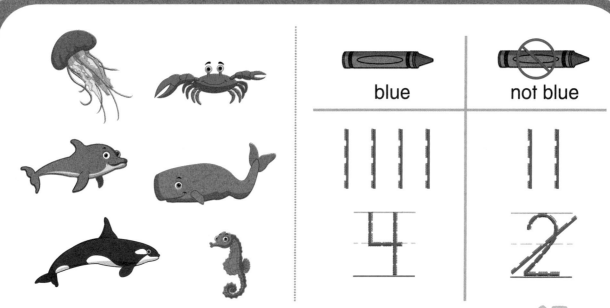

Directions: 1 Classify the animals into the categories shown. Write the marks in the chart. Count the marks and write the numbers to tell how many animals are in each category. Circle the number that is greater than the other number.

2

 2 spots	 3 spots

3

Directions: 2 Classify the frogs into the categories shown. Write the marks in the chart. Count the marks and write the numbers to tell how many frogs are in each category. Draw a line through the number that is less than the other number.
3 Classify the frogs by color. Count the number of frogs in each category. Write each number. Circle the numbers that are equal.

Name ________________________________

Performance Task 4

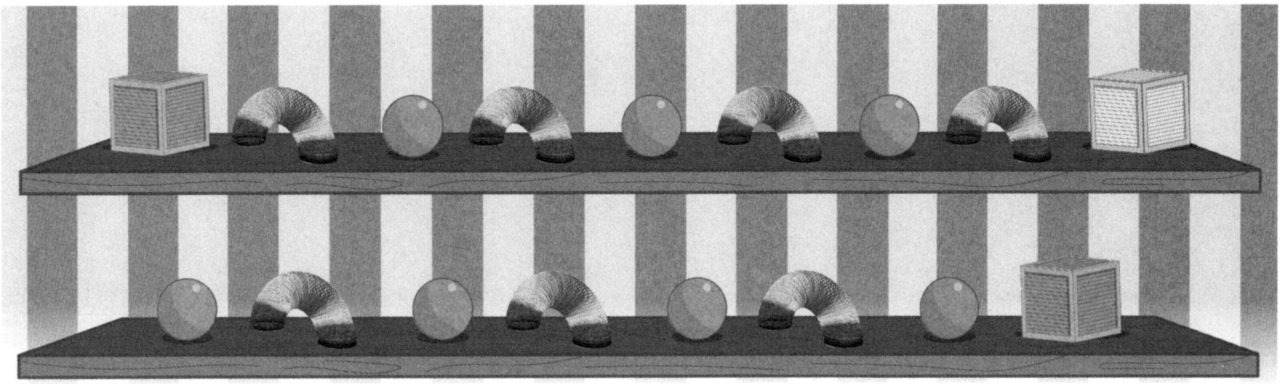

1

2

green	not green

3

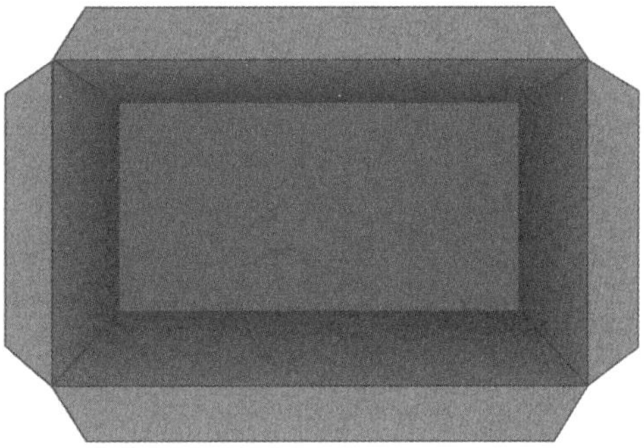

Directions: 1 Count the toys in each group. Write each number. Is the number of spring toys equal to the number of balls? Circle the thumbs up for *yes* or the thumbs down for *no*. 2 Classify the toys into the categories shown. Write the marks in the chart. Count the marks and write the numbers to tell how many toys are in each category. Circle the number that is greater than the other number. 3 More balls are delivered in a box. The number of balls in the box is less than the number of balls in the picture. Draw the balls in the box. Write the number of balls in the box.

Toss and Compare

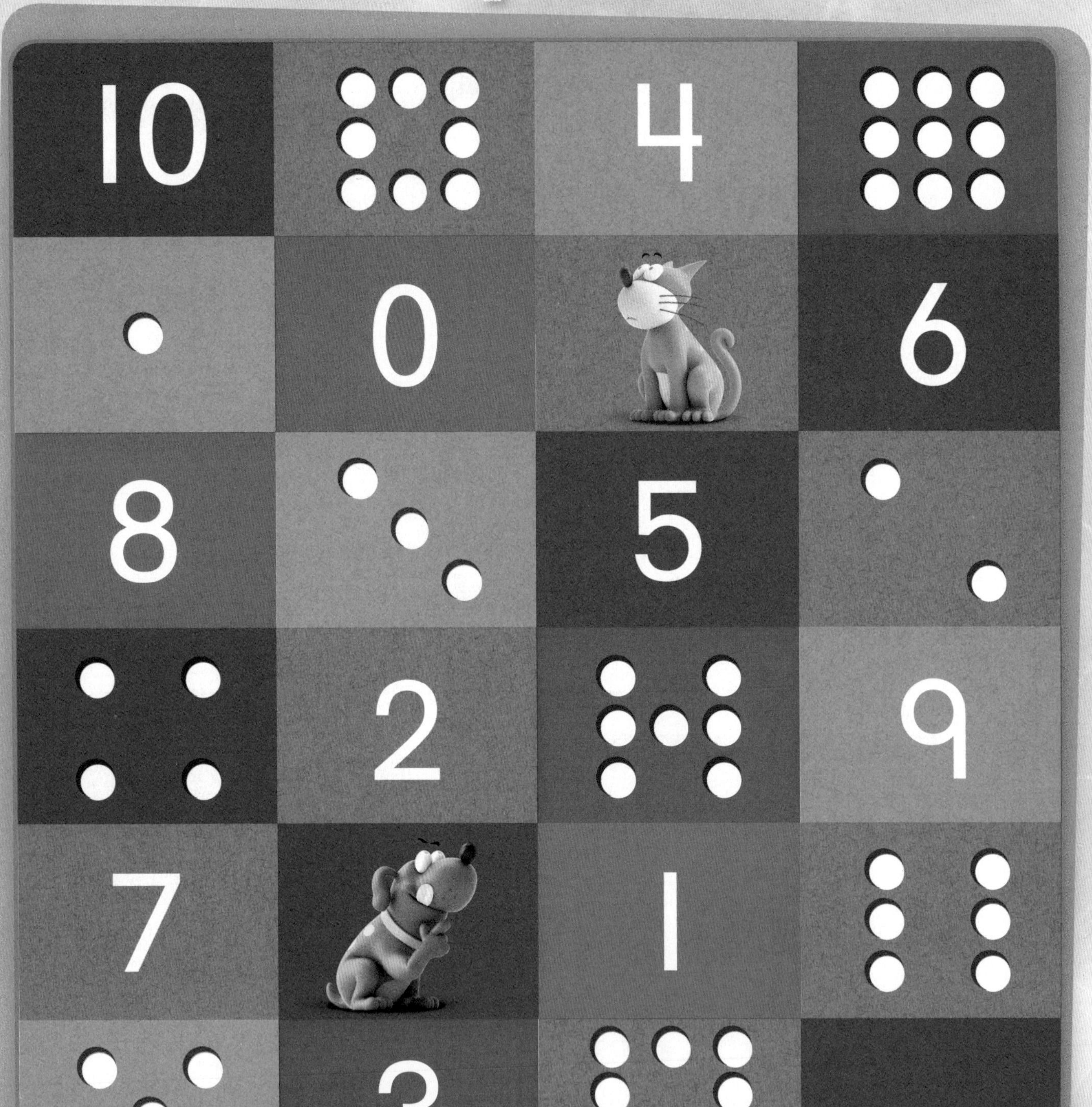

Directions: Take turns tossing a counter onto the board. If the counter lands on Newton or Descartes, choose any number from 0 to 10. Write the numbers on your Toss and Compare Numbers from 0 to 10 Recording Sheet. Circle the number that is greater than the other number. Circle both numbers if they are equal. Repeat this process until you fill your sheet.

Name ______________________________

Chapter 4 Practice

4.1 Compare Groups to 10 by Matching

1

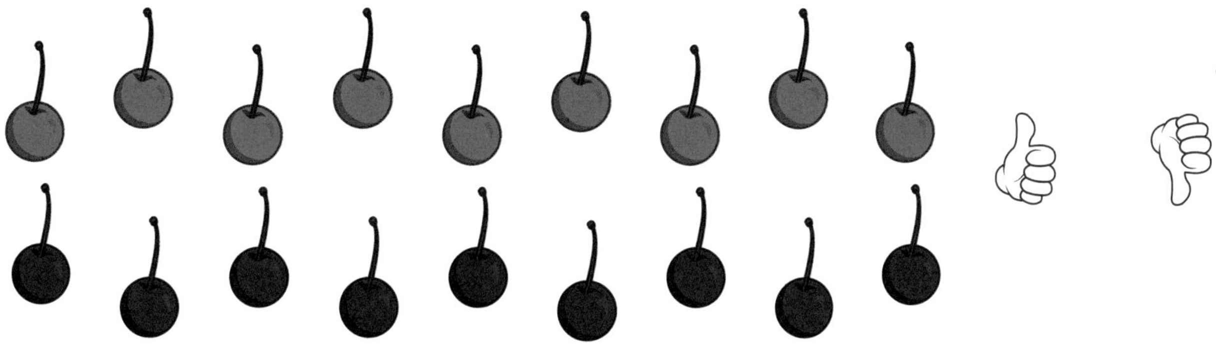

2

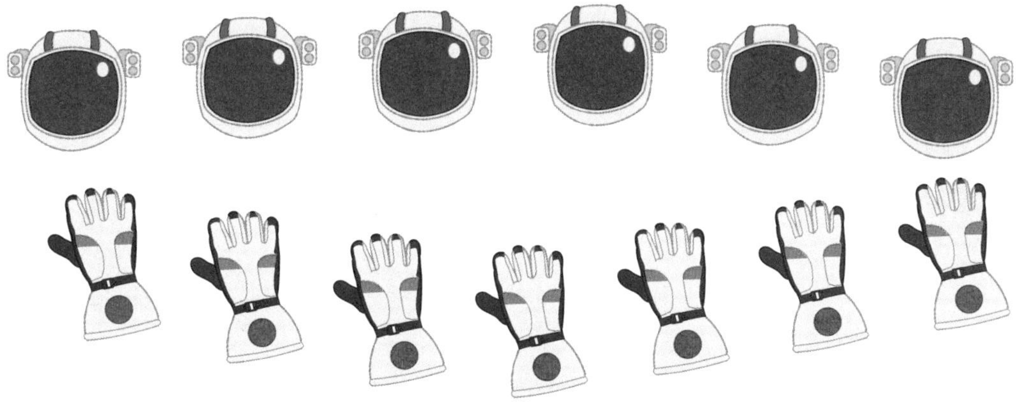

3

Directions: Draw lines between the objects in each group.
1 Is the number of red cherries equal to the number of black cherries? Circle the thumbs up for *yes* or the thumbs down for *no*. 2 Circle the group that is greater in number than the other group. 3 Draw a line through the group that is less in number than the other group.

4.2 Compare Groups to 10 by Counting

4

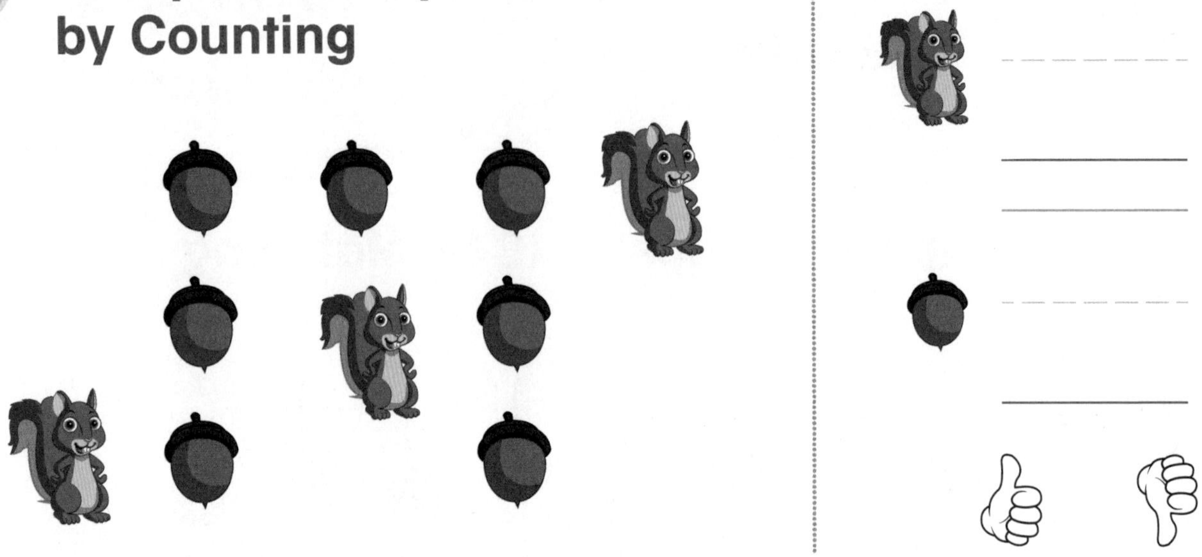

5

6

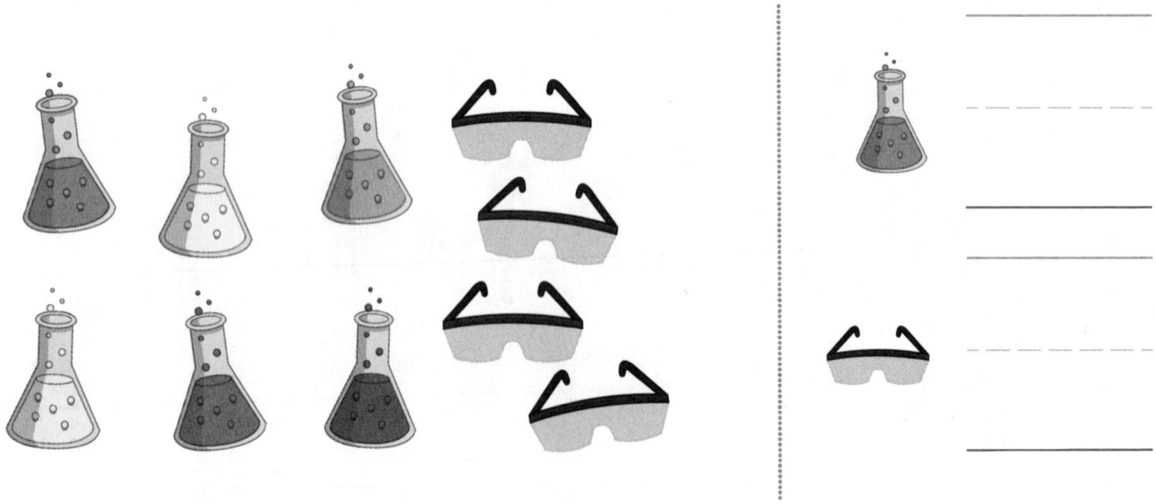

Directions: Count the objects in each group. Write each number. 4 Is the number of squirrels equal to the number of acorns? Circle the thumbs up for *yes* or the thumbs down for *no.* 5 Circle the number that is greater than the other number. 6 Draw a line through the number that is less than the other number.

4.3 Compare Numbers to 10

7

7

7

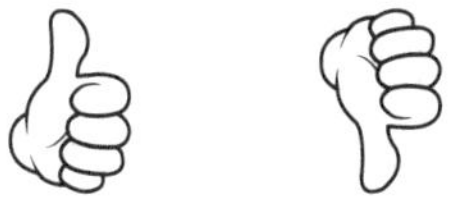

8

2

10

9

6

9

Directions: Compare the numbers. 7 Are the numbers equal? Circle the thumbs up for *yes* or the thumbs down for *no.* 8 Circle the number that is greater than the other number. Draw to show how you know. 9 Draw a line through the number that is less than the other number. Draw to show how you know.

4.4 Classify Objects into Categories

10

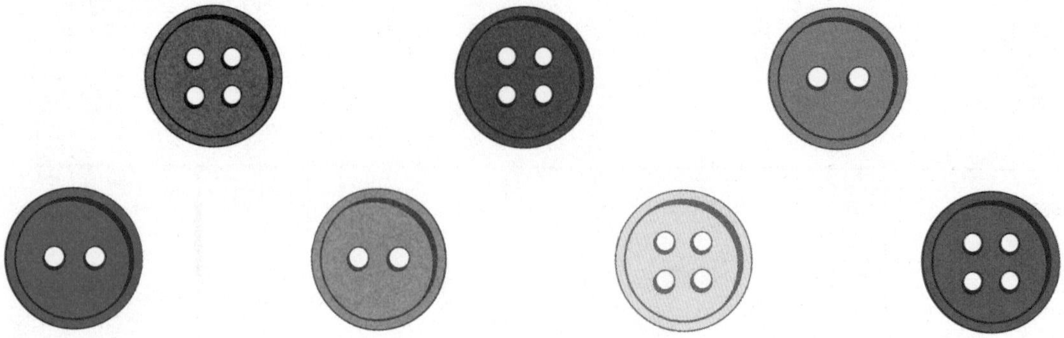

4.5 Classify and Compare by Counting

11

green	not green
____	____

Directions: 10 Circle the buttons that have 4 holes. Cross out the buttons that do *not* have 4 holes. 11 Classify the animals into the categories shown. Write the marks in the chart. Count the marks and write the numbers to tell how many animals are in each category. Circle the number that is greater than the other number.

Name ____________________

Cumulative Practice 1–4

1

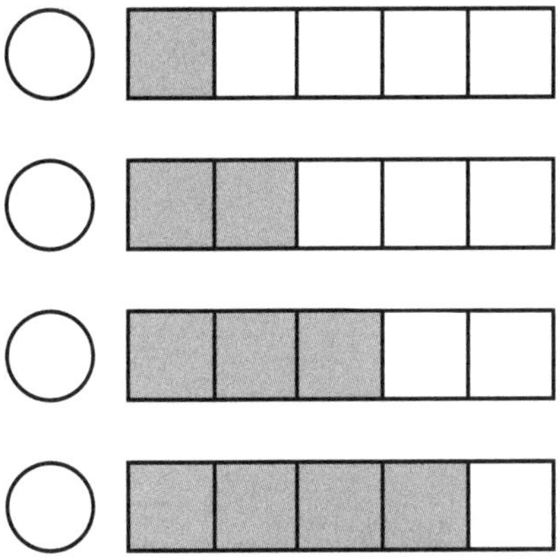

2

3

8

○ 9

○ 8

○ 0

○ 6

Directions: Shade the circle next to the answer. 1 Which five frame shows the number of puzzle pieces? 2 Which basket has 0 apples? 3 Which number is greater than 8?

4

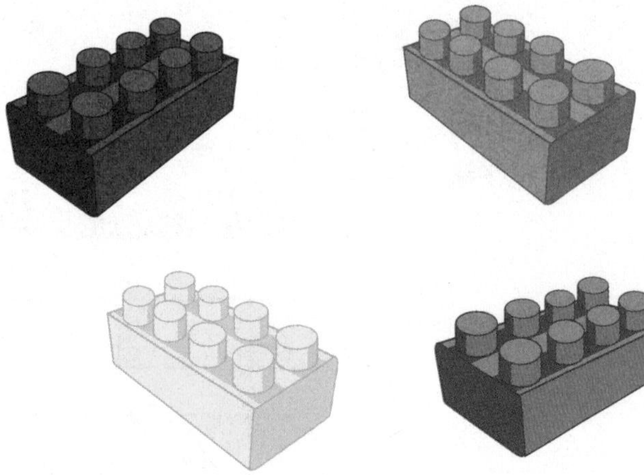

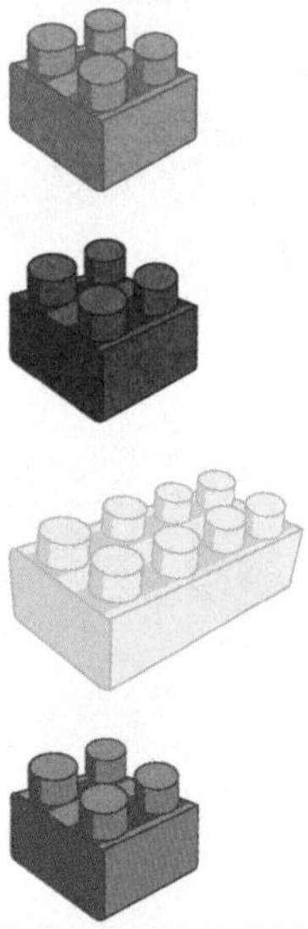

5

14325	54321	12345	25314

6

Directions: Shade the circle next to the answer. 4 Which block belongs in the group? 5 Which ticket shows the numbers 1 to 5 in order? 6 Which group does *not* have 7 balls?

7

8

9

Directions: 7 Count the flowers. Color the boxes to show how many. 8 Count the salamanders. Say the number. Write the number. 9 Draw lines between the objects in each group. Is the number of detective hats equal to the number of magnifying glasses? Circle the thumbs up for *yes* or the thumbs down for *no.*

10

11

12

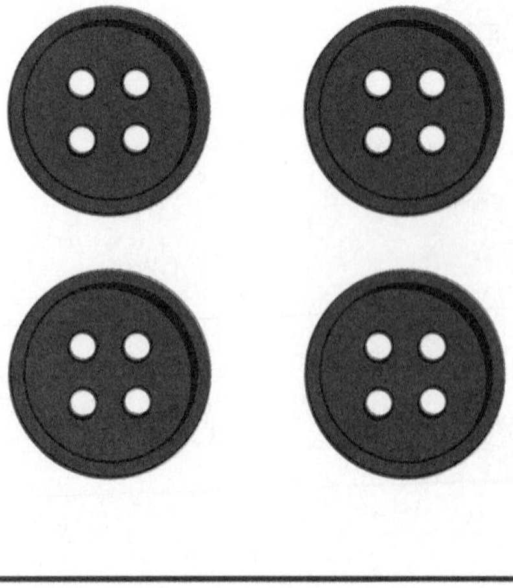

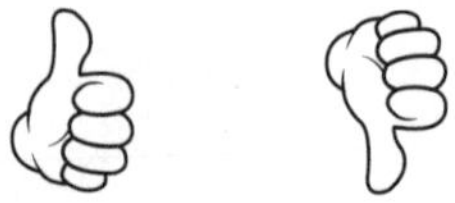

Directions: 10 Count the objects in each group. Write each number. Circle the number that is greater than the other number. 11 Draw lines between the objects in each group. Draw a line through the group that is less in number than the other group. 12 Draw 4 pieces of string. Is the number of pieces of string equal to the number of buttons? Circle the thumbs up for *yes* or the thumbs down for *no*.

5 Compose and Decompose Numbers to 10

- How many butterflies are in the picture?
- How many butterflies are on the flower? How many are flying?

Chapter Learning Target:
Understand partner numbers.

Chapter Success Criteria:
- I can identify the parts and the whole.
- I can name partner numbers.
- I can compare parts of numbers.
- I can model taking apart numbers.

Name ___________________

5 Vocabulary

Review Word
less than

____

____

Directions: Count the animals in each group. Write each number. Draw a line through the number that is less than the other number.

Chapter 5 Vocabulary Cards

number bond

part

partner numbers

put together

take apart

whole

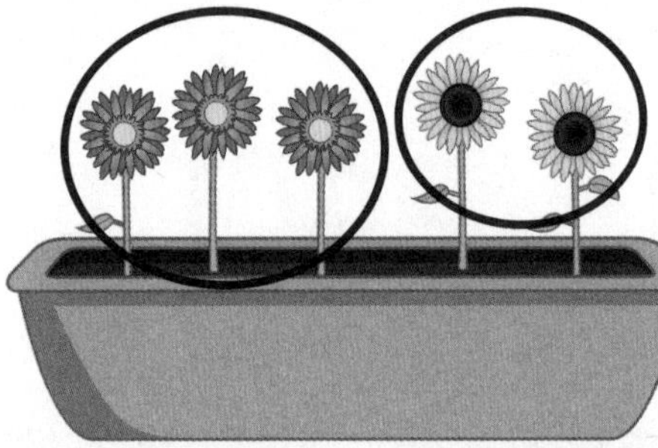

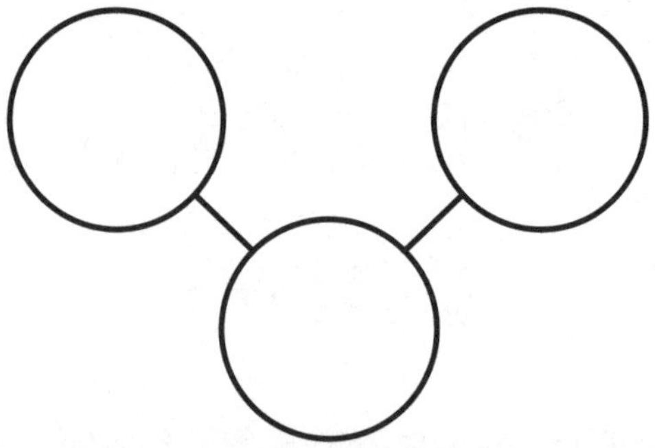

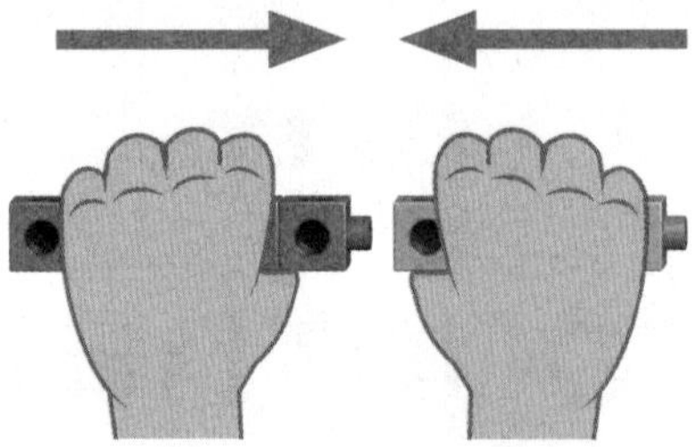

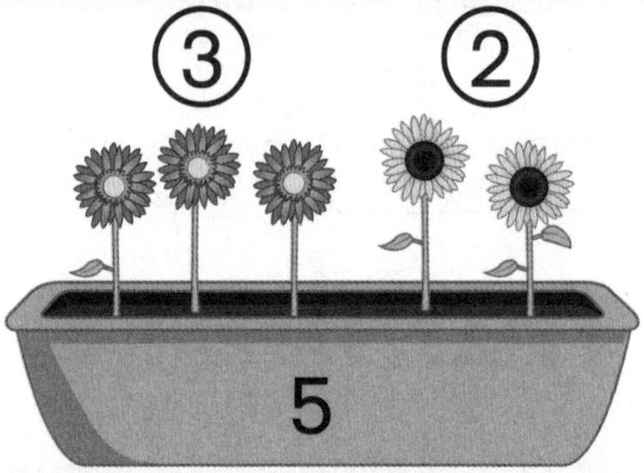
3
2
5

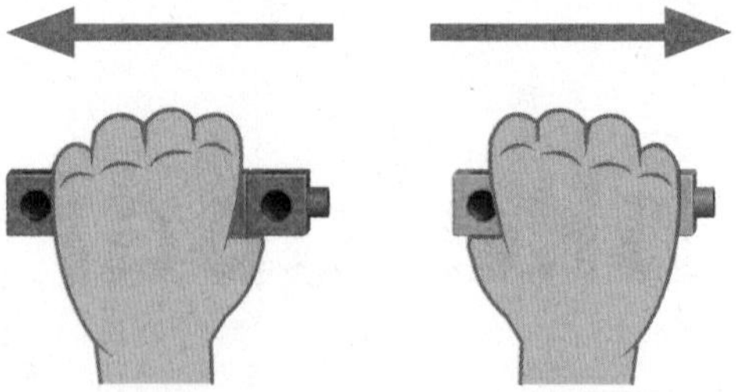

Name ______________________

Partner Numbers to 5

5.1

Learning Target: Use partner numbers to show numbers to 5.

Explore and Grow

Directions: Drop 3 two-color counters in the box. Move the counters to the correct frame. Name the parts and the whole. Repeat this process using 4 and 5 counters.

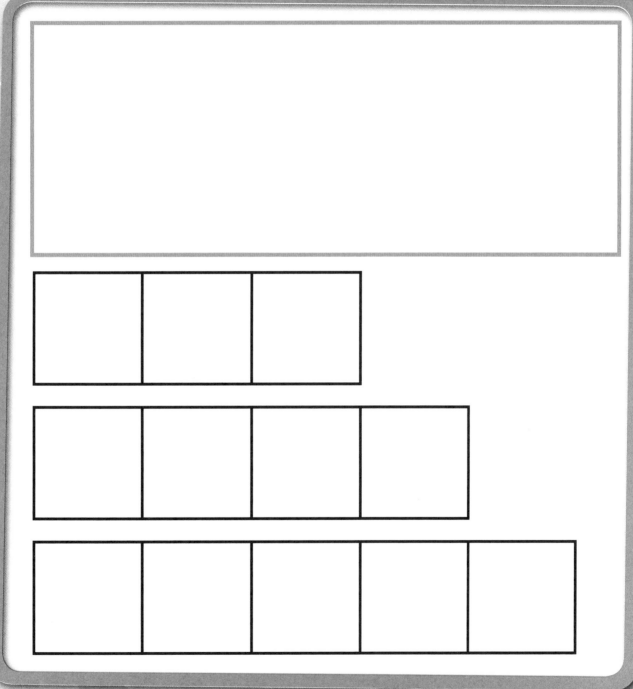

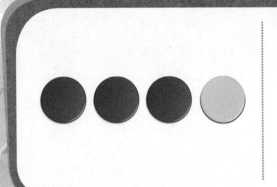

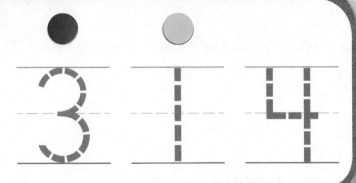

Think and Grow

3 1 4

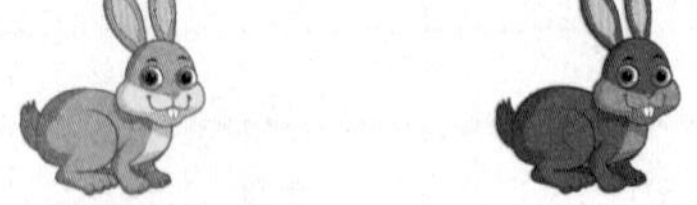

Directions: Count each type of object. Write each number. Count all of the objects. Write the number for the whole.

Name ______________________________

Apply and Grow: Practice

1

______ ______ ______

______ ______ ______

2

______ ______ ______

______ ______ ______

3

______ ______ ______

______ ______ ______

Directions: 1 – 3 Count each type of animal. Write each number. Count all of the animals. Write the number for the whole.

Think and Grow: Modeling Real Life

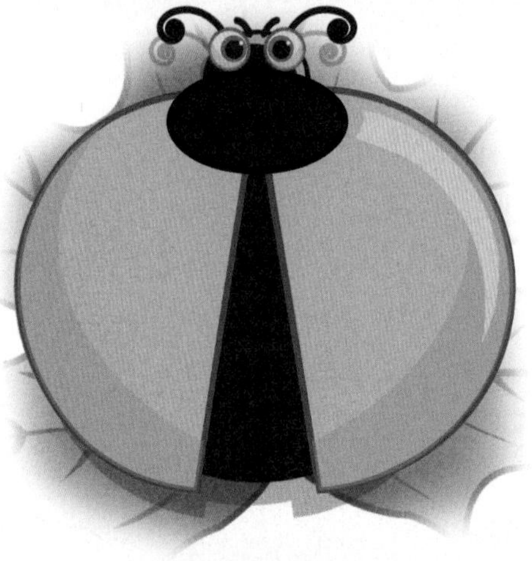

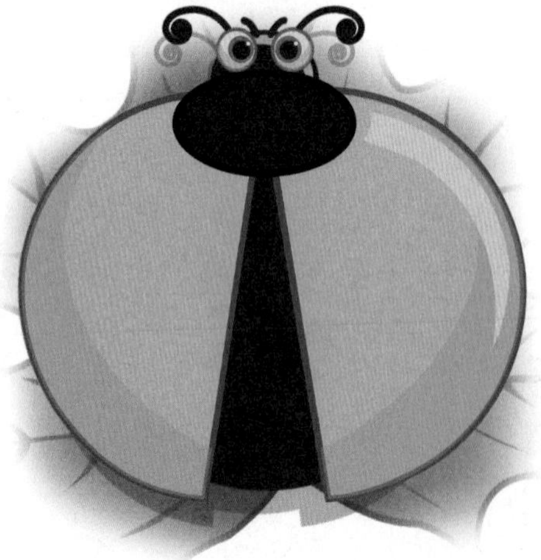

Directions:

- Show one way to draw 4 spots on the ladybug. Write the number of spots on each wing.
- Show two ways to draw 5 spots on the ladybug. Write the number of spots on each wing.

Name ________________________

Learning Target: Use partner numbers to show numbers to 5.

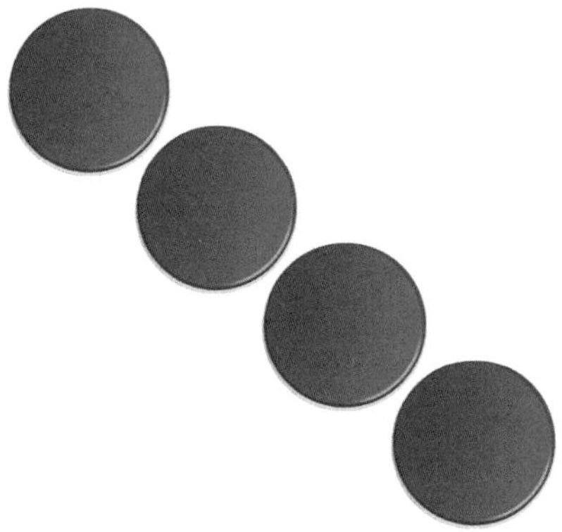

4 0 4

Directions: Count each type of object. Write each number. Count all of the objects. Write the number for the whole.

1

2

Directions: 1 and 2 Count each type of object. Write each number. Count all of the objects. Write the number for the whole.

3

4

5

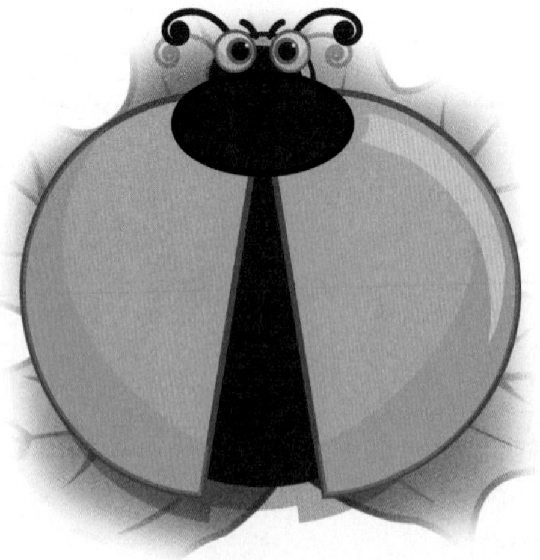

Directions: 3 and 4 Count each type of dog. Write each number. Count all of the dogs. Write the number for the whole. 5 Show one way to draw 3 spots on the ladybug. Write the number of spots on each wing.

Name ______________________________

Use Number Bonds to Represent Numbers to 5

5.2

Learning Target: Use number bonds to show the parts and the whole for numbers to 5.

Explore and Grow

Directions: Use counters to show 3 berries on one bush and 2 berries on the other bush. Slide the counters to the bottom to show the whole. Name the parts and the whole.

Think and Grow

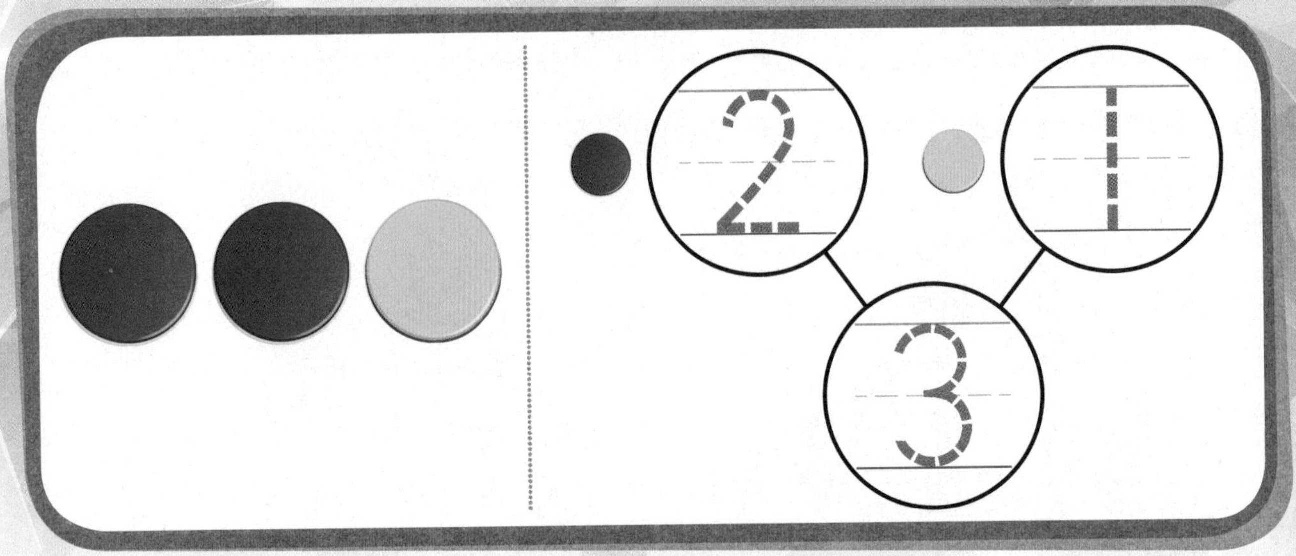

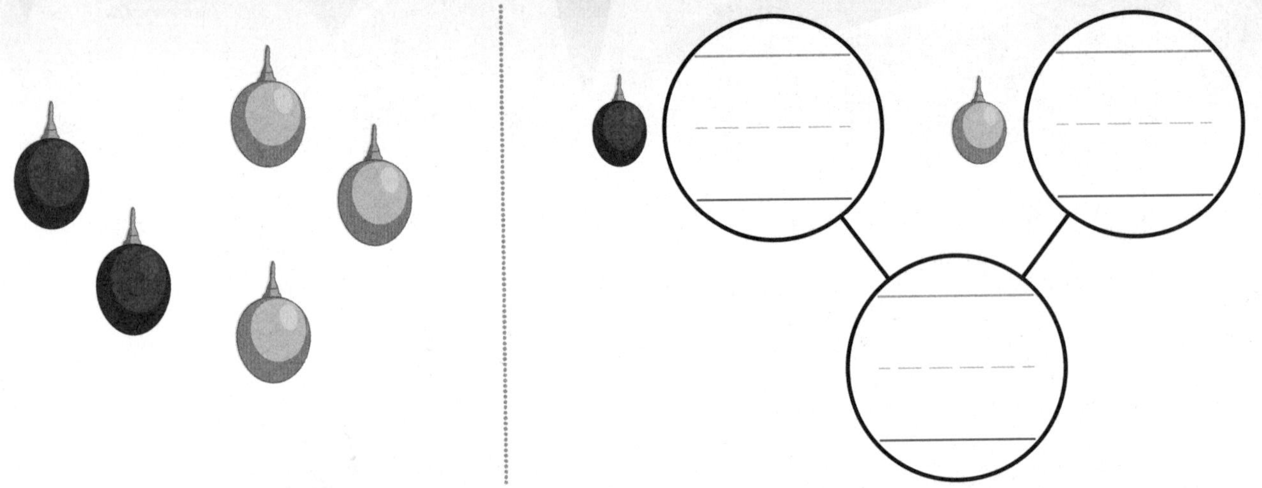

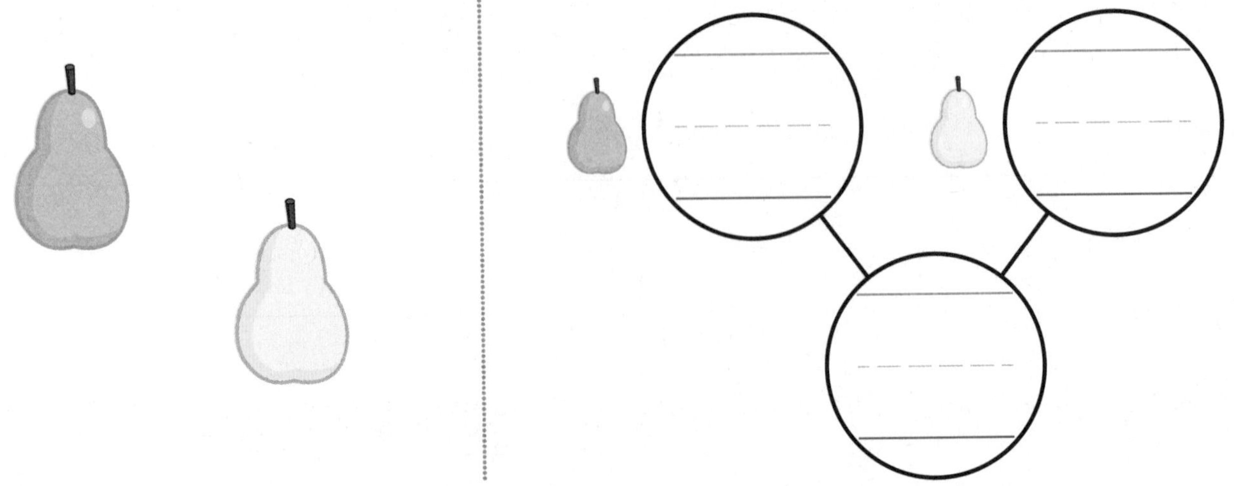

Directions: Name the parts and the whole for the group. Then complete the number bond.

Name ________________________________

Apply and Grow: Practice

1

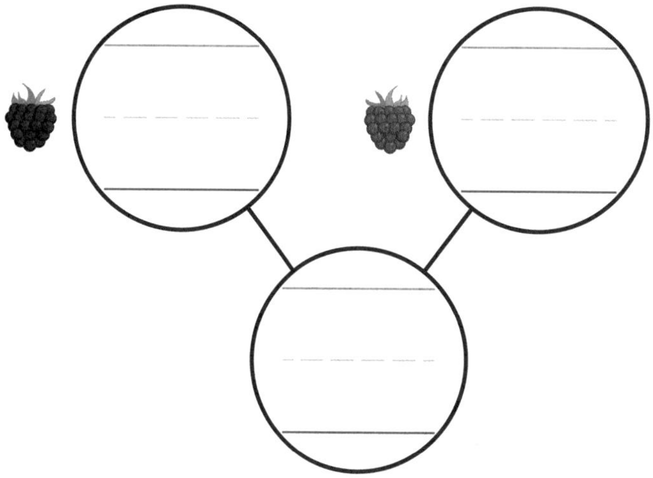

2

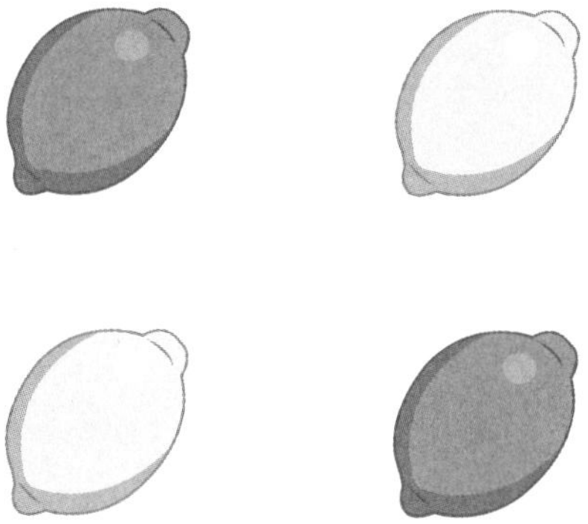

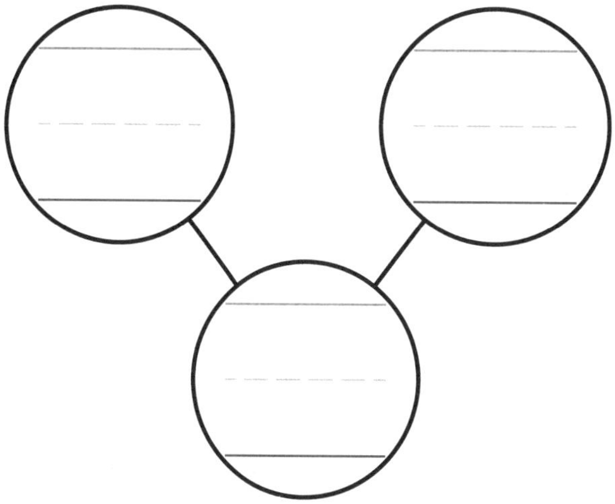

3

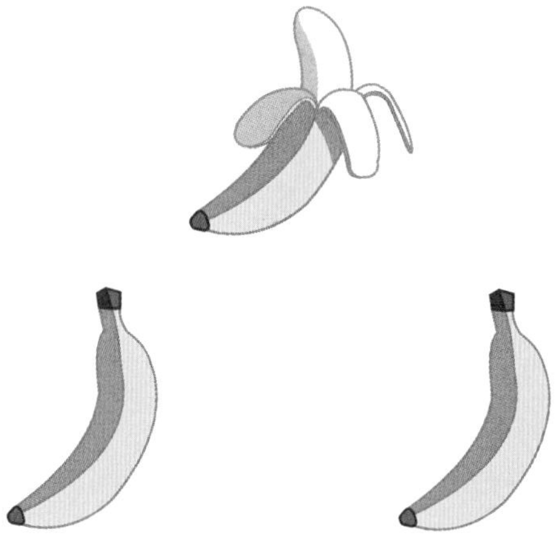

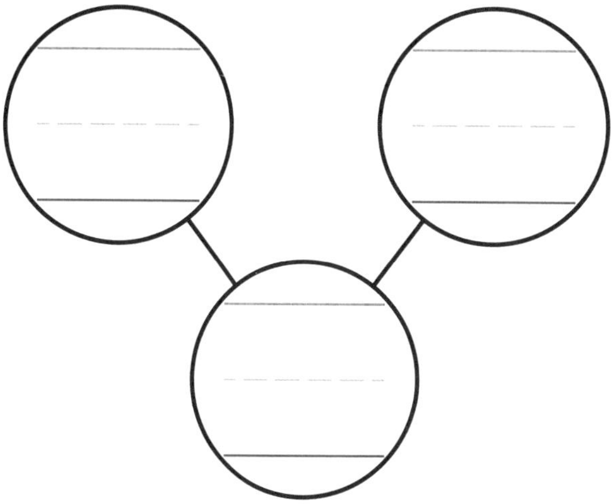

Directions: 1–3 Name the parts and the whole for the group. Then complete the number bond.

Think and Grow: Modeling Real Life

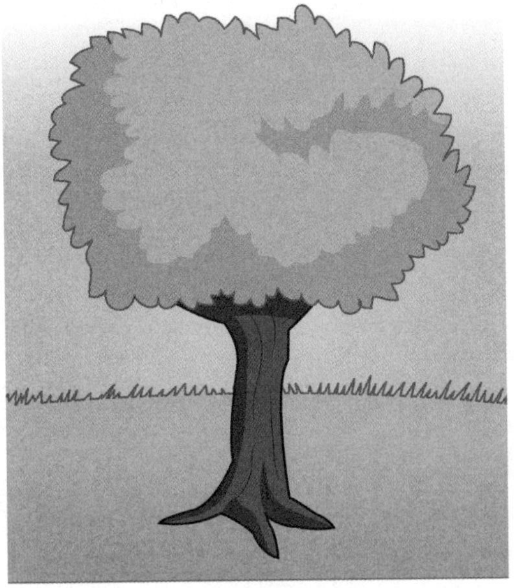

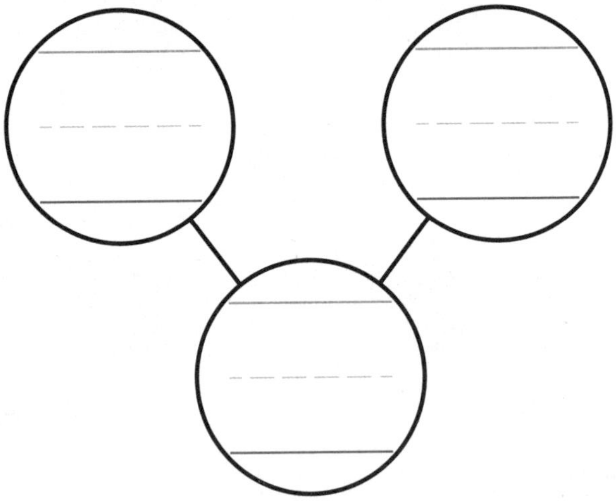

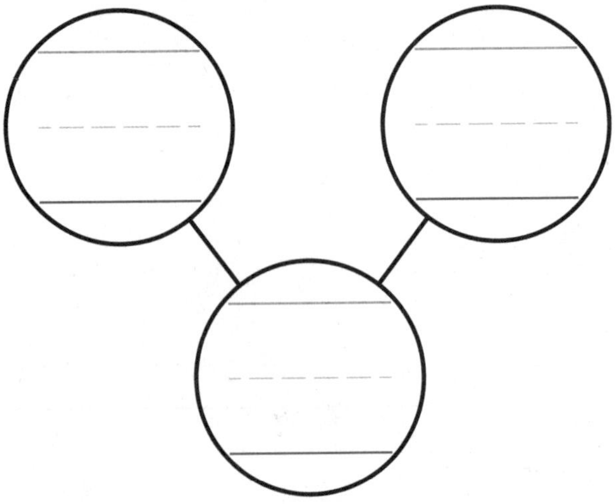

Directions:

- Draw 3 cherries on the picture. Draw some of the cherries in the tree and some of the cherries on the ground. Complete the number bond to match your picture.
- Draw 4 cherries on the picture. Draw some of the cherries in the tree and some of the cherries on the ground. Complete the number bond to match your picture.

Name ______________________

Practice 5.2

Learning Target: Use number bonds to show the parts and the whole for numbers to 5.

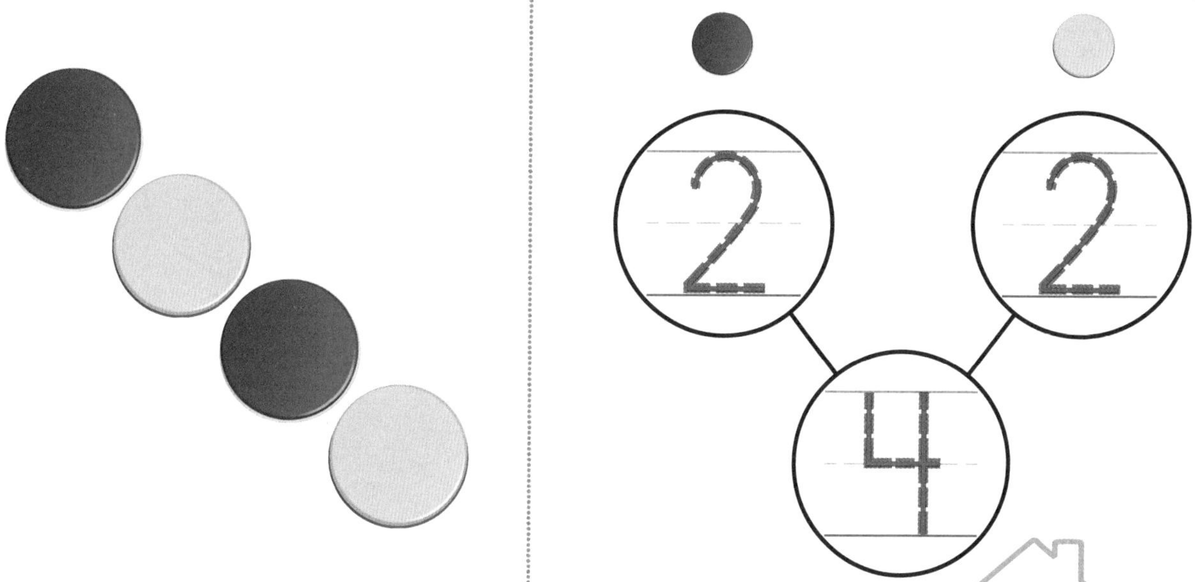

Directions: Name the parts and the whole for the group. Then complete the number bond.

1

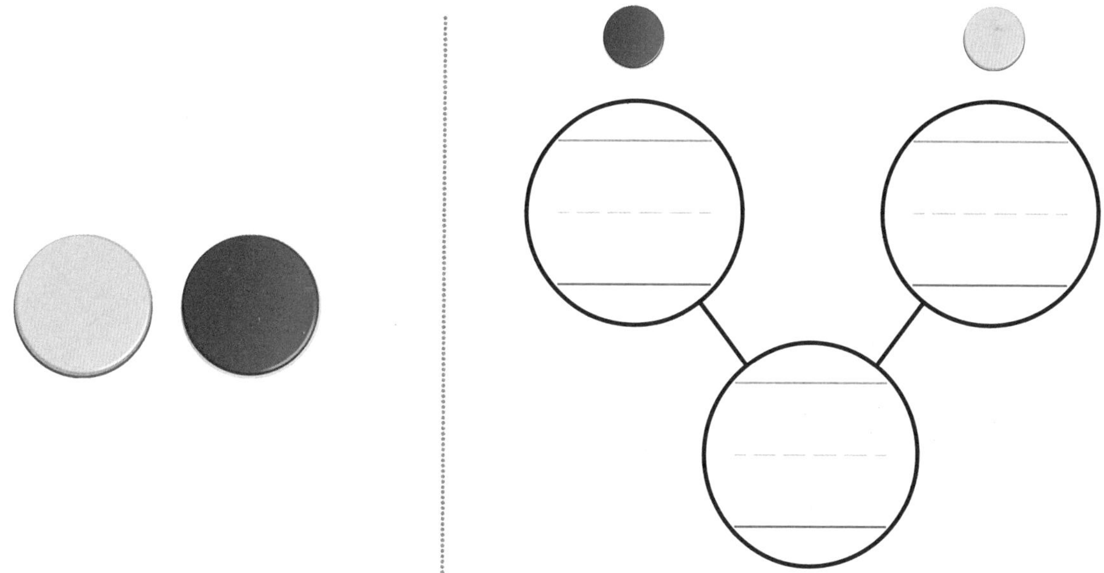

Directions: 1 Name the parts and the whole for the group. Then complete the number bond.

2

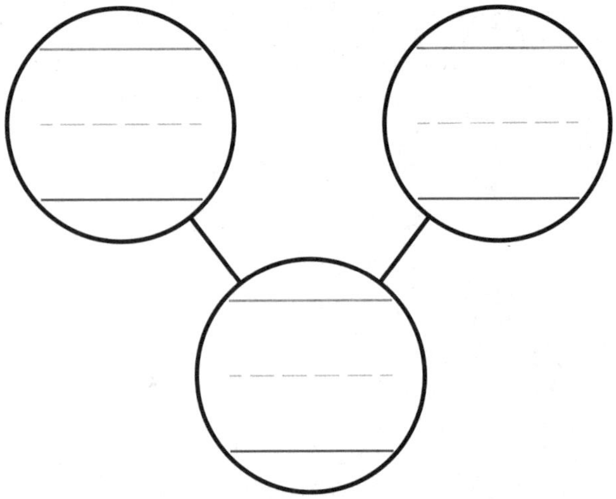

3

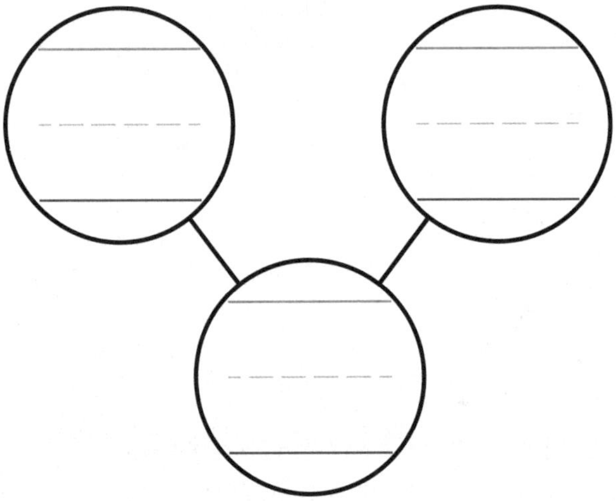

4

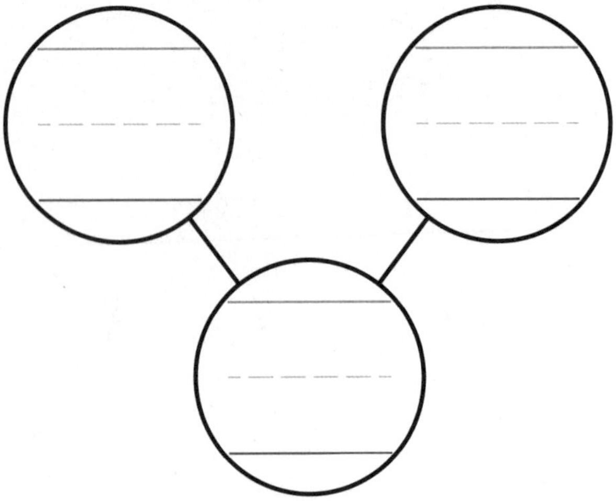

Directions: 2 and 3 Name the parts and the whole for the group. Then complete the number bond. 4 Draw 5 cherries on the picture. Draw some of the cherries in the tree and some of the cherries on the ground. Complete the number bond to match your picture.

Name ________________________________

Compose and Decompose 6

5.3

Learning Target: Use partner numbers to make and take apart the number 6.

Explore and Grow

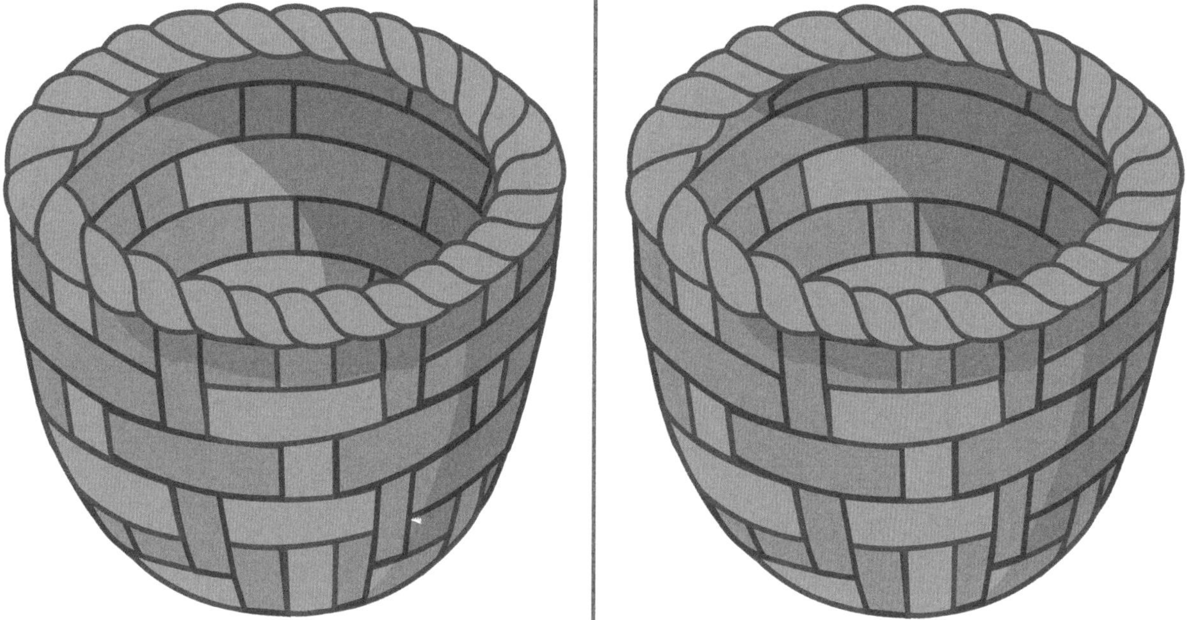

Directions: Use counters to show 2 vegetables in one basket and 4 vegetables in the other basket. Slide the counters to the top to show the whole. Name the parts and the whole.

Think and Grow

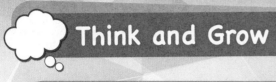

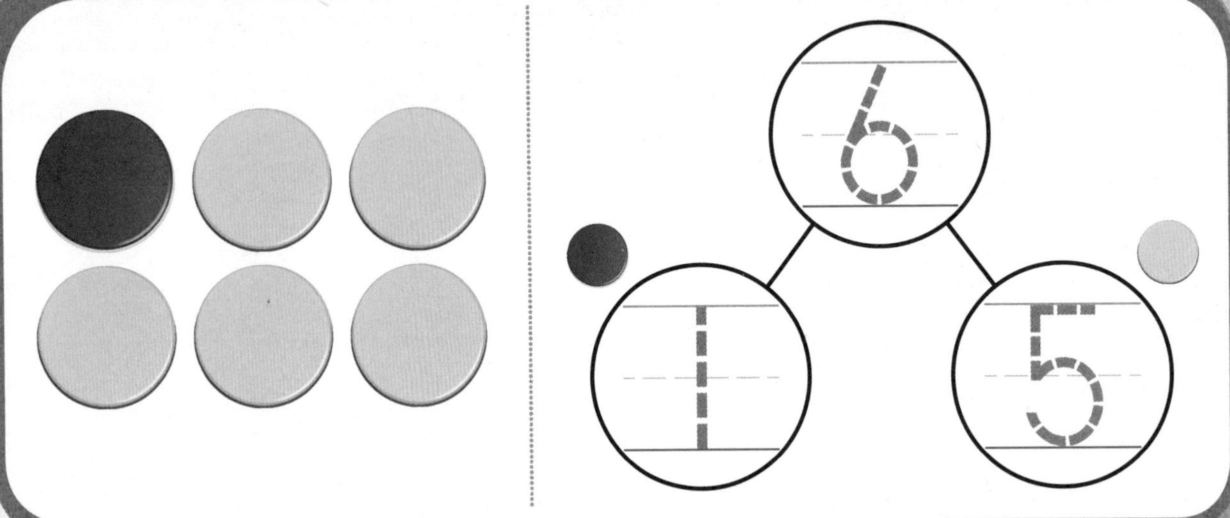

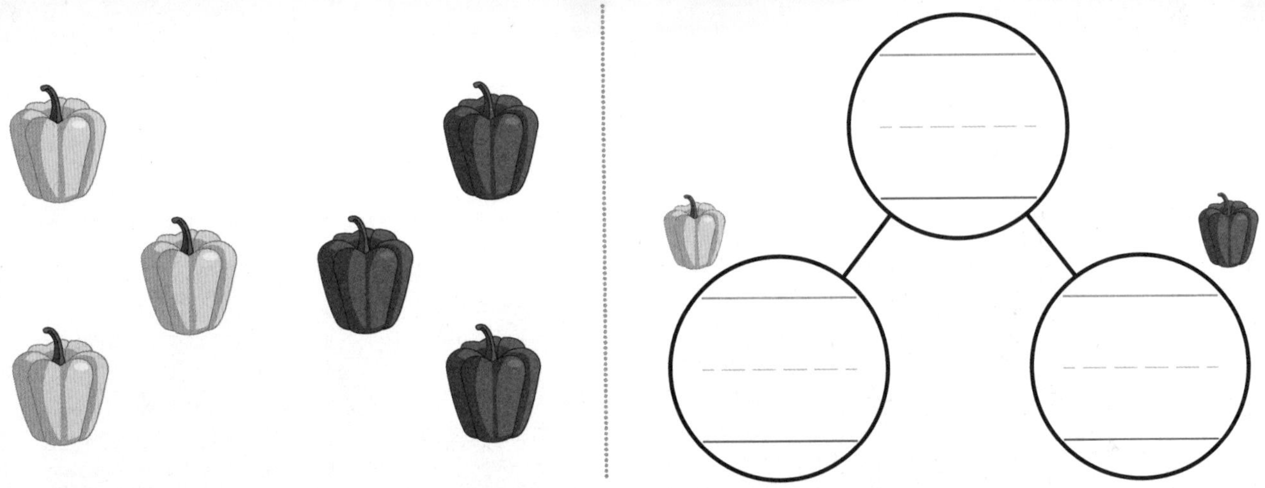

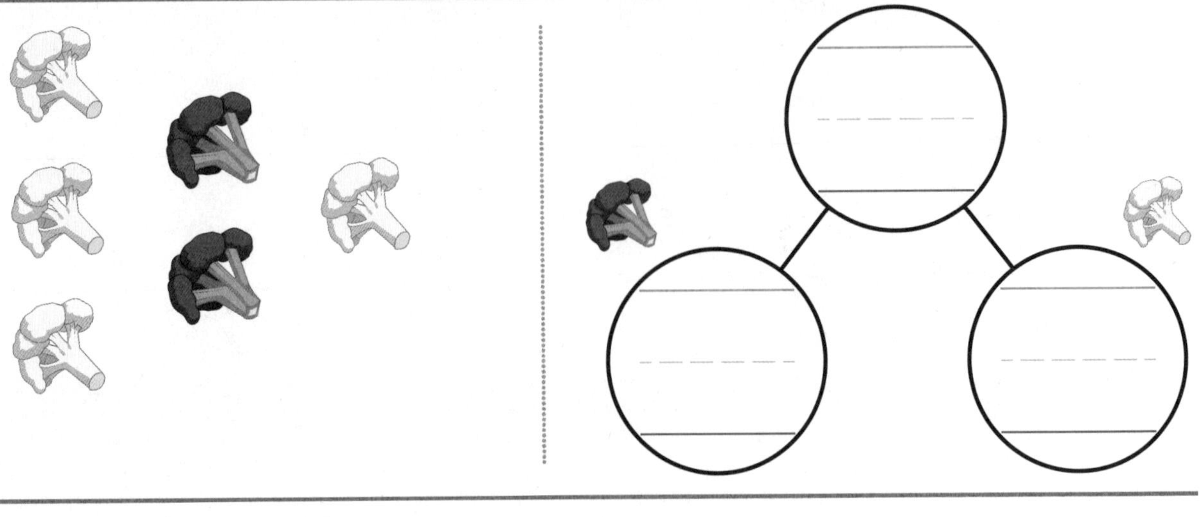

Directions: Name the parts and the whole for the group. Then complete the number bond.

Name ________________________________

Apply and Grow: Practice

1

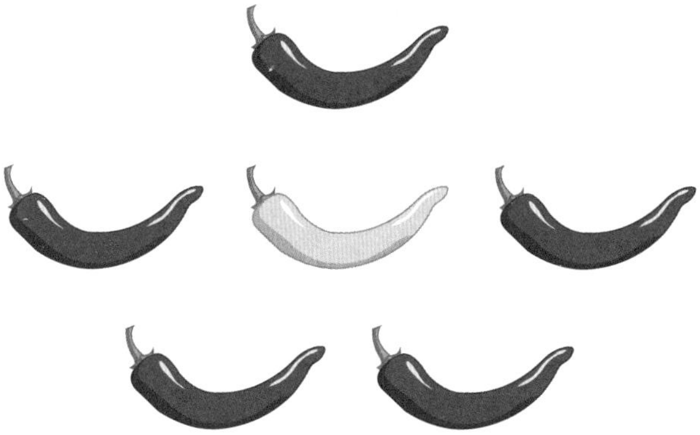

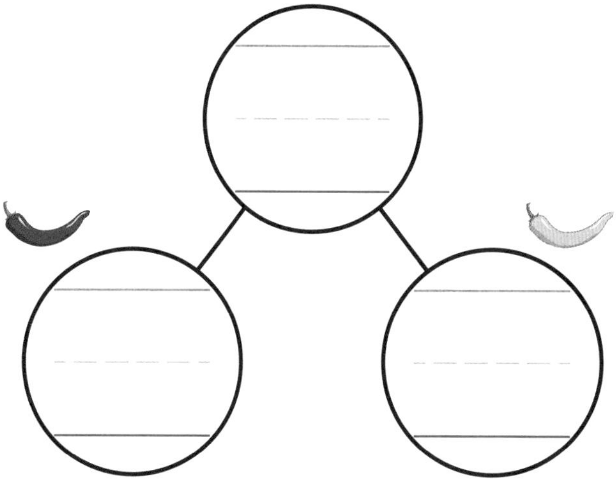

2

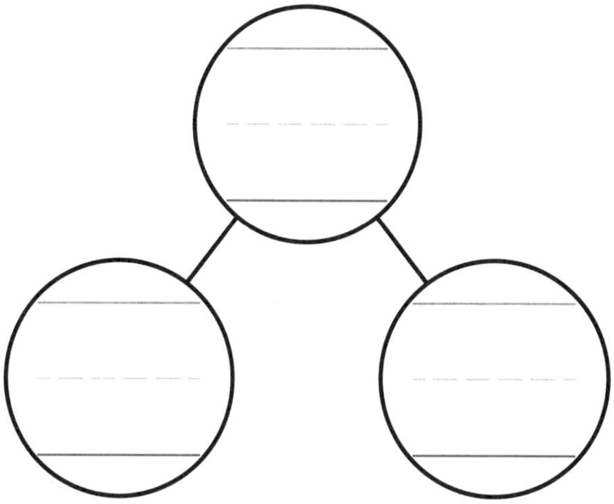

3

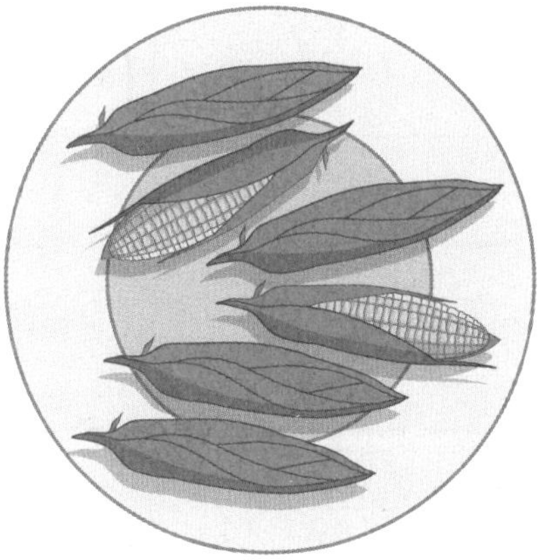

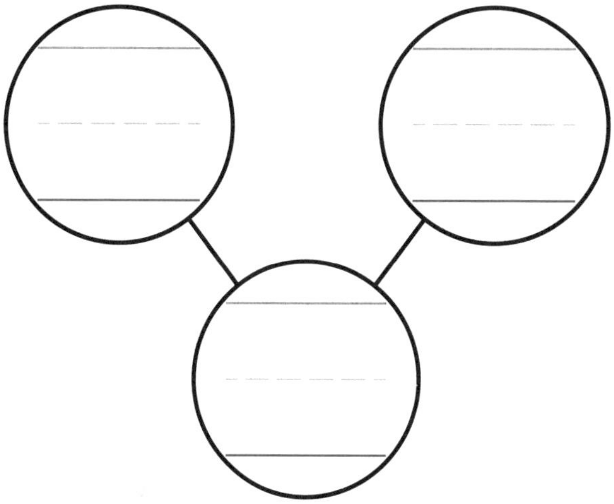

Directions: 1 – 3 Name the parts and the whole for the group. Then complete the number bond.

Think and Grow: Modeling Real Life

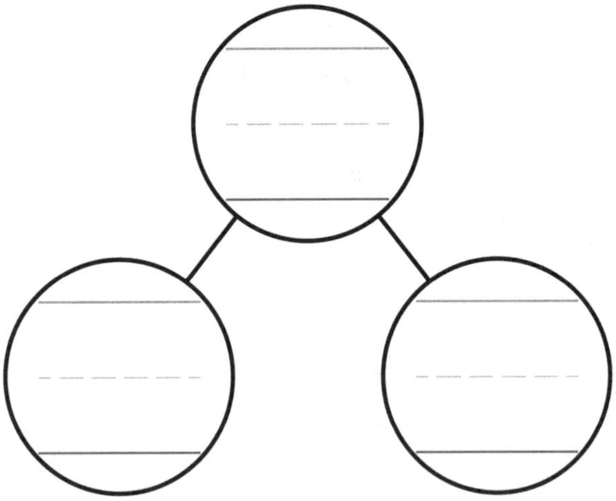

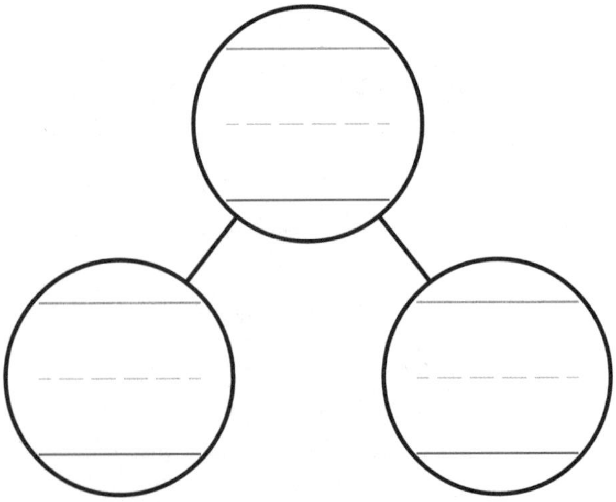

Directions: There are 6 tomatoes at a farm stand. Newton and Descartes buy all of them. Newton buys fewer tomatoes than Descartes.

- Draw tomatoes in the wagons to show how many tomatoes Newton and Descartes could buy. Then complete the number bond to match your picture.
- Draw another way to show how many tomatoes Newton and Descartes could buy. Then complete the number bond to match your picture.

Name ______________________________

Learning Target: Use partner numbers to make and take apart the number 6.

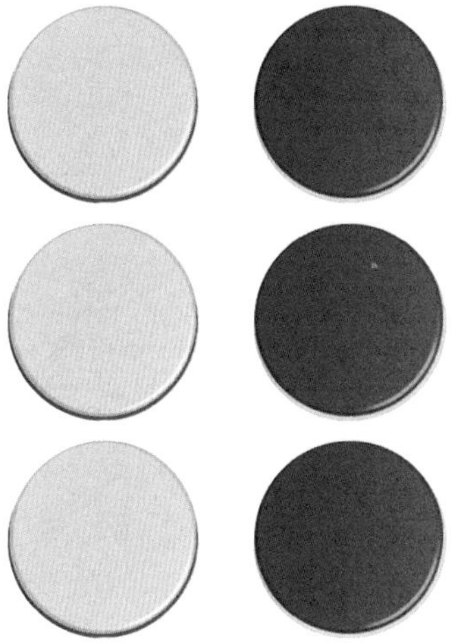

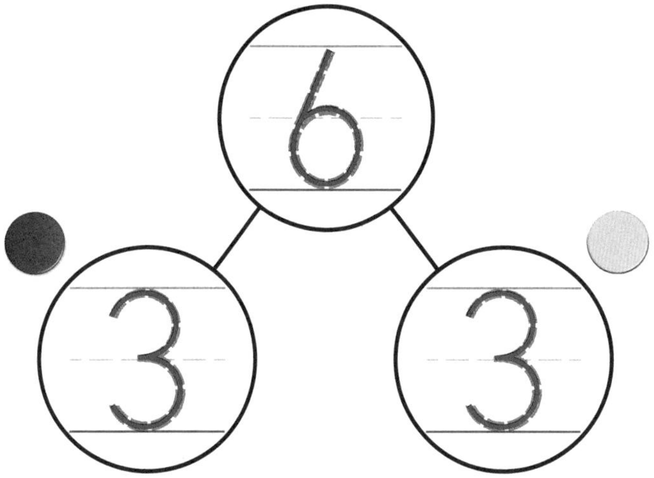

Directions: Name the parts and the whole for the group. Then complete the number bond.

1

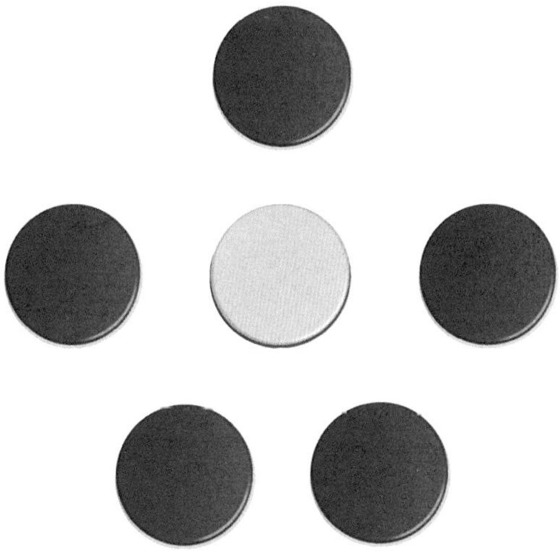

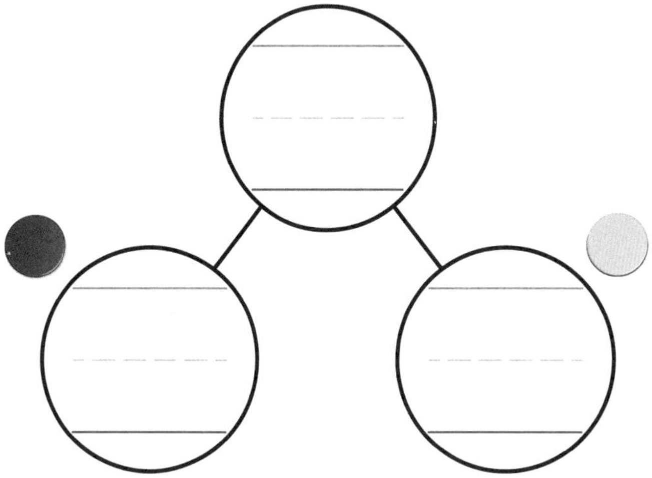

Directions: 1 Name the parts and the whole for the group. Then complete the number bond.

2

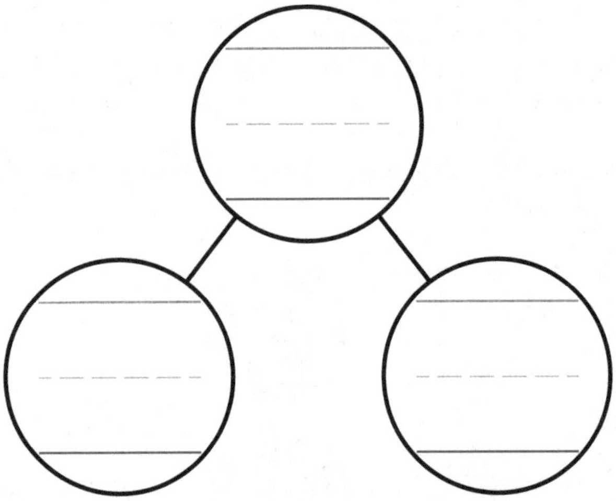

3

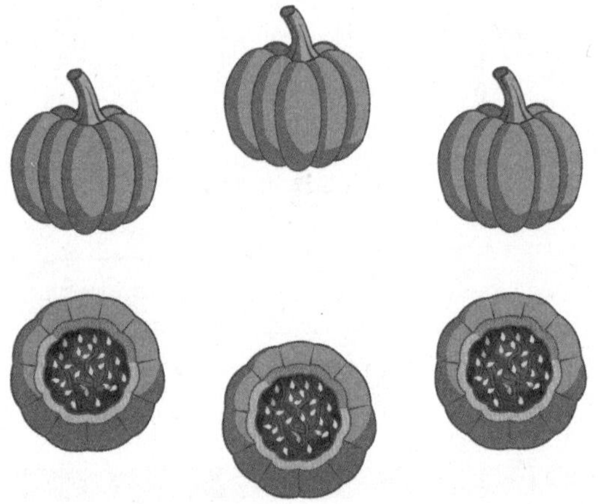

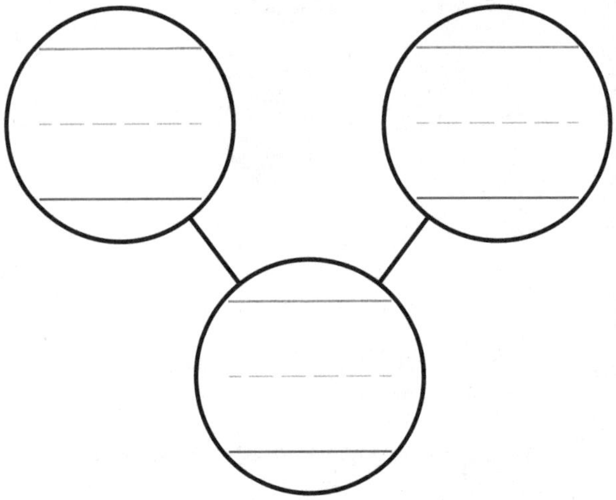

4

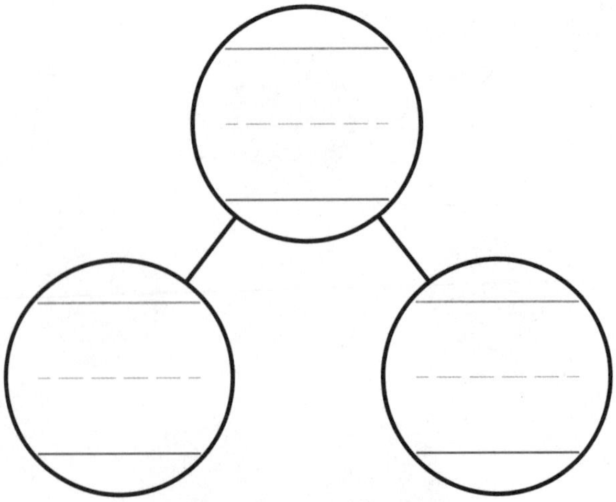

Directions: 2 and 3 Name the parts and the whole for the group. Then complete the number bond. 4 There are 6 tomatoes at a farm stand. Newton and Descartes buy all of them. Newton buys more tomatoes than Descartes. Draw tomatoes in the wagons to show how many tomatoes Newton and Descartes could buy. Then complete the number bond to match your picture.

Name ___________________________

Compose and Decompose 7 5.4

Learning Target: Use partner numbers to make and take apart the number 7.

Explore and Grow

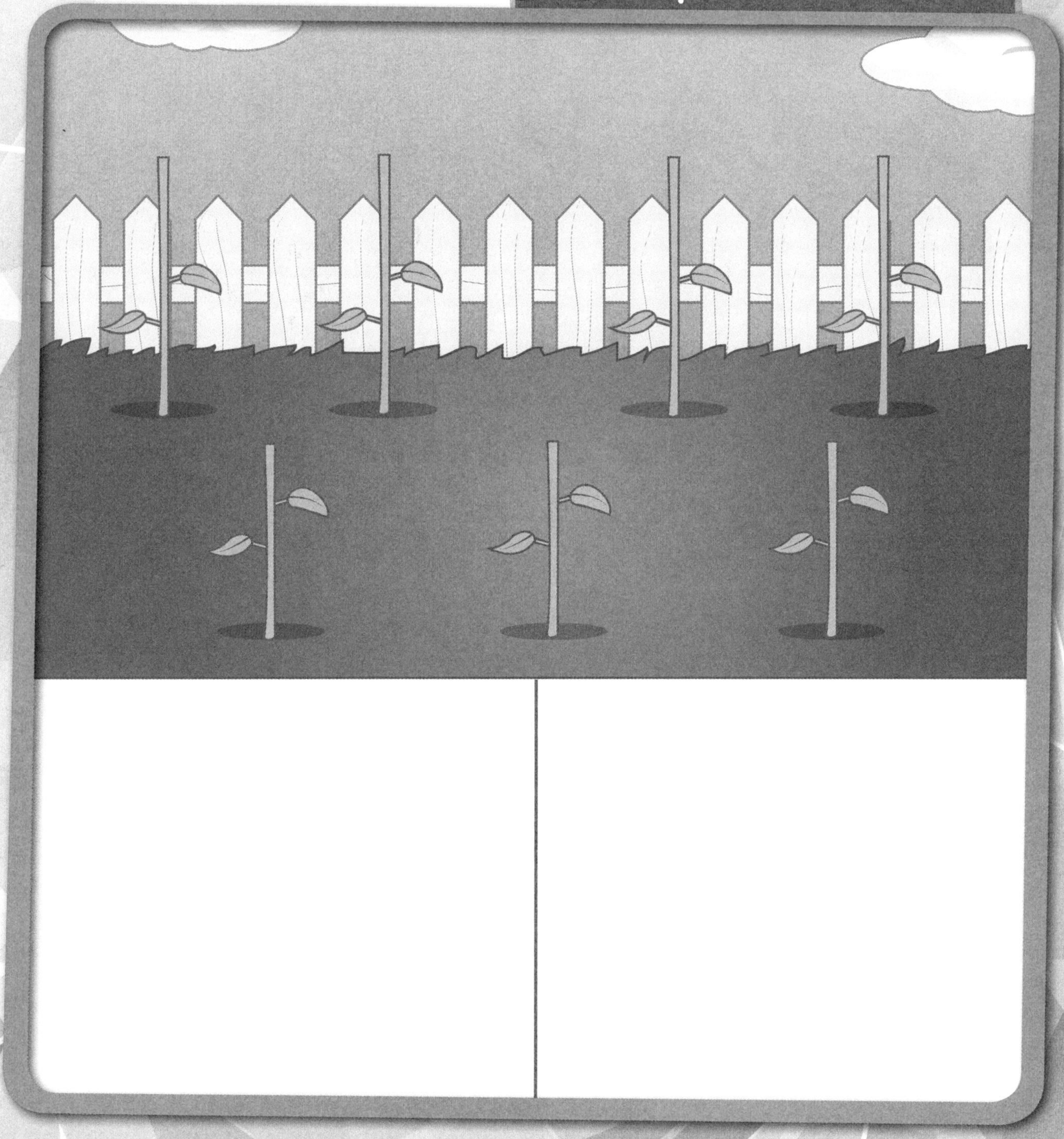

Directions: Use counters to show 7 flowers. Slide the counters to the bottom to show 2 groups. Name the parts and the whole.

Think and Grow

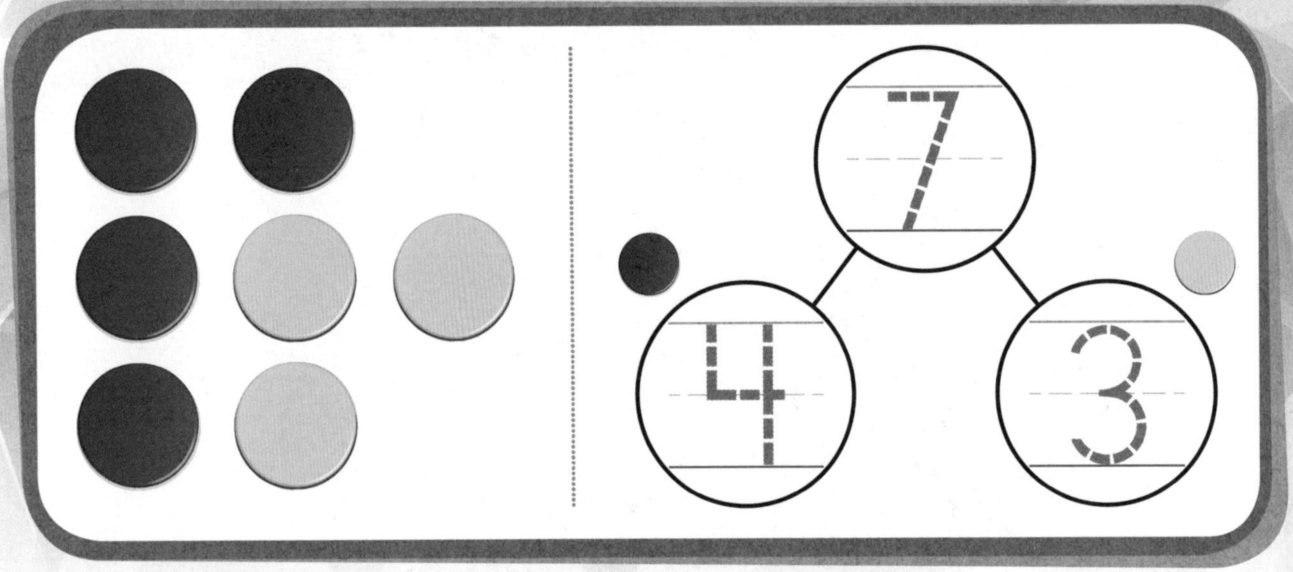

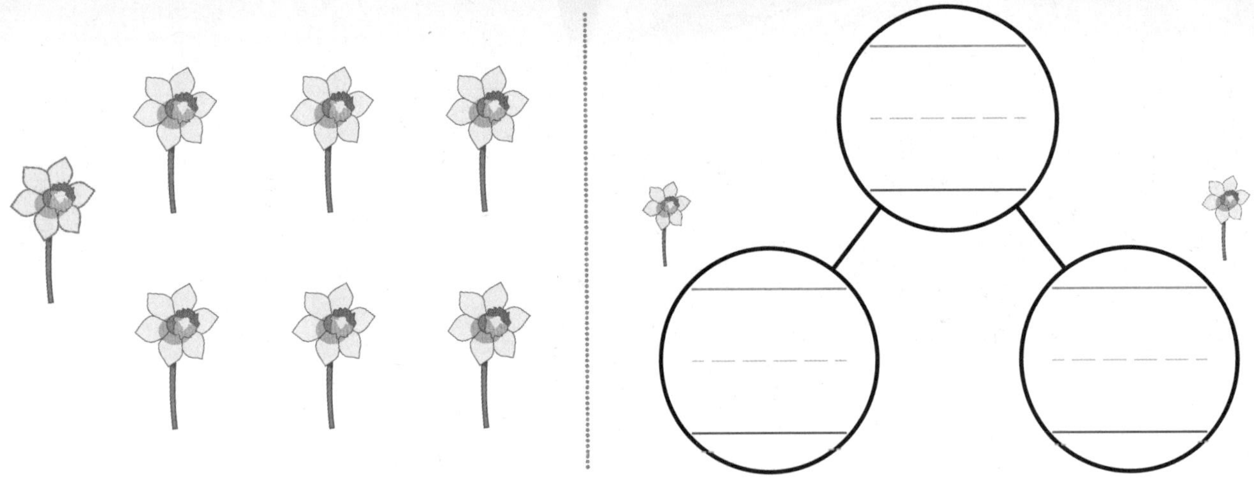

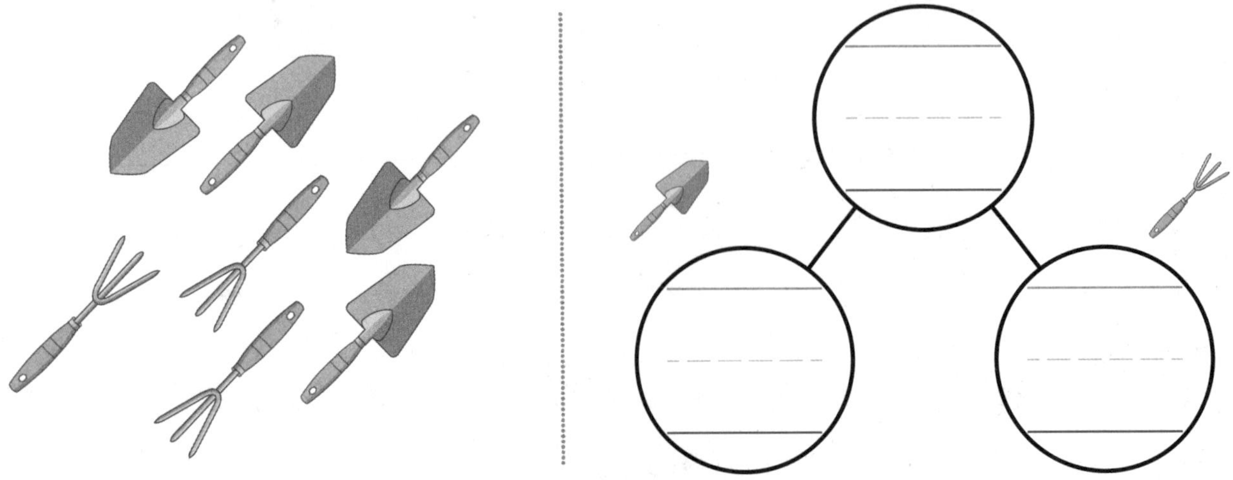

Directions: Name the parts and the whole for the group. Then complete the number bond.

Name ______________________________

Apply and Grow: Practice

1

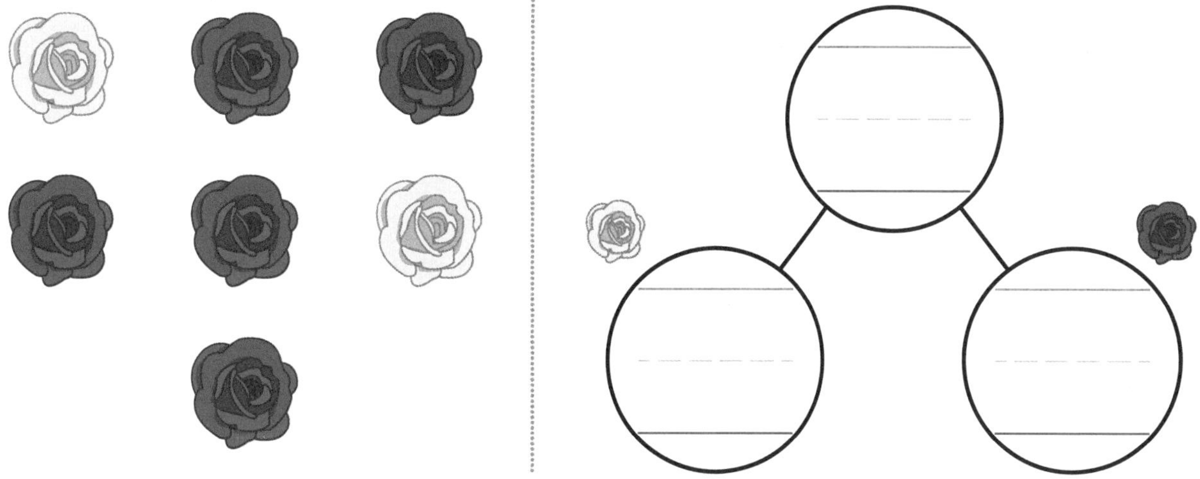

2

3

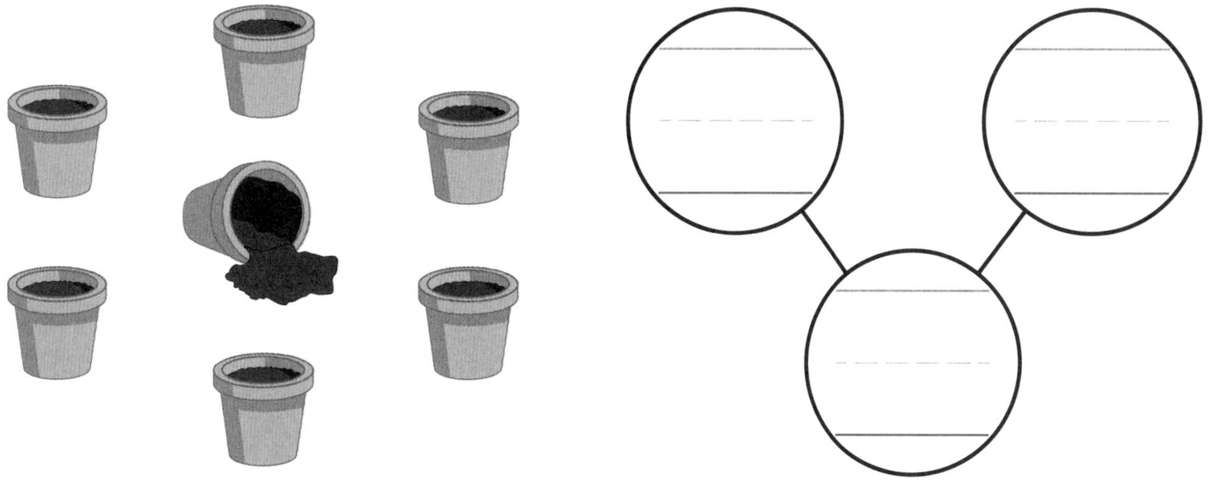

Directions: 1–3 Name the parts and the whole for the group. Then complete the number bond.

Think and Grow: Modeling Real Life

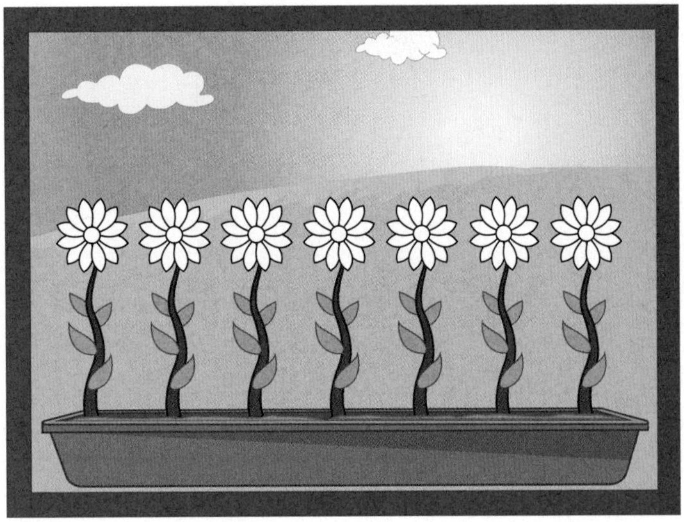

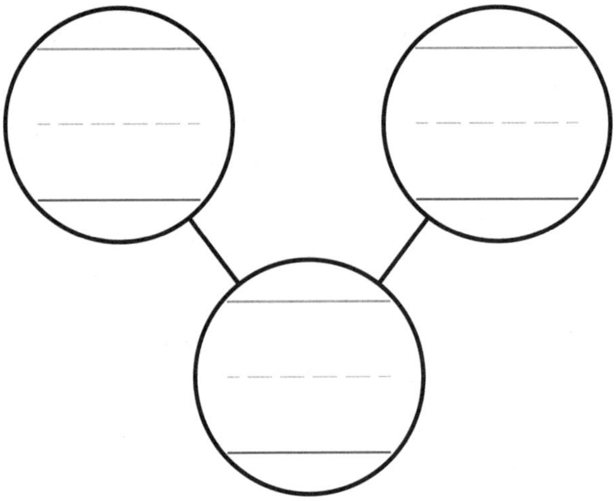

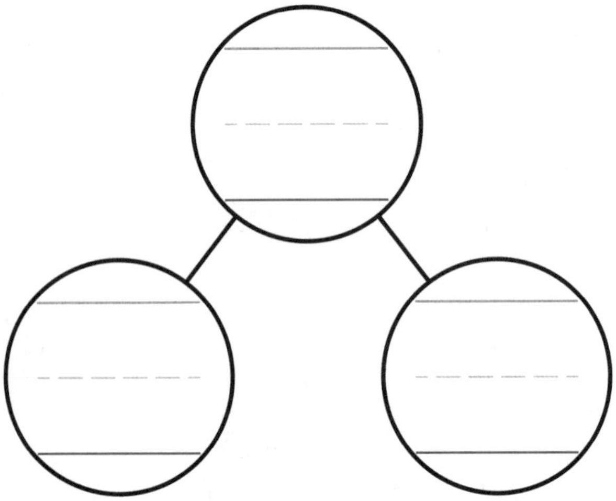

Directions:

- Color some of the flowers purple and some of the flowers yellow. Complete the number bond to match your picture.
- Color to show another way. Complete the number bond to match your picture.

Name ______________________

Practice 5.4

Learning Target: Use partner numbers to make and take apart the number 7.

Directions: Name the parts and the whole for the group. Then complete the number bond.

1

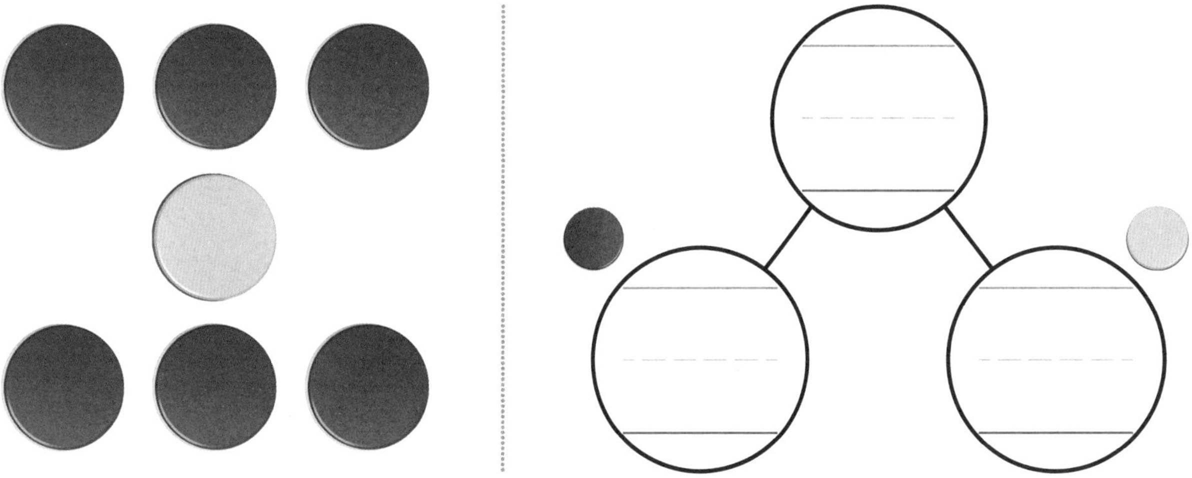

Directions: 1 Name the parts and the whole for the group. Then complete the number bond.

2

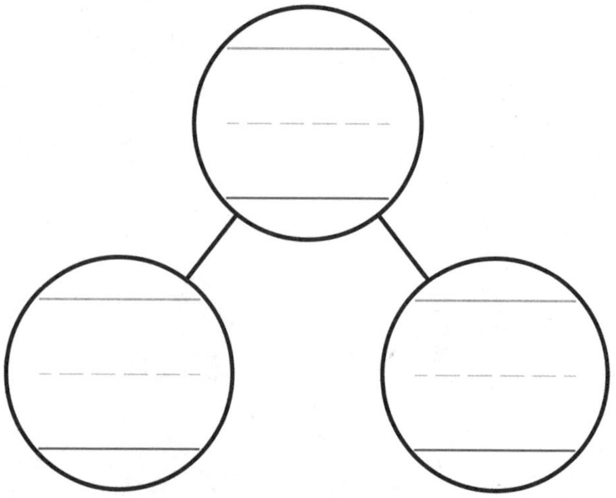

3

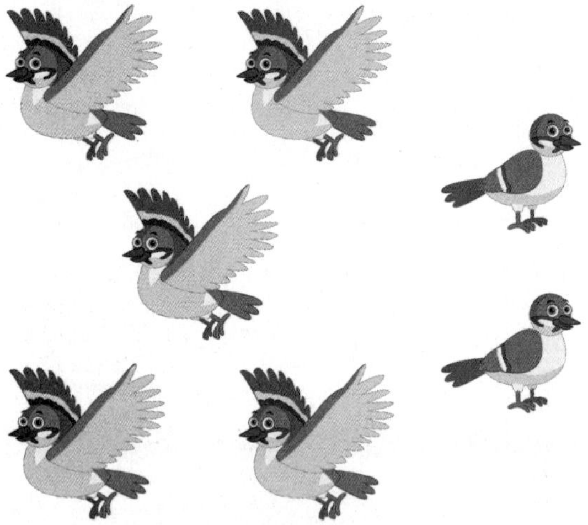

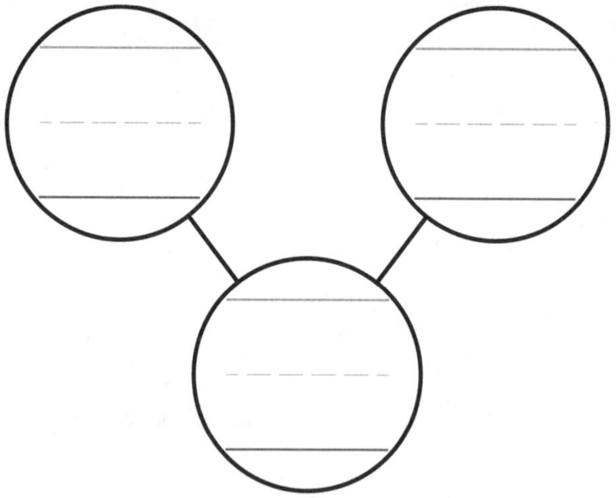

4

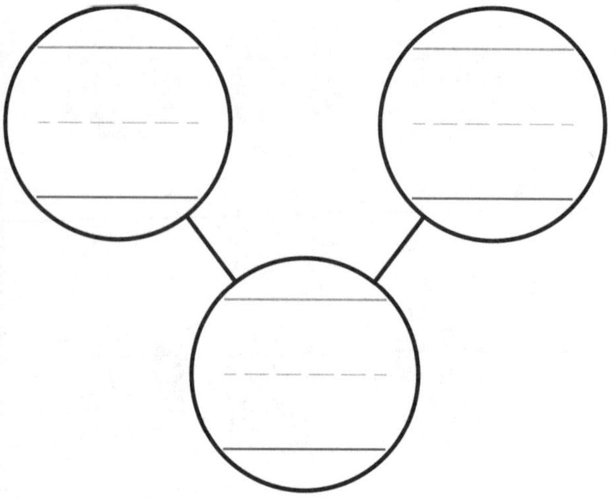

Directions: 2 and 3 Name the parts and the whole for the group. Then complete the number bond. 4 Color some of the flowers yellow and some of the flowers purple. Complete the number bond to match your picture.

Name ___________________________________

Compose and Decompose 8 5.5

Learning Target: Use partner numbers to make and take apart the number 8.

Explore and Grow

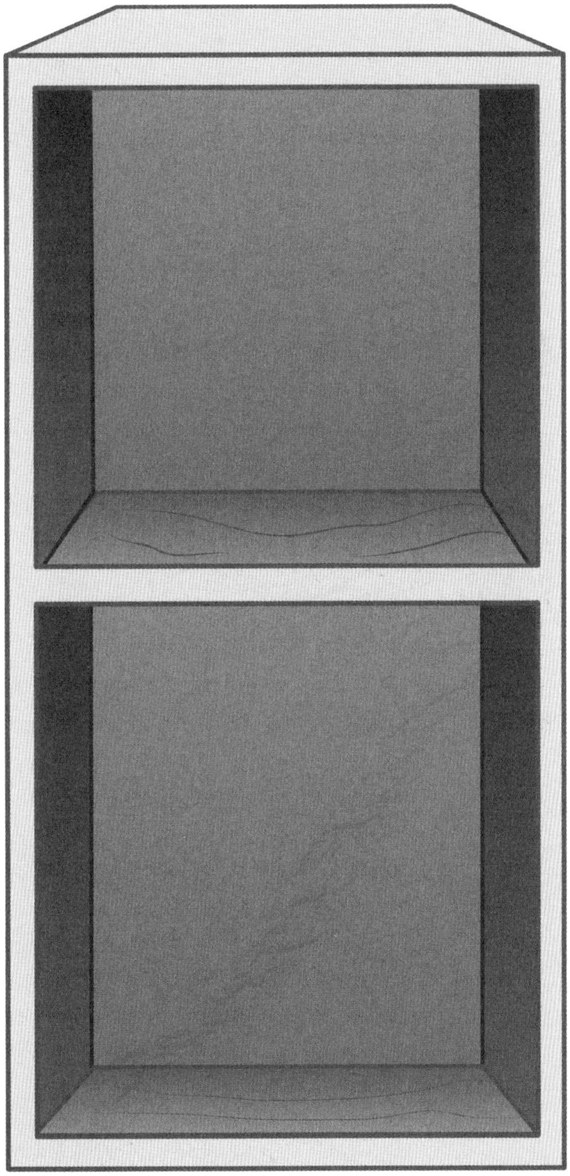

Directions: Use counters to show 5 toys on the top shelf and 3 toys on the bottom shelf. Slide the counters to the side to show the whole. Name the parts and the whole.

Think and Grow

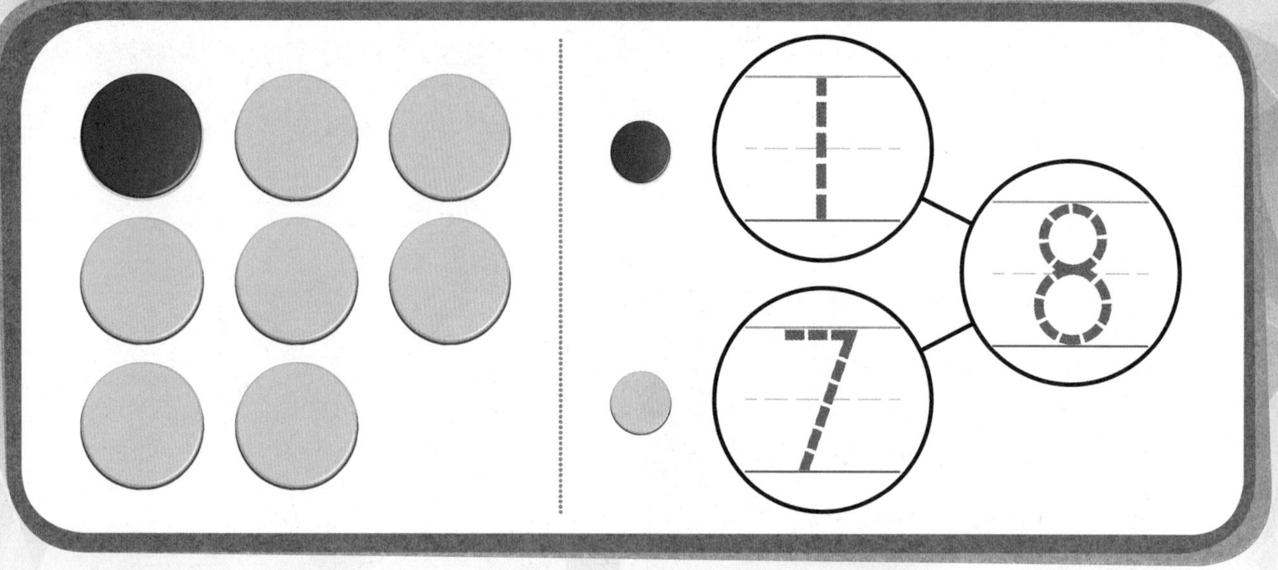

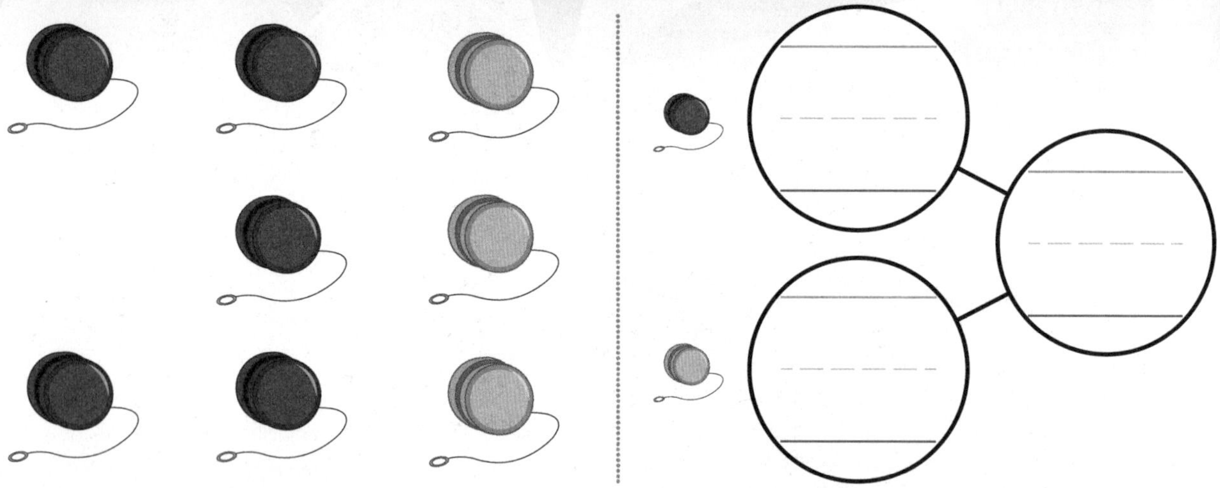

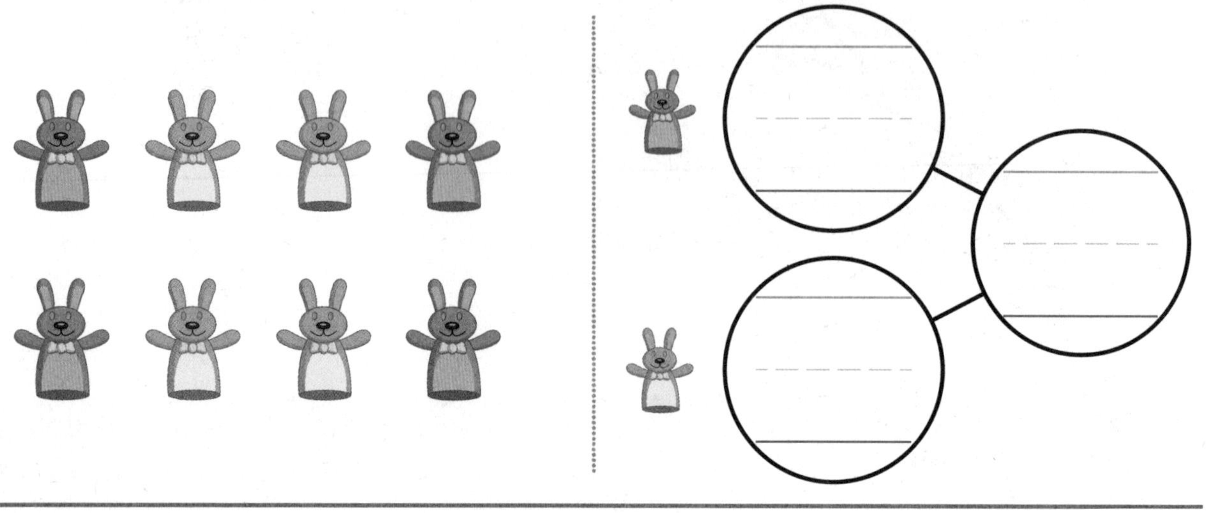

Directions: Name the parts and the whole for the group. Then complete the number bond.

Name ____________________

Apply and Grow: Practice

1

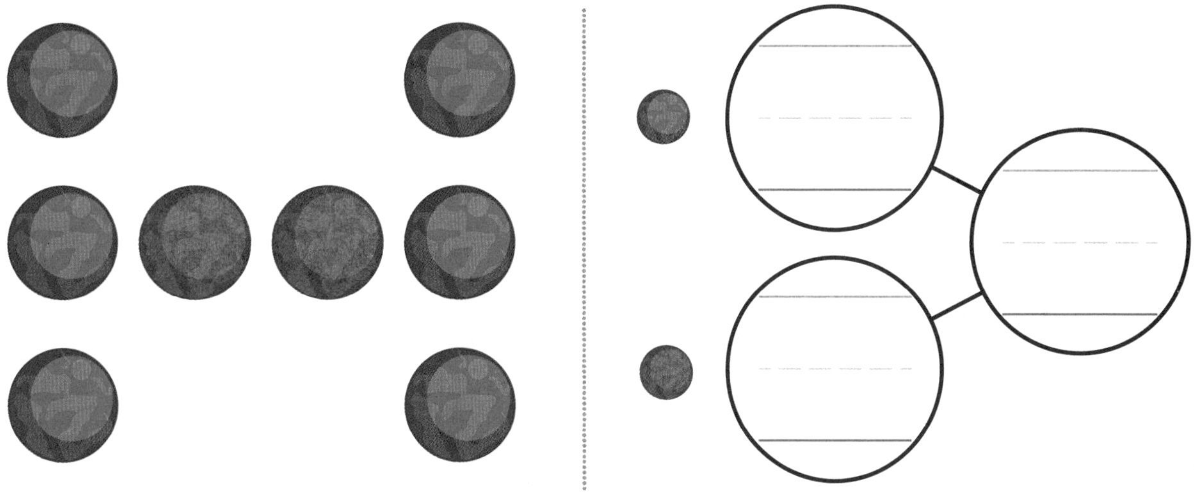

2

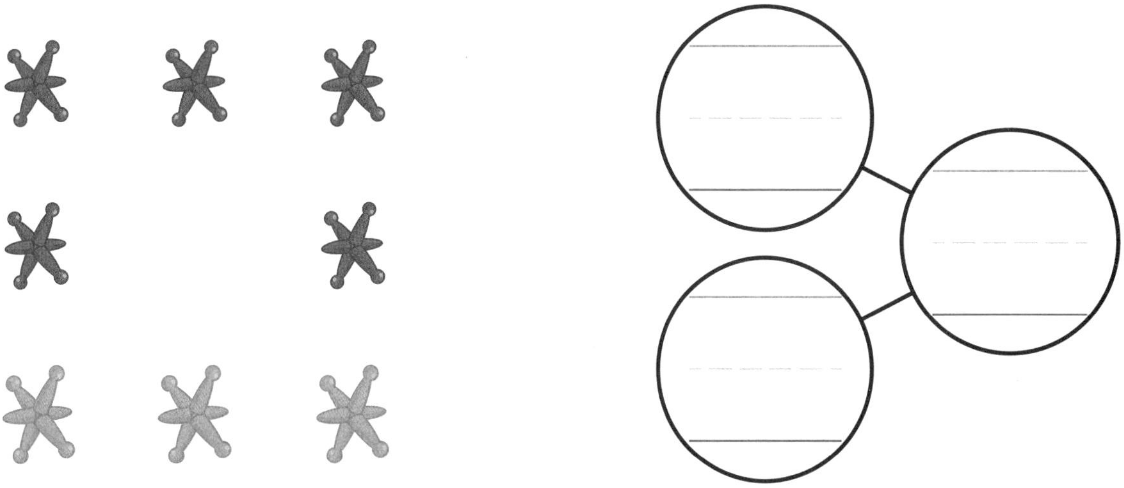

3

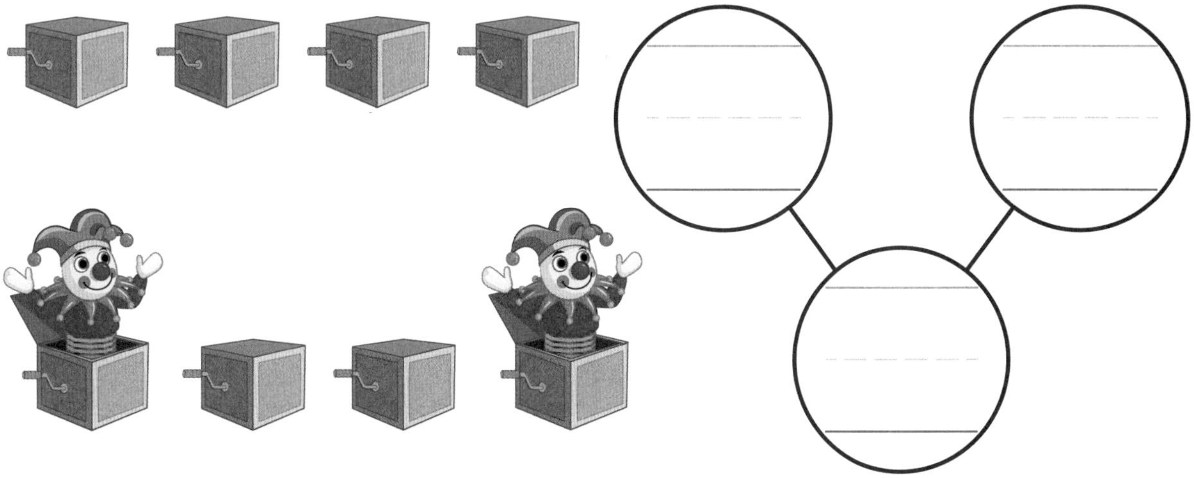

Directions: 1 – 3 Name the parts and the whole for the group. Then complete the number bond.

Think and Grow: Modeling Real Life

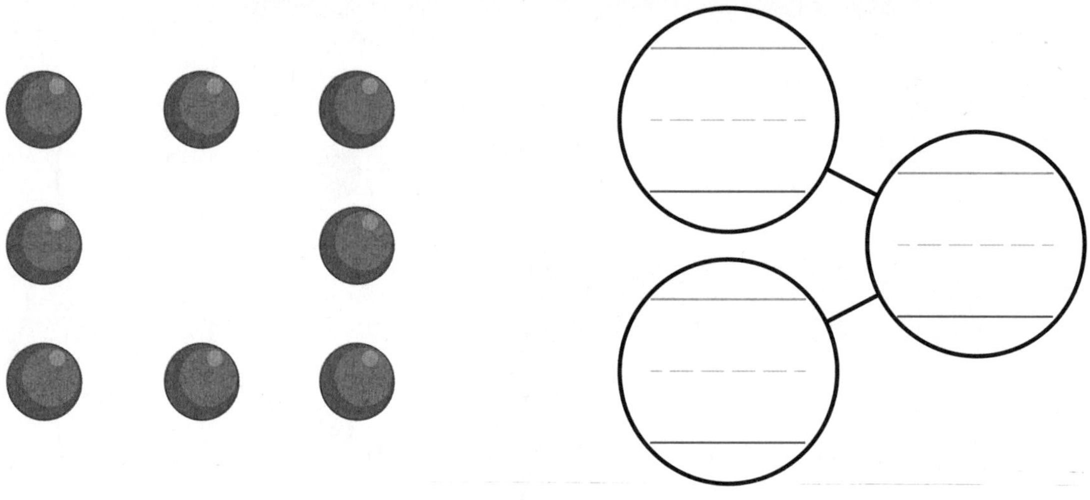

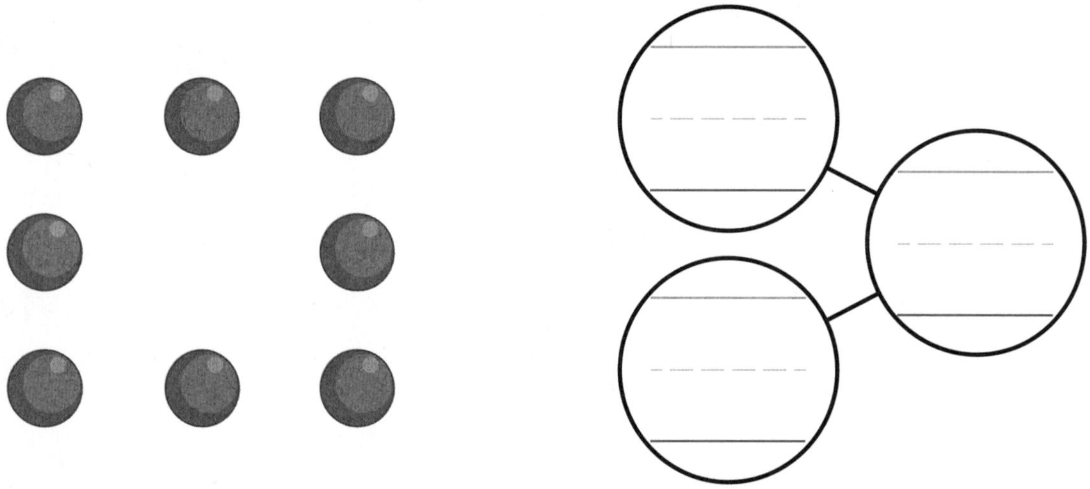

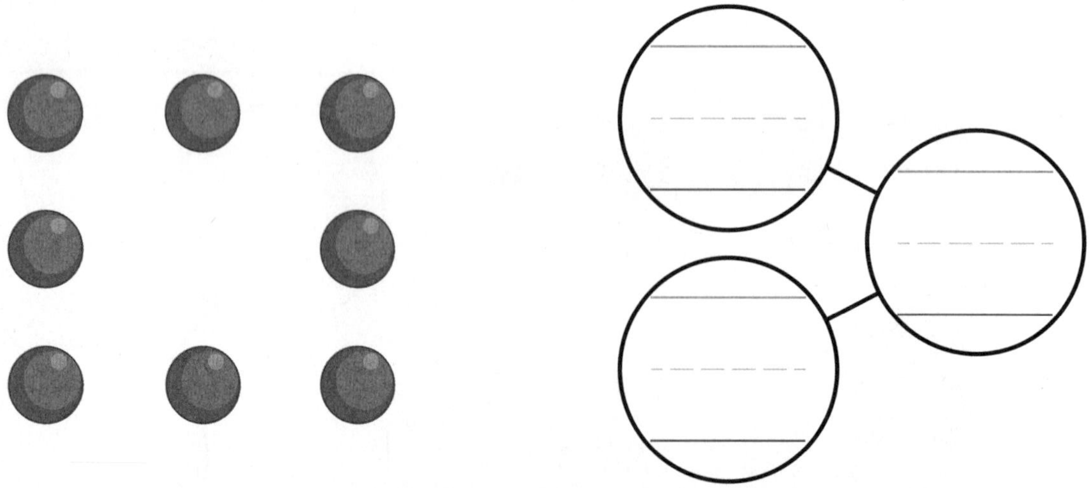

Directions:

- Put the marbles into 2 groups. Circle the groups. Then complete the number bond to match your picture.
- Show 2 other ways you can put the marbles into 2 groups. Then complete the number bonds to match your pictures.

Name ______________________________

Practice 5.5

Learning Target: Use partner numbers to make and take apart the number 8.

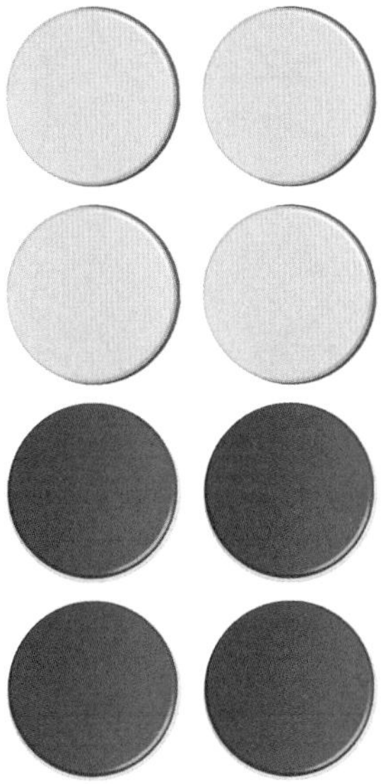

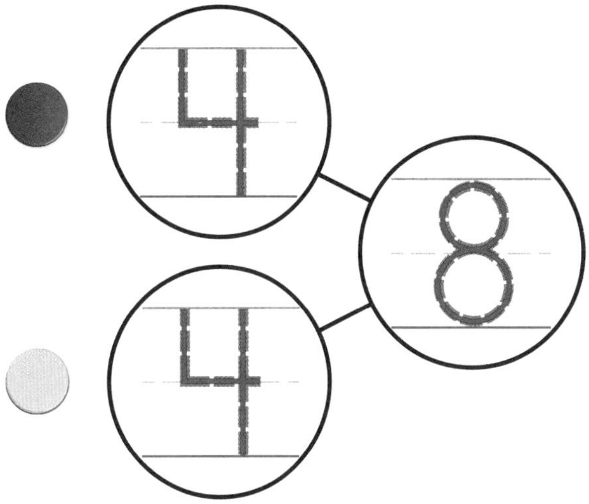

Directions: Name the parts and the whole for the group. Then complete the number bond.

1

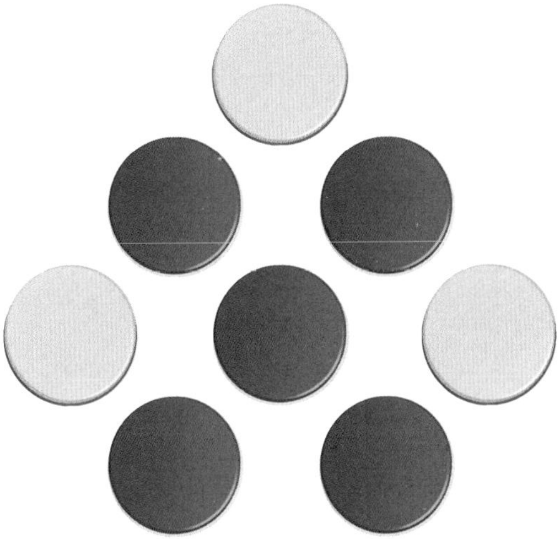

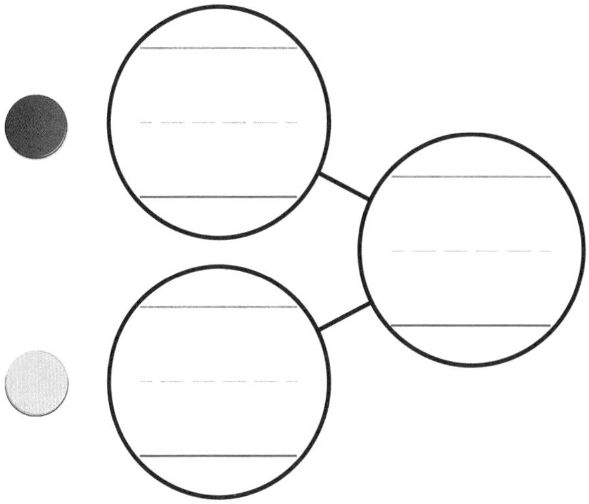

Directions: 1 Name the parts and the whole for the group. Then complete the number bond.

2

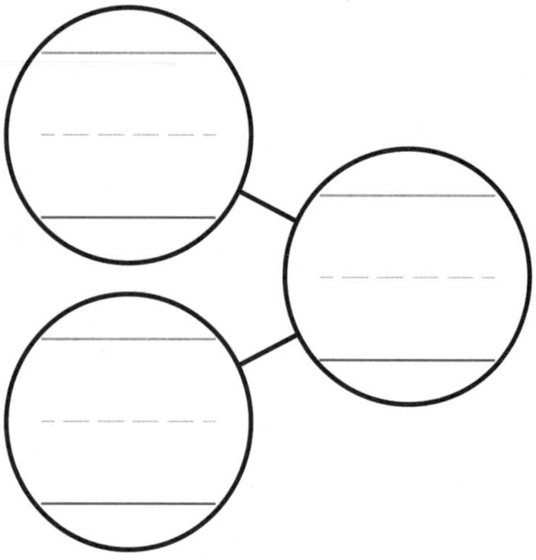

3

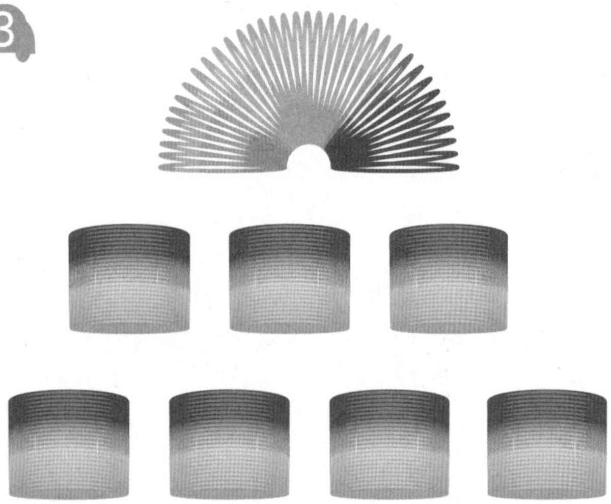

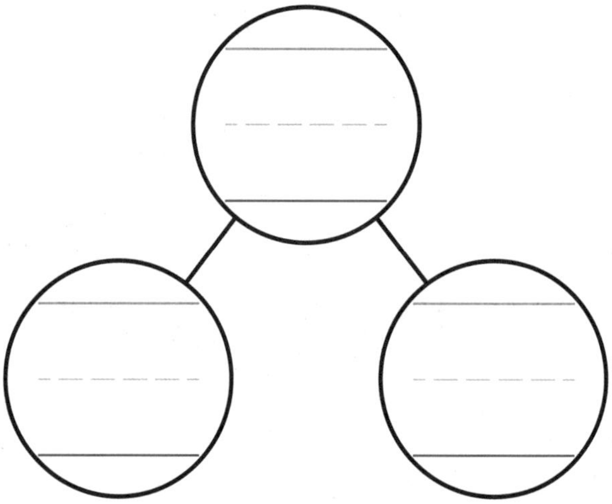

4

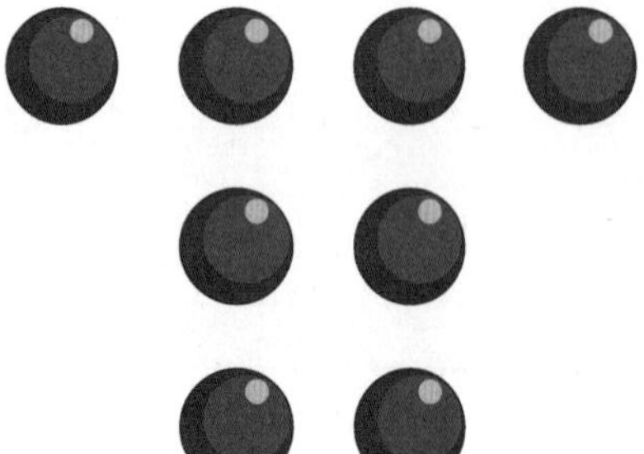

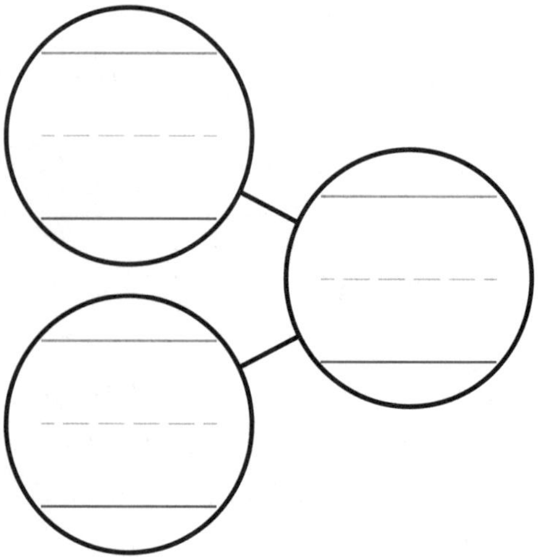

Directions: 2 and 3 Name the parts and the whole for the group. Then complete the number bond. 4 Put the marbles into 2 equal groups. Circle the groups. Then complete the number bond to match your picture.

Name ______________________________

Compose and Decompose 9

5.6

Learning Target: Use partner numbers to make and take apart the number 9.

Explore and Grow

Directions: Use counters to show 3 fish in one scene of underwater vegetation and 6 fish in the other scene of underwater vegetation. Slide the counters to the side to show the whole. Name the parts and the whole.

Think and Grow

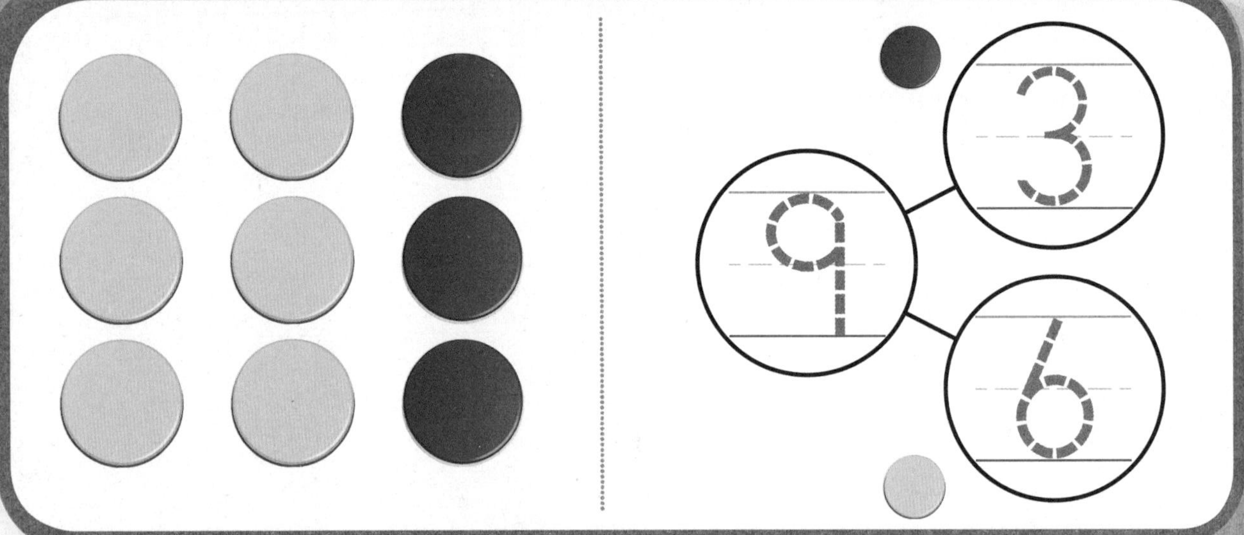

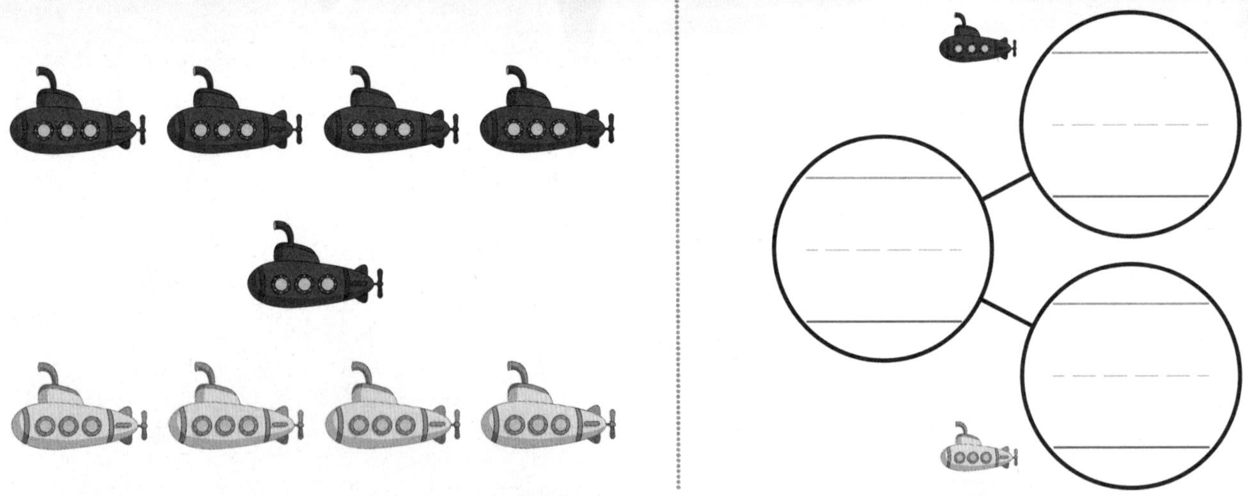

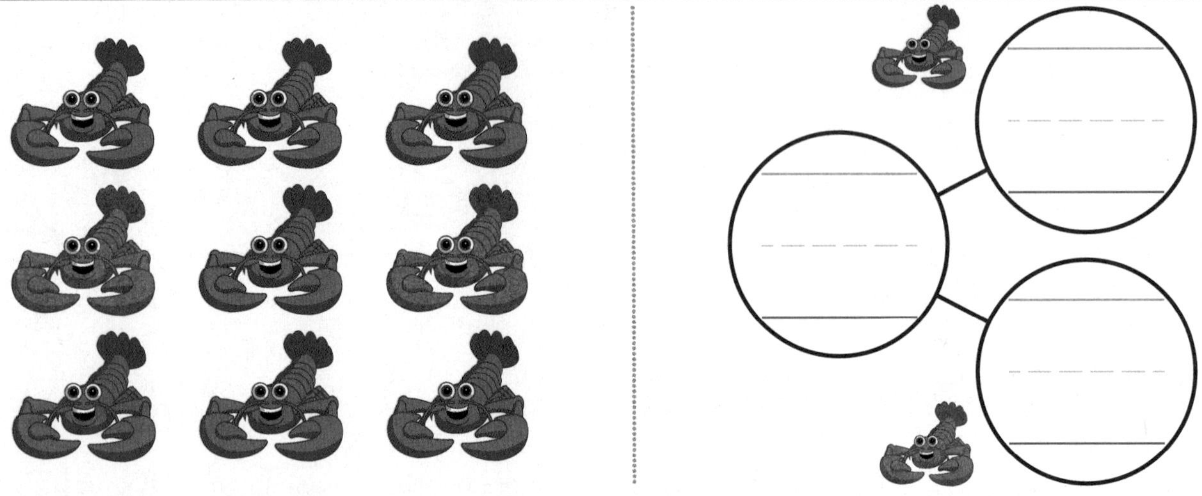

Directions: Name the parts and the whole for the group. Then complete the number bond.

Name ____________________

Apply and Grow: Practice

1

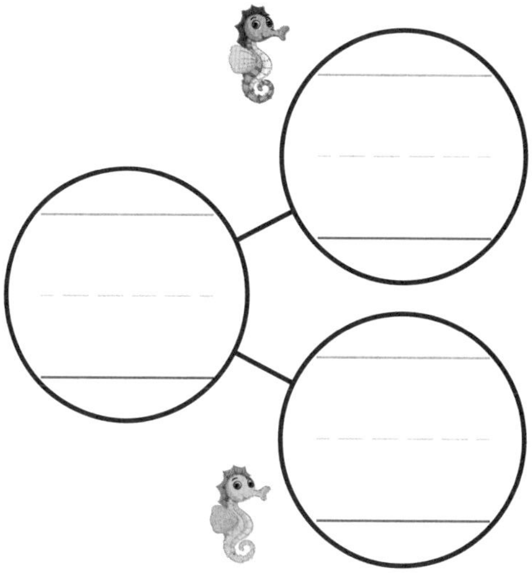

2

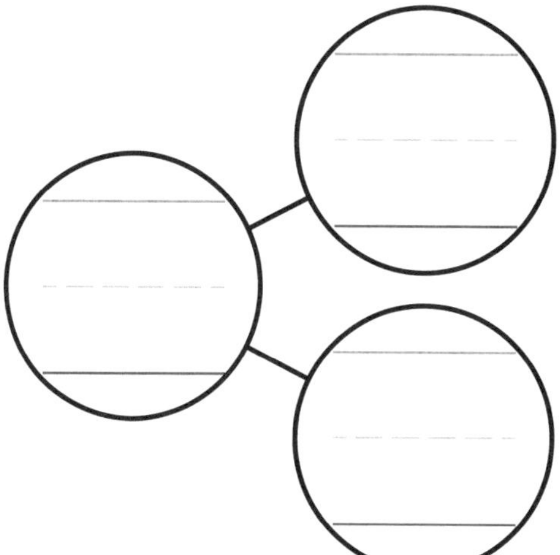

3
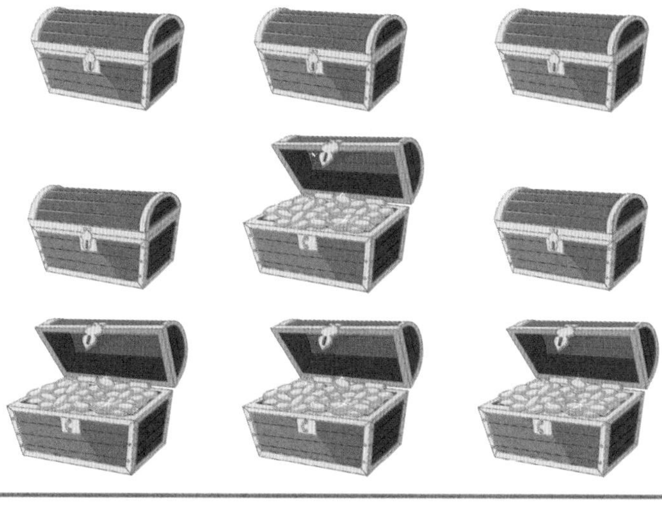
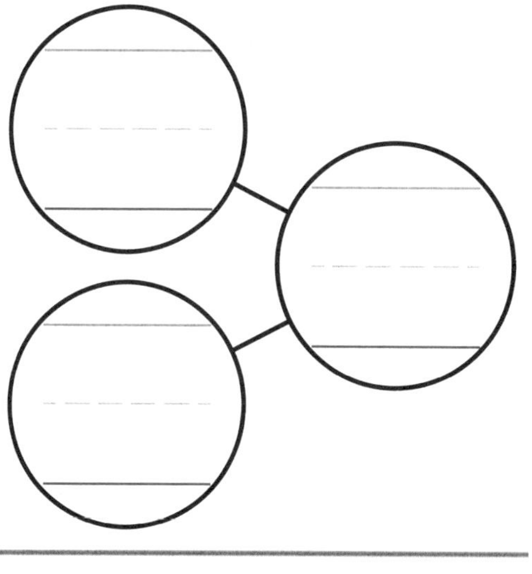

Directions: 1–3 Name the parts and the whole for the group. Then complete the number bond.

Think and Grow: Modeling Real Life

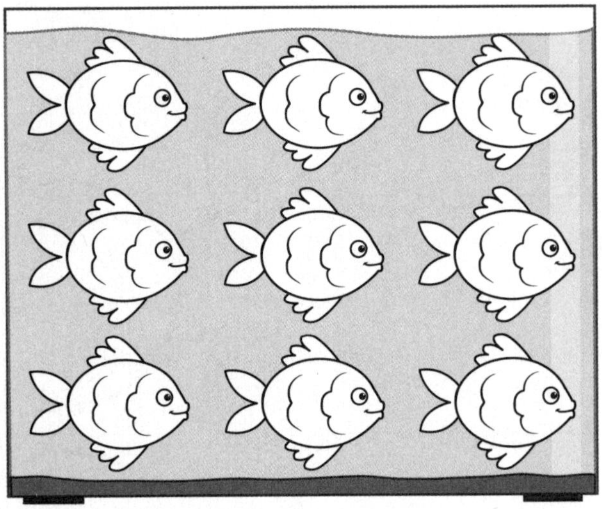

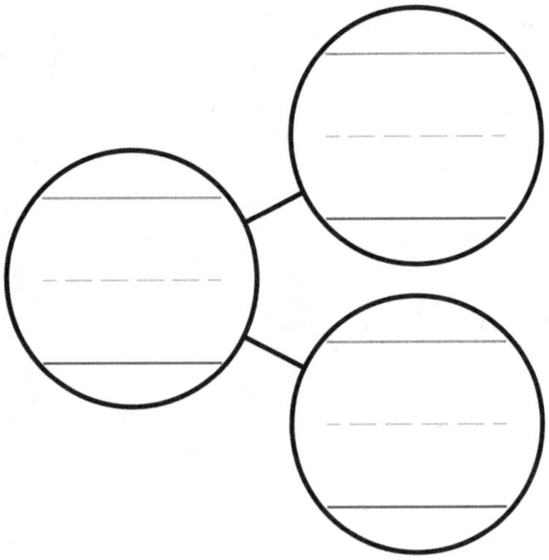

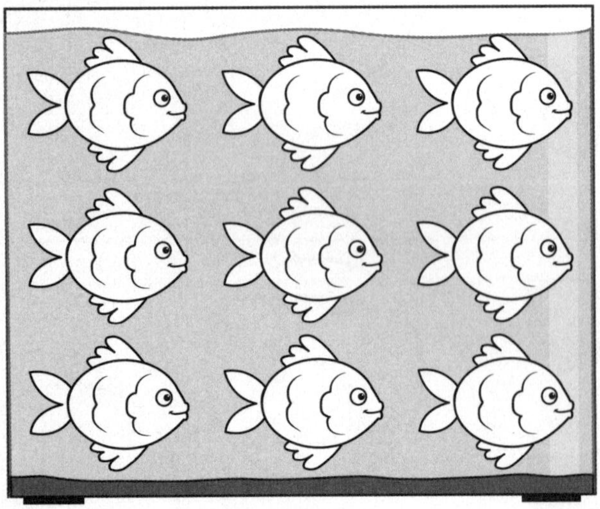

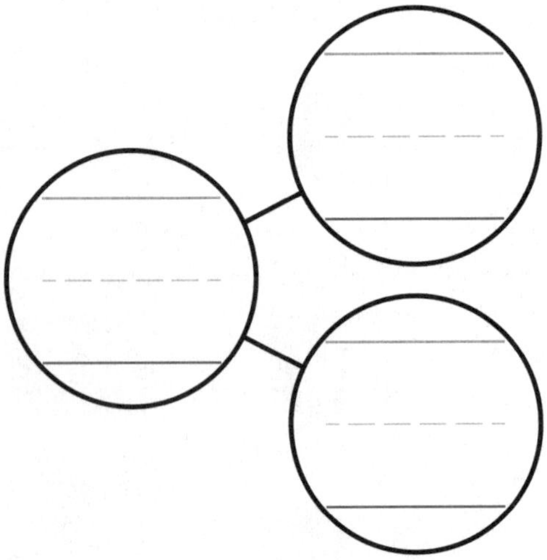

Directions: You buy 9 fish for your fish tank. You buy more orange fish than yellow fish.

- Color to show how many orange fish and yellow fish you could buy. Then complete the number bond to match your picture.
- Color to show another way. Then complete the number bond to match your picture.

Name ____________________

Practice 5.6

Learning Target: Use partner numbers to make and take apart the number 9.

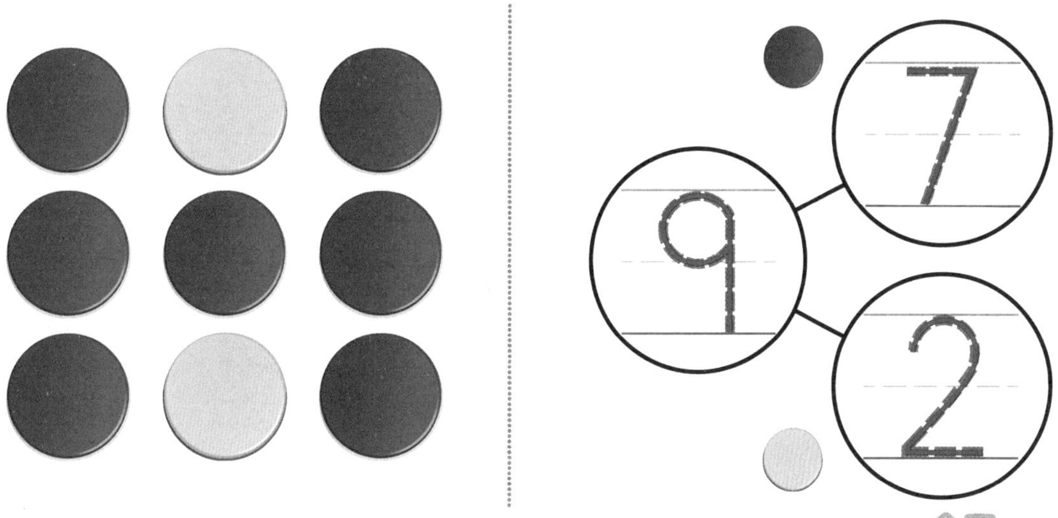

Directions: Name the parts and the whole for the group. Then complete the number bond.

1

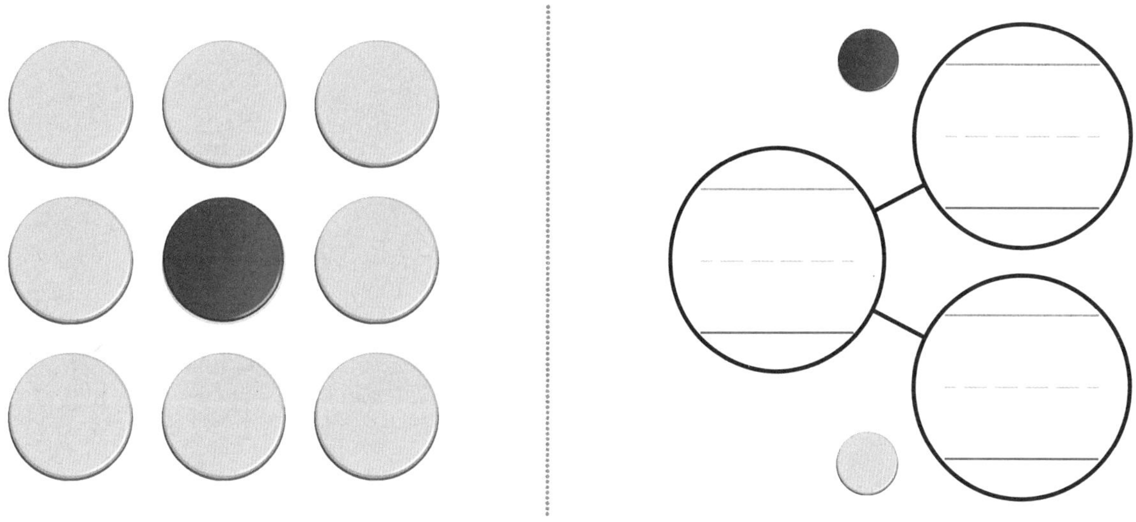

Directions: 1 Name the parts and the whole for the group. Then complete the number bond.

2

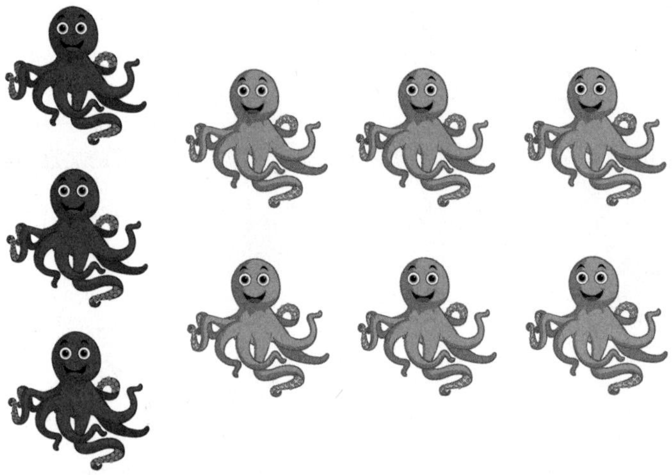

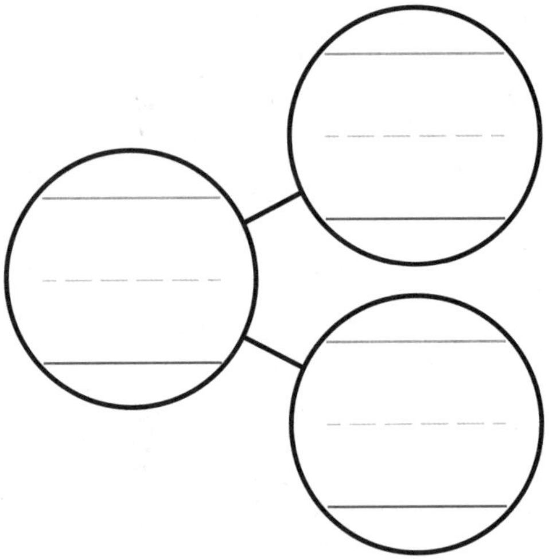

3

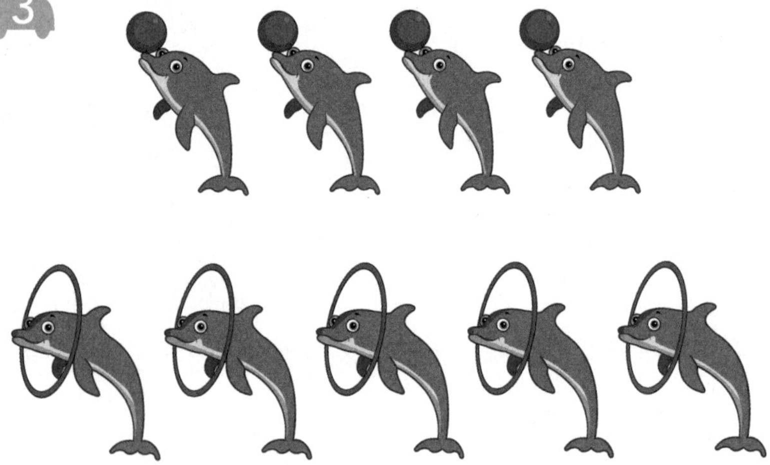

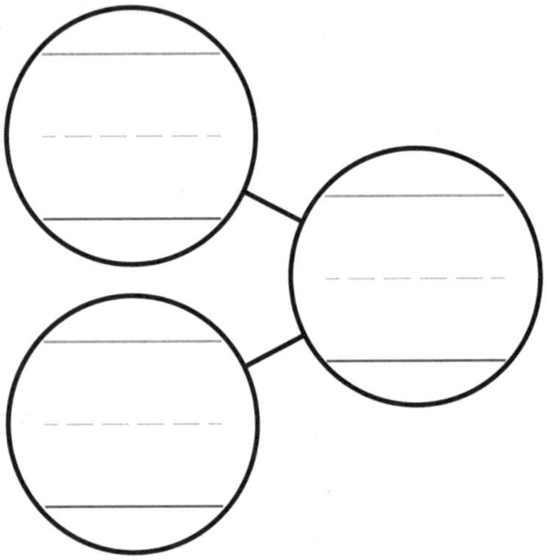

4

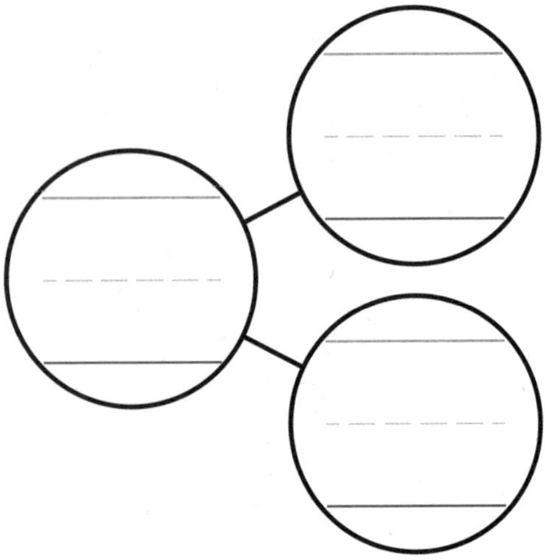

Directions: 2 and 3 Name the parts and the whole for the group. Then complete the number bond. 4 You buy 9 fish for your fish tank. You buy fewer red fish than purple fish. Color to show how many red fish and purple fish you could buy. Then complete the number bond to match your picture.

Name ____________________

Compose and Decompose 10 5.7

Learning Target: Use partner numbers to make and take apart the number 10.

Explore and Grow

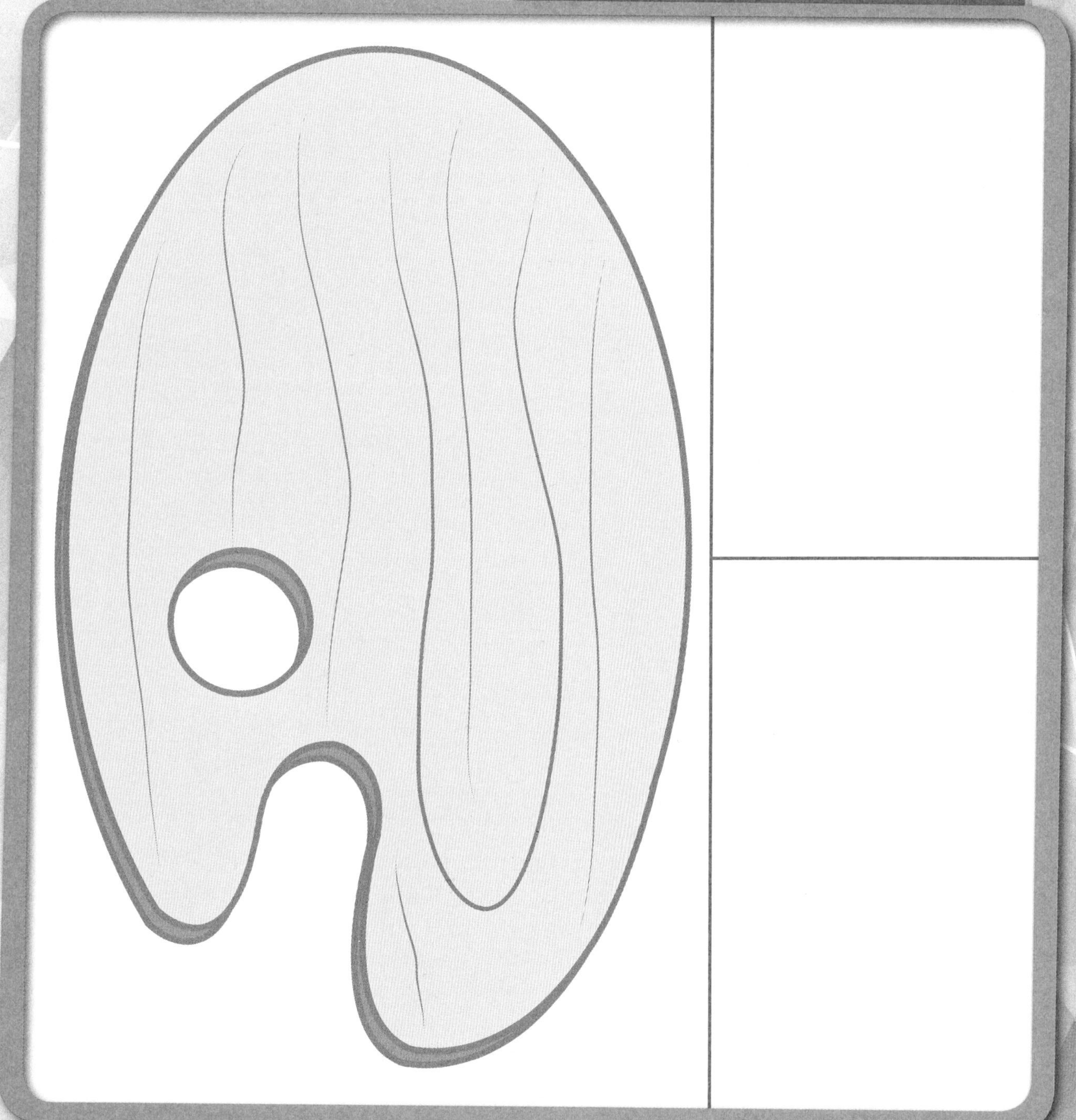

Directions: Use counters to show 10 paint spots. Slide the counters to the side to show 2 groups. Name the parts and the whole.

Think and Grow

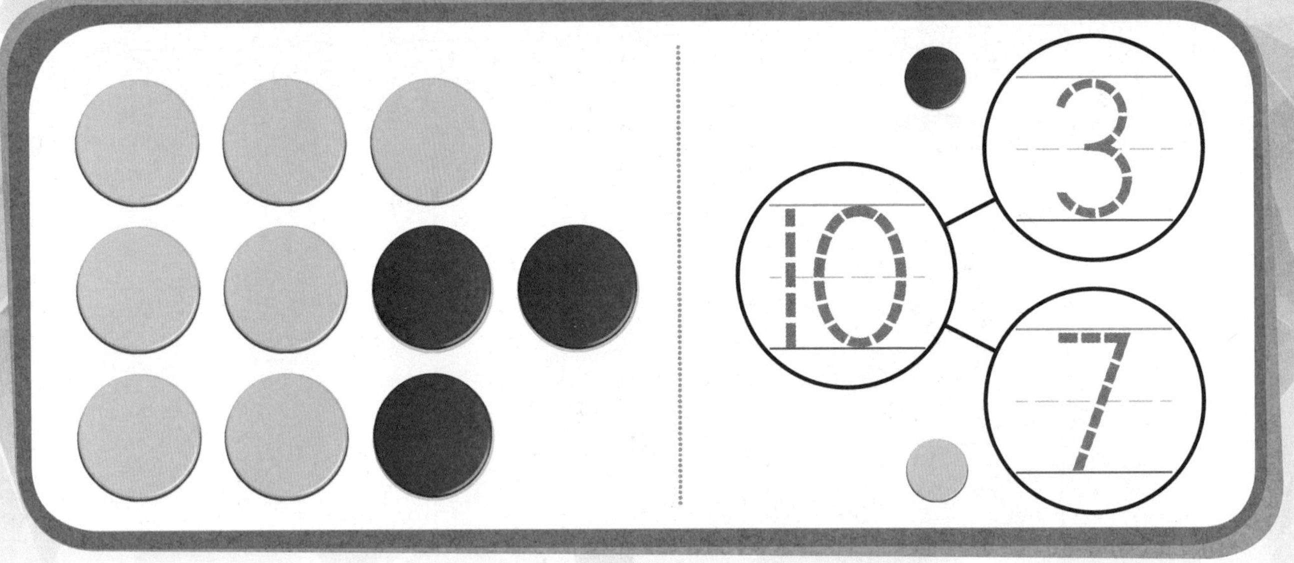

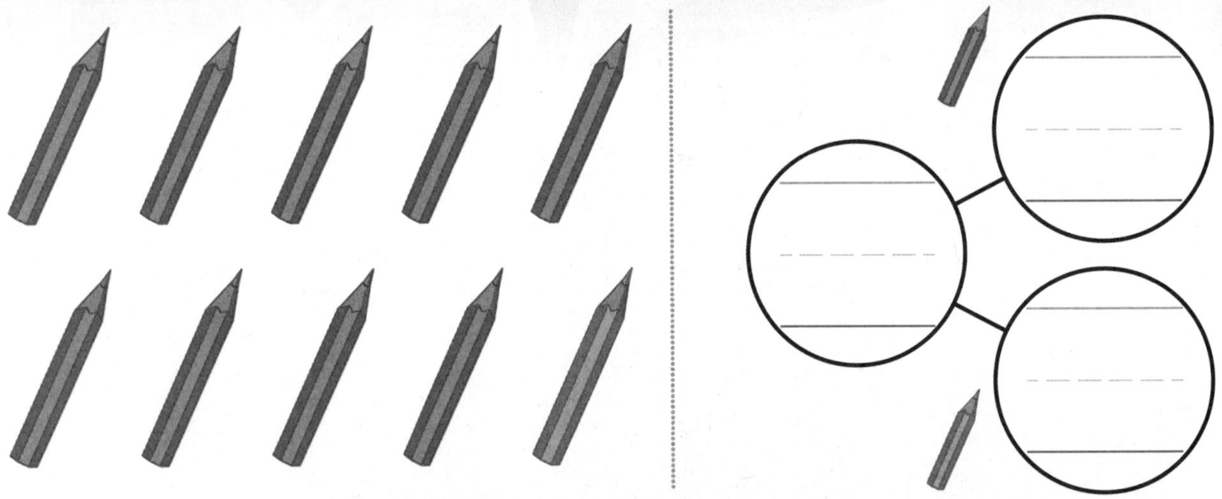

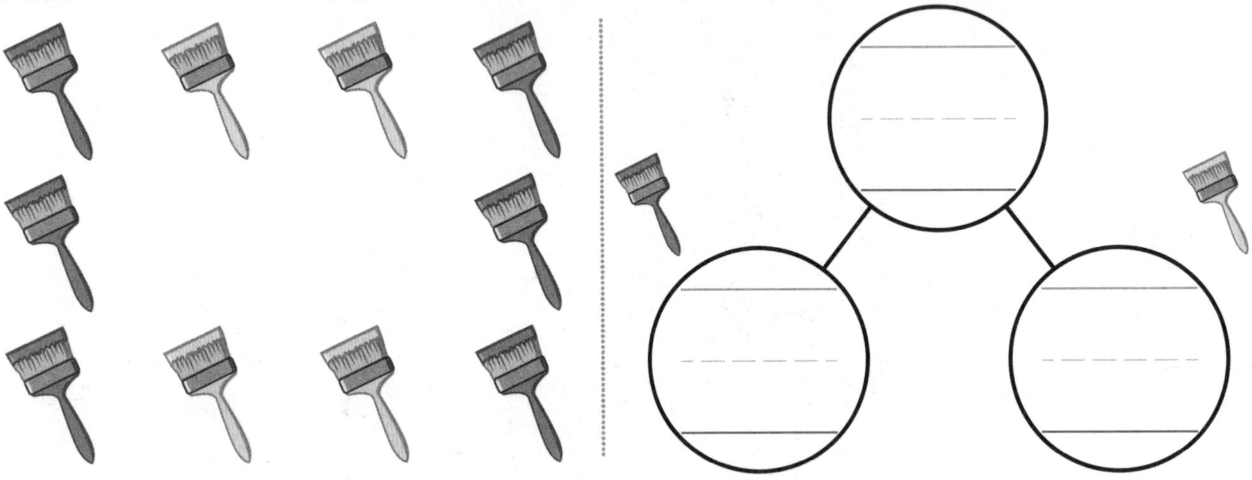

Directions: Name the parts and the whole for the group. Then complete the number bond.

Name ______________________________

Apply and Grow: Practice

1

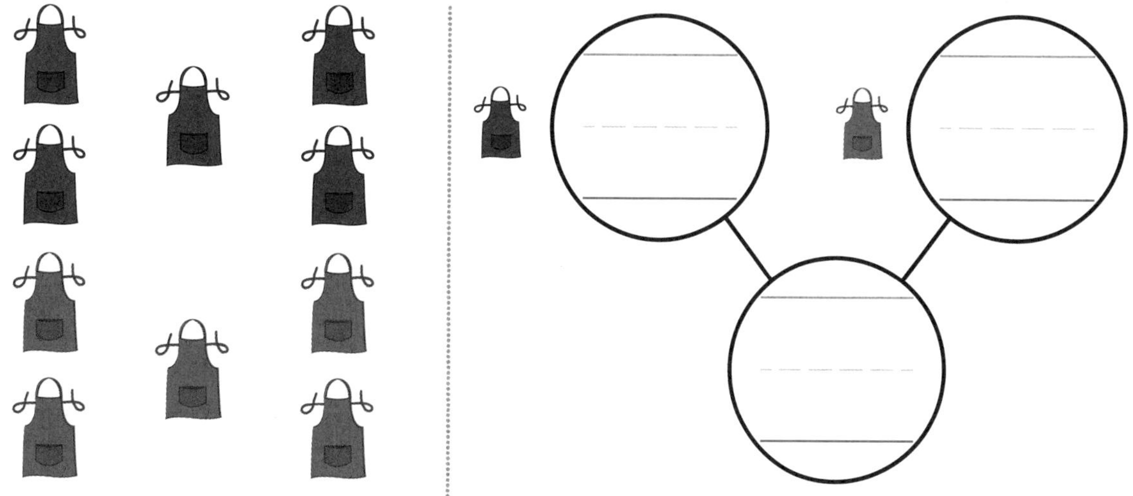

2

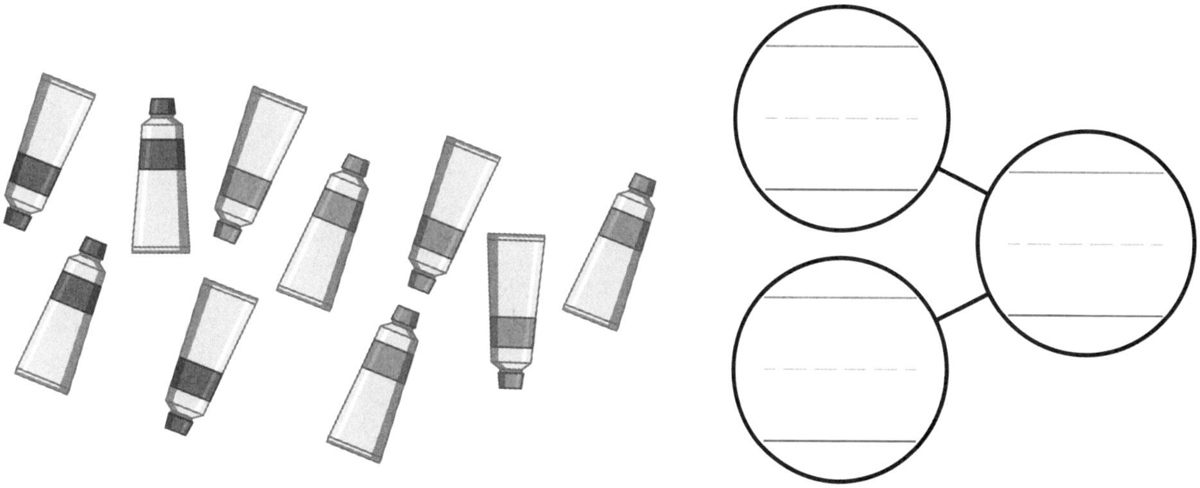

3

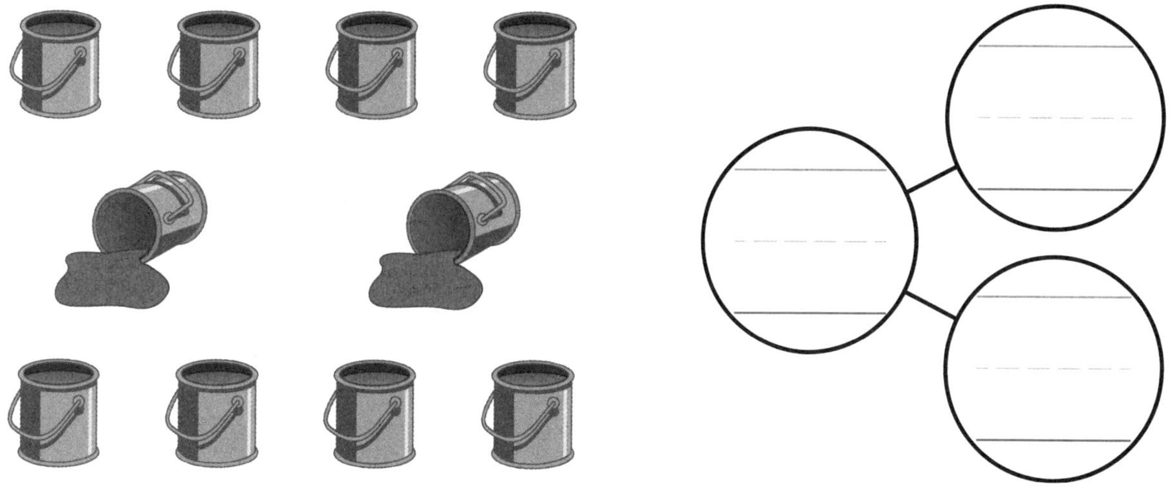

Directions: 1–3 Name the parts and the whole for the group. Then complete the number bond.

Think and Grow: Modeling Real Life

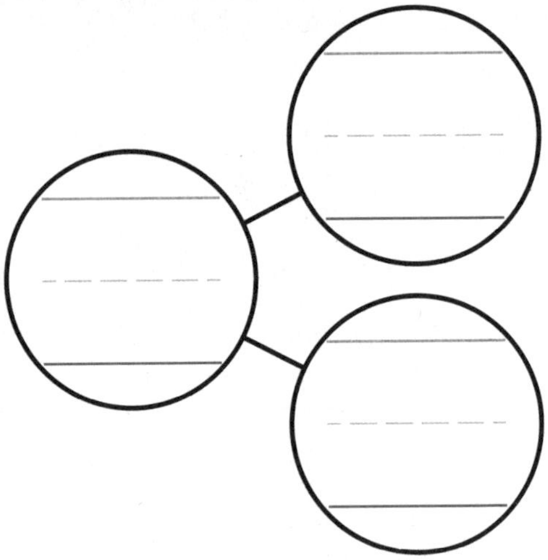

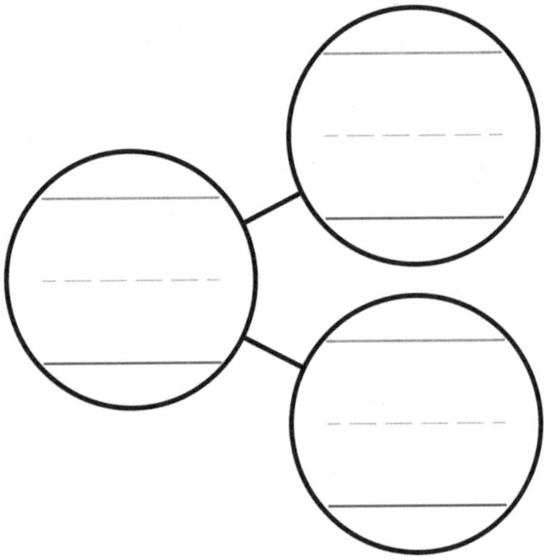

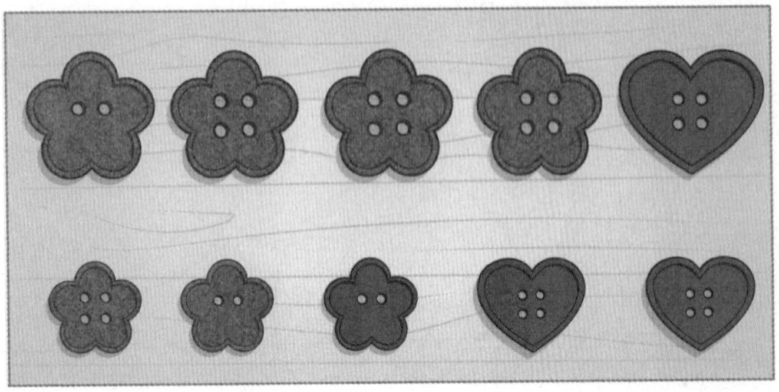

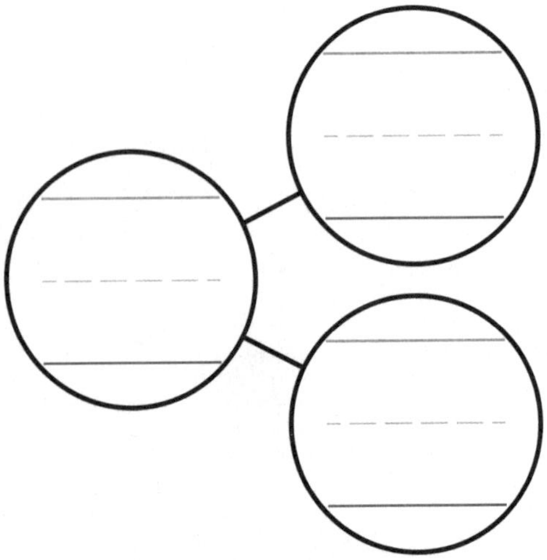

Directions:

- You have 10 buttons. Classify the buttons into 2 categories. Circle the groups. Then complete the number bond to match your picture.
- Show 2 other ways you can classify the buttons into 2 categories. Then complete the number bonds to match your pictures.

Name ______________________

Practice 5.7

Learning Target: Use partner numbers to make and take apart the number 10.

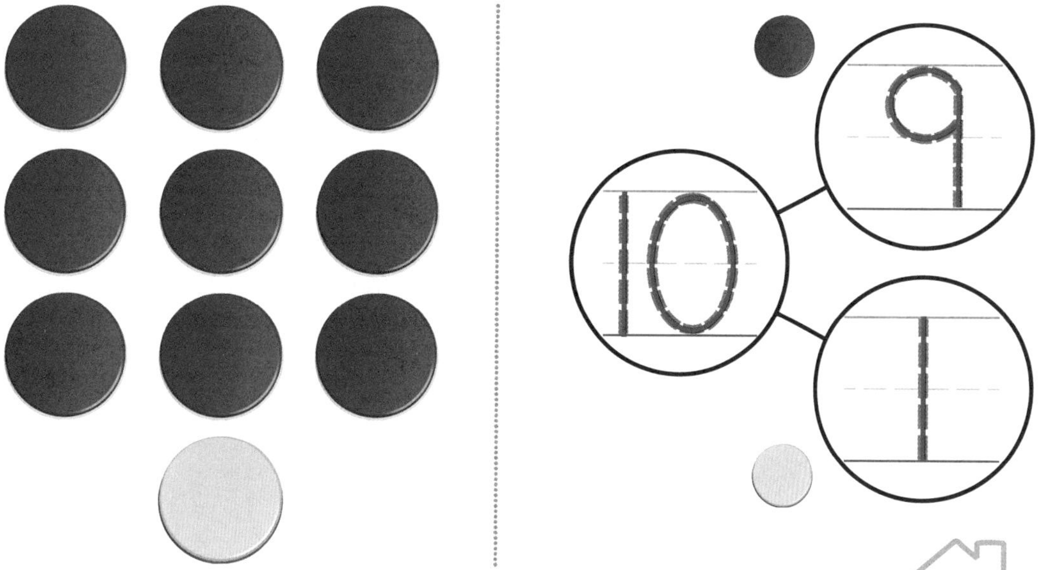

Directions: Name the parts and the whole for the group. Then complete the number bond.

1

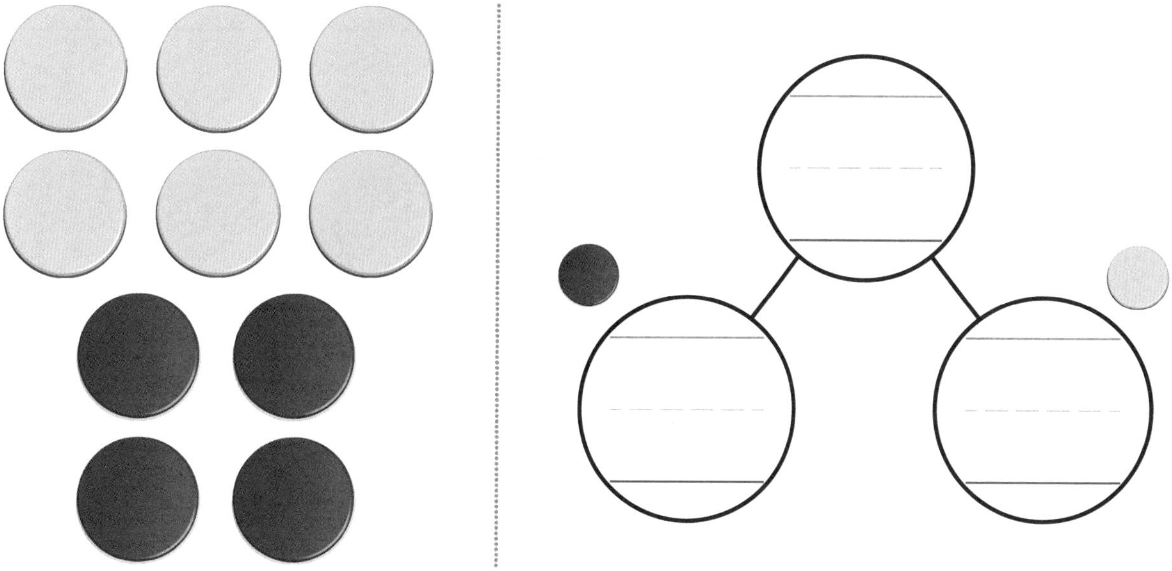

Directions: 1 Name the parts and the whole for the group. Then complete the number bond.

2

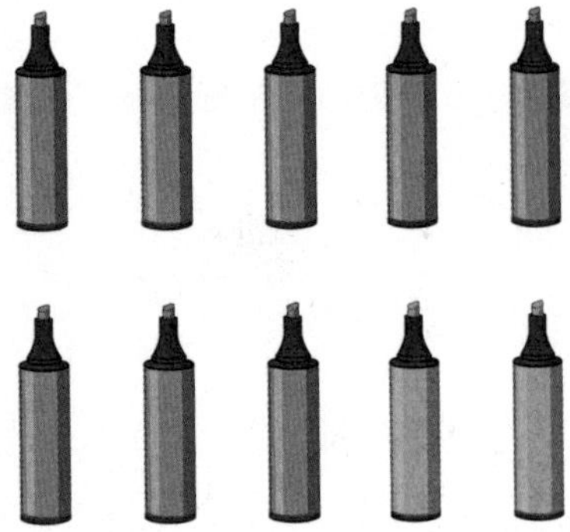

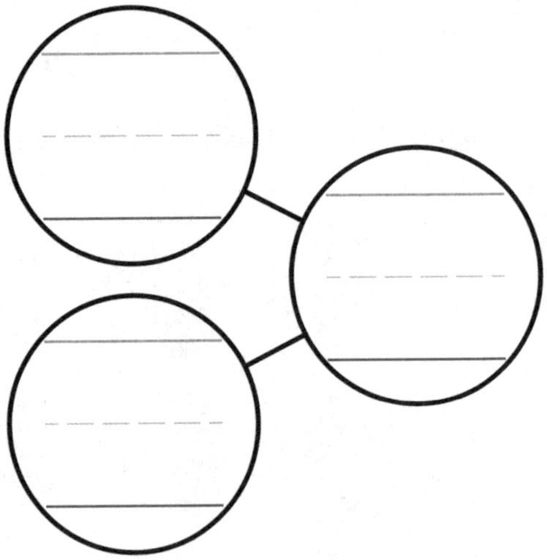

3

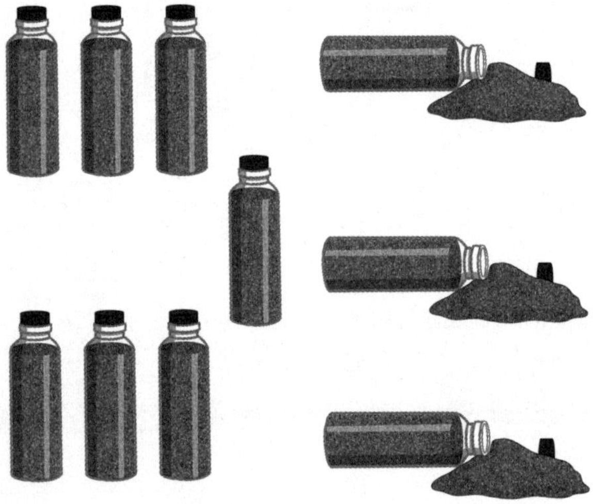

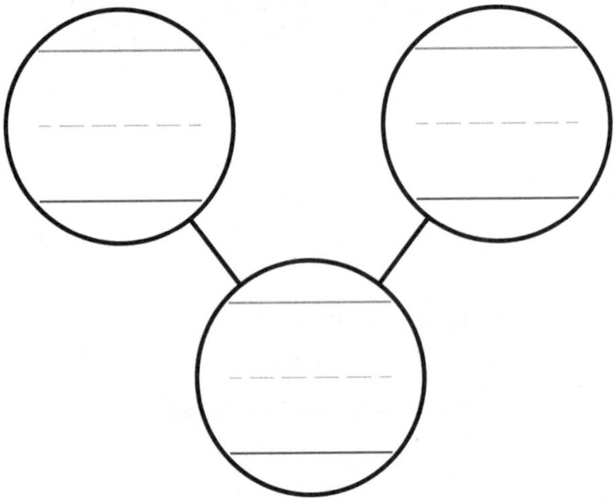

4

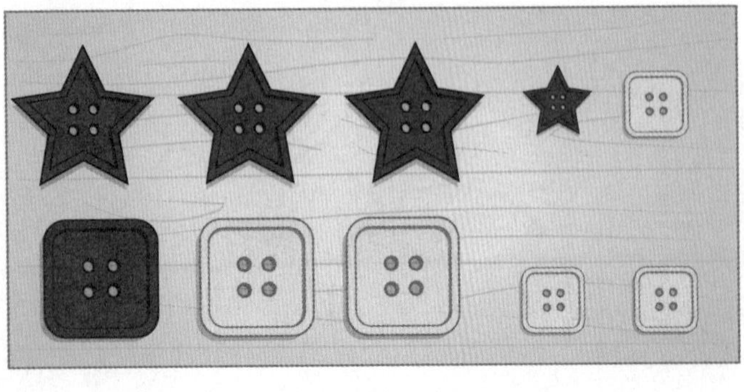

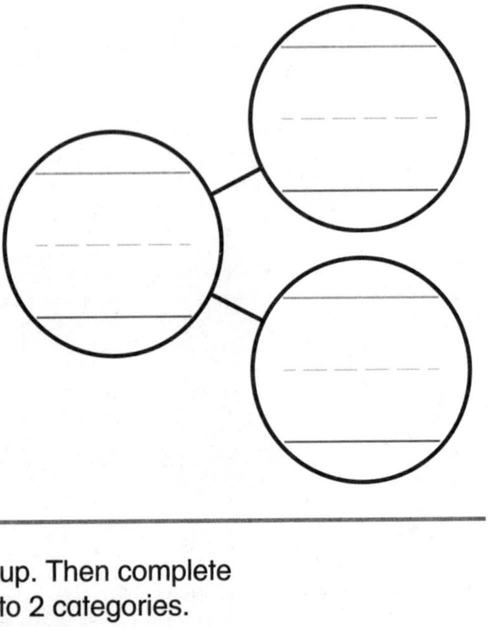

Directions: 2 and 3 Name the parts and the whole for the group. Then complete the number bond. 4 You have 10 buttons. Classify the buttons into 2 categories. Circle the groups. Then complete the number bond to match your picture.

Name ______________________________

Compose and Decompose Using a Group of 5

5.8

Learning Target: Use a group of 5 to put together and take apart numbers to 10.

Explore and Grow

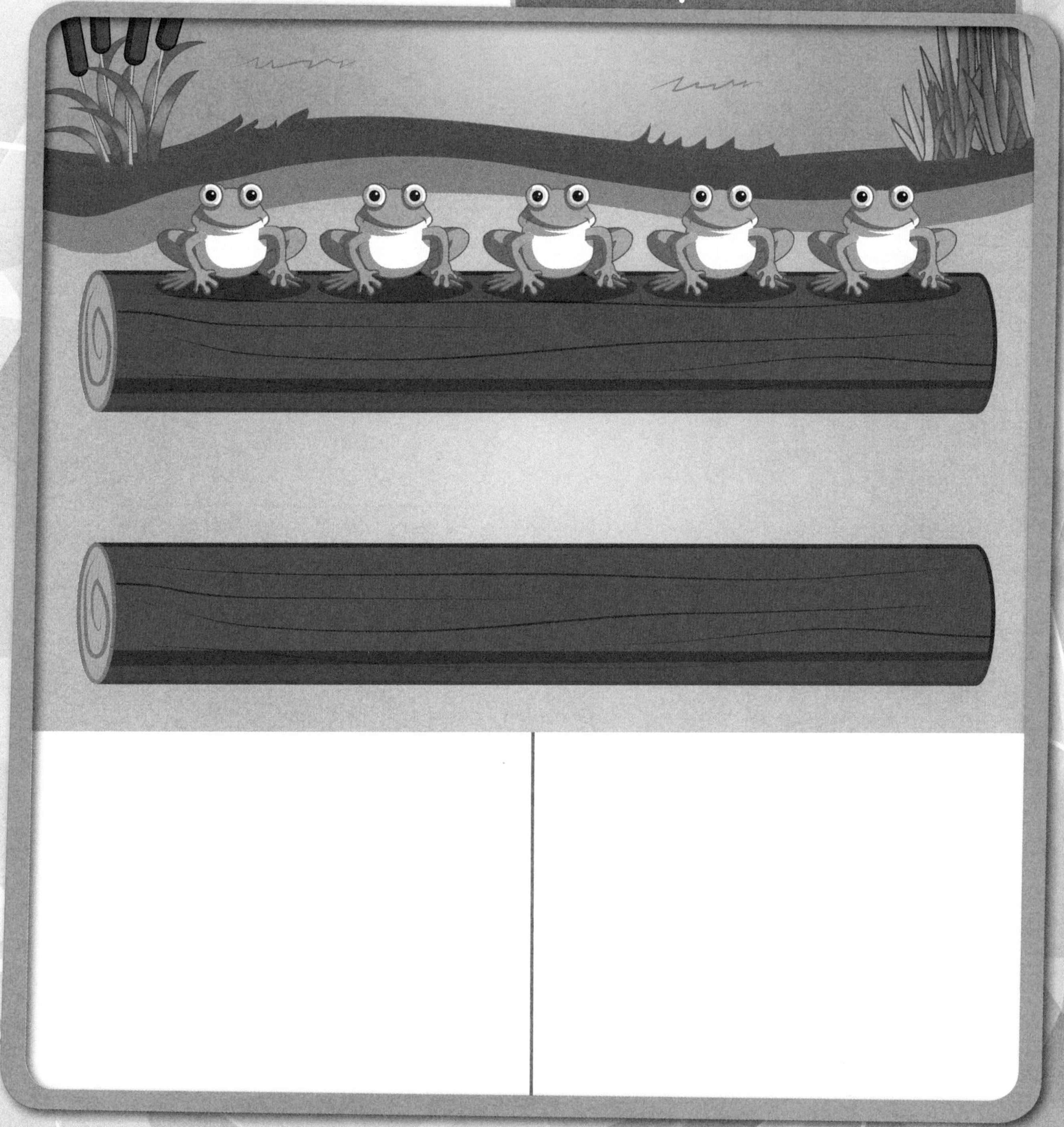

Directions: How many frogs are on the log? Place a counter on each frog. Use more counters to show 9 frogs. Slide the counters to the bottom to show the 2 groups. Name the parts and the whole.

Think and Grow

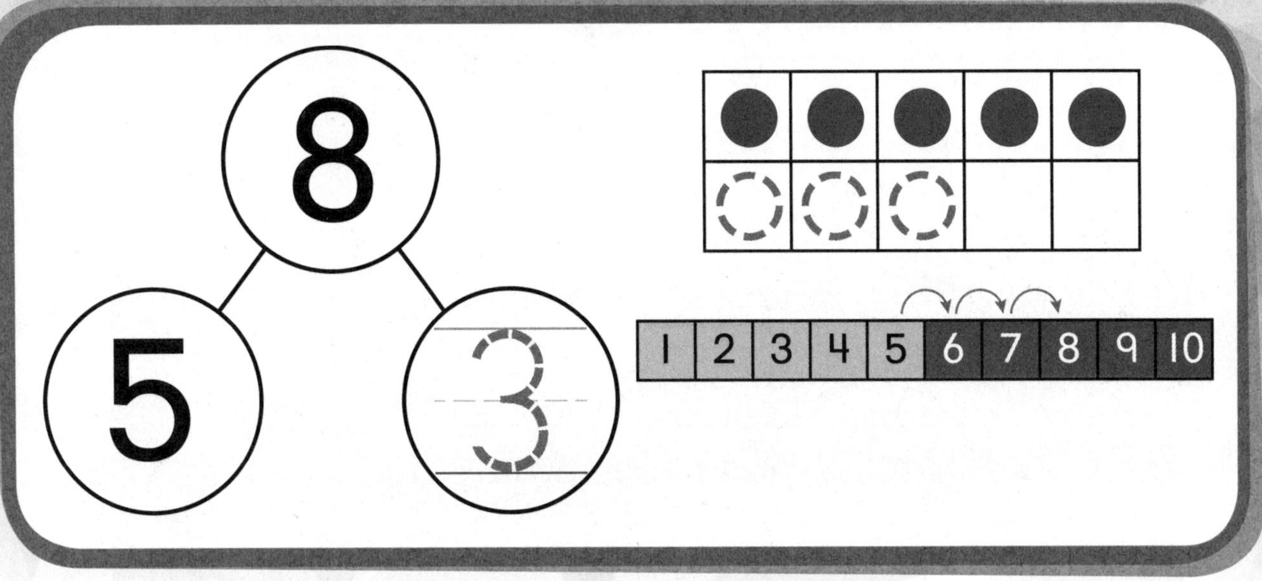

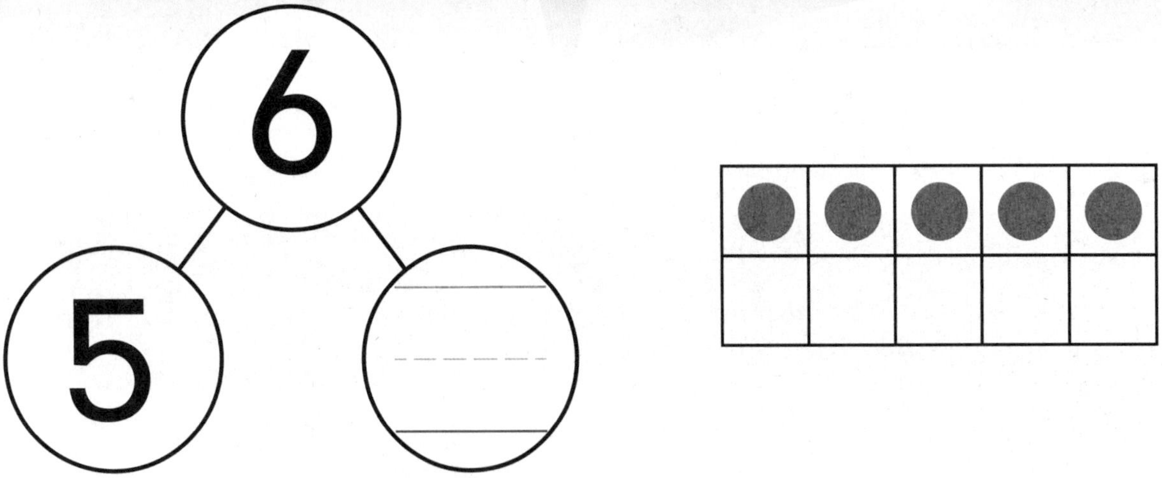

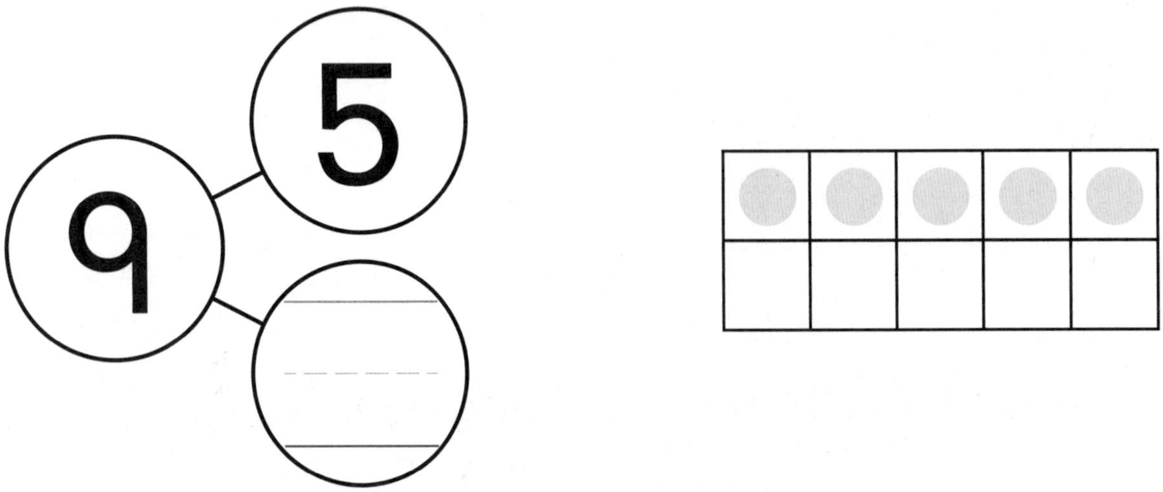

Directions: Draw dots in the ten frame to make the whole. Use the ten frame to complete the number bond.

Name ______________________________

✓ Apply and Grow: Practice

1

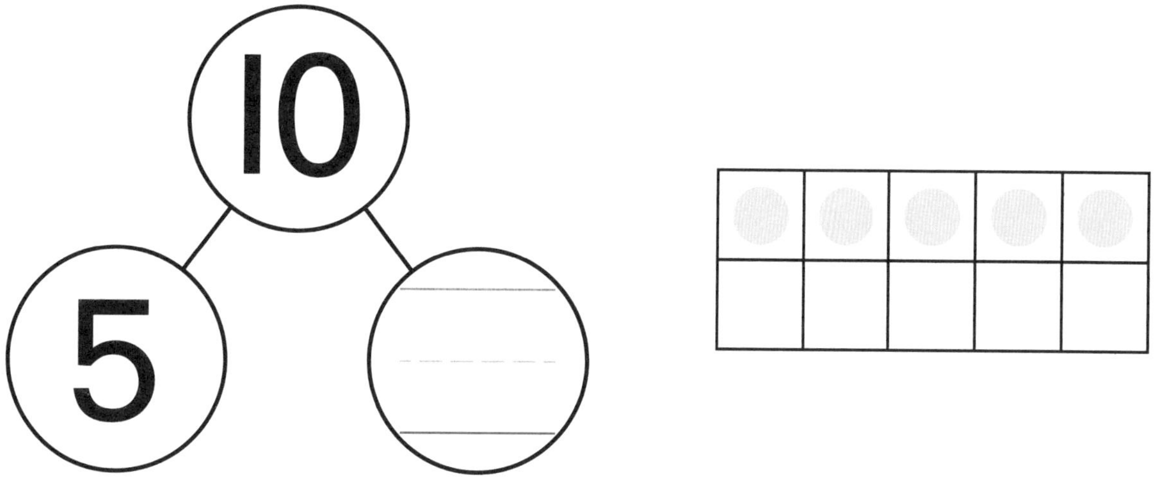

2

3

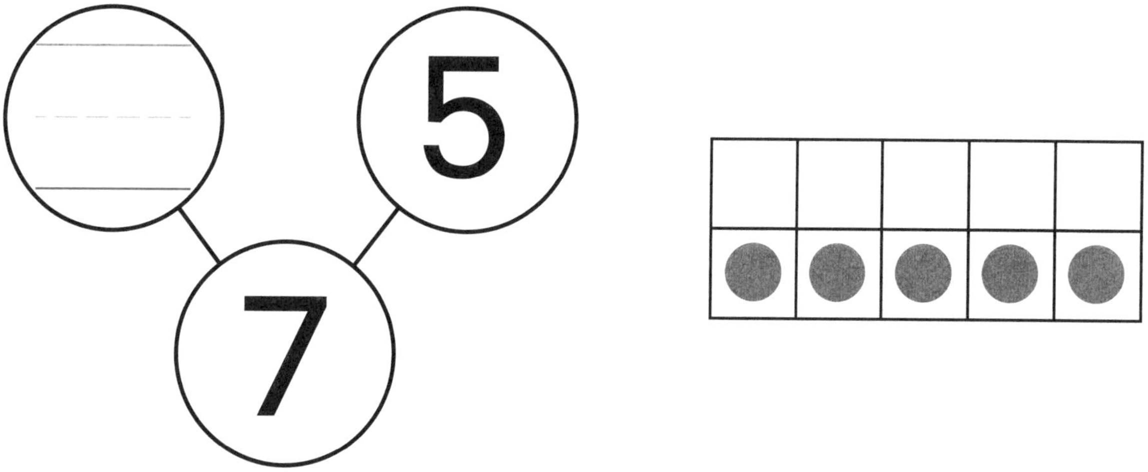

Directions: 1 – 3 Draw dots in the ten frame to make the whole. Use the ten frame to complete the number bond.

Think and Grow: Modeling Real Life

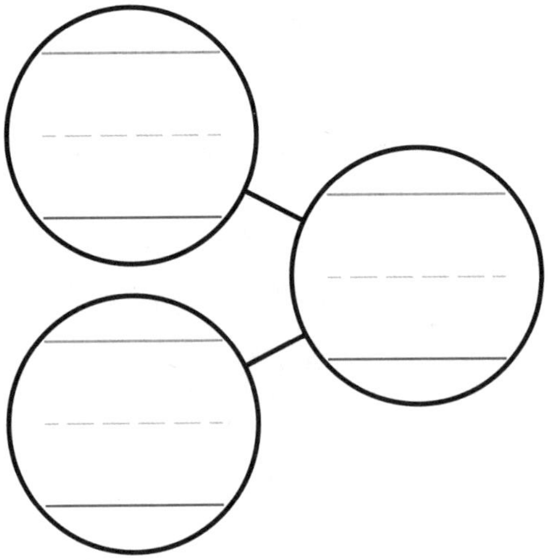

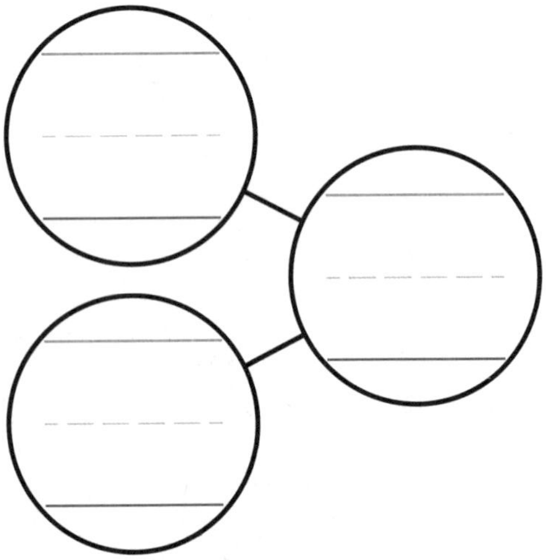

Directions: Newton has 5 balloons. Descartes has fewer balloons than Newton.

- Draw Descartes's balloons. Complete the number bond to match your picture.
- Draw to show another way. Then complete the number bond to match your picture.

Name ______________________________

Learning Target: Use a group of 5 to put together and take apart numbers to 10.

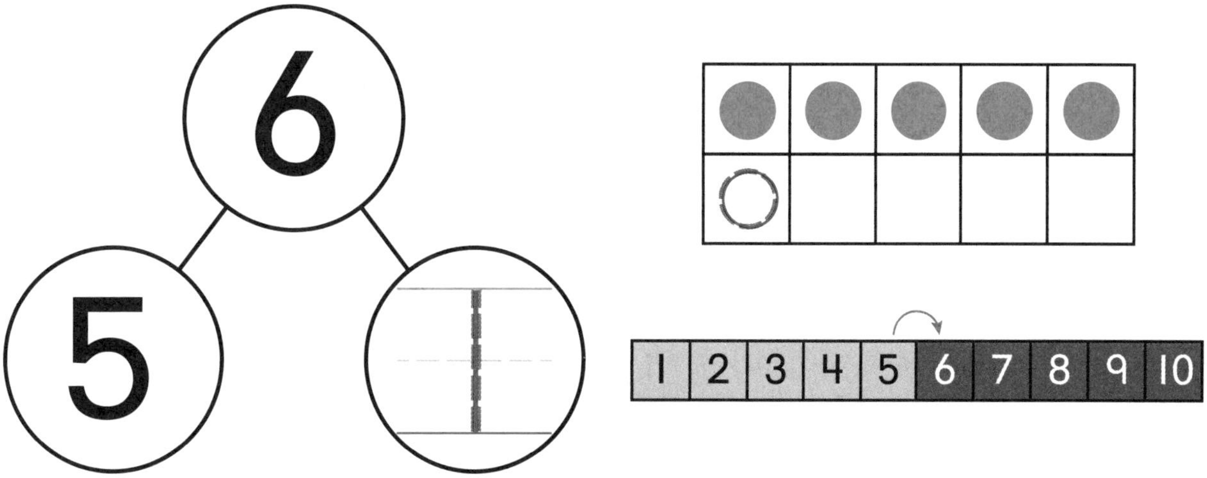

Directions: Draw dots in the ten frame to make the whole. Use the ten frame to complete the number bond.

1

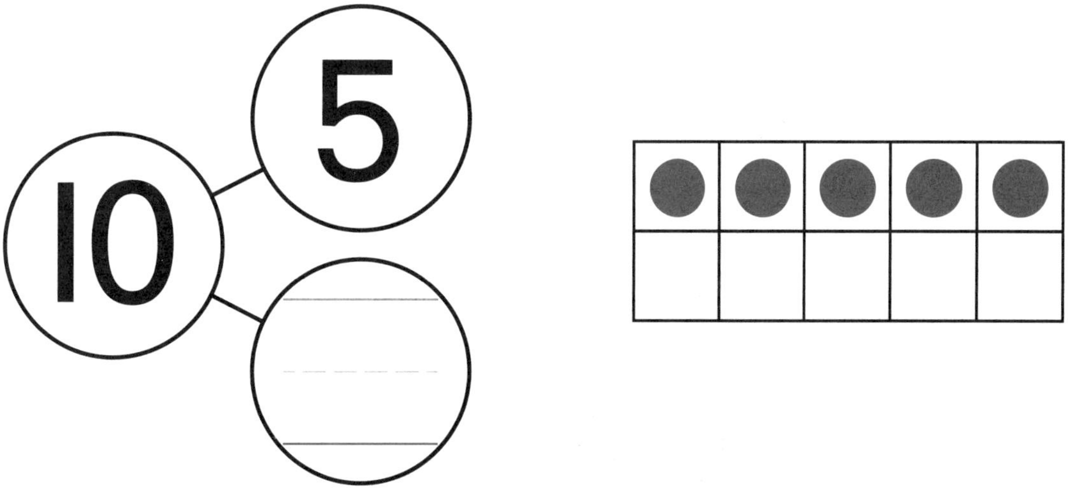

Directions: 1 Draw dots in the ten frame to make the whole. Use the ten frame to complete the number bond.

2

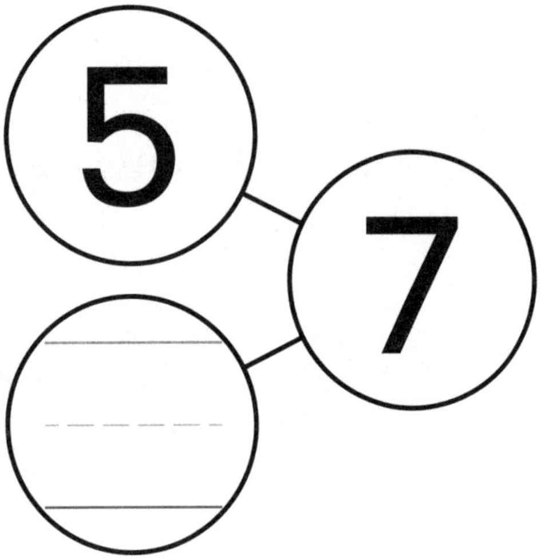

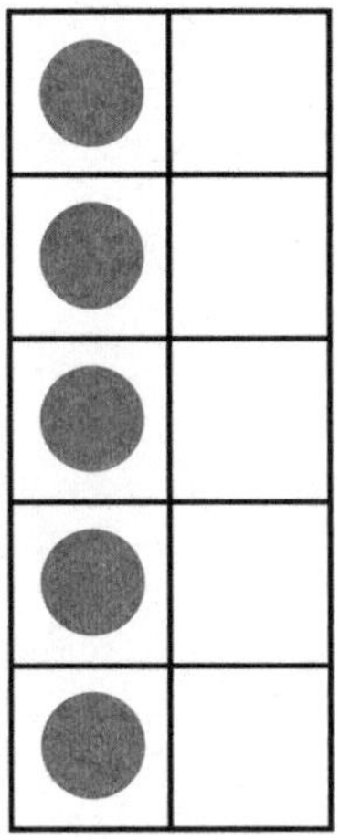

3

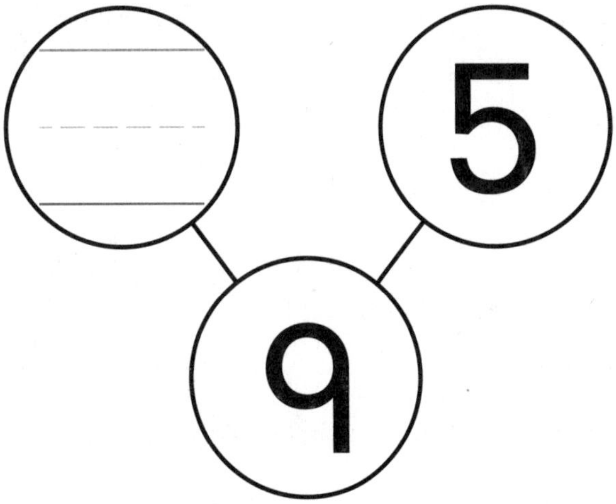

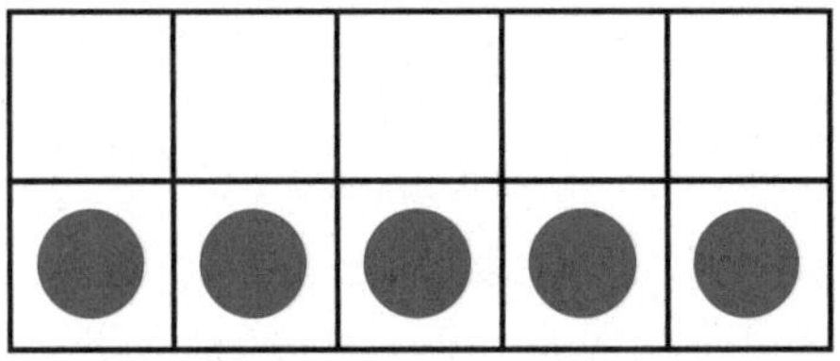

4

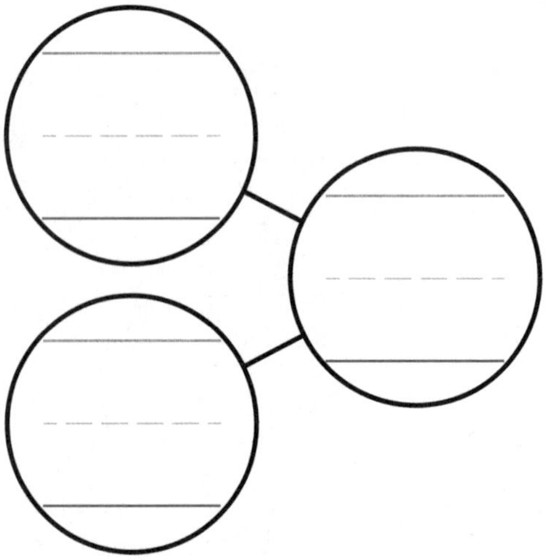

Directions: 2 and 3 Draw dots in the ten frame to make the whole. Use the ten frame to complete the number bond. 4 Newton has 5 balloons. Descartes has the same number of balloons as Newton. Draw Descartes's balloons. Complete the number bond to match your picture.

Name ________________________________

Performance Task 5

1

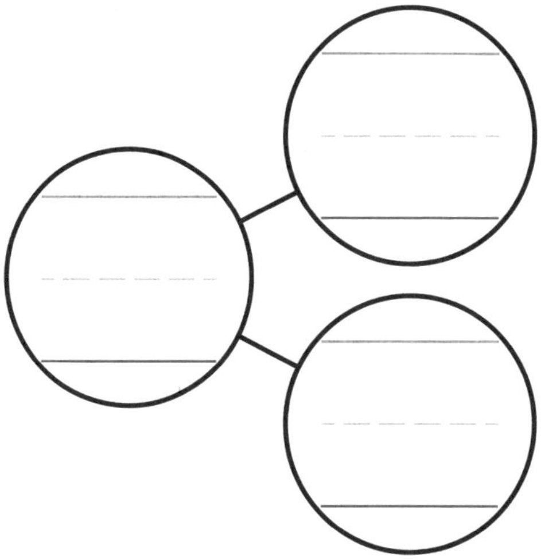

2

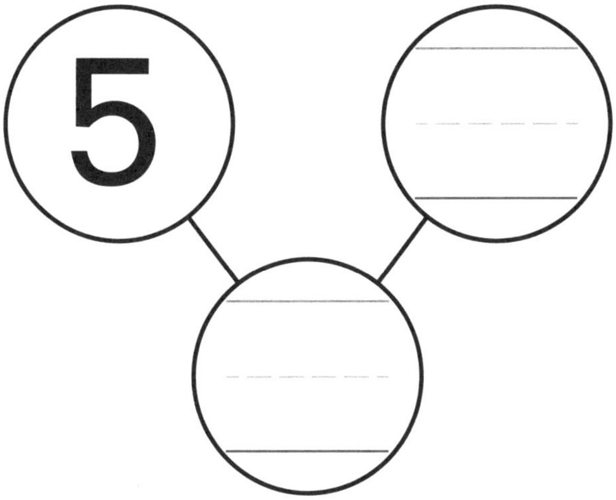

3

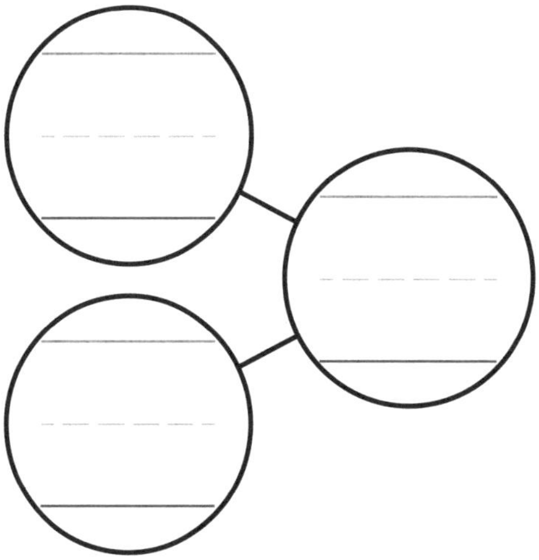

Directions: 1 Color to show fewer red ladybugs than yellow ladybugs. Then complete the number bond to match your picture. 2 Use the number bond to classify the butterflies. Then complete the number bond. 3 Classify the butterflies another way. Then complete the number bond.

Number Bond Spin and Cover

Directions: Take turns using the spinner to find your partner number with 5. Use your partner numbers to find the whole on the game board. Cover the whole with a counter. Repeat this process until you have covered all of the numbers.

Name ______________________________

Chapter Practice 5

5.1 Partner Numbers to 5

1

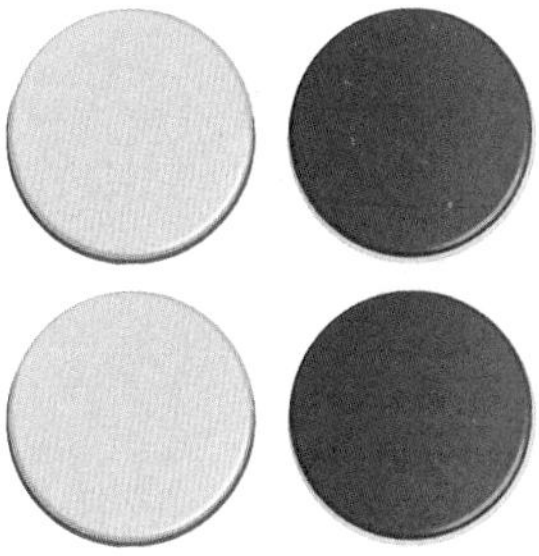

2

5.2 Use Number Bonds to Represent Numbers to 5

3

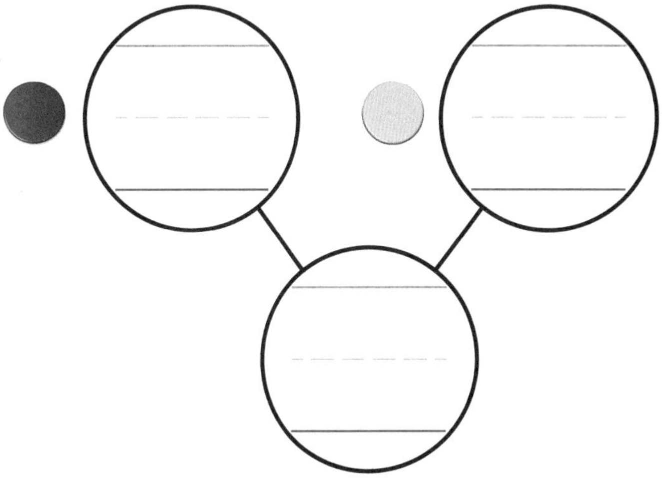

Directions: 1 and 2 Count each type of object. Write each number. Count all of the objects. Write the number for the whole. 3 Name the parts and the whole for the group. Then complete the number bond.

5.3 Compose and Decompose 6

4

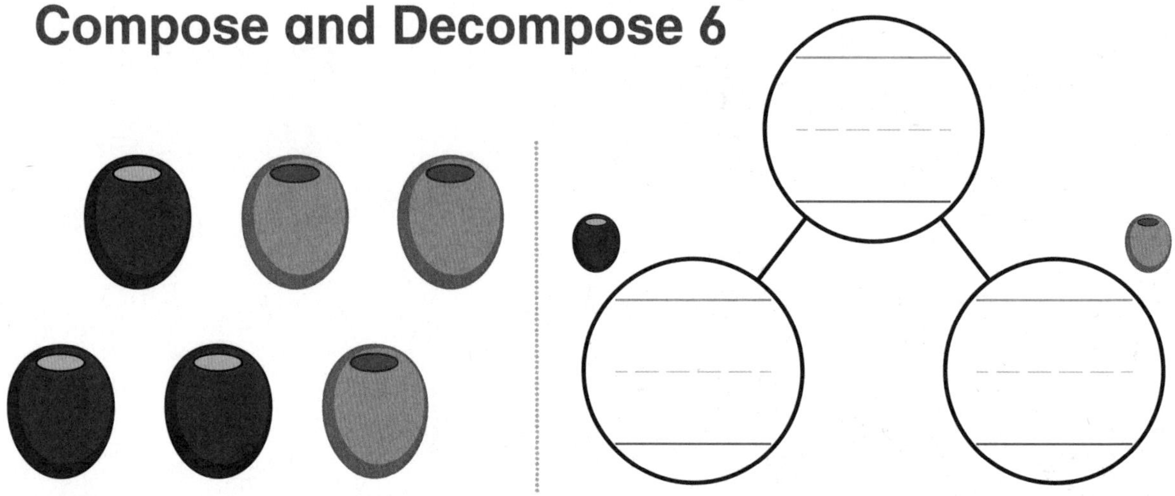

5.4 Compose and Decompose 7

5

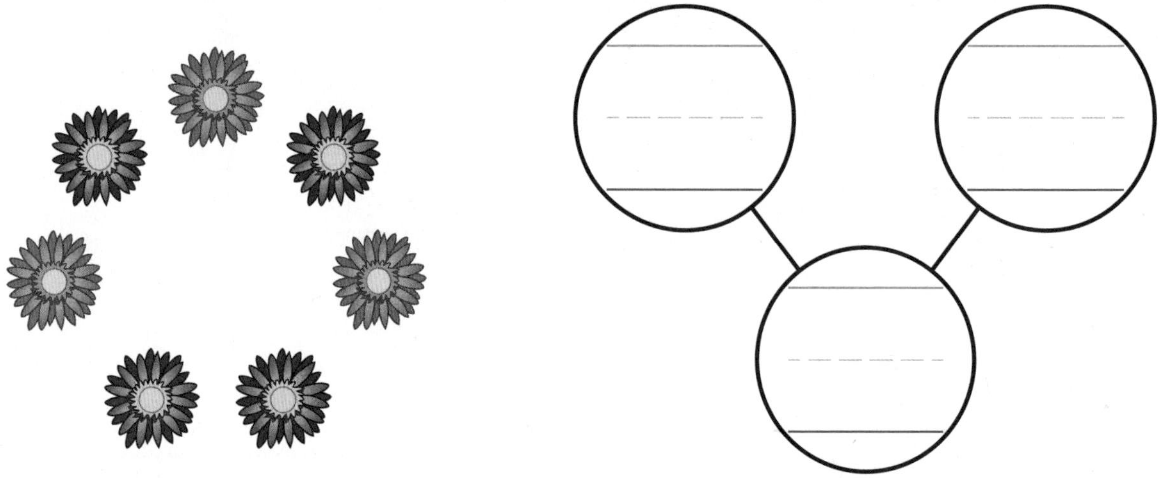

5.5 Compose and Decompose 8

6

Directions: 4–6 Name the parts and the whole for the group. Then complete the number bond.

5.6 Compose and Decompose 9

7

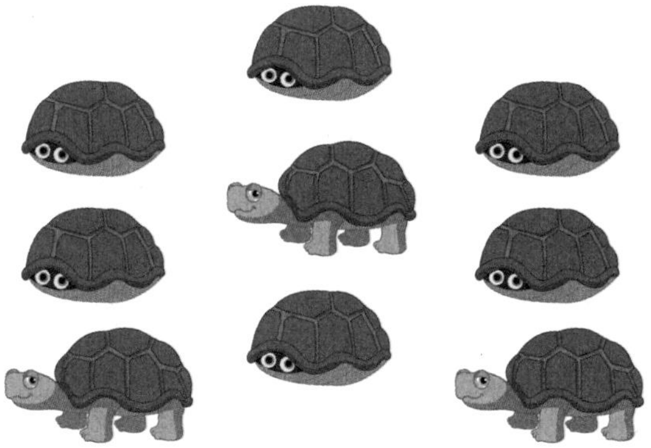

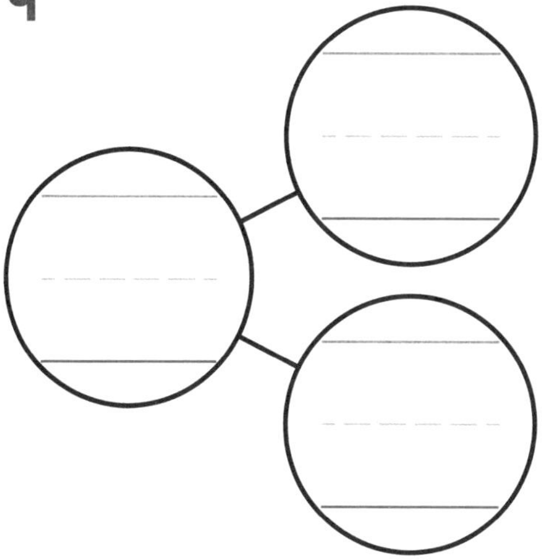

5.7 Compose and Decompose 10

8

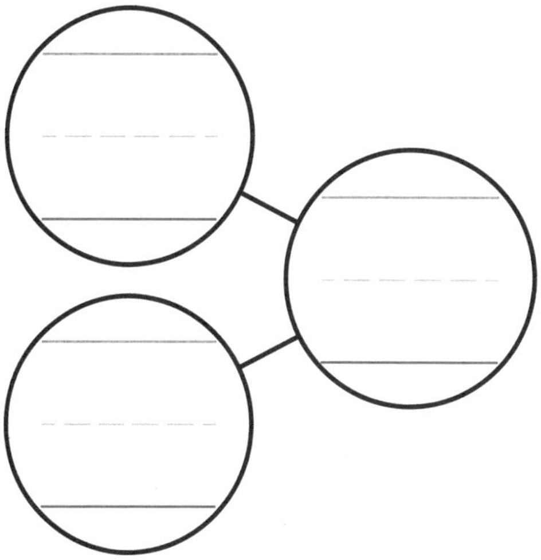

9

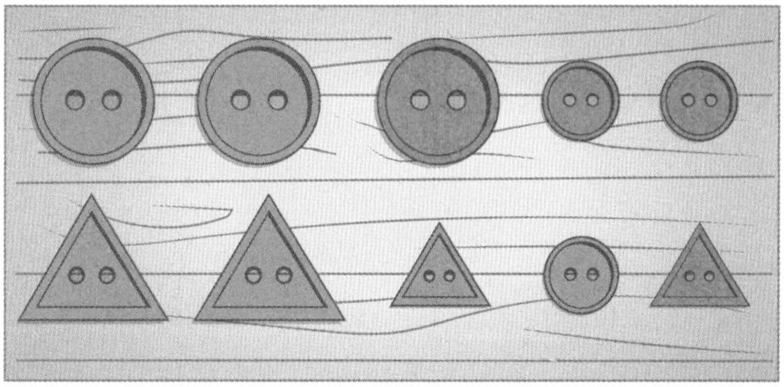

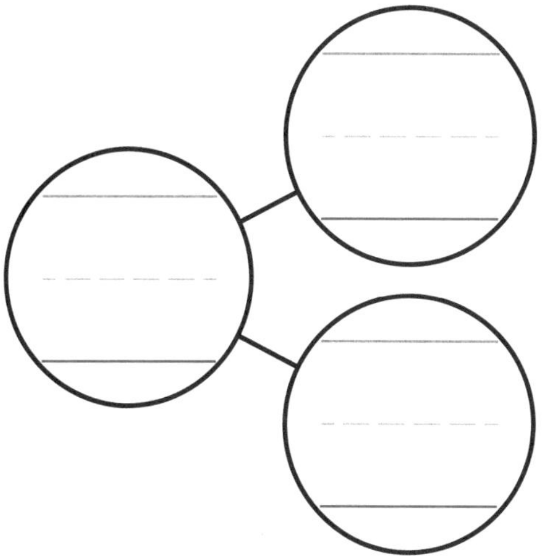

Directions: 7 and 8 Name the parts and the whole for the group. Then complete the number bond. 9 You have 10 buttons. Classify the buttons into 2 categories. Circle the groups. Then complete the number bond to match your picture.

5.8 Compose and Decompose Using a Group of 5

10

11

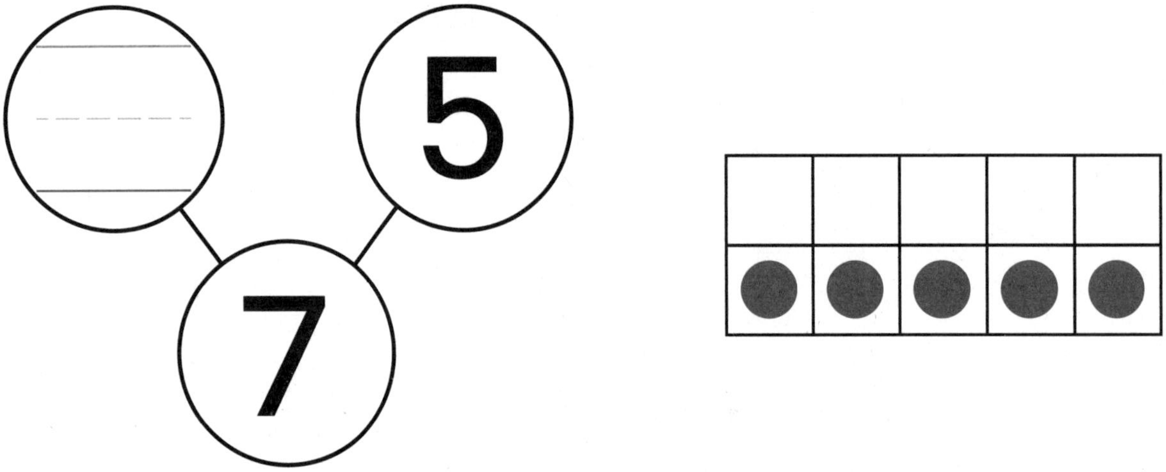

12

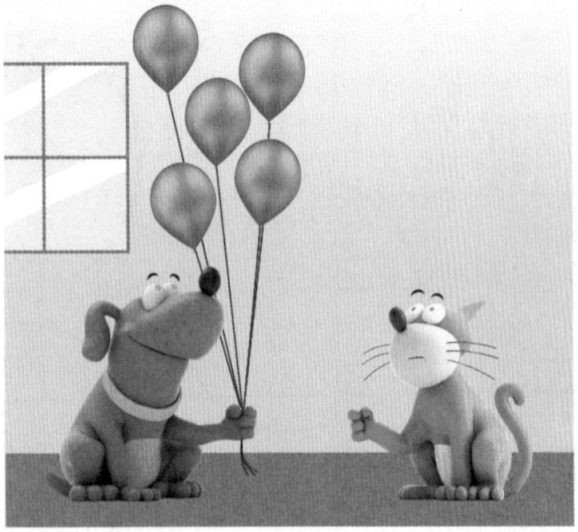

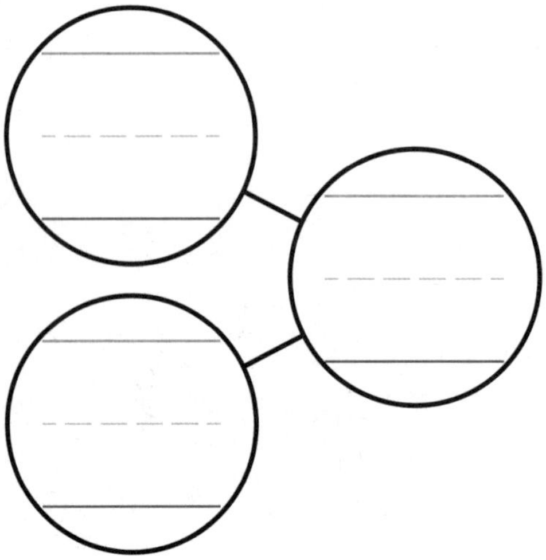

Directions: 10 and 11 Draw dots in the ten frame to make the whole. Use the ten frame to complete the number bond. 12 Newton has 5 balloons. Descartes has fewer balloons than Newton. Draw Descartes's balloons. Complete the number bond to match your picture.

6 Add Numbers within 10

- What kinds of animals live in the ocean?
- How many turtles are in the picture? If another turtle joins the group, how many turtles will there be in all?

Chapter Learning Target:
Understand addition patterns.

Chapter Success Criteria:
- I can identify a number sentence.
- I can describe a pattern.
- I can write an addition sentence.
- I can explain addition sentences.

Name ______________________________

6 Vocabulary

Review Words
part
number bond
whole

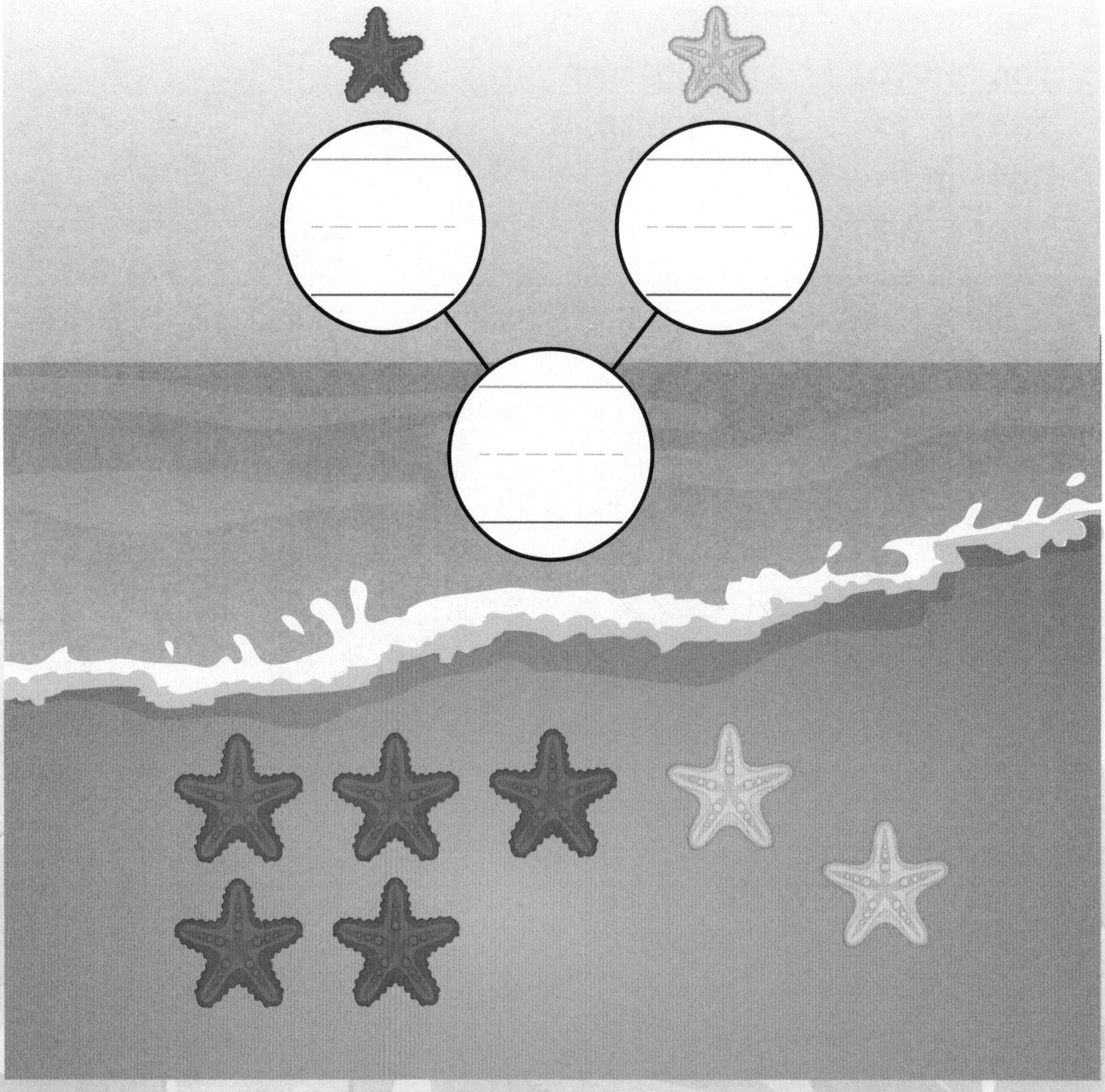

Directions: Name the parts and the whole for the group. Then complete the number bond.

Chapter 6 Vocabulary Cards

add

addition sentence

equal sign

in all

join

pattern

plus sign

$2 + 3 = 5$

$2 + 4 = 6$

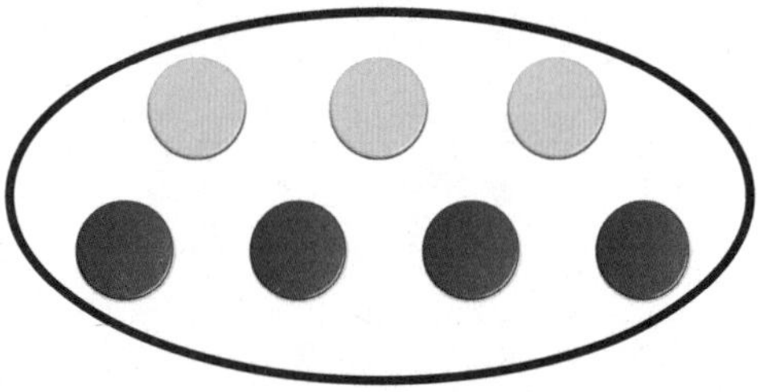

$3 + 4 = 7$

$1 + 1 = 2$ 

$2 + 1 = 3$ 

$3 + 1 = 4$ 

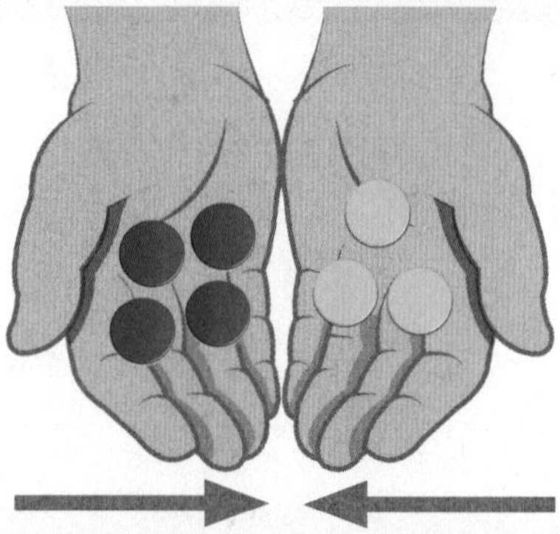

$2 + 1 = 3$

Name ______________________

Understand Addition 6.1

Learning Target: Add to a group of objects and tell how many.

Explore and Grow

______ and ______

Directions: Use counters to act out the story.

- There are 3 students on the bus. Write the number.
- 2 more students get on the bus. Write the number.
- Tell how many students are on the bus now.

Think and Grow

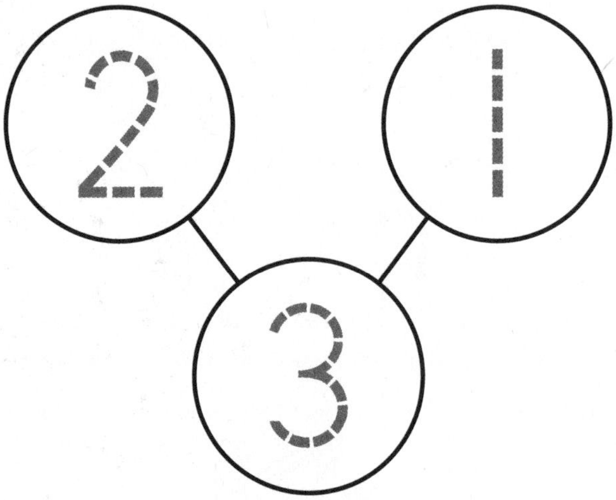

2 and 1 is 3 in all.

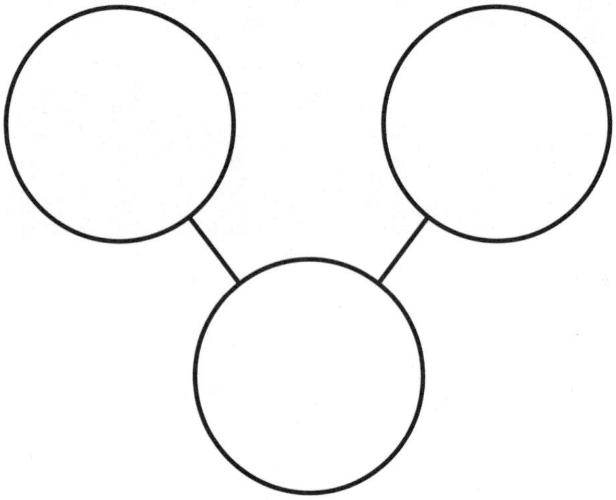

_____ and _____ is _____ in all.

Directions: Complete the sentence to tell how many students are in the group to start, how many join, and how many there are in all.

Name ____________________

Apply and Grow: Practice

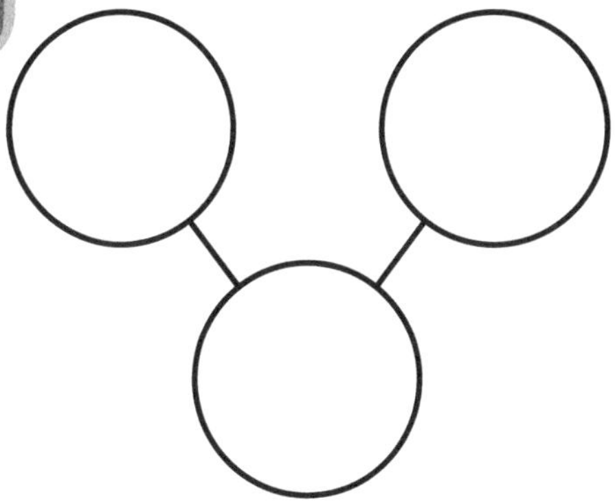

1

______ ______ ______

______ and ______ is ______ in all.

2

______ ______ ______

______ and ______ is ______ in all.

3

______ ______ ______

______ and ______ is ______ in all.

Directions: 1–3 Complete the sentence to tell how many students are in the group to start, how many join, and how many there are in all.

Think and Grow: Modeling Real Life

______ and ______ is ______ in all.

Directions: 5 students are playing basketball. 5 more students join them. Draw the students who join the group. Then complete the sentence to tell how many students are in the group to start, how many join, and how many there are in all.

Name ____________________

Practice **6.1**

Learning Target: Add to a group of objects and tell how many.

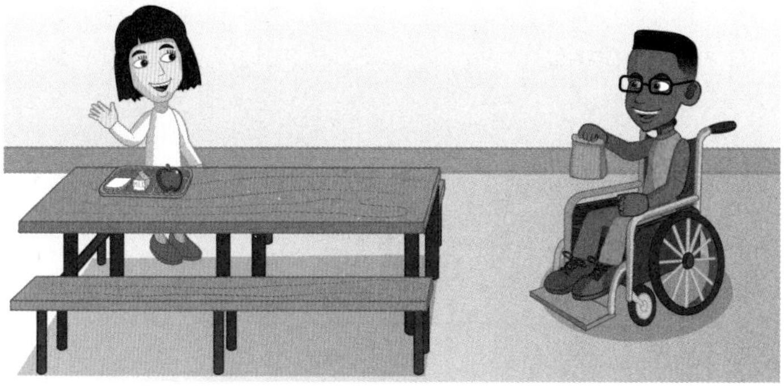

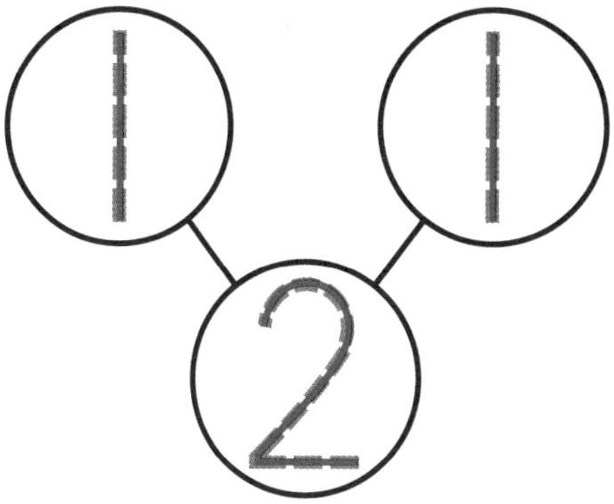

1 and 1 is 2 in all.

Directions: Complete the sentence to tell how many students are in the group to start, how many join, and how many there are in all.

1

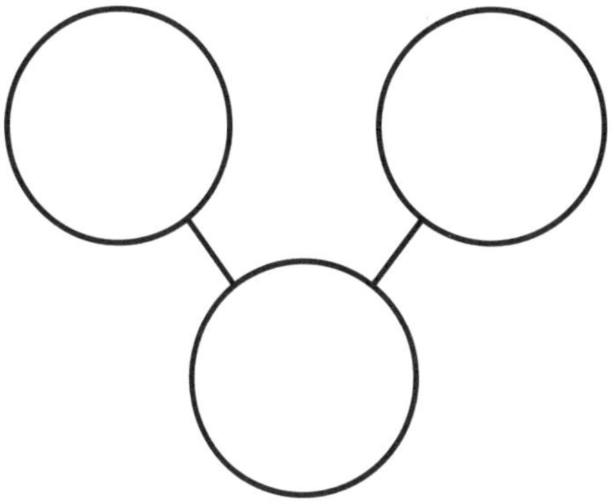

____ and ____ is ____ in all.

Directions: 1 Complete the sentence to tell how many students are in the group to start, how many join, and how many there are in all.

2

_____ and _____ is _____ in all.

3

_____ and _____ is _____ in all.

4

_____ and _____ is _____ in all.

Directions: 2 and 3 Complete the sentence to tell how many students are in the group to start, how many join, and how many there are in all. 4 Draw 3 students who join the group. Then complete the sentence to tell how many students are in the group to start, how many join, and how many there are in all.

Name ______________________

Learning Target: Add to a group of objects and complete an addition sentence.

Explore and Grow

____ + ____

Directions: Use counters to act out the story.

- There are 4 elephants in the water. Write the number.
- 2 more elephants join them. Write the number.
- Tell how many elephants are in the water now.

Think and Grow

2 and 3 is 5.

2 + 3 = 5

____ and ____ is ____.

____ + ____ = ____

Directions: Complete the sentence to tell how many animals are in the group to start, how many join, and how many there are in all. Then complete the addition sentence to match.

Name ______________________________

Apply and Grow: Practice

1

______ and ______ is ______.

______ + ______ = ______

2

______ + ______ = ______

3

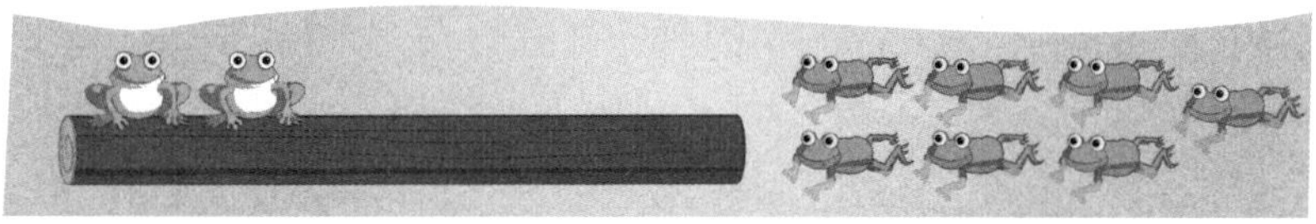

______ + ______ = ______

Directions: 1 Complete the sentence to tell how many ducks are in the group to start, how many join, and how many there are in all. Then complete the addition sentence to match. 2 and 3 Complete the addition sentence to tell how many animals there are in all.

Think and Grow: Modeling Real Life

____ + ____ = ____

Directions: There are 3 rabbits in a burrow. 6 more rabbits join them. Draw the rabbits that join the group. Then complete the addition sentence to tell how many rabbits there are in all.

Name ______________________

Practice 6.2

Learning Target: Add to a group of objects and complete an addition sentence.

1 and 2 is 3.

$1 + 2 = 3$

Directions: Complete the sentence to tell how many otters are in the group to start, how many join, and how many there are in all. Then complete the addition sentence to match.

1

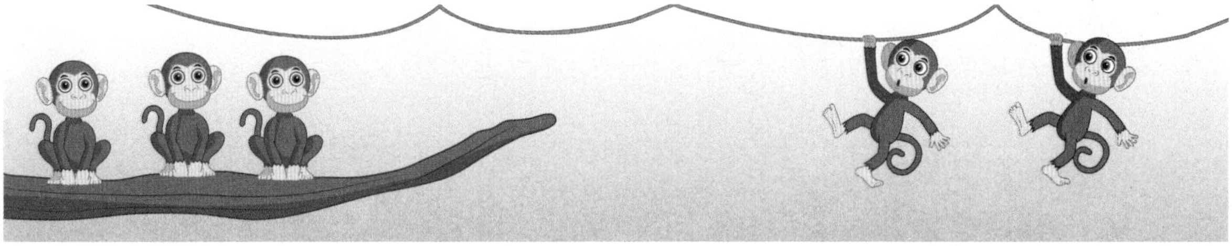

____ and ____ is ____.

____ + ____ = ____

Directions: 1 Complete the sentence to tell how many monkeys are in the group to start, how many join, and how many there are in all. Then complete the addition sentence to match.

2

___ + ___ = ___

3

___ + ___ = ___

4

___ + ___ = ___

Directions: 2 and 3 Complete the addition sentence to tell how many animals there are in all. 4 Draw 4 mice that join the group. Then complete the addition sentence to tell how many mice there are in all.

Name ______________________

Addition: Put Together 6.3

Learning Target: Put two groups of objects together and complete an addition sentence.

Explore and Grow

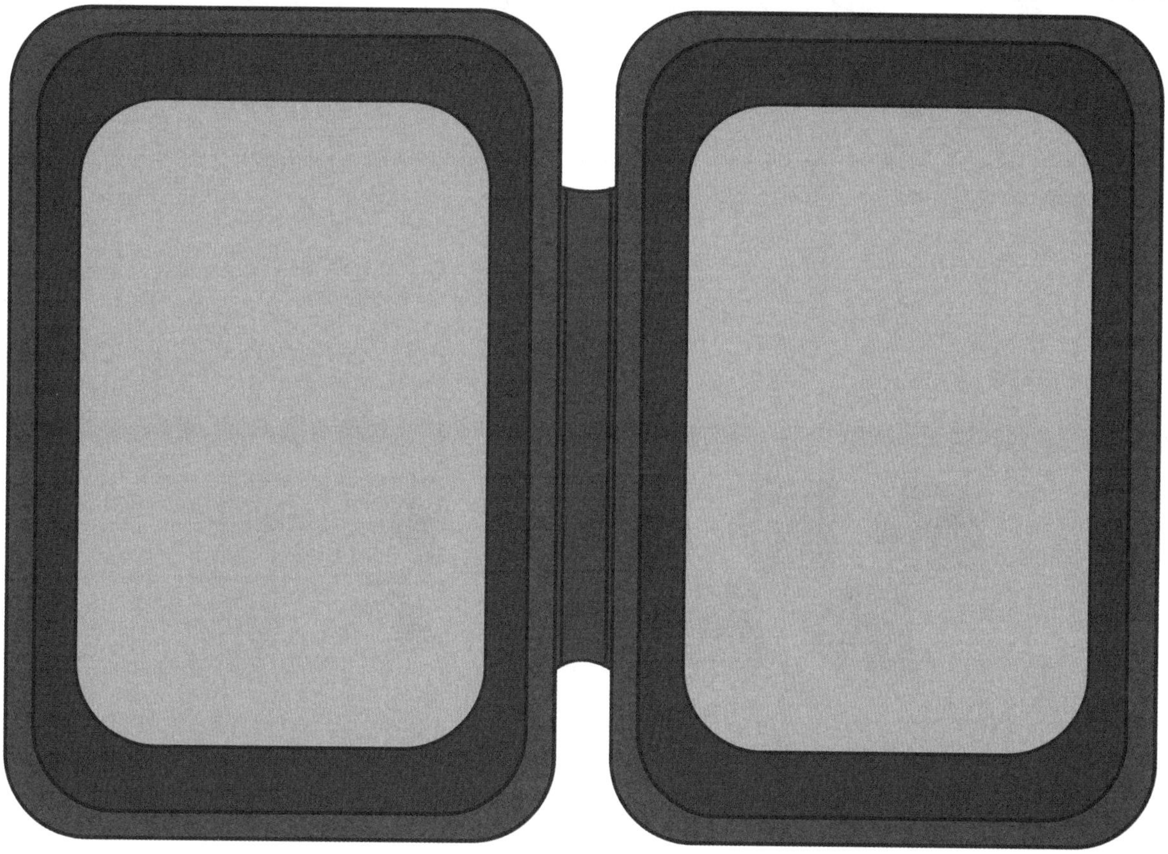

_____ + _____

Directions: Use counters to act out the story.

- There are 4 pencils in the case. Write the number.
- There are 3 crayons in the case. Write the number.
- Tell how many objects are in the case now.

Think and Grow

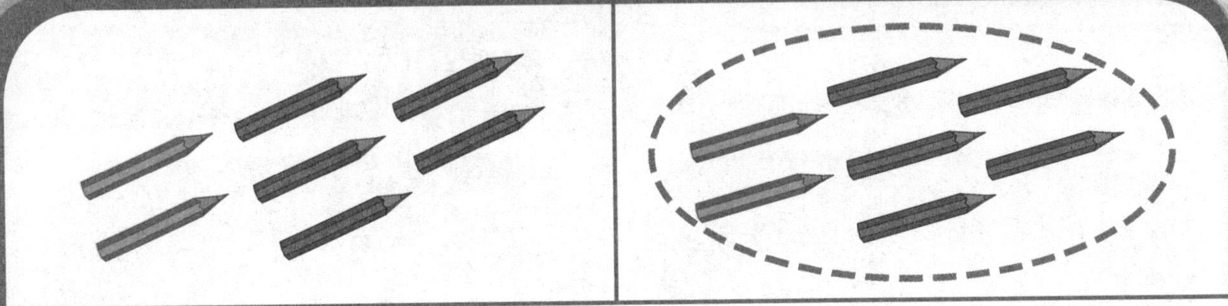

2 + 5 = 7

___ + ___ = ___

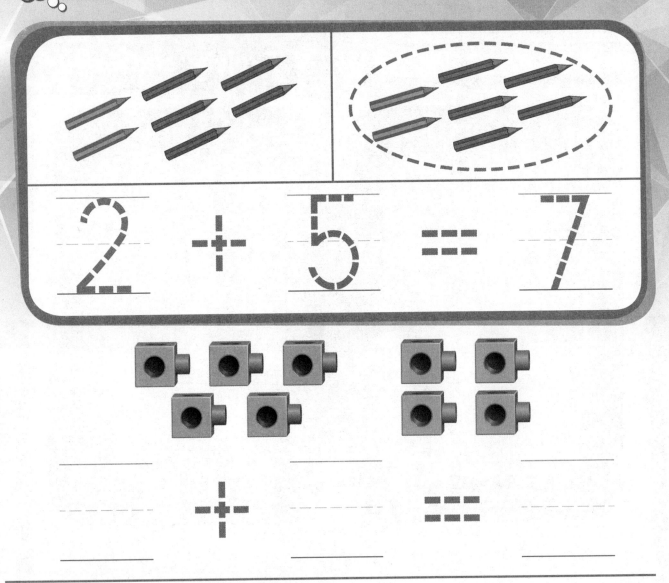

___ + ___ = ___

Directions: Circle the groups to put them together. Then write an addition sentence to tell how many objects there are in all.

Name ______________________________

Apply and Grow: Practice

1

_____ + _____ = _____

2

_____ + _____ = _____

3

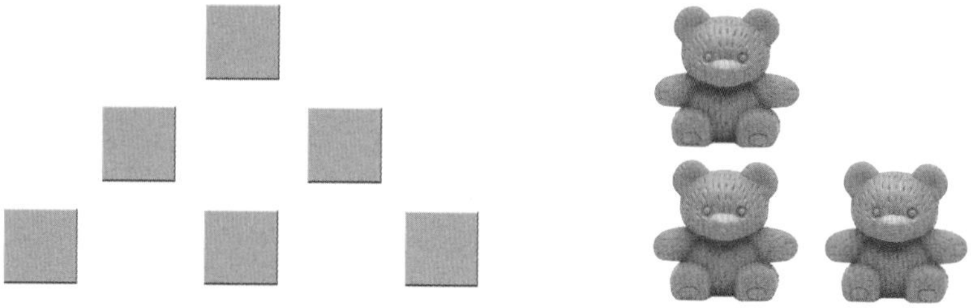

_____ + _____ = _____

Directions: 1 – 3 Circle the groups to put them together. Then write an addition sentence to tell how many objects there are in all.

Think and Grow: Modeling Real Life

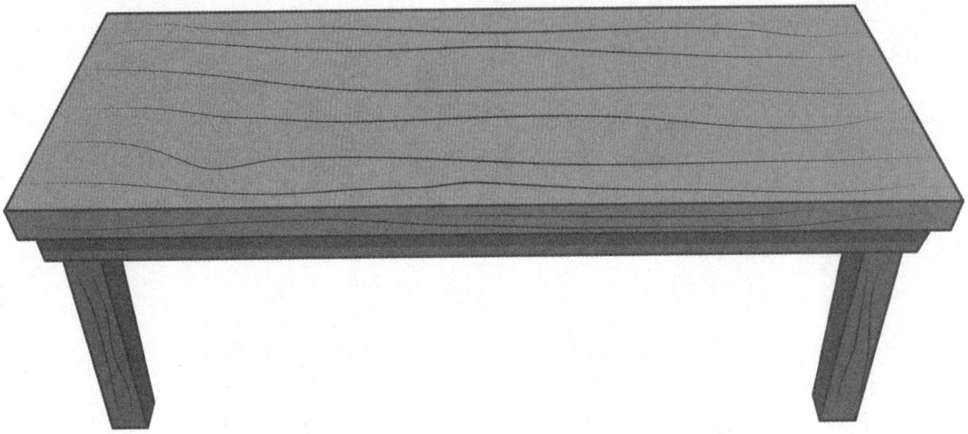

_____ + _____ = _____

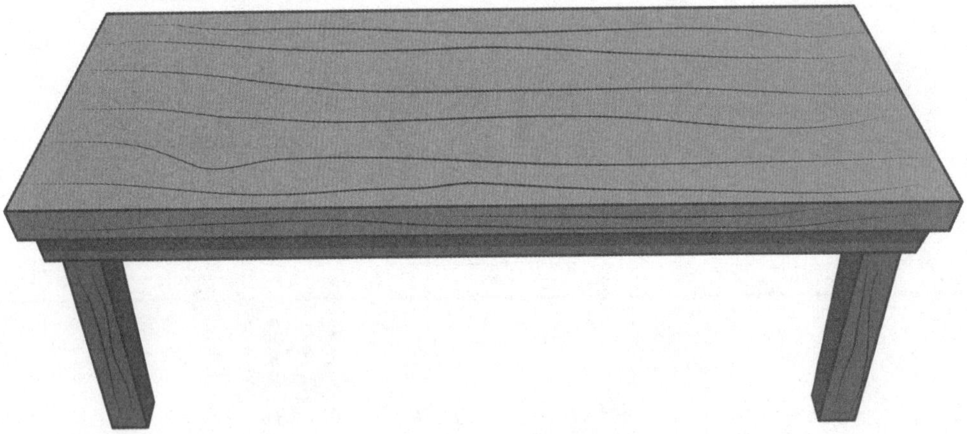

_____ + _____ = _____

Directions:

- You have 5 balls of red clay and 1 ball of blue clay. Draw and color the balls of clay. Then write an addition sentence to tell how many balls of clay you have in all.
- Your friend has 2 balls of red clay and 6 balls of blue clay. Draw and color the balls of clay. Then write an addition sentence to tell how many balls of clay your friend has in all.

Name ____________________

Practice 6.3

Learning Target: Put two groups of objects together and complete an addition sentence.

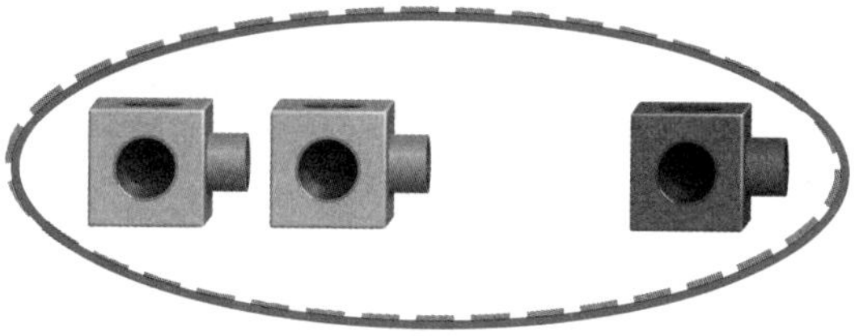

$$2 + 1 = 3$$

Directions: Circle the groups to put them together. Then complete the addition sentence to tell how many linking cubes there are in all.

1

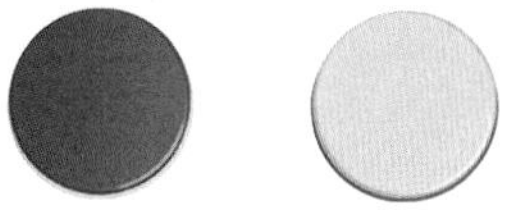

___ + ___ = ___

2

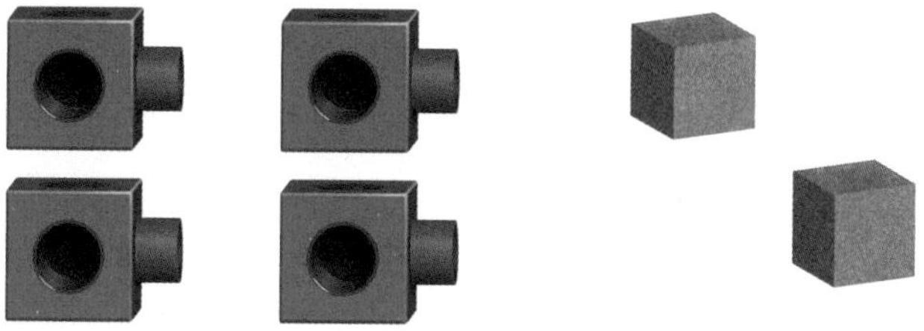

___ + ___ = ___

Directions: 1 and 2 Circle the groups to put them together. Then write an addition sentence to tell how many objects there are in all.

3

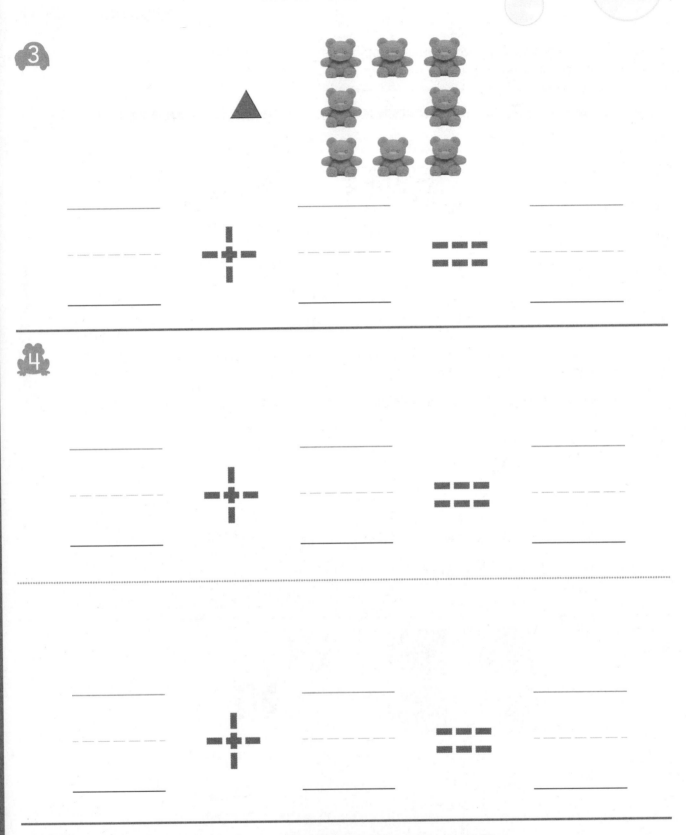

____ + ____ = ____

4

____ + ____ = ____

____ + ____ = ____

Directions: 3 Circle the groups to put them together. Then write an addition sentence to tell how many objects there are in all. 4 You have 4 orange marbles and 4 purple marbles. Your friend has 7 orange marbles and 2 purple marbles. Draw and color your marbles and your friend's marbles. Then write addition sentences to tell how many marbles you each have in all.

Name ____________________

Addition: Partner Numbers 6.4

Learning Target: Find partner numbers for a number and write an addition sentence.

Explore and Grow

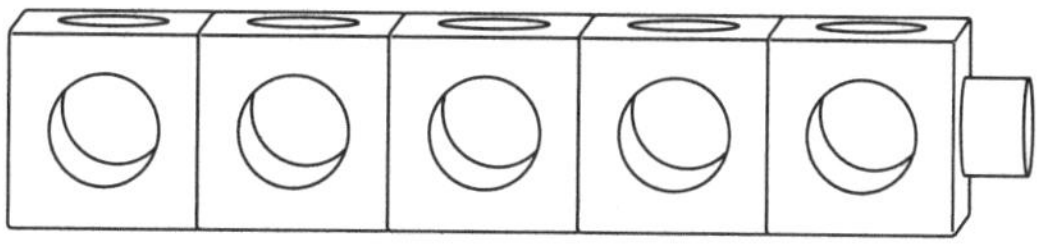

5 = ____ + ____

Directions: You have 5 linking cubes. Some are red and some are blue. Color to show how many are red and how many are blue. Then complete the addition sentence to match your picture.

Think and Grow

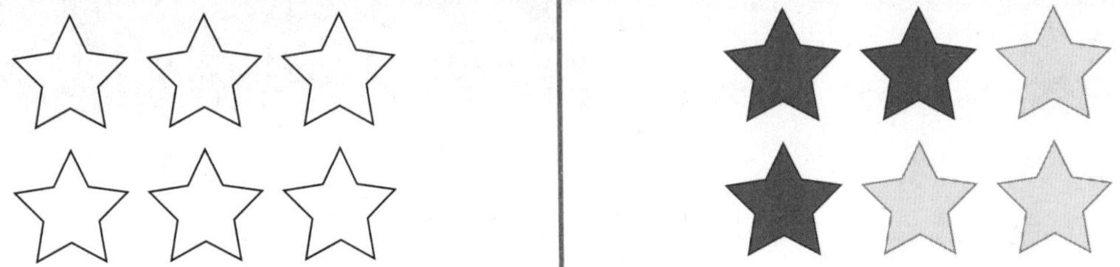

6 = 3 + 3

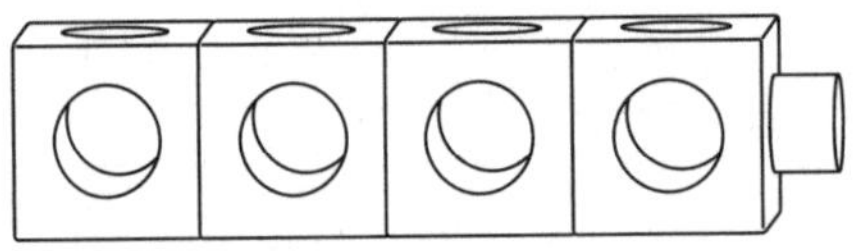

4 = ___ + ___

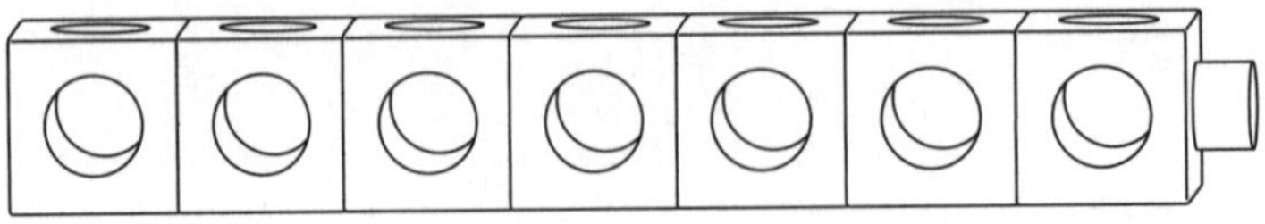

7 = ___ + ___

Directions: Use 2 colors to show partner numbers that make the whole. Then complete the addition sentence to match your picture.

Name ____________________

Apply and Grow: Practice

1

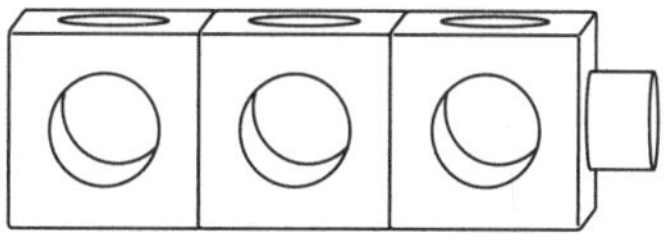

3 = ___ + ___

2

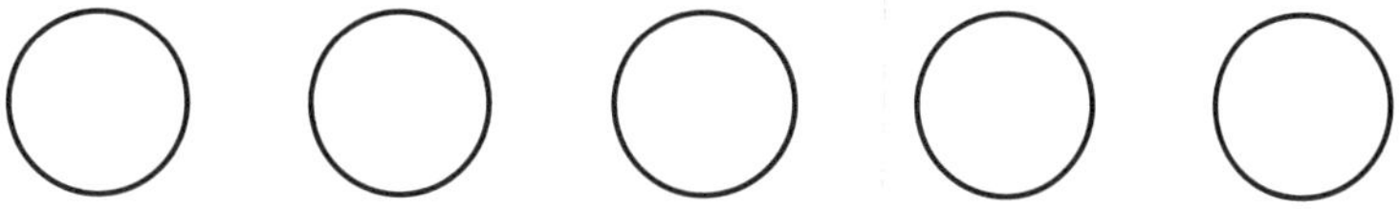

5 = ___ + ___

3

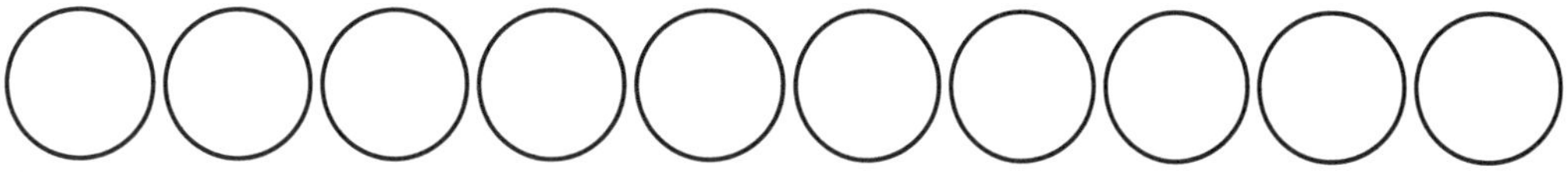

10 = ___ + ___

4

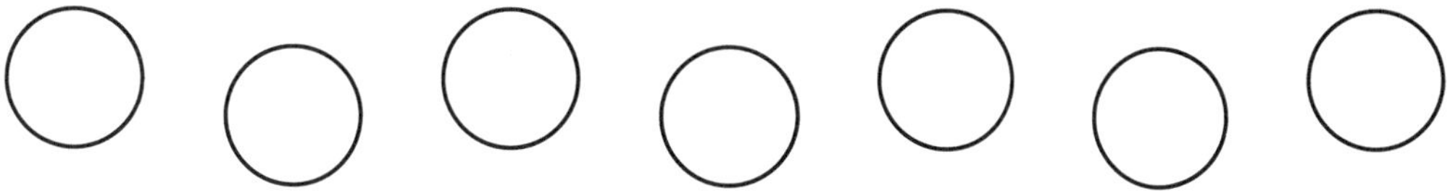

7 = ___ + ___

Directions: 1–4 Use 2 colors to show partner numbers that make the whole. Then complete the addition sentence to match your picture.

Think and Grow: Modeling Real Life

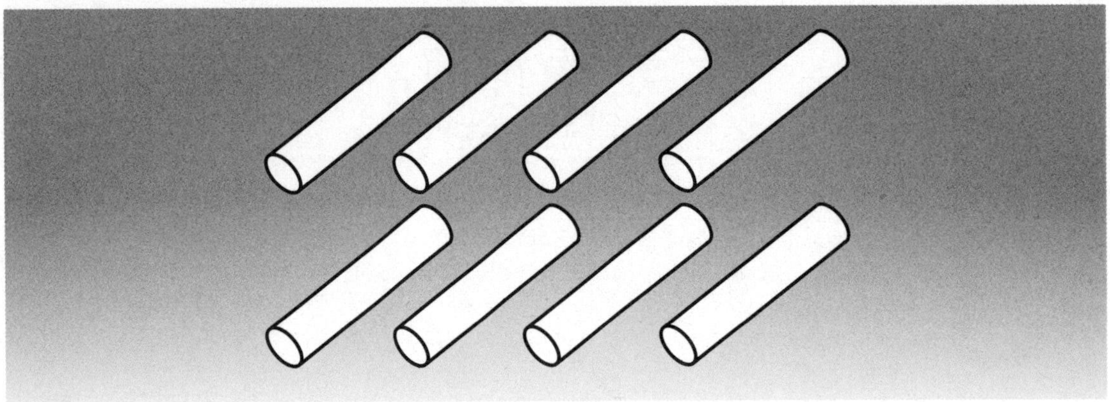

____ + ____ = ____

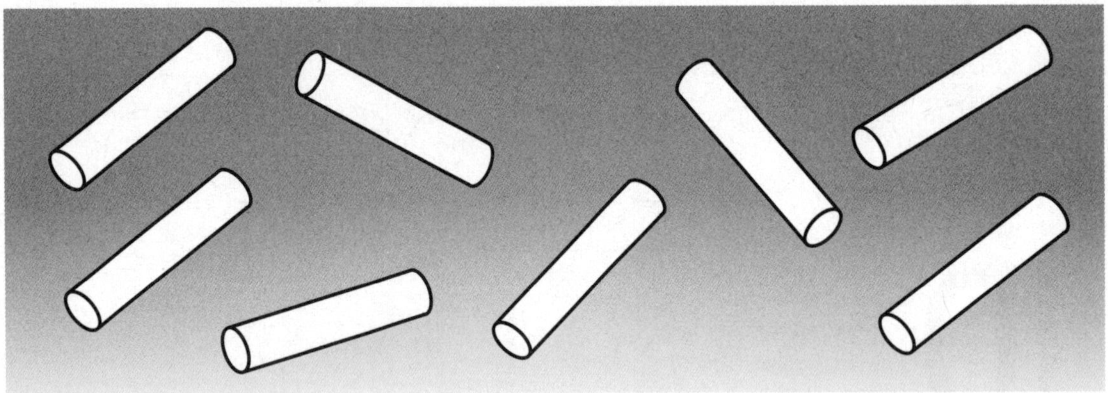

____ + ____ = ____

Directions: You have 8 pieces of sidewalk chalk. Some are red and some are blue.

- Color the pieces of chalk to show partner numbers that make 8. Then write an addition sentence to match your picture.
- Color to show another way to make 8. Then write an addition sentence to match your picture.

Name ______________________

Practice 6.4

Learning Target: Find partner numbers for a number and write an addition sentence.

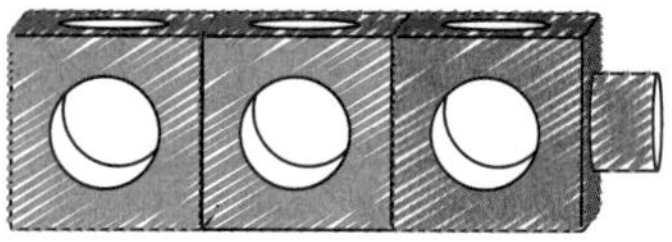

3 = 2 + 1

Directions: Use 2 colors to show partner numbers that make the whole. Then complete the addition sentence to match your picture.

1

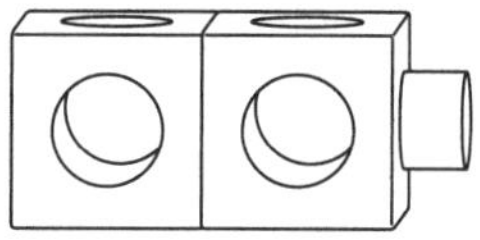

2 = ____ + ____

2

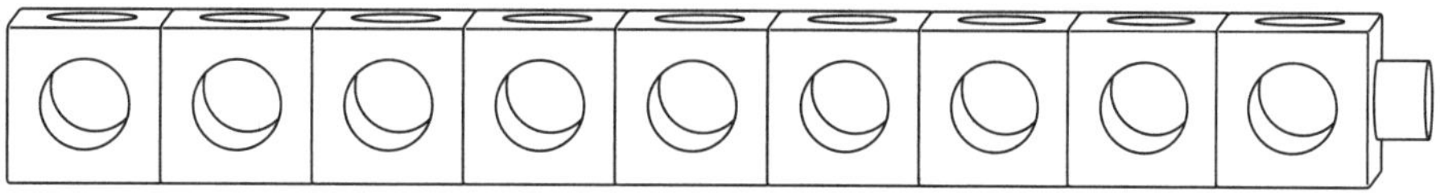

9 = ____ + ____

Directions: 1 and 2 Use 2 colors to show partner numbers that make the whole. Then complete the addition sentence to match your picture.

3

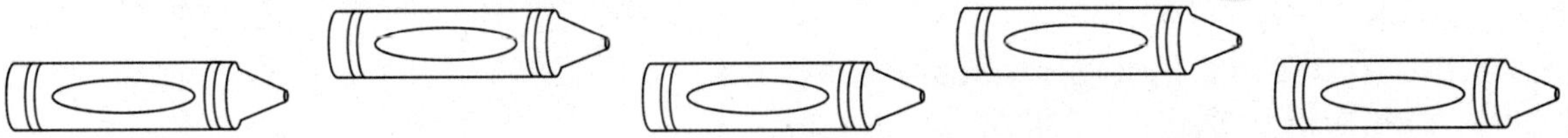

5 = ____ + ____

4

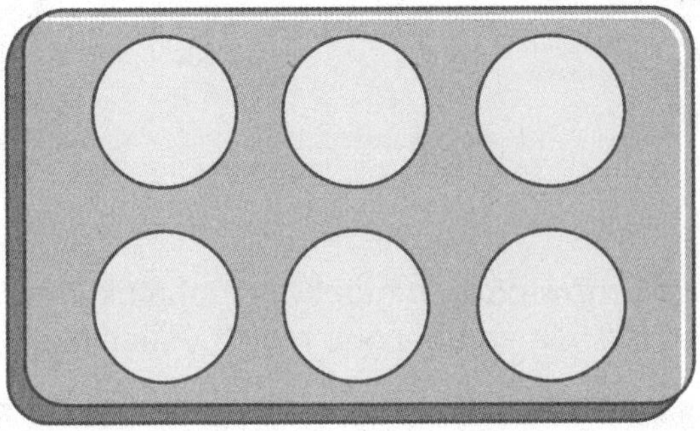

____ = ____ + ____

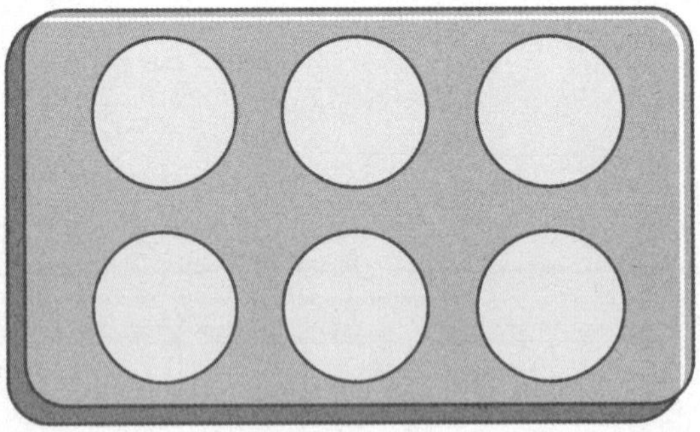

____ = ____ + ____

Directions: 3 Use 2 colors to show partner numbers that make the whole. Then complete the addition sentence to match your picture. 4 There are 6 paint spots on a paint tray. Some are purple and some are green. Color the paint spots to show partner numbers that make 6. Then color the paint spots to show another way to make 6. Write addition sentences to match your pictures.

Name ______________________

Learning Target: Explain addition patterns with 0 and 1.

Explore and Grow

$1 + 1 =$ □□□□□

$2 + 1 =$ □□□□□

$3 + 1 =$ □□□□□

$1 + 0 =$ □□□□□

$2 + 0 =$ □□□□□

$3 + 0 =$ □□□□□

Directions: Color the boxes to show how many in all. Tell what you notice.

Think and Grow

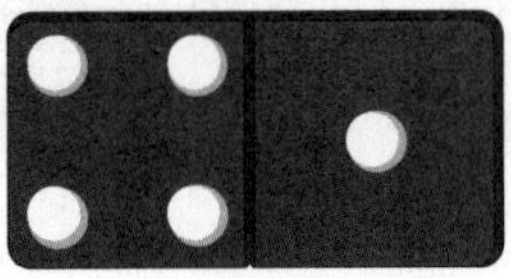

4 + 1 = 5

4 + 0 = 4

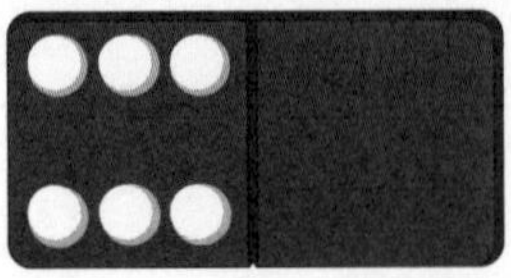

____ + ____ = ____

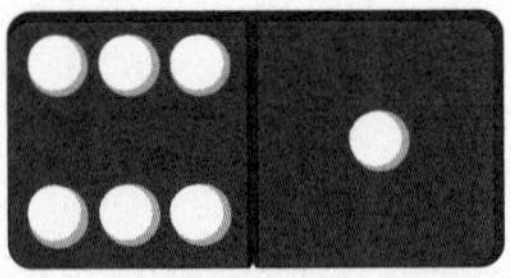

____ + ____ = ____

Directions: Write an addition sentence to tell how many dots there are in all. Tell what you notice.

Name ____________________

Apply and Grow: Practice

1  ____ + ____ = ____

2 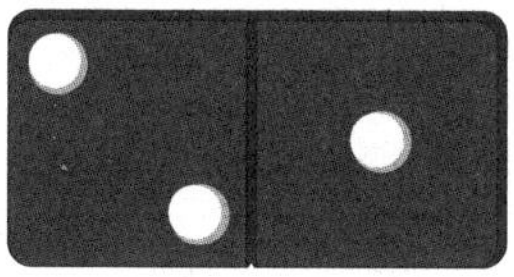 ____ + ____ = ____

3 5 + 0 = ____

4 5 + 1 = ____

5 9 + 1 = ____

6 10 + 0 = ____

Directions: 1 and 2 Write an addition sentence to tell how many dots there are in all. Tell what you notice. 3–6 Complete the addition sentence. Tell what you notice.

Think and Grow: Modeling Real Life

_____ + _____ = _____

_____ + _____ = _____

Directions: You find 7 coins to put in your piggy bank.

- You cannot find any more coins. Draw and color all of your coins. Then write an addition sentence to tell how many coins you have in all.
- Your friend gives you a coin to put in your piggy bank. Draw and color all of your coins. Then write an addition sentence to tell how many coins you have in all.

Name ______________________________

Practice 6.5

Learning Target: Explain addition patterns with 0 and 1.

1 + 1 = 2   next number when counting

same number   1 + 0 = 1

Directions: Write an addition sentence to tell how many dots there are in all. Tell what you notice.

1

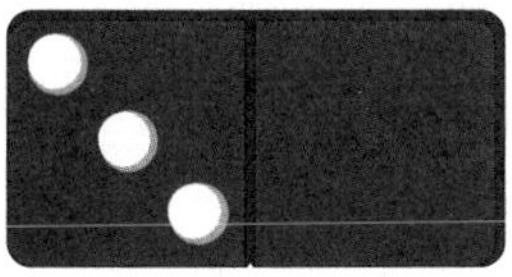

____ + ____ = ____

2

____ + ____ = ____

Directions: 1 and 2 Write an addition sentence to tell how many dots there are in all. Tell what you notice.

3 4 + 0 = ____

4 4 + 1 = ____

5 8 + 1 = ____

6 9 + 0 = ____

7

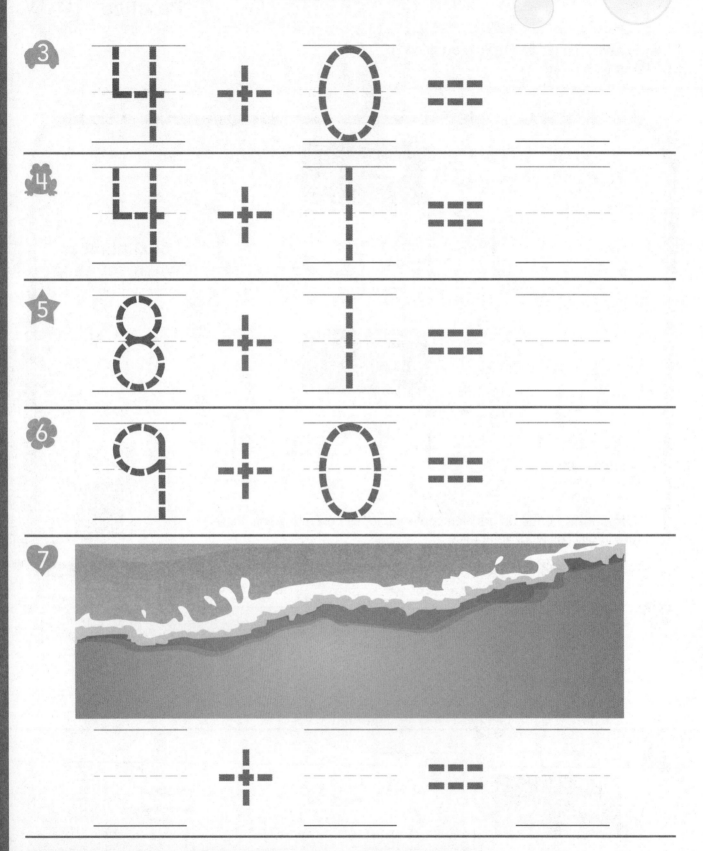

____ + ____ = ____

Directions: 3–6 Complete the addition sentence. Tell what you notice.
7 You found 8 seashells at the beach yesterday. You do not find any more seashells today. Draw and color all of your seashells. Then write an addition sentence to tell how many seashells you have in all.

Name ______________________

Practice Addition 6.6

Learning Target: Add partner numbers to 5.

Explore and Grow

$1 + 2 =$ ____

$3 + 2 =$ ____

$0 + 4 =$ ____

Directions: Use counters in the five frame to show how many there are in all. Complete the addition sentences.

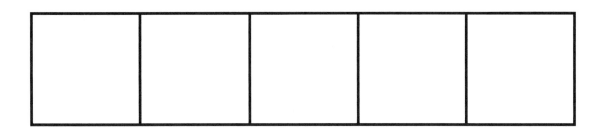

Think and Grow

$2 + 3 = ?$

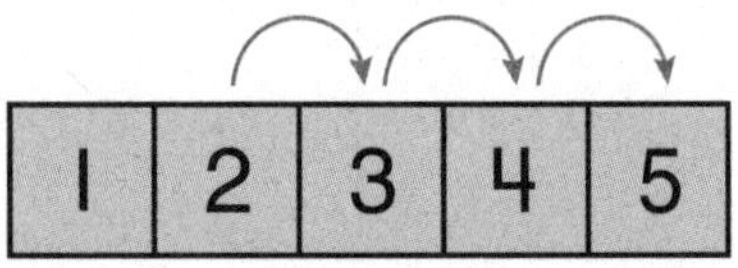

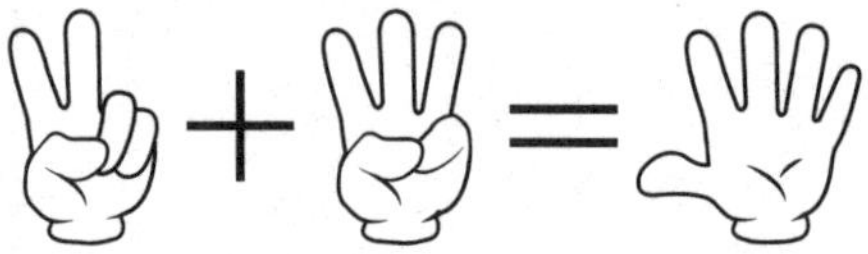

$2 + 3 = 5$

$1 + 4 =$ ____

$0 + 3 =$ ____

$1 + 3 =$ ____

Directions: Complete the addition sentence. Tell how you found your answer.

Name ________________________________

Apply and Grow: Practice

1 $1 + 2 =$ ____

2 $0 + 5 =$ ____

3 $2 + 2 =$ ____

4 $0 + 0 =$ ____

5 $2 + 3 =$ ____

$3 + 2 =$ ____

Directions: 1–4 Complete the addition sentence. Tell how you found your answer. 5 Complete the addition sentences. Tell what you notice.

Think and Grow: Modeling Real Life

____ = ____ + ____

____ + ____ = ____

____ + ____ = ____

Directions:

- You have 4 game pieces. Some are green and some are yellow. Write an addition sentence to show partner numbers that make the whole. Color to show how you know.
- There is 1 game piece on a game board. You put 2 more game pieces on the board. Write an addition sentence to tell how many game pieces are on the game board. Draw to show how you know.
- You have 3 blue game pieces and 2 red game pieces. Write an addition sentence to show how many game pieces you have in all. Draw to show how you know.

Name ____________________

Learning Target: Add partner numbers to 5.

$3 + 2 = 5$

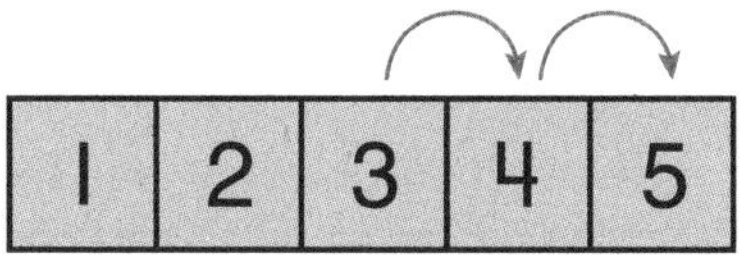

Directions: Complete the addition sentence. Tell how you found your answer.

1. $0 + 2 =$ ____

2. $1 + 3 =$ ____

3. $1 + 2 =$ ____

Directions: 1–3 Complete the addition sentence. Tell how you found your answer.

4

$1 + 4 =$ ____

$4 + 1 =$ ____

5

____ = ____ + ____

○ ○ ○ ○ ○

6

____ + ____ = ____

Directions: 4 Complete the addition sentences. Tell what you notice. 5 You have 5 game pieces. Some are red and some are black. Write an addition sentence to show partner numbers that make the whole. Color to show how you know. 6 There are no game pieces on a game board. You put 1 game piece on the board. Write an addition sentence to tell how many game pieces are on the game board. Draw to show how you know.

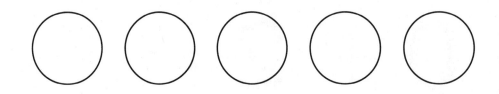

Name ______________________

Use a Group of 5 to Add 6.7

Learning Target: Use a group of 5 to write an addition sentence.

Explore and Grow

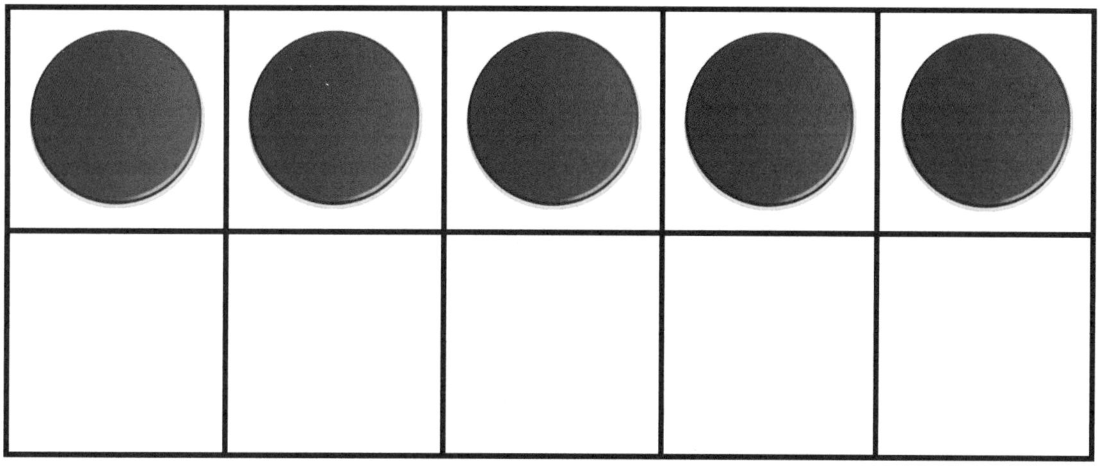

5 + ___ = 8

Directions: Add more counters to make 8. Then complete the addition sentence.

Think and Grow

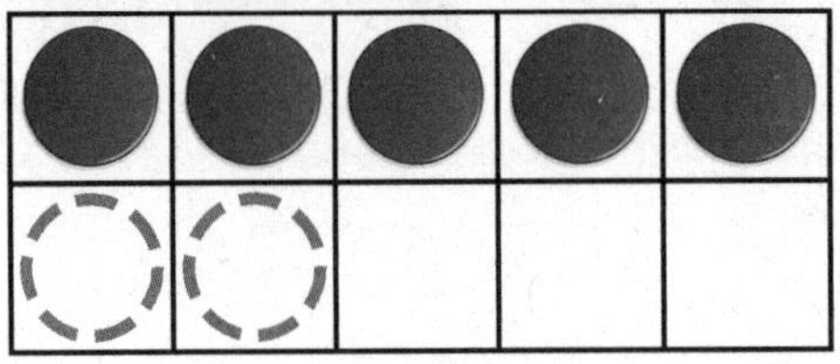

1	2	3	4	5	6	7	8	9	10

5 + 2 = 7

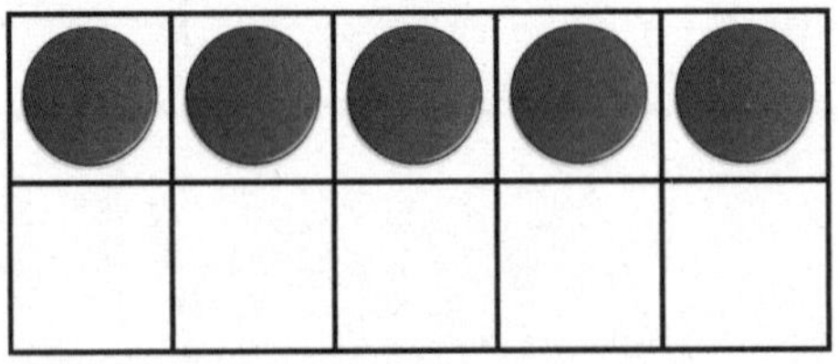

5 + ___ = 6

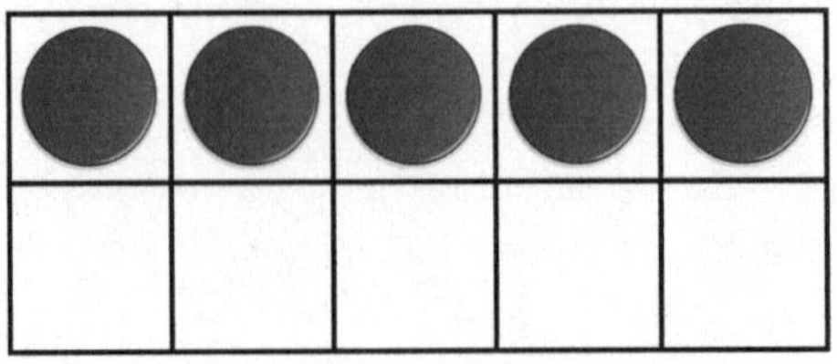

5 + ___ = 9

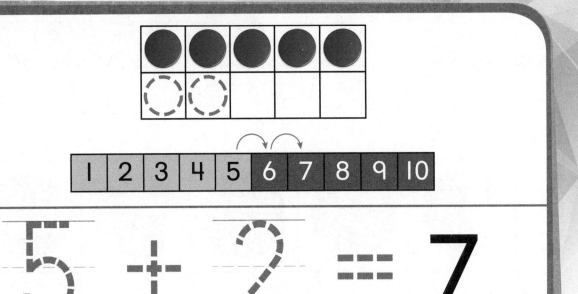

Directions: Draw more counters to show how many in all. Use the ten frame to complete the addition sentence.

Name ______________________________

Apply and Grow: Practice

1

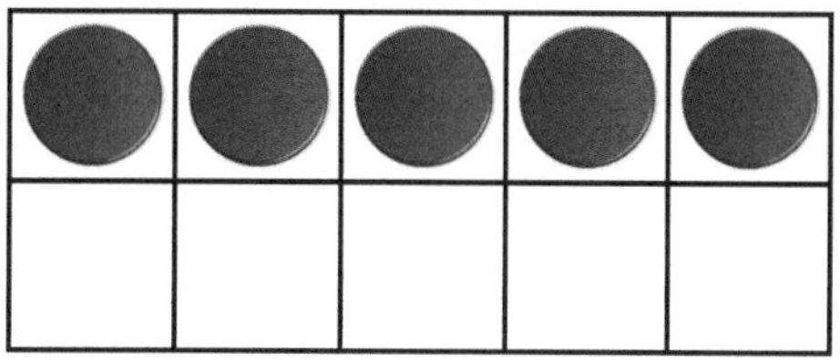

$5 + \_\_\_ = 8$

2

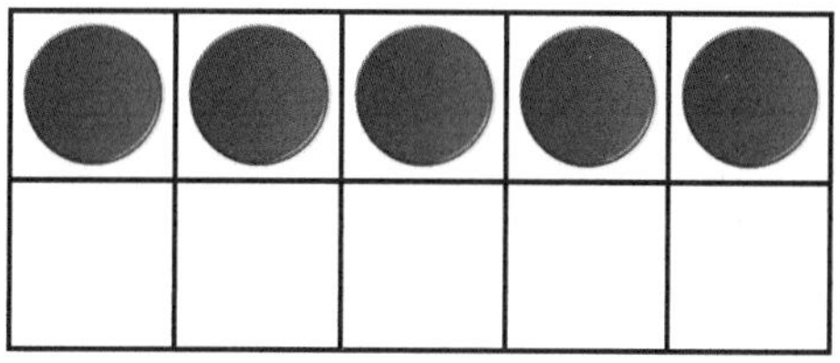

$5 + \_\_\_ = 10$

3

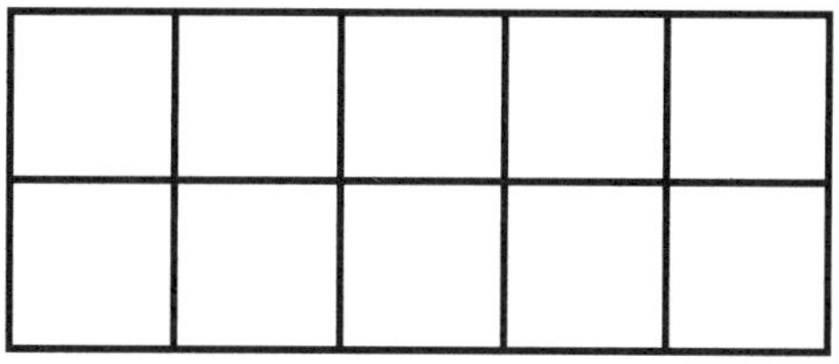

$5 + \_\_\_ = 7$

Directions: 1 and 2 Draw more counters to show how many in all. Use the ten frame to complete the addition sentence. 3 Draw 5 counters. Draw more counters to show how many in all. Use the ten frame to complete the addition sentence.

Think and Grow: Modeling Real Life

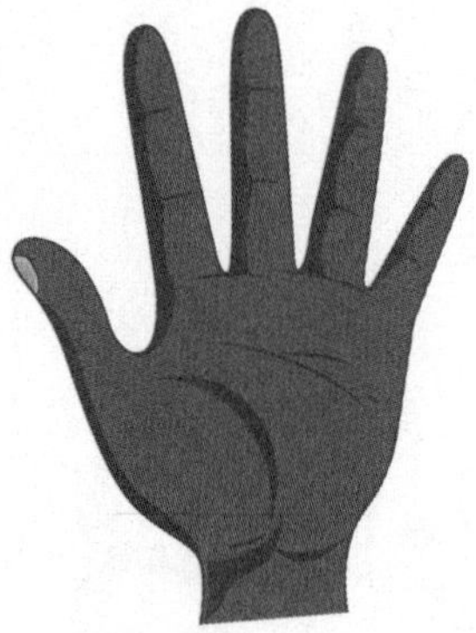

____ + ____ = ____

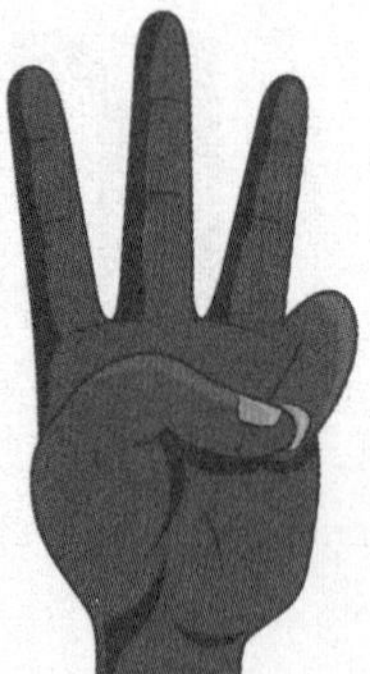

____ + ____ = ____

Directions:

- A boy holds up 5 fingers to tell his age. His sister is 9 years old. Draw more fingers to show his sister's age. Then write an addition sentence to match your picture.
- A girl holds up 3 fingers to tell her age. Her brother is 8 years old. Draw more fingers to show her brother's age. Then write an addition sentence to match your picture.

Name ____________________

Practice 6.7

Learning Target: Use a group of 5 to write an addition sentence.

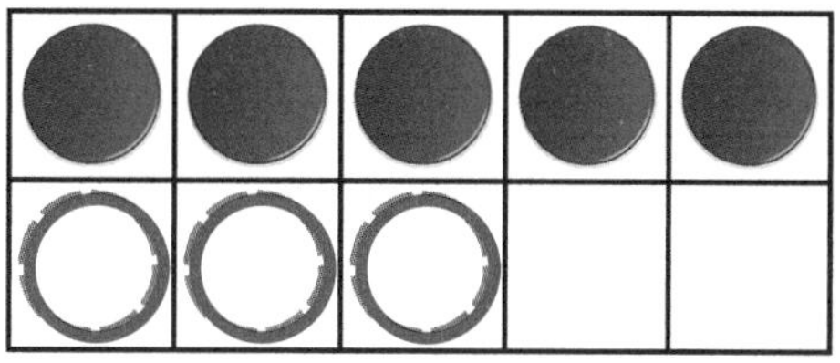

5 + 3 = 8

Directions: Draw more counters to show how many in all. Use the ten frame to complete the addition sentence.

1

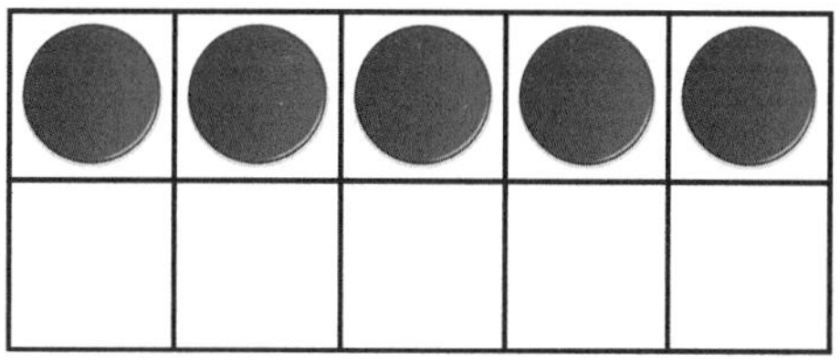

5 + ____ = 6

2

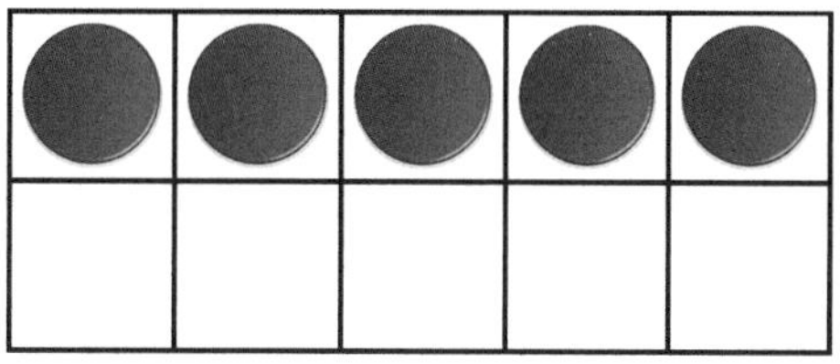

5 + ____ = 9

Directions: 1 and 2 Draw more counters to show how many in all. Use the ten frame to complete the addition sentence.

3

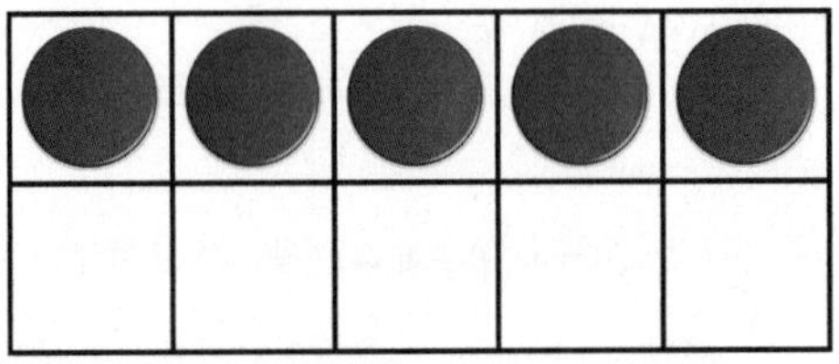

5 + ___ = 5

4

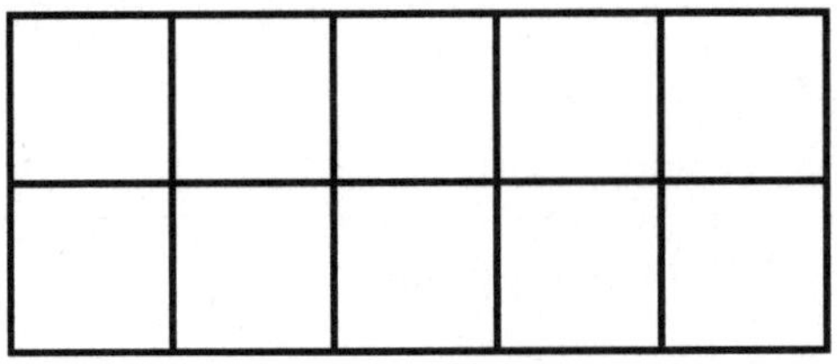

5 + ___ = 10

5

___ + ___ = ___

Directions: 3 Draw more counters to show how many in all. Use the ten frame to complete the addition sentence. 4 Draw 5 counters. Draw more counters to show how many in all. Use the ten frame to complete the addition sentence. 5 You are decorating your friend's cubby. You blow up 5 balloons. You need 7 balloons in all. Draw more balloons to make 7. Then write an addition sentence to match your picture.

Name ______________________

Learning Target: Find partner numbers for 10 and write an addition sentence.

Explore and Grow

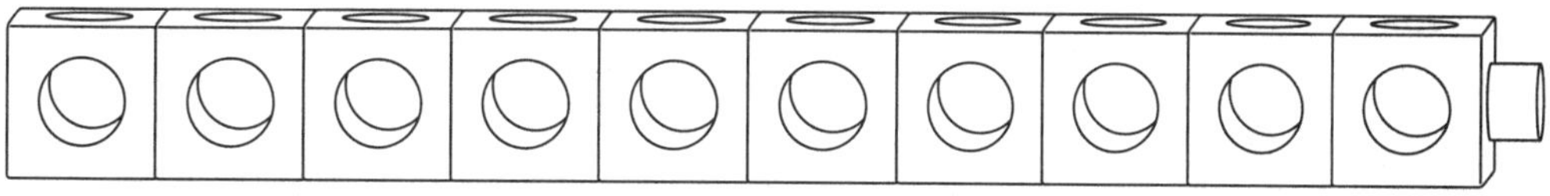

____ + ____ = 10

____ + ____ = 10

Directions: You have 10 linking cubes. Some are red and some are blue. Color to show how many are red and how many are blue. Then color to show another way. Complete the addition sentences to match your pictures.

Think and Grow

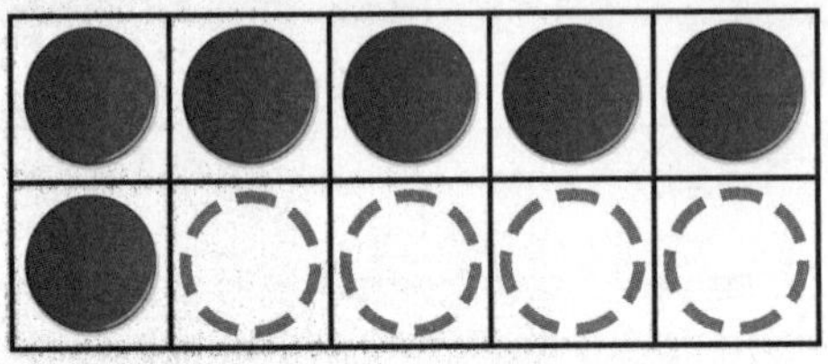

1	2	3	4	5	6	7	8	9	10

6 + 4 = 10

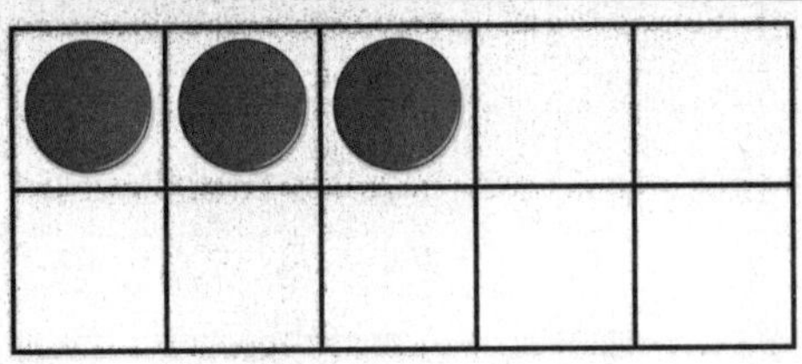

3 + ____ = 10

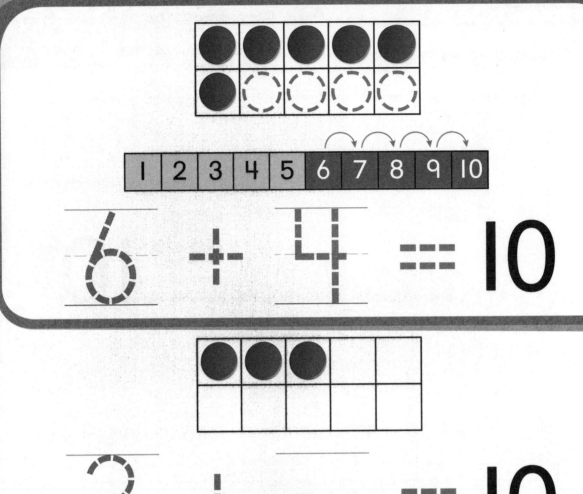

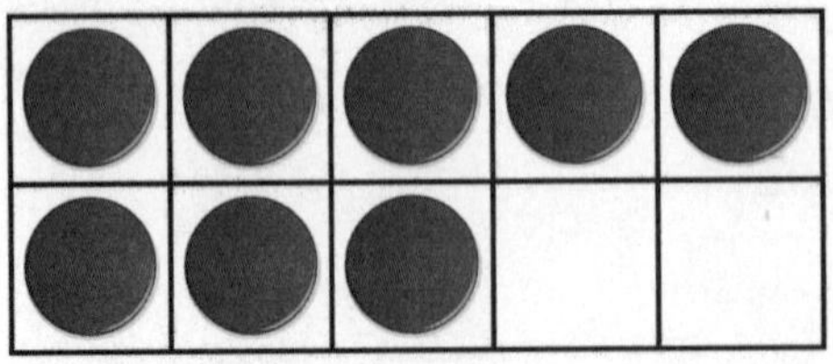

8 + ____ = 10

Directions: Draw more counters to make 10. Use the ten frame to complete the addition sentence.

Name ____________________

Apply and Grow: Practice

1

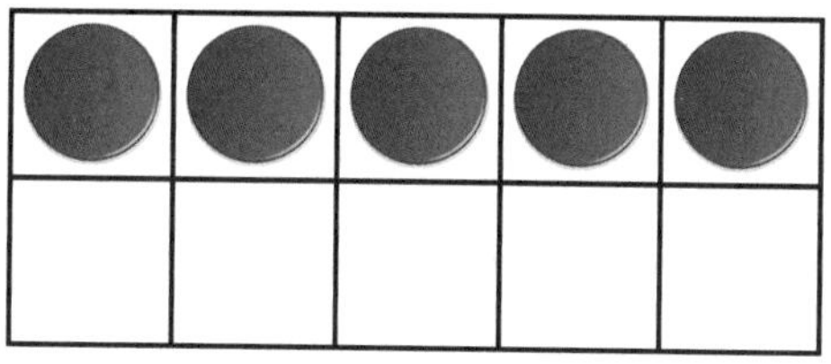

5 + ____ = 10

2

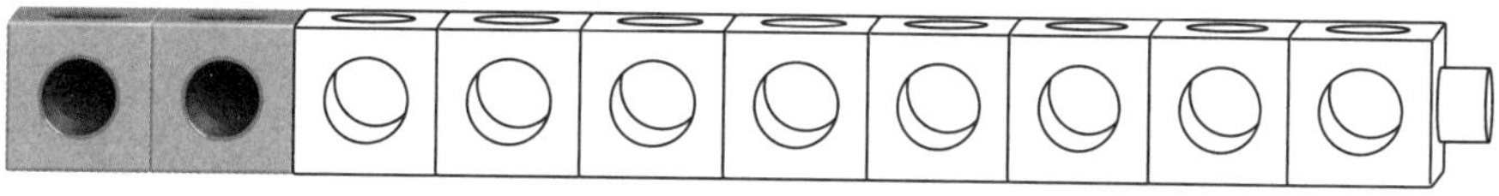

____ + ____ = 10

3

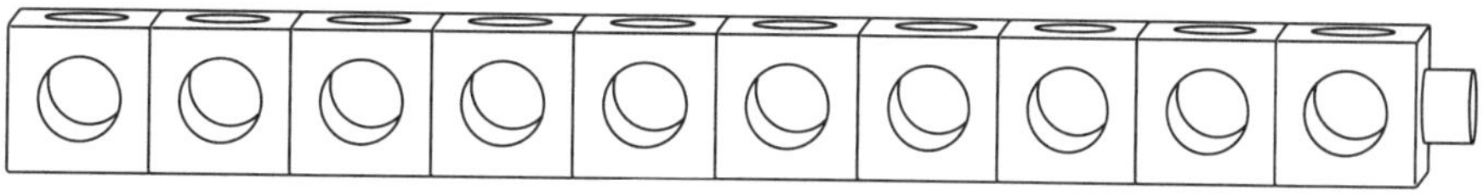

____ + ____ = 10

Directions: 1 Draw more counters to make 10. Use the ten frame to complete the addition sentence. 2 Color more linking cubes to make 10. Use the linking cubes to complete the addition sentence. 3 Color 4 linking cubes yellow. Color more linking cubes blue to make 10. Use the linking cubes to complete the addition sentence.

Think and Grow: Modeling Real Life

____ + ____ = ____

____ + ____ = ____

Directions: You need 10 tickets in all to win a prize.

- You win 1 ticket. Draw more tickets to make 10. Then write an addition sentence to match your picture.
- Your friend wins 3 tickets. Draw more tickets to make 10. Then write an addition sentence to match your picture.
- Who needs more tickets? Circle your answer.

Name ____________________

Practice 6.8

Learning Target: Find partner numbers for 10 and write an addition sentence.

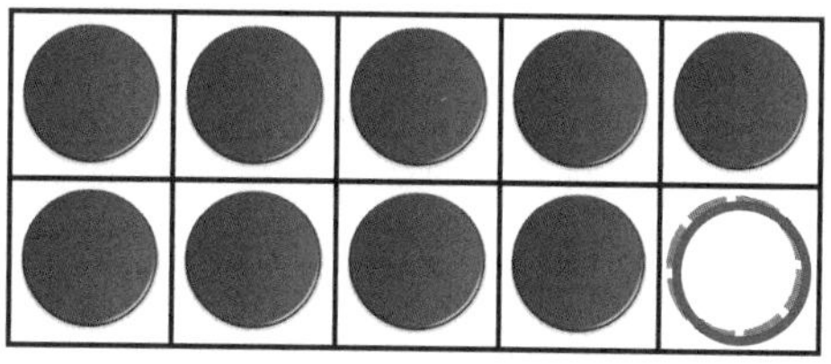

9 + 1 = 10

Directions: Draw more counters to make 10. Use the ten frame to complete the addition sentence.

1

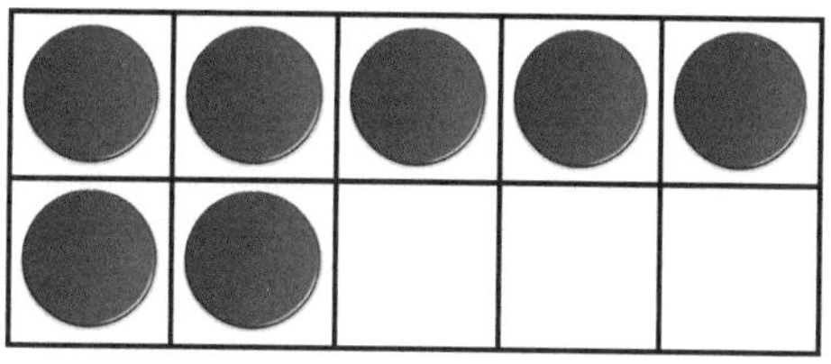

7 + ___ = 10

2

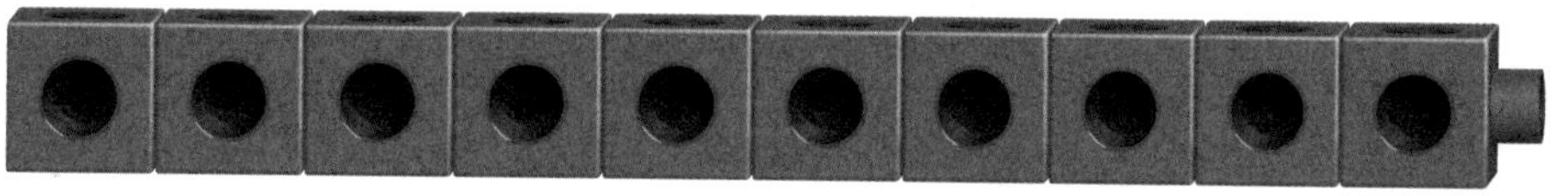

10 + ___ = 10

Directions: 1 Draw more counters to make 10. Use the ten frame to complete the addition sentence. 2 Color more linking cubes to make 10. Use the linking cubes to complete the addition sentence.

3

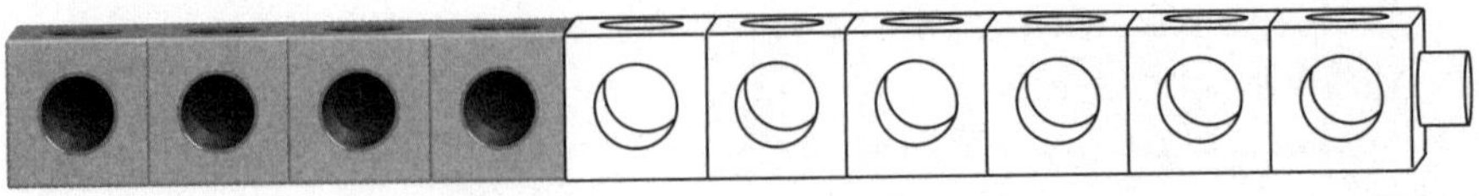

____ + ____ = 10

4

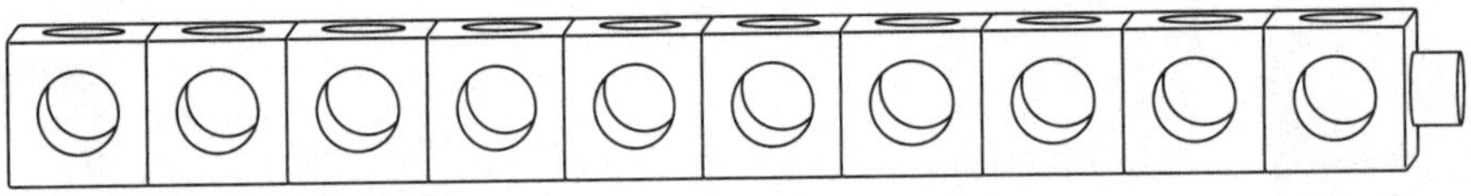

____ + ____ = 10

5

____ + ____ = ____

Directions: 3 Color more linking cubes to make 10. Use the linking cubes to complete the addition sentence. 4 Color 6 linking cubes yellow. Color more linking cubes blue to make 10. Use the linking cubes to complete the addition sentence. 5 You need 10 stickers in all to win a prize. You have 8 stickers. Draw more stickers to make 10. Write an addition sentence to match your picture.

Name ________________________________

Performance Task 6

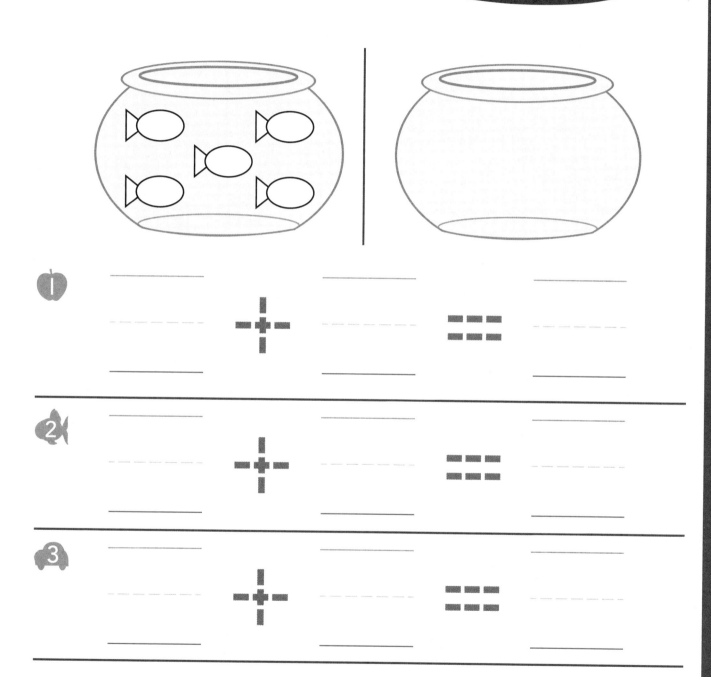

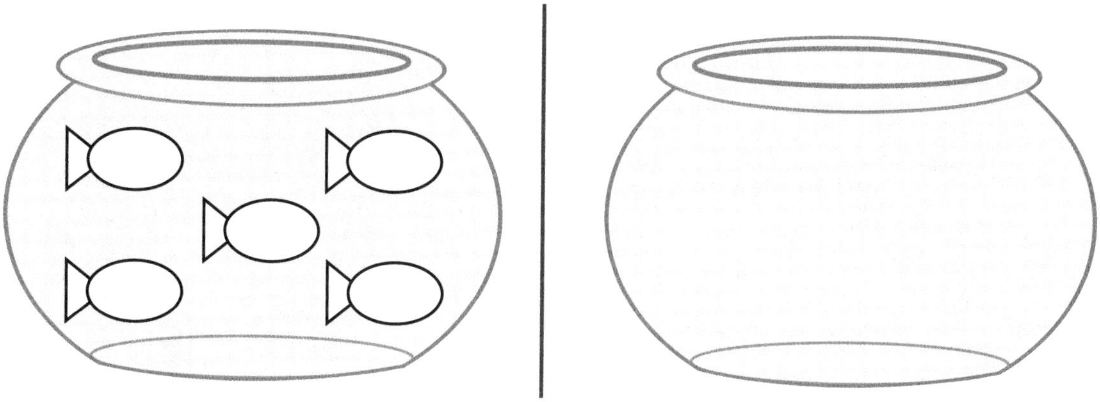

1 ______ + ______ = ______

2 ______ + ______ = ______

3 ______ + ______ = ______

Directions: 1 You buy more red fish than blue fish at a pet store. Color to show the fish that you buy. Then write an addition sentence to match your picture. 2 Your friend buys 5 fish. Draw and color your friend's fish to show fewer red fish than blue fish. Then write an addition sentence to match your picture. 3 You put food pellets into your fishbowl to feed *your* fish. The number of food pellets is equal to the number of fish. Draw the food pellets. Then write an addition sentence to tell how many objects are in your fishbowl in all.

Add and Cover

Directions: Start at Newton. Roll a die and move forward that number of spaces. Use the numbers on the space to find how many in all. Place a counter on a cloud with that number. If you land on a sun, cover a cloud of your choice. Repeat this process until you cover all of the clouds.

Name ____________________

Chapter Practice 6

6.1 Understand Addition

1

_____ and _____ is _____ in all.

6.2 Addition: Add To

2

_____ and _____ is _____.

_____ + _____ = _____

Directions: 1 Complete the sentence to tell how many students are in the group to start, how many join, and how many there are in all. 2 Complete the sentence to tell how many owls are in the group to start, how many join, and how many there are in all. Then complete the addition sentence to match.

6.3 Addition: Put Together

3

___ + ___ = ___

6.4 Addition: Partner Numbers

4

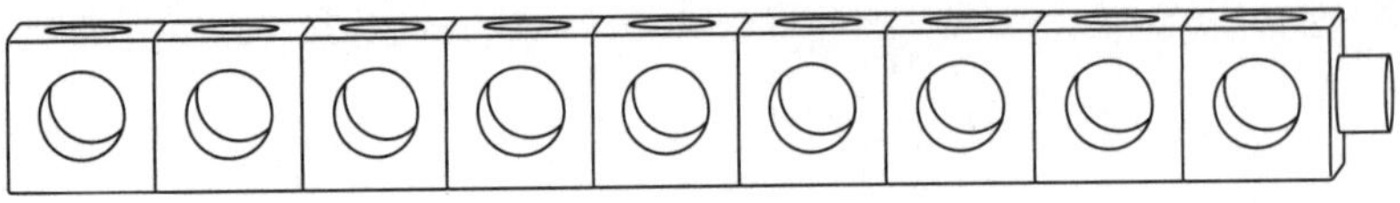

9 = ___ + ___

5

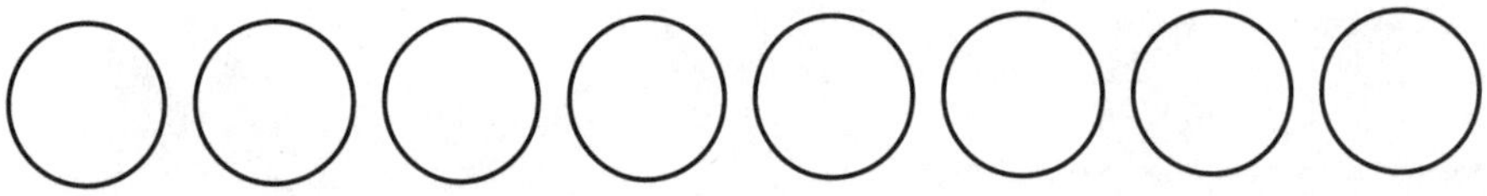

___ + ___ = 8

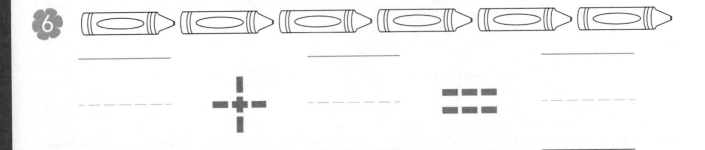

6

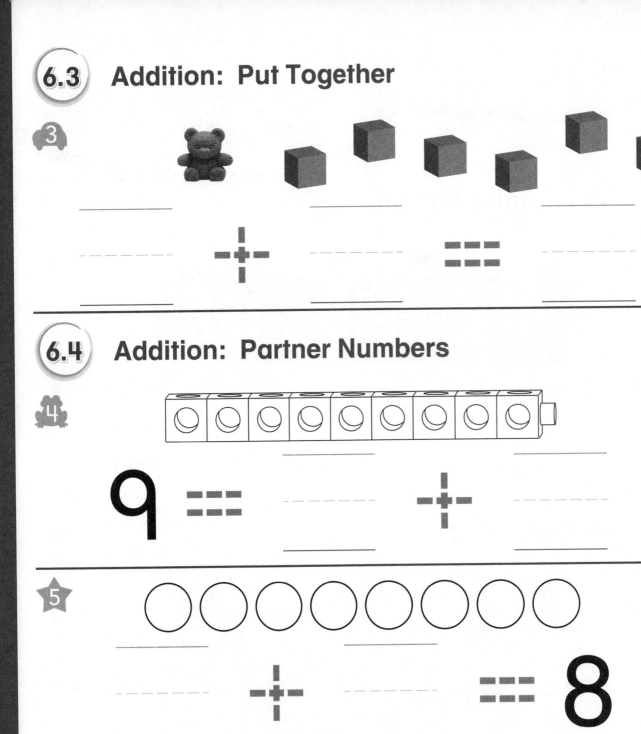

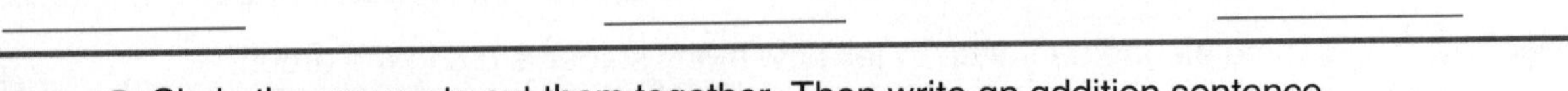

___ + ___ = ___

Directions: 3 Circle the groups to put them together. Then write an addition sentence to tell how many objects there are in all. 4–6 Use 2 colors to show partner numbers that make the whole. Then complete the addition sentence to match your picture.

6.5 Addition Number Patterns

7

___ + ___ = ___

8

8 + 0 = ___

6.6 Practice Addition

9

2 + 2 = ___

10

0 + 0 = ___

11

2 + 1 = ___

1 + 2 = ___

Directions: 7 Write an addition sentence to tell how many dots there are in all. Tell what you notice. 8 Complete the addition sentence. Tell what you notice. 9 and 10 Complete the addition sentence. Tell how you found your answer. 11 Complete the addition sentences. Tell what you notice.

6.7 Use a Group of 5 to Add

12

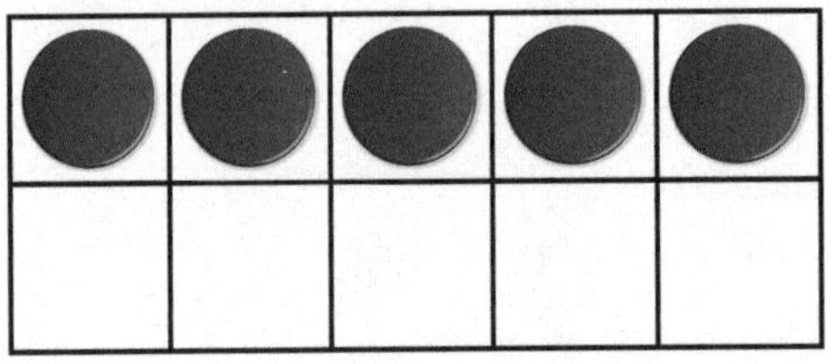

5 + ___ = 9

6.8 Add to Make 10

13

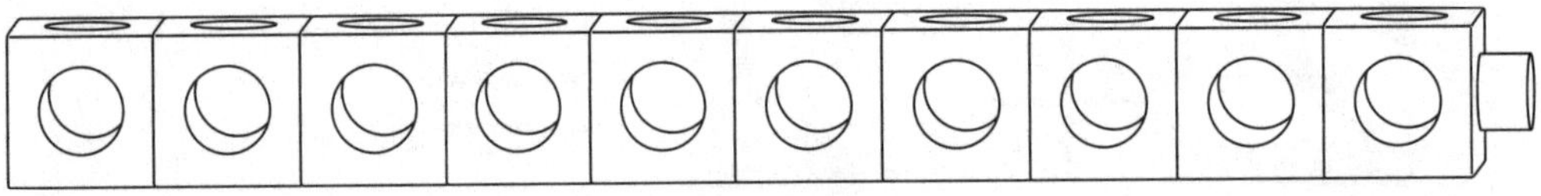

___ + ___ = 10

14

___ + ___ = ___

Directions: 12 Draw more counters to show how many in all. Use the ten frame to complete the addition sentence. 13 Color 3 linking cubes yellow. Color more linking cubes blue to make 10. Use the linking cubes to complete the addition sentence. 14 You need 10 tickets in all to win a prize. You win 2 tickets. Draw more tickets to make 10. Then write an addition sentence to match your picture.

7 Subtract Numbers within 10

- Where have you seen bubbles before?
- How many bubbles are in the picture? If 5 bubbles pop, how many bubbles will be left?

Chapter Learning Target:
Understand subtraction.

Chapter Success Criteria:
- I can identify a number sentence.
- I can describe how objects can be taken away.
- I can write a subtraction sentence.
- I can explain subtraction sentences.

Name ______________________________

7 Vocabulary

Review Words
parts
whole
number bond

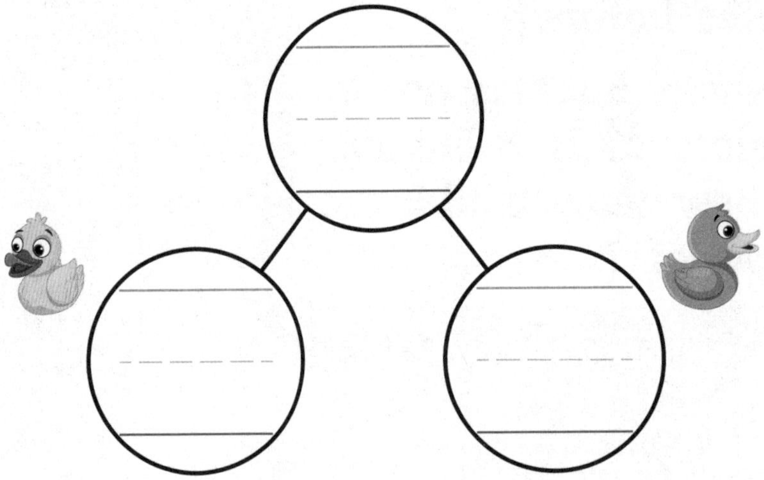

Directions: Name the parts and the whole for the group. Then complete the number bond.

Chapter 7 Vocabulary Cards

left

minus sign

separate

subtract

subtraction sentence

take away

$3 - 2 = 1$

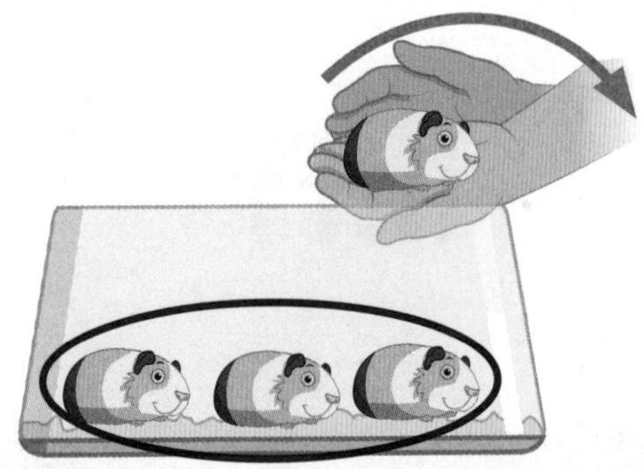

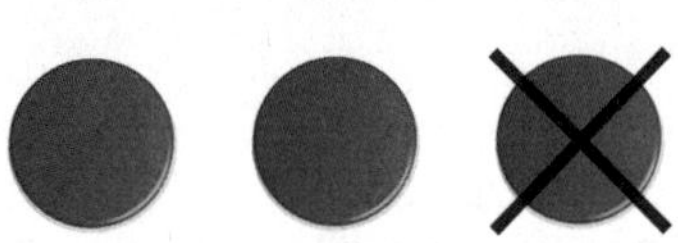

$3 - 1 = 2$

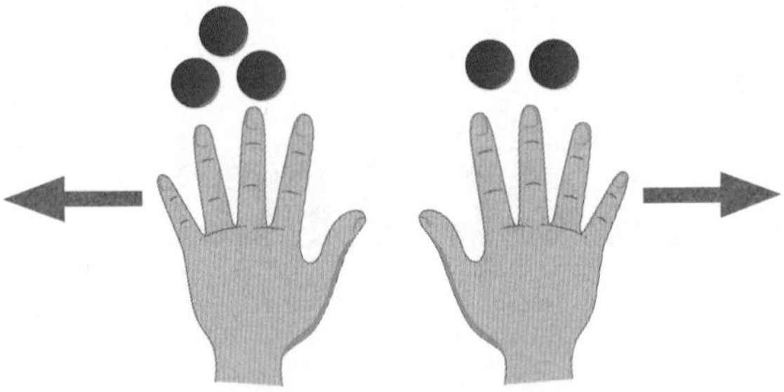

$4 - 1 = 3$

Name ______________________

Learning Target: Subtract a group of objects and tell how many are left.

Explore and Grow

_____ take away _____

Directions: Use counters to act out the story.
- There are 4 students in the school. Write the number.
- 3 students leave the school. Write the number.
- Tell how many students are left in the school.

Think and Grow

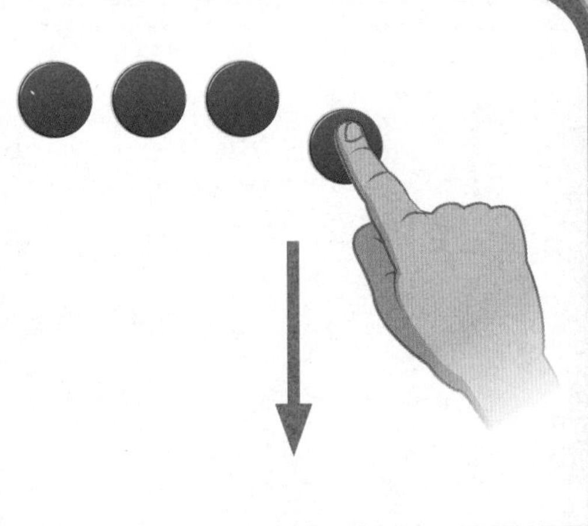

4 take away 1 is 3.

5 take away ______ is ______.

Directions: Complete the sentence to tell how many students there are in all, how many are leaving, and how many are left.

Name ________________

Apply and Grow: Practice

1

6 take away ______ is ______.

2

______ take away ______ is ______.

3

______ take away ______ is ______.

Directions: 1 – 3 Complete the sentence to tell how many students there are in all, how many are leaving, and how many are left.

Think and Grow: Modeling Real Life

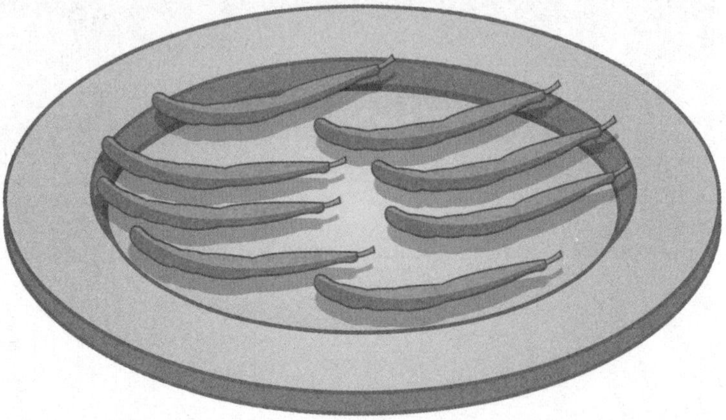

______ take away ______ is ______ .

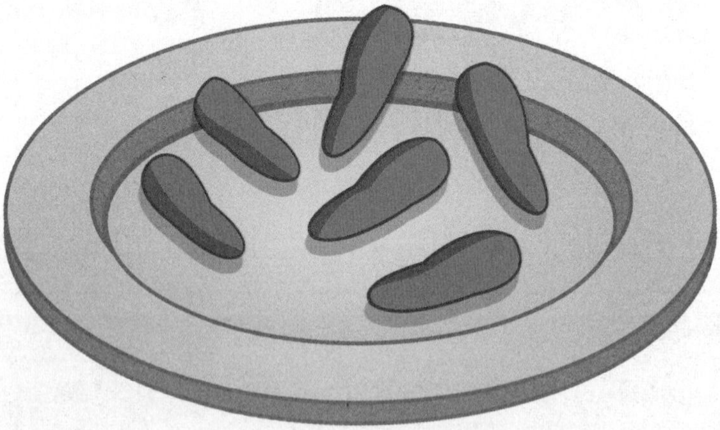

______ take away ______ is ______ .

Directions:

- You have 8 green beans on your plate. You eat 6 of them. Cross out the green beans you eat. Then complete the sentence to match your picture.
- You have 6 carrots on your plate. You eat some of them. Cross out the carrots you eat. Then complete the sentence to match your picture.

Name ____________________

Practice 7.1

Learning Target: Subtract a group of objects and tell how many are left.

5 take away 2 is 3.

Directions: Complete the sentence to tell how many students there are in all, how many are leaving, and how many are left.

1

3 take away ____ is ____.

2

____ take away ____ is ____.

Directions: 1 and 2 Complete the sentence to tell how many students there are in all, how many are leaving, and how many are left.

3

_______ take away _______ is _______.

4

_______ take away _______ is _______.

5

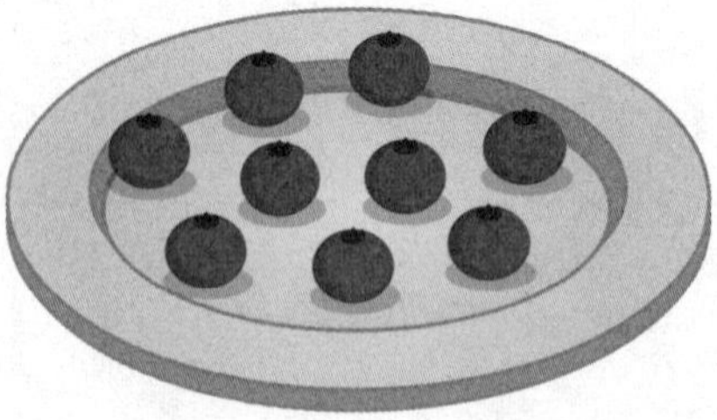

_______ take away _______ is _______.

Directions: 3 and 4 Complete the sentence to tell how many students there are in all, how many are leaving, and how many are left. 5 You have 9 blueberries on your plate. You eat some of them. Cross out the blueberries you eat. Then complete the sentence to tell how many blueberries there are in all, how many you eat, and how many are left.

Name ______________________________

Learning Target: Take from a group of objects and write a subtraction sentence.

Explore and Grow

_______ _______

_______ — _______

_______ _______

Directions: Use counters to act out the story.

- There are 5 birds in the cage. Write the number.
- 3 of the birds fly away. Write the number.
- Tell how many birds are left in the cage.

Think and Grow

3 take away 2 is 1.

$3 - 2 = 1$

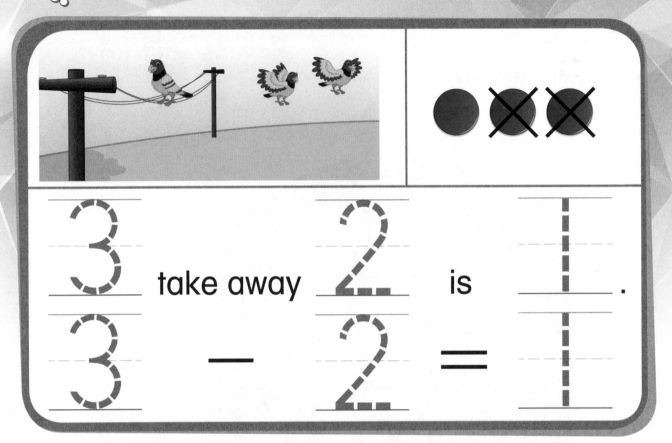

_____ take away _____ is _____.

_____ $-$ _____ $=$ _____

Directions: Complete the sentence to tell how many animals there are in all, how many are leaving, and how many are left. Then complete the subtraction sentence to match.

Name ______________________________

Apply and Grow: Practice

1

_____ take away _____ is _____.

_____ − _____ = _____

2

_____ − _____ = _____

3

_____ − _____ = _____

Directions: 1 Complete the sentence to tell how many deer there are in all, how many are leaving, and how many are left. Then complete the subtraction sentence to match. 2 and 3 Complete the subtraction sentence to tell how many animals are left.

Think and Grow: Modeling Real Life

_____ − _____ = _____

Directions: Some of the bats in a cave fly away. Cross out the bats that fly away. Then complete the subtraction sentence to tell how many are left.

Name ______________________

Practice 7.2

Learning Target: Take from a group of objects and write a subtraction sentence.

4 take away 3 is 1.

4 − 3 = 1

Directions: Complete the sentence to tell how many cheetahs there are in all, how many are leaving, and how many are left. Then complete the subtraction sentence to match.

1

______ take away ______ is ______.

______ − ______ = ______

Directions: 1 Complete the sentence to tell how many panthers there are in all, how many are leaving, and how many are left. Then complete the subtraction sentence to match.

2

___ − ___ = ___

3

___ − ___ = ___

4

___ − ___ = ___

Directions: 2 and 3 Complete the subtraction sentence to tell how many animals are left. 4 Some of the wolves leave the group. Cross out the wolves that leave. Then complete the subtraction sentence to tell how many wolves are left.

Name ______________________

Subtraction: Take Apart 7.3

Learning Target: Take apart a group of objects and write a subtraction sentence.

Explore and Grow

Directions: There are 7 apples in the tree. Some are red and some are yellow. Use counters to show the apples in the tree. Write the number above the tree. Take apart the group of apples by placing the red apples in one group and the yellow apples in another group. Write the numbers.

Think and Grow

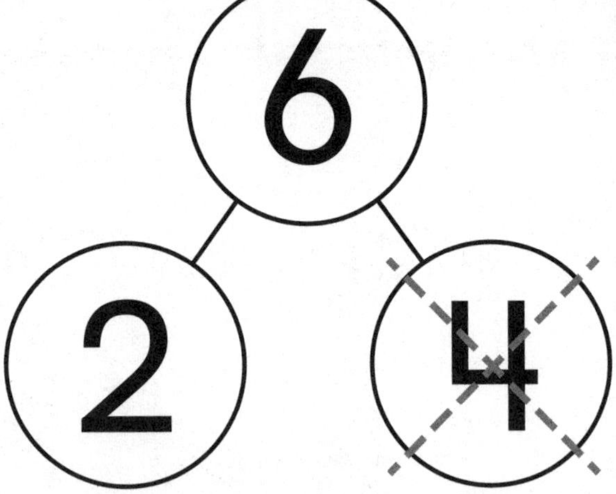

$6 - 4 = 2$

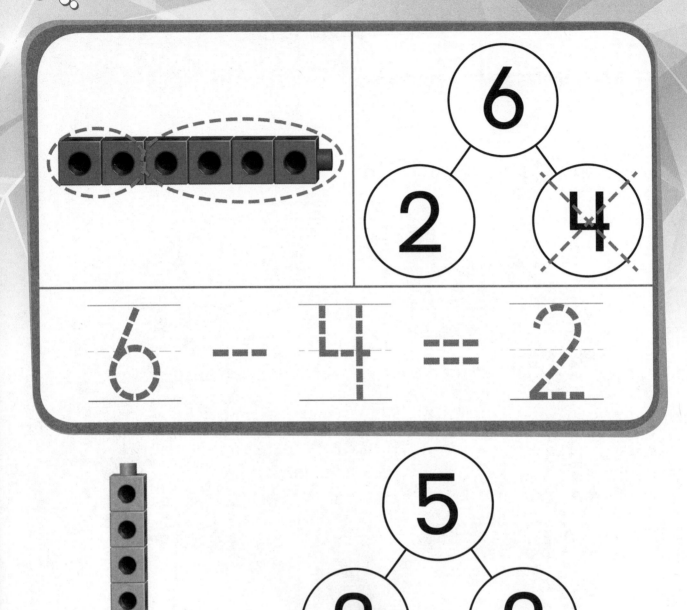

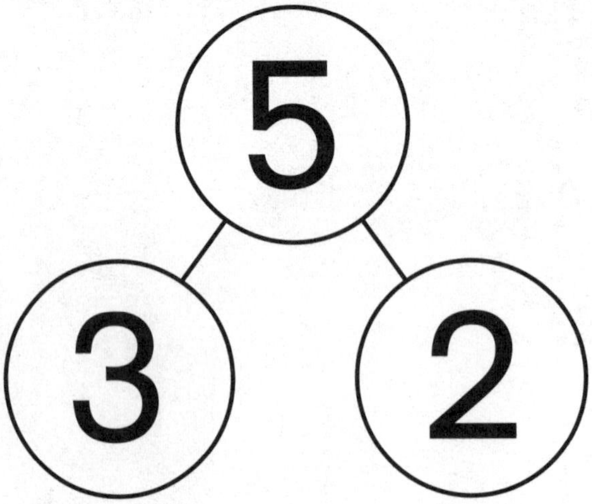

____ − ____ = ____

Directions: Circle the linking cubes to show the parts in the number bond. Then write a subtraction sentence by taking one of the parts from the whole. Cross out the part on the number bond that you take away.

Name

Apply and Grow: Practice

1

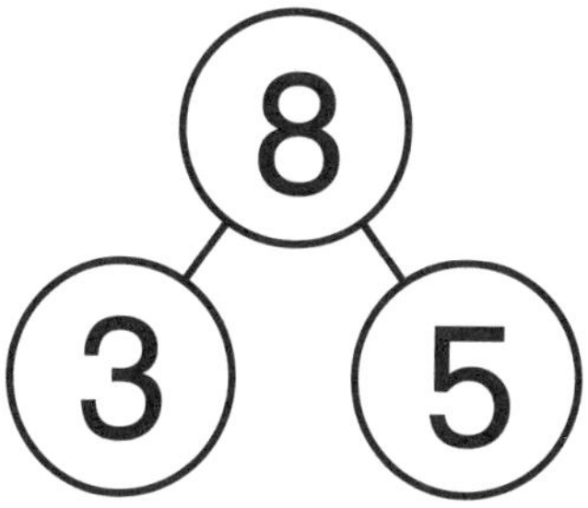

2

Directions: 1 Circle the linking cubes to show the parts in the number bond. Then write a subtraction sentence by taking one of the parts from the whole. Cross out the part on the number bond that you take away. 2 Take apart the linking cubes. Circle the parts. Write a subtraction sentence by taking one of the parts from the whole. Then write another subtraction sentence by taking the other part from the whole.

Think and Grow: Modeling Real Life

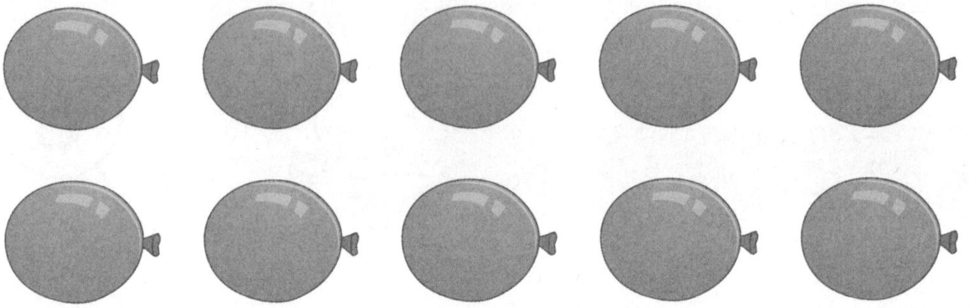

____ − ____ = ____

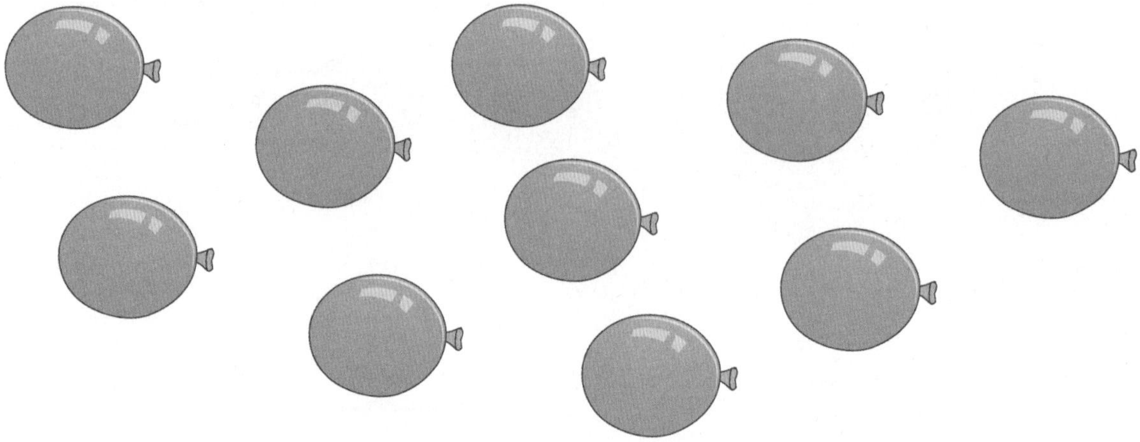

____ − ____ = ____

Directions: You have 10 balloons. You want to share some with your friend.

- Put the balloons into 2 groups. Circle the groups. Then cross out the group you give to your friend. Write a subtraction sentence to match your picture. Circle the number that shows how many balloons you have left.
- Show another way you can share the balloons. Then write a subtraction sentence to match your picture. Circle the number that shows how many balloons you have left.

Name ______________________

Learning Target: Take apart a group of objects and write a subtraction sentence.

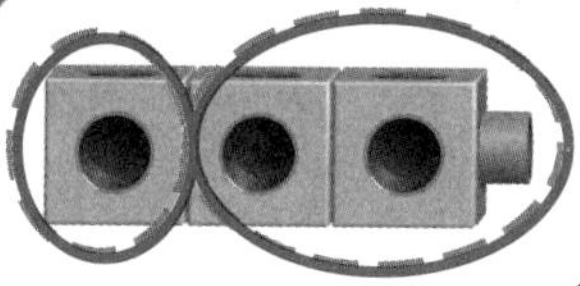

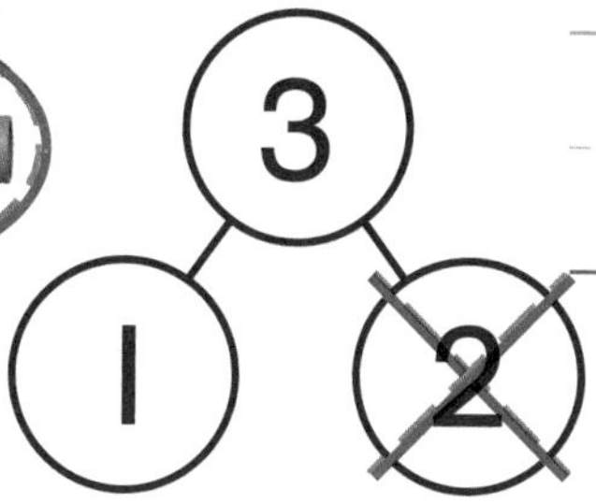

3 − 2 = 1

Directions: Circle the linking cubes to show the parts in the number bond. Then write a subtraction sentence by taking one of the parts from the whole. Cross out the part on the number bond that you take away.

1

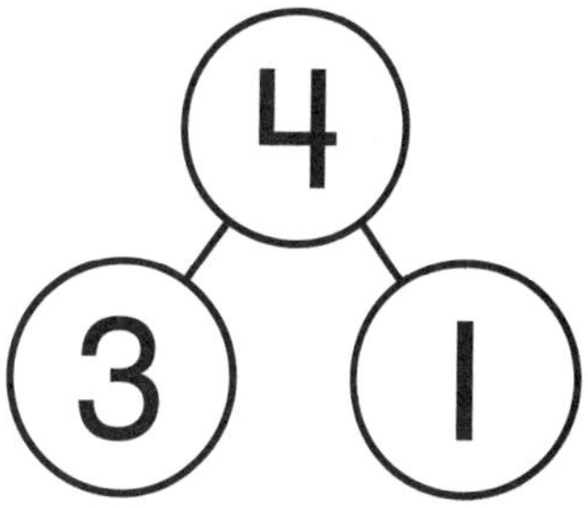

_____ − _____ = _____

2

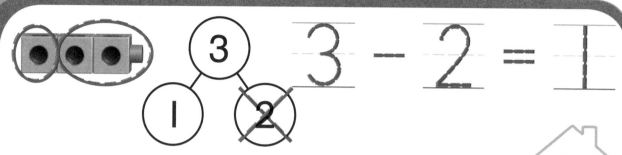

_____ − _____ = _____

Directions: 1 Circle the linking cubes to show the parts in the number bond. Then write a subtraction sentence by taking one of the parts from the whole. Cross out the part on the number bond that you take away. 2 Take apart the linking cubes. Circle the parts. Then write a subtraction sentence by taking one of the parts from the whole.

3

4

Directions: 3 Take apart the linking cubes. Circle the parts. Write a subtraction sentence by taking one of the parts from the whole. Then write another subtraction sentence by taking the other part from the whole. 4 You pick 8 flowers. You want to give some to your friend. Put the flowers into 2 groups. Circle the groups. Then cross out the group you give to your friend. Write a subtraction sentence to match your picture. Circle the number that shows how many flowers you have left.

Name ____________________

Learning Target: Find and explain subtraction patterns.

Explore and Grow

$3 - 0 =$

$2 - 0 =$

$1 - 0 =$

$3 - 1 =$

$2 - 1 =$

$1 - 1 =$

Directions: Shade the boxes to show how many there are to start. Cross out the shaded boxes to show how many are being taken away. Tell how many are left.

Think and Grow

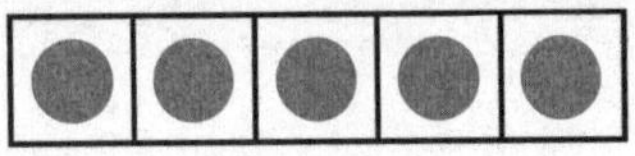

$5 - 0 = 5$

$5 - 5 = 0$

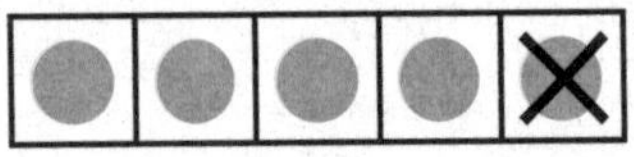

$5 - 1 = 4$

$4 - \_\_\_ = \_\_\_$

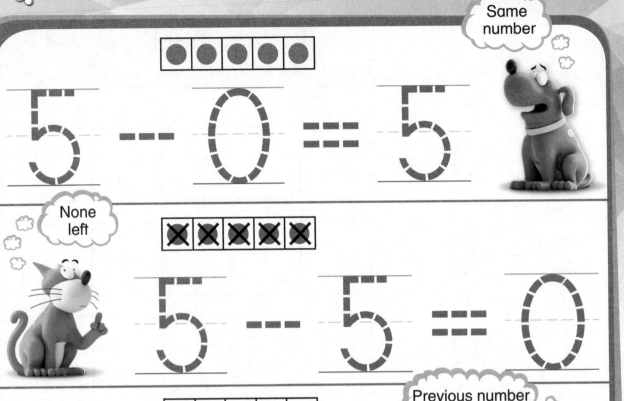

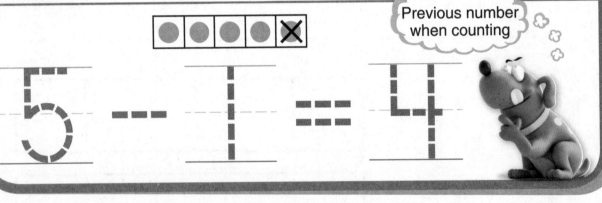

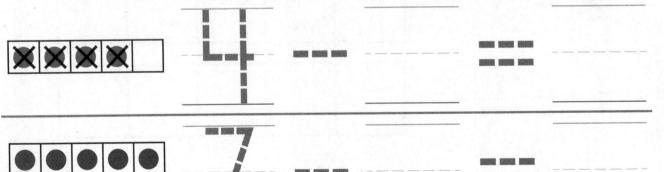

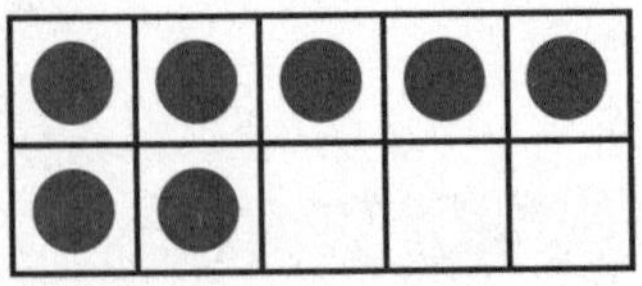

$7 - \_\_\_ = \_\_\_$

Directions: Complete the subtraction sentence to tell how many dots are left. Tell what you notice.

Name ______________________________

Apply and Grow: Practice

1
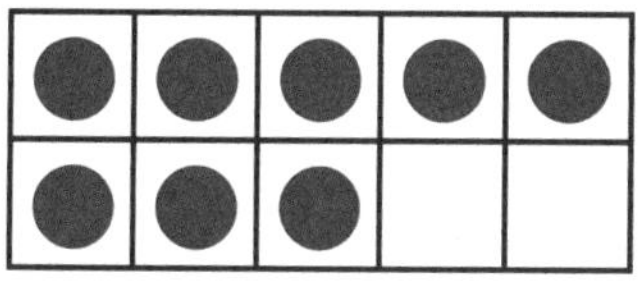
8 − ___ = ___

2

8 − ___ = ___

3
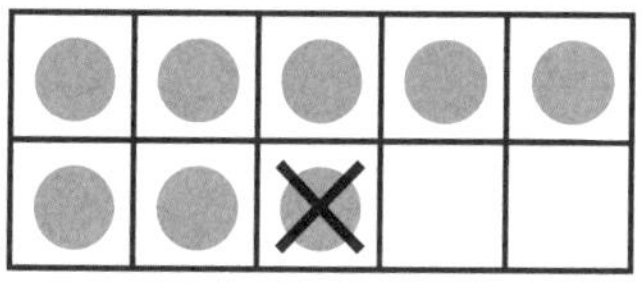
8 − ___ = ___

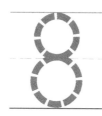

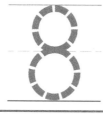

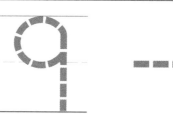

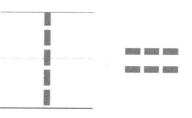

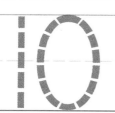

4 6 − 6 = ___

5 9 − 1 = ___

6 10 − 0 = ___

Directions: 1–3 Complete the subtraction sentence to tell how many dots are left. Tell what you notice. 4–6 Complete the subtraction sentence. Tell what you notice.

Think and Grow: Modeling Real Life

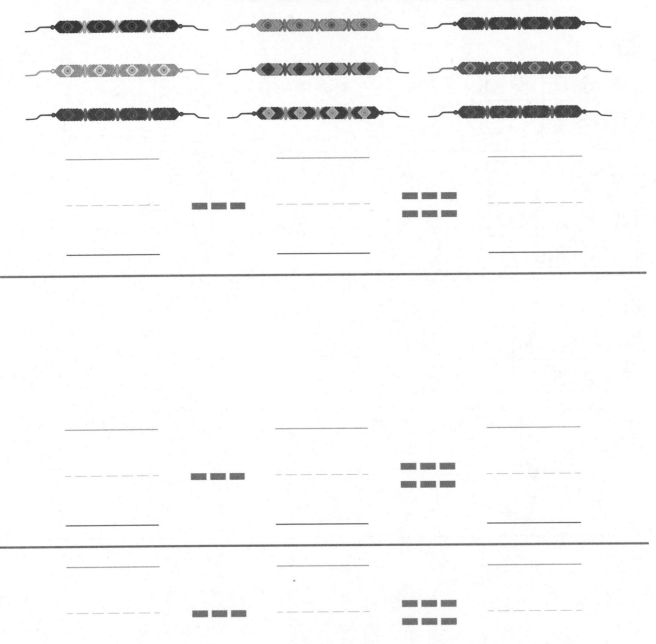

Directions:

- You make 9 bracelets. You give all of them away. Cross out the bracelets you give away. Then write a subtraction sentence to tell how many bracelets you have left.
- Your friend makes 6 bracelets. She does not give away any of her bracelets. Draw and color your friend's bracelets. Then write a subtraction sentence to tell how many bracelets she has left.
- Your friend gives you a bracelet. Write a subtraction sentence to tell how many bracelets she has left now.

Name ________________________

Practice 7.4

Learning Target: Find and explain subtraction patterns.

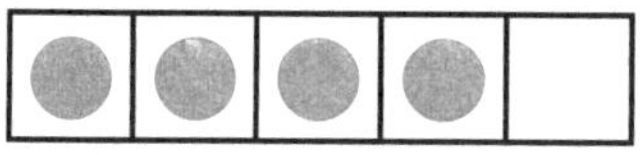

4 − 0 = 4 same number

4 − 4 = 0 none left

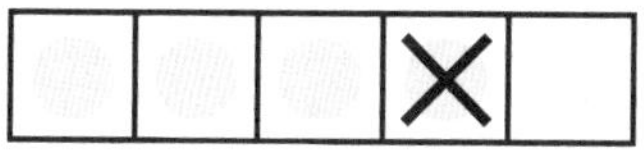

4 − 1 = 3 previous number when counting

Directions: Complete the subtraction sentence to tell how many dots are left. Tell what you notice.

1

3 − ____ = ____

2

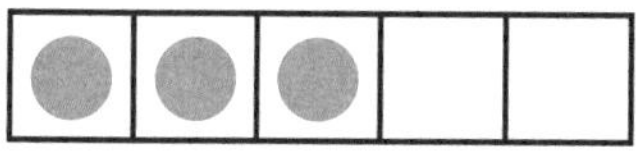

3 − ____ = ____

3

3 − ____ = ____

Directions: 1–3 Complete the subtraction sentence to tell how many dots are left. Tell what you notice.

4 10 − 10 = ___

5 7 − 1 = ___

6 9 − 0 = ___

7

___ − ___ = ___

___ − ___ = ___

Directions: 4–6 Complete the subtraction sentence. Tell what you notice.
7 Your friend makes 10 cards. She does not give away any of her cards. Draw and color your friend's cards. Then write a subtraction sentence to tell how many cards she has left. Your friend gives you a card. Write a subtraction sentence to tell how many cards she has left now.

Name ______________________

Practice Subtraction 7.5

Learning Target: Subtract within 5.

Explore and Grow

$2 - 1 =$ ____

$3 - 2 =$ ____

$4 - 4 =$ ____

Directions: Use counters in the five frame to show how many there are to start. Show how many counters are being taken away. Tell and write how many are left.

Think and Grow

$5 - 2 = ?$

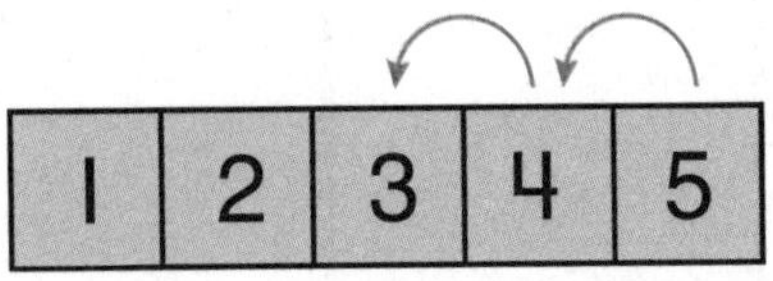

$5 - 2 = 3$

$3 - 1 =$ ____

$4 - 3 =$ ____

$5 - 4 =$ ____

Directions: Complete the subtraction sentence. Tell how you found your answer.

Name ______________________________

Apply and Grow: Practice

1

$2 - 2 =$ ____

2

$5 - 0 =$ ____

3

$4 - 2 =$ ____

4

$5 - 3 =$ ____

5

$4 - 1$ $2 - 1$ $3 - 0$

Directions: 1 – 4 Complete the subtraction sentence. Tell how you found your answer. 5 Circle all of the subtraction problems that equal 3.

Think and Grow: Modeling Real Life

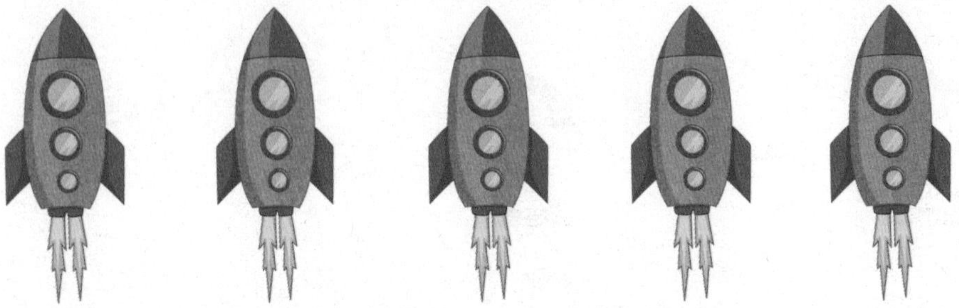

_____ − _____ = _____

_____ − _____ = _____

Directions: You are playing a video game.

- You have 5 spaceships. Some of them are captured. Cross out the spaceships that are captured. Then write a subtraction sentence to tell how many spaceships you have left.
- You need to capture 5 aliens to win. You capture some aliens. Cross out the aliens that you capture. Then write a subtraction sentence to tell how many aliens you still need to capture.

Name ____________________

Learning Target: Subtract within 5.

$$5 - 1 = 4$$

1	2	3	4	5

Directions: Complete the subtraction sentence. Tell how you found your answer.

1. $5 - 5 =$ ____

2. $4 - 0 =$ ____

3. $5 - 2 =$ ____

Directions: 1–3 Complete the subtraction sentence. Tell how you found your answer.

4

$4 - 3 =$ ____

5

$3 - 1 =$ ____

6

$1 - 1$ $4 - 2$ $5 - 3$

7

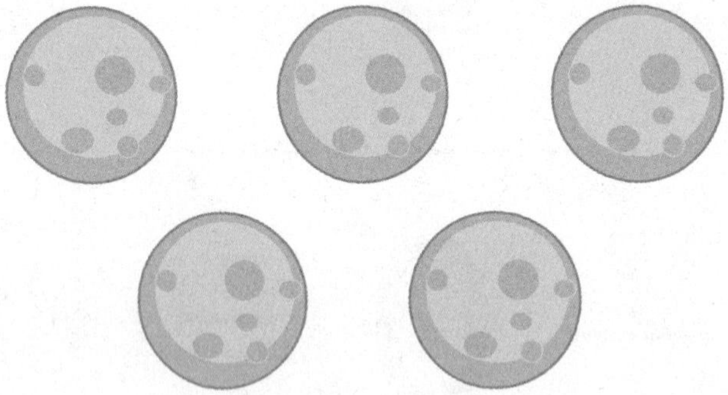

____ $-$ ____ $=$ ____

Directions: 4 and 5 Complete the subtraction sentence. Tell how you found your answer. 6 Circle all of the subtraction problems that equal 2. 7 You are playing a video game. You need to visit 5 moons. You visit some moons. Cross out the moons you visit. Then write a subtraction sentence to tell how many moons you have left to visit.

Name ______________________

Use a Group of 5 to Subtract 7.6

Learning Target: Use a group of 5 to write a subtraction sentence.

Explore and Grow

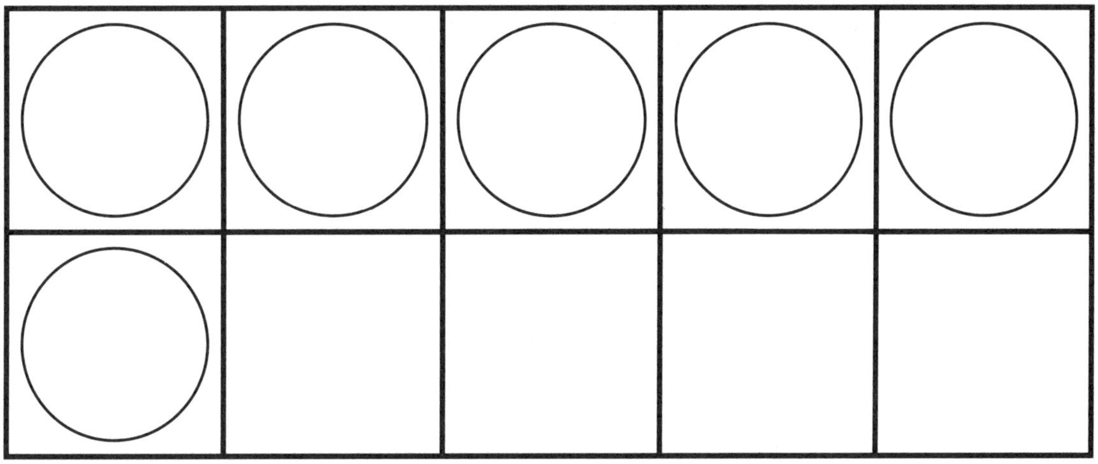

6 − 5 = ____

Directions: Color the counters to show how many there are in all. Cross out counters to take away 5. Complete the subtraction sentence.

Think and Grow

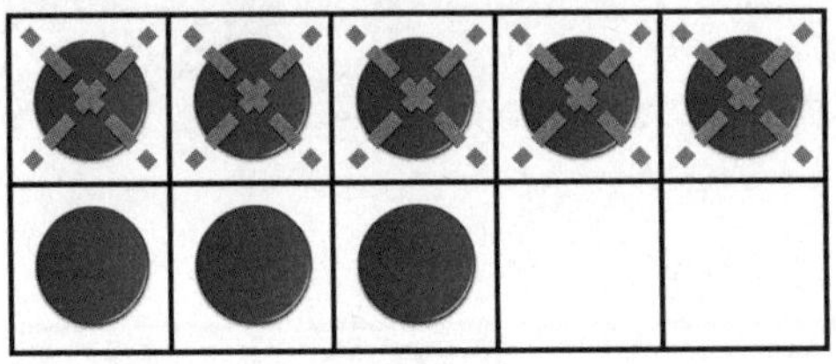

8 − 5 = 3

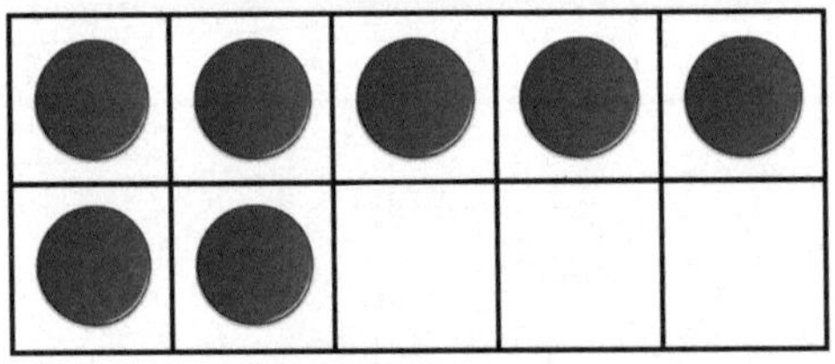

7 − 5 = ____

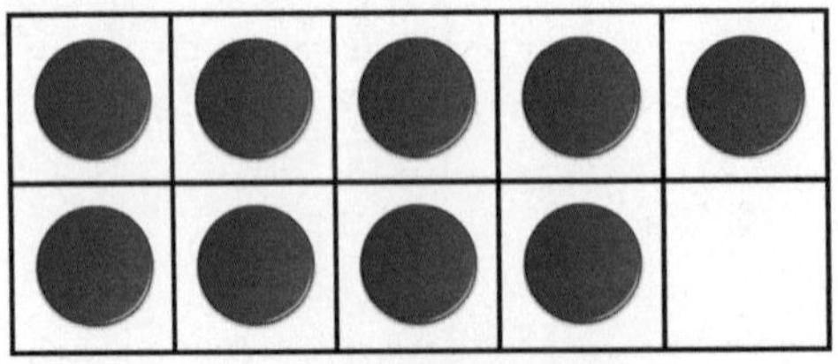

9 − 5 = ____

Directions: Cross out 5 counters to show how many to take away. Use the ten frame to complete the subtraction sentence.

Name ______________________________

Apply and Grow: Practice

1

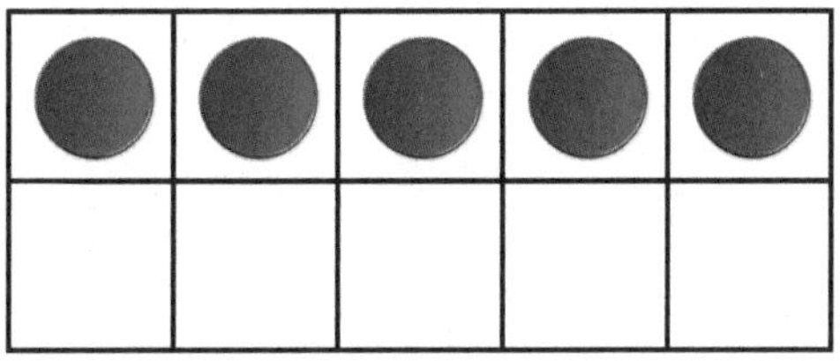

5 − 5 = ______

2

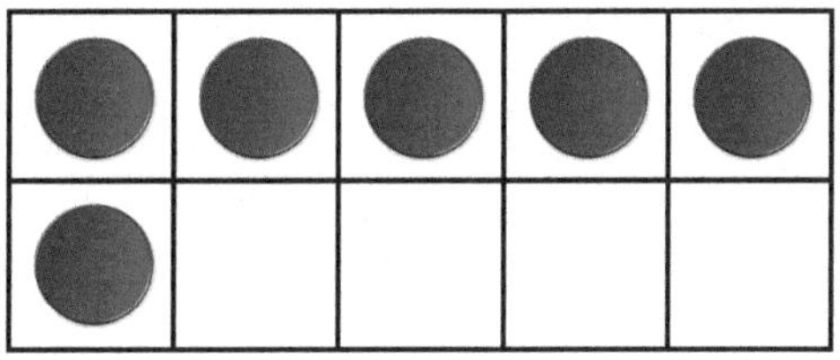

6 − 5 = ______

3

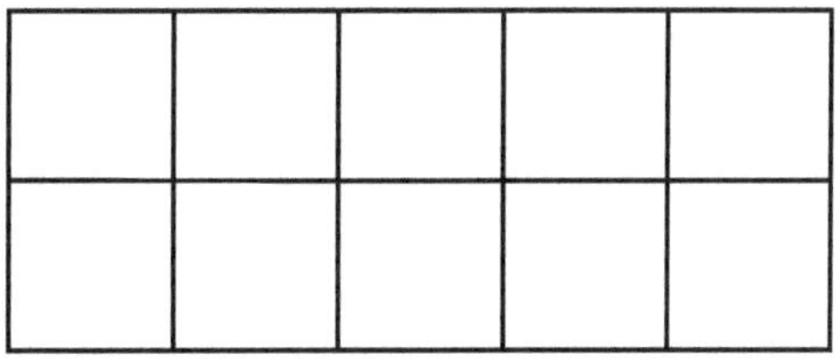

10 − 5 = ______

Directions: 1 and 2 Cross out 5 counters to show how many to take away. Use the ten frame to complete the subtraction sentence. 3 Draw 10 counters. Cross out 5 counters to show how many to take away. Use the ten frame to complete the subtraction sentence.

Think and Grow: Modeling Real Life

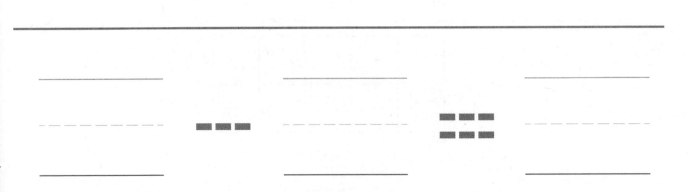

______ − ______ = ______

______ − ______ = ______

Directions: You have 2 rolls to knock down 10 bowling pins.

- On your first roll, you knock down 5 pins. Cross out the pins you knock down. Then write a subtraction sentence to match your picture. How many pins do you need to knock down on your second roll? Circle the answer.
- On your second roll, you knock down the pins that are left. Write a subtraction sentence to show how many pins you have left now.

Name ______________________

Practice 7.6

Learning Target: Use a group of 5 to write a subtraction sentence.

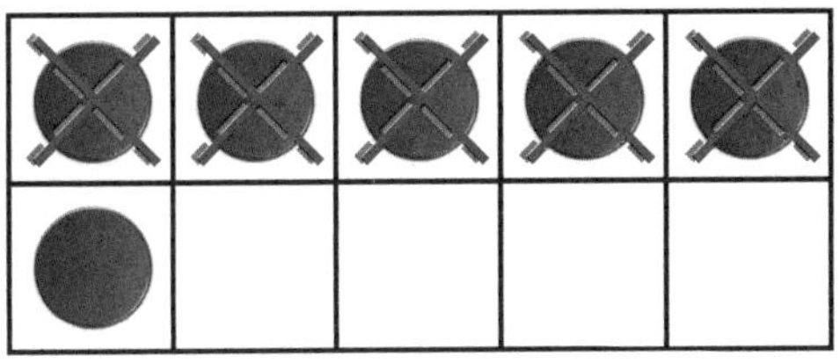

6 − 5 = 1

Directions: Cross out 5 counters to show how many to take away. Use the ten frame to complete the subtraction sentence.

1

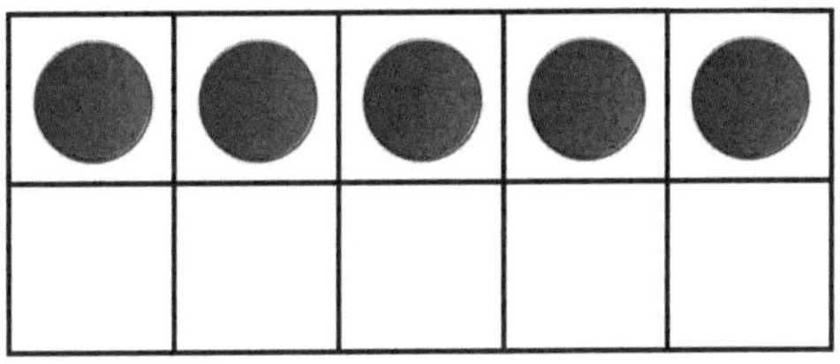

5 − 5 = ____

2

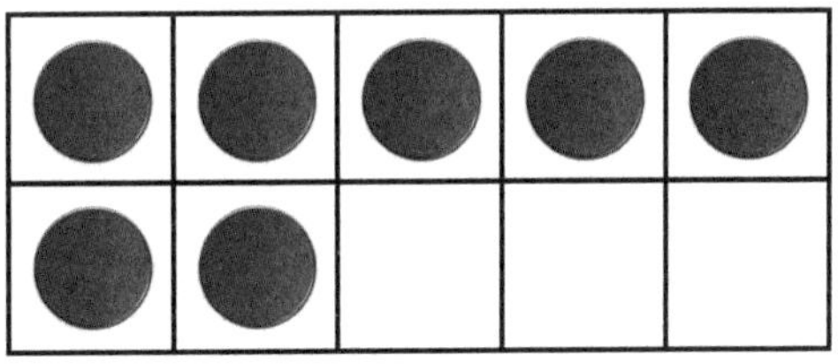

7 − 5 = ____

Directions: 1 and 2 Cross out 5 counters to show how many to take away. Use the ten frame to complete the subtraction sentence.

3

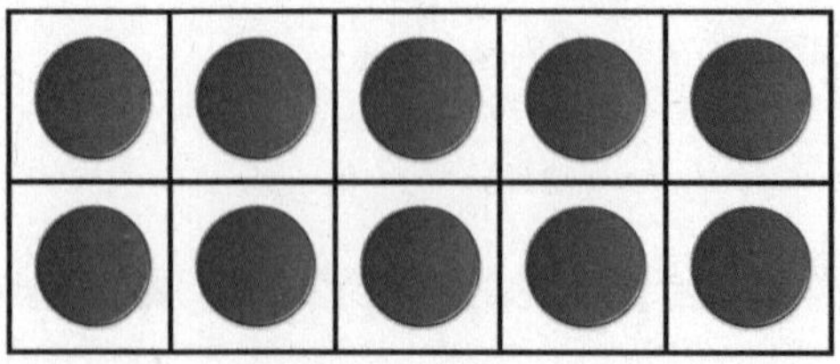

10 − 5 = ____

4

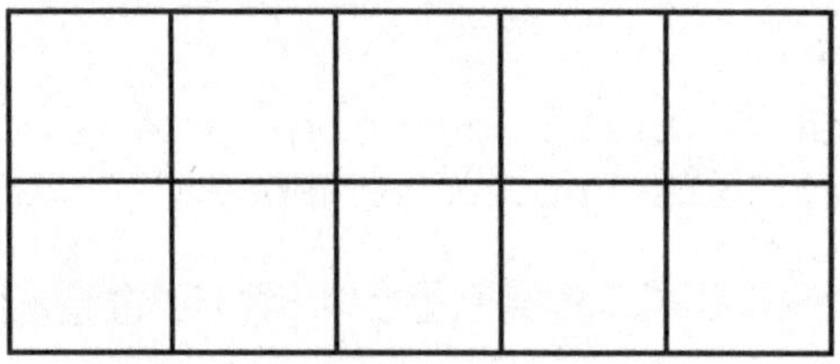

8 − 5 = ____

5

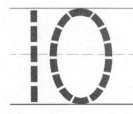

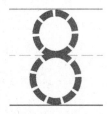

____ − ____ = ____

Directions: 3 Cross out 5 counters to show how many to take away. Use the ten frame to complete the subtraction sentence. 4 Draw 8 counters. Cross out 5 counters to show how many to take away. Use the ten frame to complete the subtraction sentence. 5 You have 2 throws to knock down 9 bottles. On your first throw, you knock down 5 bottles. Cross out the bottles you knock down. Then write a subtraction sentence to match your picture. How many more bottles do you need to knock down? Circle the answer.

Name ____________________

Related Facts 7.7

Learning Target: Use related facts to add or subtract within 5.

Explore and Grow

____ + ____ = ____

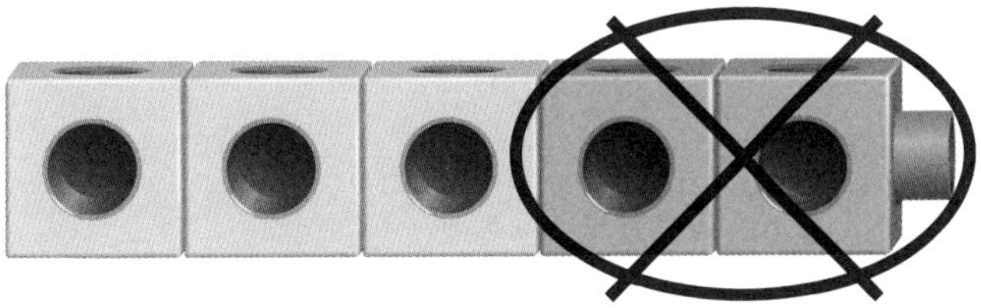

____ − ____ = ____

Directions:

- You have 3 yellow linking cubes and 2 green linking cubes. How many linking cubes do you have in all? Write an addition sentence to match the picture.
- You have 5 linking cubes. You give your friend 2 linking cubes. How many linking cubes do you have left? Write a subtraction sentence to match the picture.

Think and Grow

3 + 1 = 4

4 − 1 = 3

____ ◯ ____ = ____

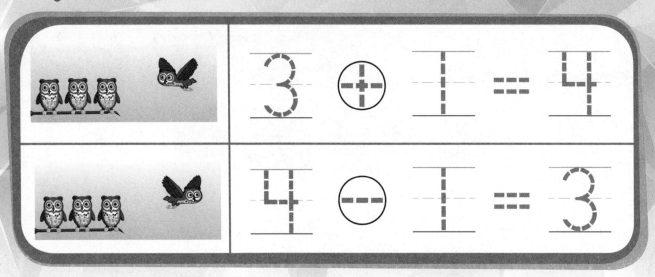

____ ◯ ____ = ____

Directions: Tell whether the pictures show addition or subtraction. Then write addition and subtraction sentences to show the related facts.

Name ______________________

Apply and Grow: Practice

1

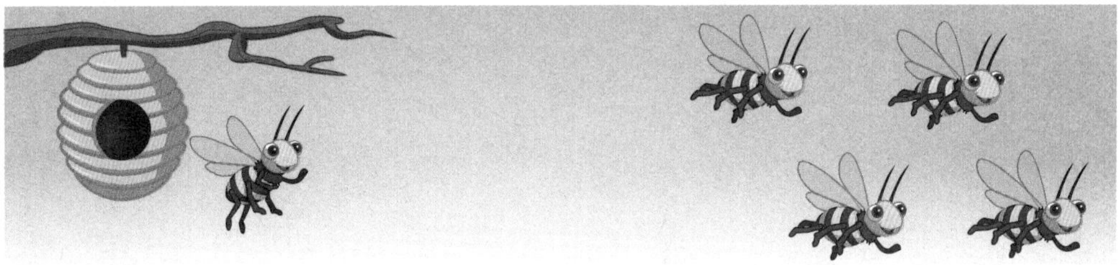

____ ◯ ____ = ____

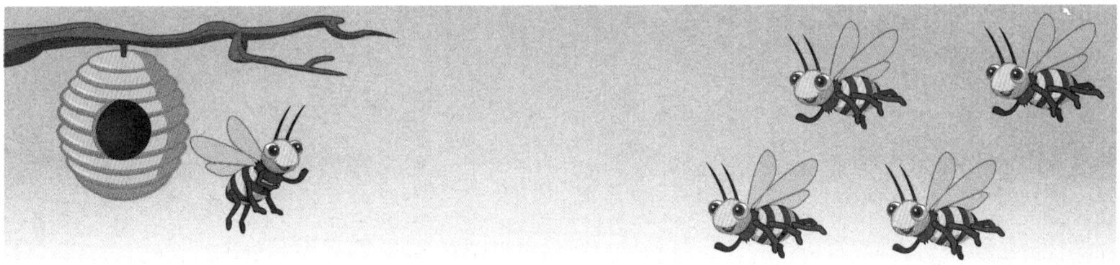

____ ◯ ____ = ____

2

$2 + 1 = 3$	$5 + 3 = 8$
$3 - 1 = 2$	$5 - 3 = 2$

3

$5 + 2 = 7$	$3 + 1 = 4$
$5 - 2 = 3$	$4 - 1 = 3$

Directions: 1 Tell whether the pictures show addition or subtraction. Then write addition and subtraction sentences to show the related facts. 2 and 3 Circle the addition and subtraction sentences that show related facts. Tell how you know.

Think and Grow: Modeling Real Life

Directions:

- A zoo has 5 lizards. Some are green and some are brown. Color the lizards. Then write an addition sentence to match your picture.
- Write a subtraction sentence that shows the related fact. Tell a story to match your subtraction sentence.

Name ______________________________

Practice 7.7

Learning Target: Use related facts to add or subtract within 5.

$1 + 2 = 3$

$3 - 2 = 1$

Directions: Tell whether the pictures show addition or subtraction. Then write addition and subtraction sentences to show the related facts.

1

____ ◯ ____ = ____

____ ◯ ____ = ____

Directions: 1 Tell whether the pictures show addition or subtraction. Then write addition and subtraction sentences to show the related facts.

2

3 + 2 = 5   1 + 3 = 4

3 − 2 = 1   4 − 3 = 1

3

1 + 2 = 3   6 + 2 = 8

3 − 2 = 1   6 − 2 = 4

4

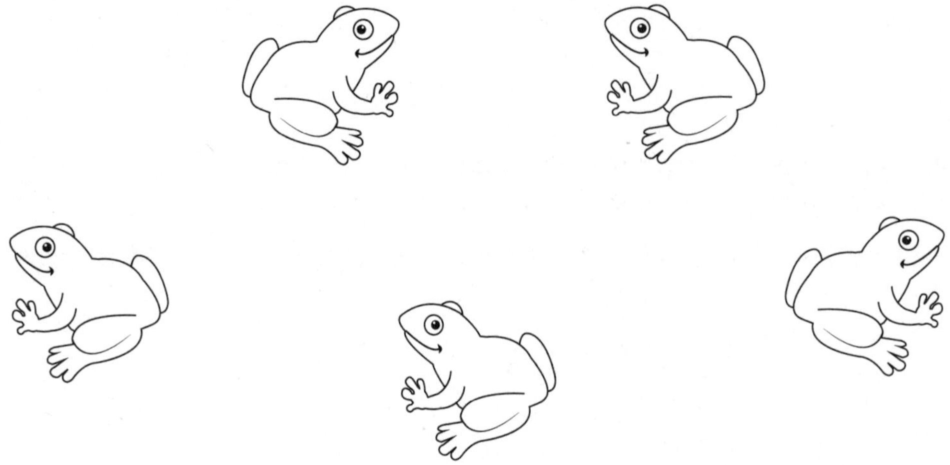

____ ◯ ____ = ____

____ ◯ ____ = ____

Directions: 2 and 3 Circle the group of addition and subtraction sentences that shows related facts. Tell how you know. 4 A tank at a pet store has 5 tree frogs. Some are blue and some are red. Color the frogs. Then write an addition sentence to match your picture. Write a subtraction sentence that shows the related fact. Tell a story to match your subtraction sentence.

Name ______________________

Performance Task 7

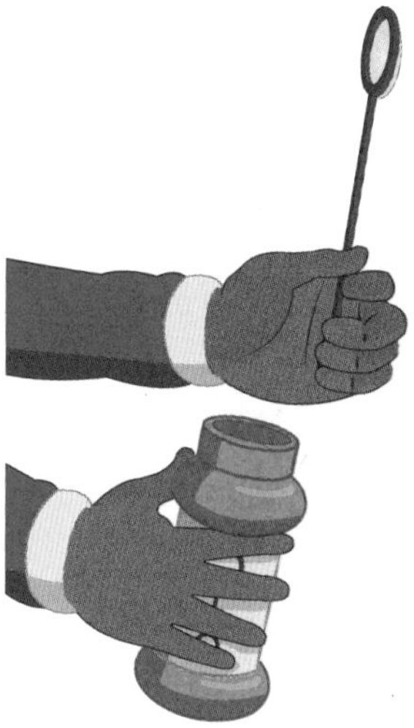

1 ____ − ____ = ____

2 ____ − ____ = ____

3 ____ − ____ = ____

Directions: 1 You blow 9 bubbles in the air. There are more big bubbles than small bubbles. Draw the bubbles. Then write a subtraction sentence to tell how many small bubbles are in the air. 2 Some of the bubbles pop. Cross out the bubbles that pop. Then write a subtraction sentence to tell how many bubbles are left. 3 All of the remaining bubbles pop. Write a subtraction sentence to tell how many bubbles are left now.

Losing Teeth

Directions: Spin the blue spinner. Put that many counters on the ten frame. Spin the red spinner. Take away that many counters from the ten frame. Tell how many counters are left. Complete the subtraction sentence on your Subtraction Recording Sheet. Repeat this process until you fill your sheet.

Name ______________________________

Chapter Practice 7

7.1 Understand Subtraction

1

______ take away ______ is ______.

7.2 Subtraction: Take From

2

______ take away ______ is ______.

______ − ______ = ______

Directions: 1 Complete the sentence to tell how many students there are in all, how many are leaving, and how many are left. 2 Complete the sentence to tell how many lions there are in all, how many are leaving, and how many are left. Then complete the subtraction sentence to match.

7.3 Subtraction: Take Apart

3

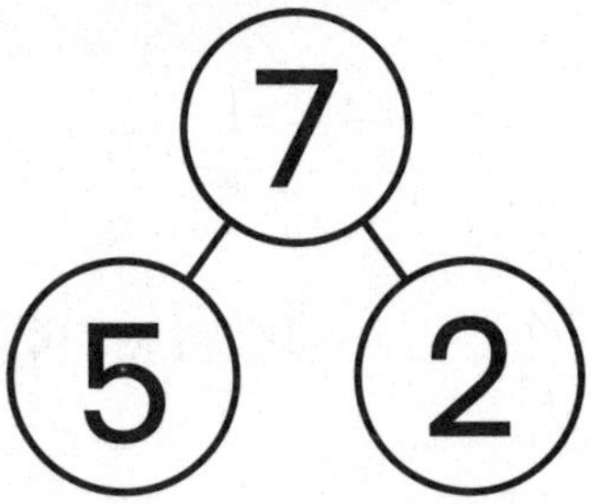

___ − ___ = ___

4

___ − ___ = ___

7.4 Subtraction Number Patterns

5

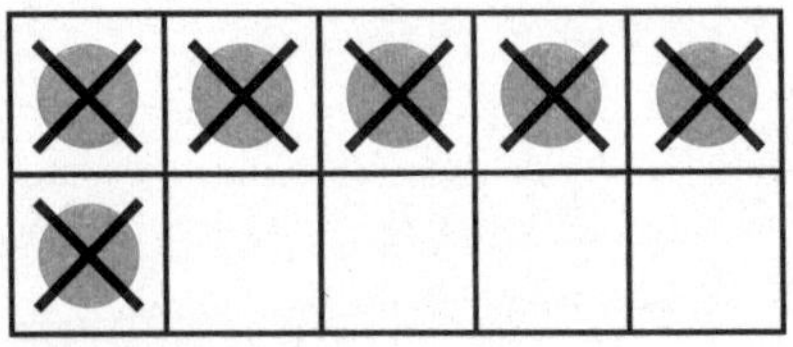

6 − ___ = ___

Directions: 3 Circle the linking cubes to show the parts in the number bond. Then write a subtraction sentence by taking one of the parts from the whole. Cross out the part on the number bond that you take away. 4 You have 9 toys. You want to give some to your friend. Put the toys into 2 groups. Circle the groups. Then cross out the group you give to your friend. Write a subtraction sentence to match your picture. Circle the number that shows how many toys you have left. 5 Complete the subtraction sentence to tell how many dots are left. Tell what you notice.

6 $3 - 0 =$ ____

7 $8 - 1 =$ ____

7.5 Practice Subtraction

8

$3 - 1 =$ ____

9

$4 - 2 =$ ____

10

$4 - 0$ $5 - 1$ $2 - 2$

Directions: 6 and 7 Complete the subtraction sentence. Tell what you notice. 8 and 9 Complete the subtraction sentence. Tell how you found your answer. 10 Circle all of the subtraction problems that equal 4.

7.6 Use a Group of 5 to Subtract

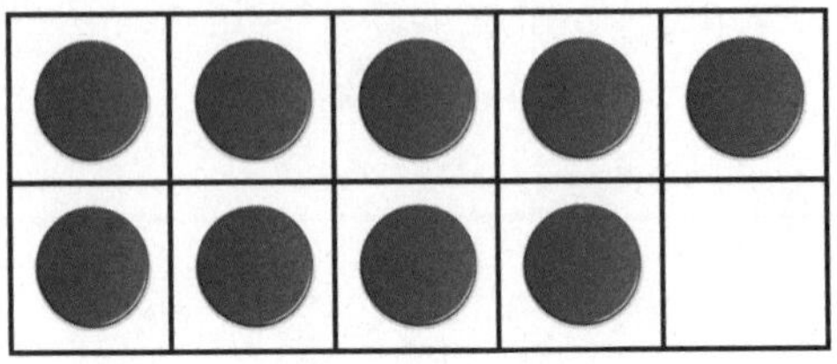

9 − 5 = ____

7.7 Related Facts

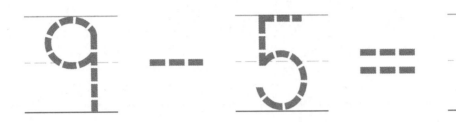

____ ◯ ____ = ____

____ ◯ ____ = ____

Directions: 11 Cross out 5 counters to show how many to take away. Use the ten frame to complete the subtraction sentence. 12 An aquarium has 5 starfish. Some are orange and some are purple. Color the starfish. Then write an addition sentence to match your picture. Write a subtraction sentence that shows the related fact. Tell a story to match your subtraction sentence.

Name ____________________

Cumulative Practice 1–7

1

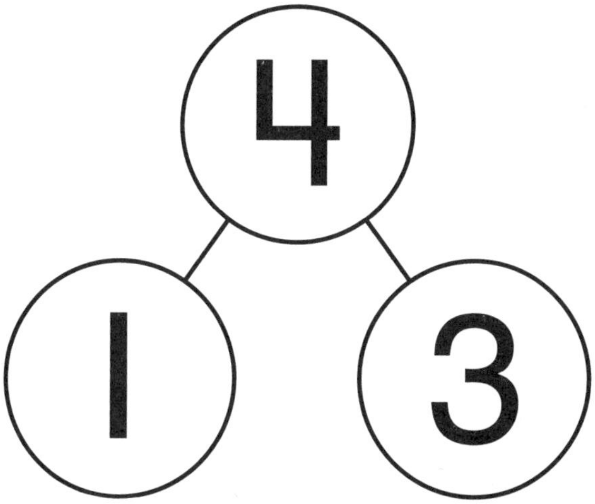

2

3

○ 0 and 5 ○ 4 and 1

○ 2 and 2 ○ 2 and 3

Directions: Shade the circle next to the answer. 1 Which group of animals matches the number bond? 2 Which animal is shown 2 times? 3 Which partner numbers do *not* make 5?

4

○ 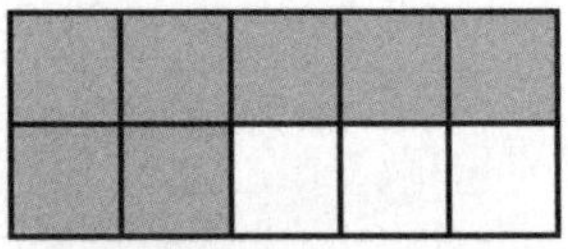

○ 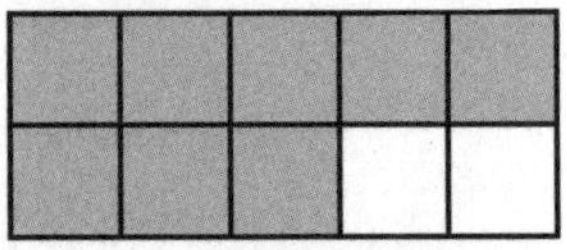

○ 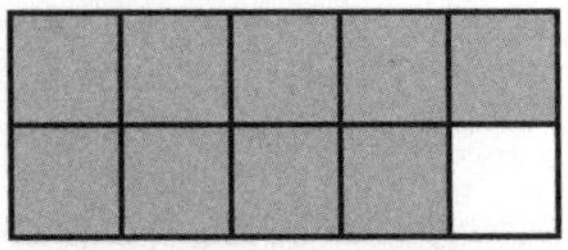

○ 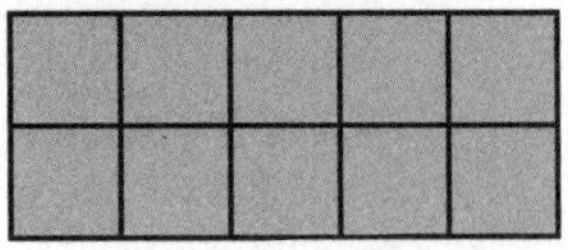

5

○ 5 and 4 is 9 in all.

○ 6 and 4 is 10 in all.

○ 5 and 3 is 8 in all.

○ 6 and 3 is 9 in all.

6

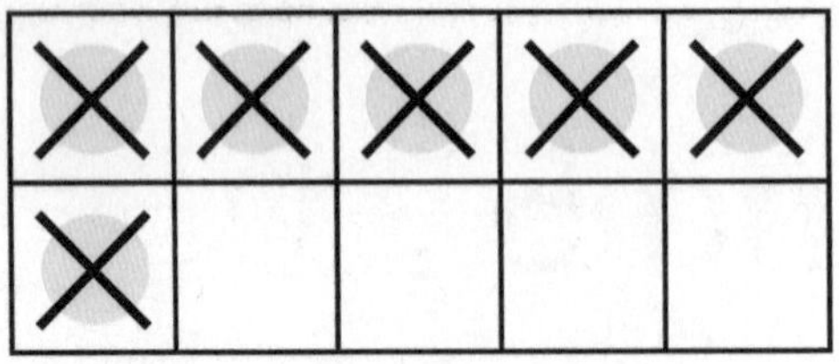

○ $6 - 0 = 6$ ○ $6 - 6 = 0$ ○ $6 - 1 = 5$

Directions: Shade the circle next to the answer. 4 Which ten frame shows the number of camels? 5 Which sentence tells how many students are in the group to start, how many join, and how many there are in all? 6 Which subtraction sentence tells how many dots are left?

7

$5 - 2 = 3$ 

$3 - 1 = 2$ 

$5 - 1 = 4$ 

8

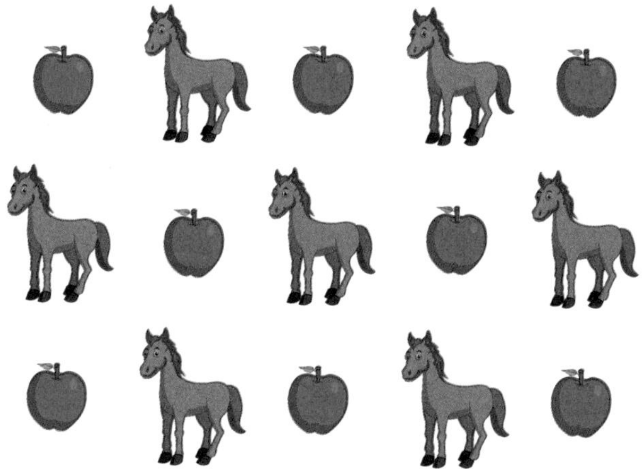

 ______

 ______

9

______ ○ ______ = ______

Directions: 7 Match the subtraction sentences with the pictures that show how many there are in all, how many are leaving, and how many are left. 8 Count the objects in each group. Write each number. Draw a line through the number that is less than the other number. 9 Circle 2 groups of bear counters that make 10 bear counters in all. Then write an addition sentence.

10

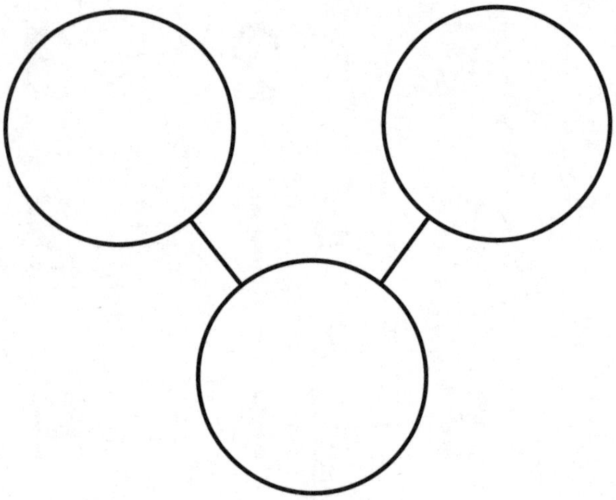

11

12

_____ − _____ = _____

Directions: 10 Color 5 cars blue and the rest red. Then complete the number bond to match your picture. 11 Draw lines between the objects in each group. Circle the group that is greater in number than the other group. 12 You are playing a video game. You need to catch 5 pigs that escaped. You catch some of the pigs. Cross out the pigs you catch. Then write a subtraction sentence to tell how many pigs you have left to catch.

Glossary

A

above [arriba, encima]

add [sumar]

$$2 + 4 = 6$$

addition sentence [enunciado suma]

$$2 + 3 = 5$$

B

balance scale [balanza]

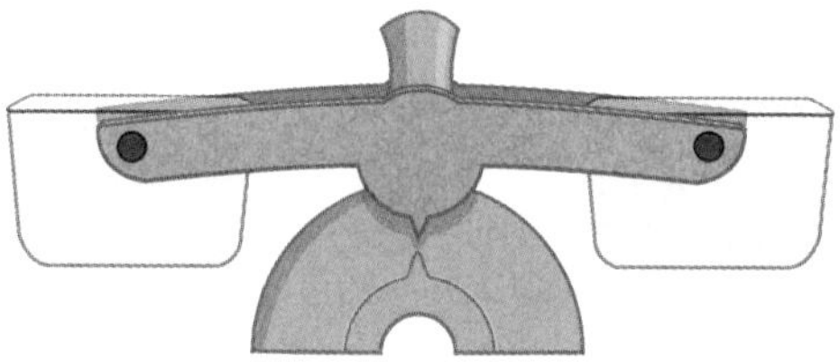

behind [detrás]

below [debajo]

beside [al lado]

C

capacity [capacidad]

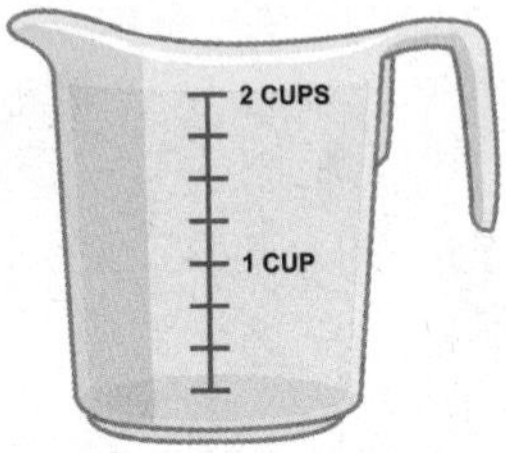

category [categoría]

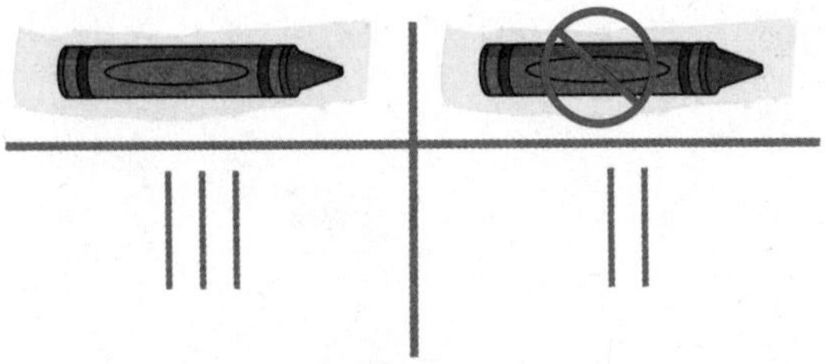

chart [gráfico]

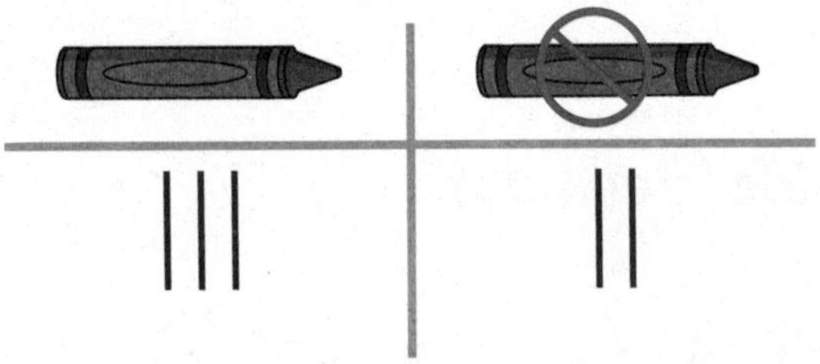

circle [círculo]

classify [clasificar]

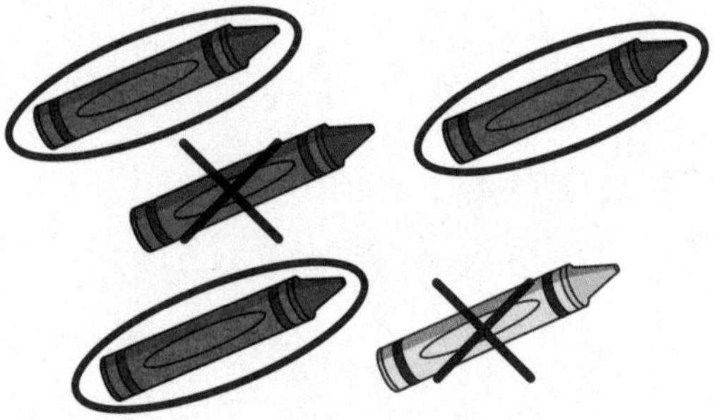

column [columna]

1	2	3	4	5	6	7	8	9	10
11	12	13	14	15	16	17	18	19	20
21	22	23	24	25	26	27	28	29	30
31	32	33	34	35	36	37	38	39	40
41	42	43	44	45	46	47	48	49	50
51	52	53	54	55	56	57	58	59	60
61	62	63	64	65	66	67	68	69	70
71	72	73	74	75	76	77	78	79	80
81	82	83	84	85	86	87	88	89	90
91	92	93	94	95	96	97	98	99	100

compare [comparar]

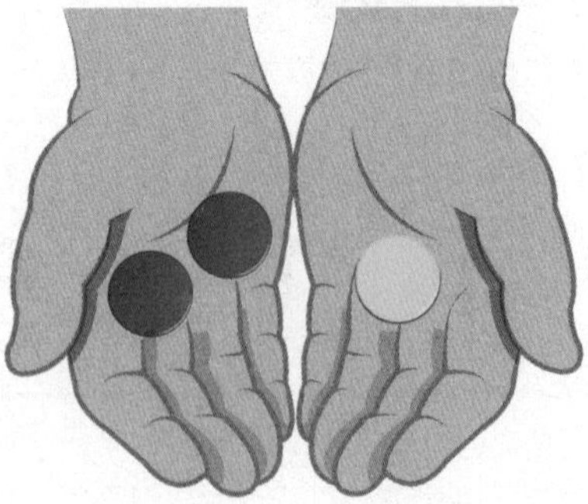

cone [cono]

count [contar]

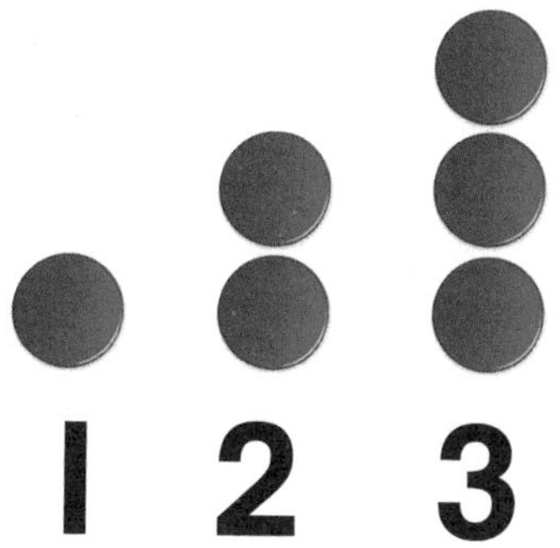

cube [cubo]

curve [curva]

curved surface [superficie curva]

cylinder [cilindro]

D

decade number
[número de década]

1	2	3	4	5	6	7	8	9	10
11	12	13	14	15	16	17	18	19	20
21	22	23	24	25	26	27	28	29	30
31	32	33	34	35	36	37	38	39	40
41	42	43	44	45	46	47	48	49	50
51	52	53	54	55	56	57	58	59	60
61	62	63	64	65	66	67	68	69	70
71	72	73	74	75	76	77	78	79	80
81	82	83	84	85	86	87	88	89	90
91	92	93	94	95	96	97	98	99	100

E

eight [ocho]

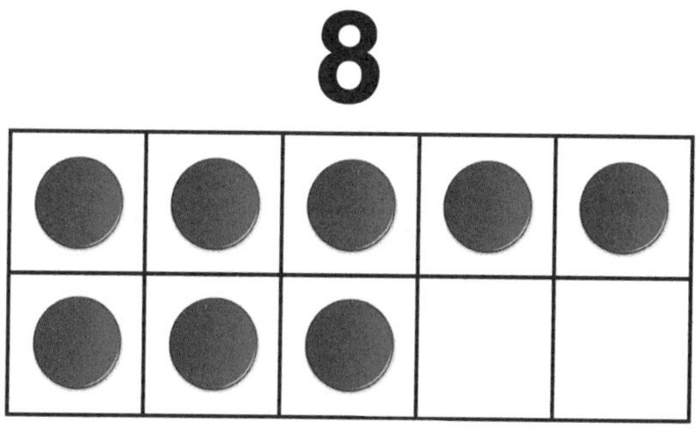

eighteen [dieciocho]

18

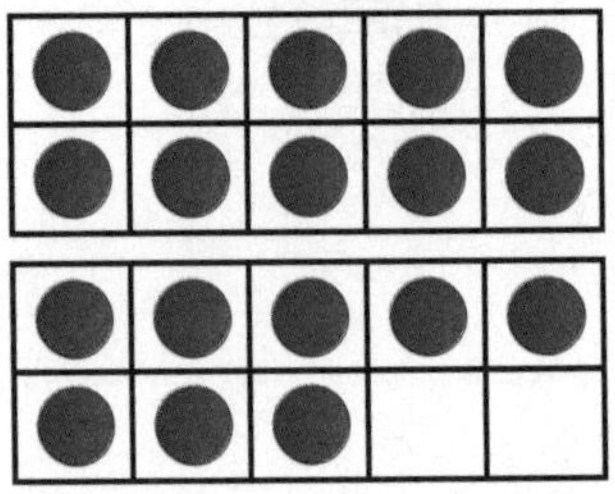

eleven [once]

11

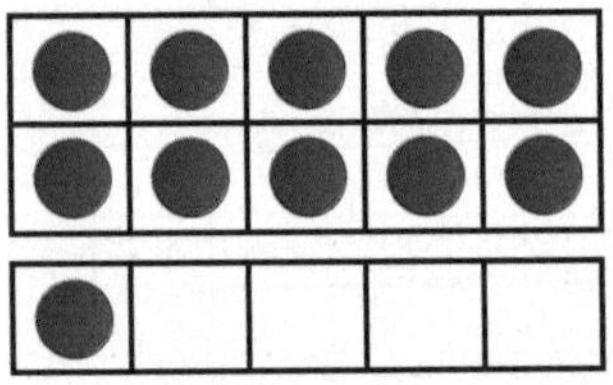

equal [igual]

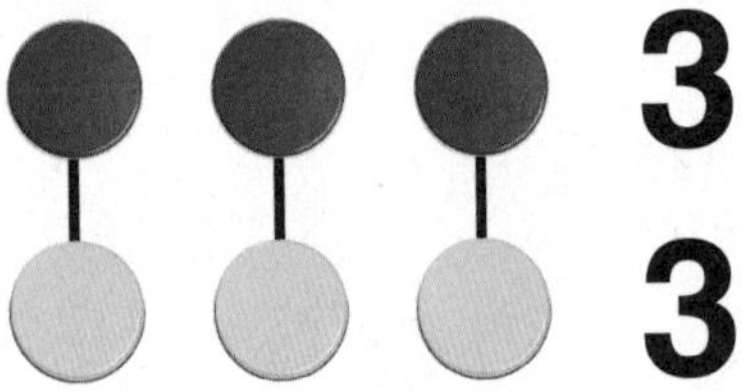

equal sign [signo igual]

$3 + 4 = 7$

F

fewer [menos]

fifteen [quince]

15

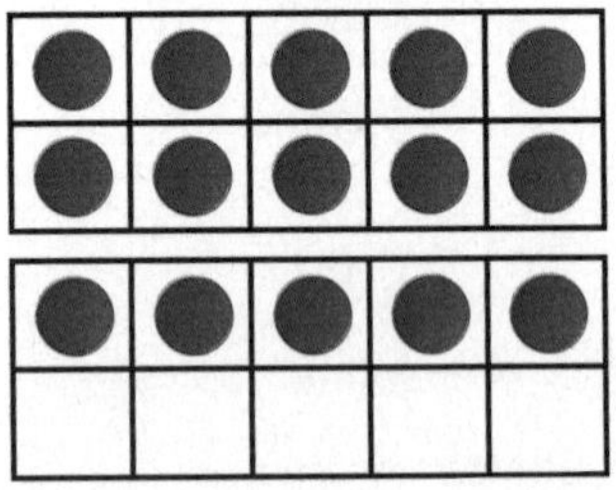

five [cinco]

5

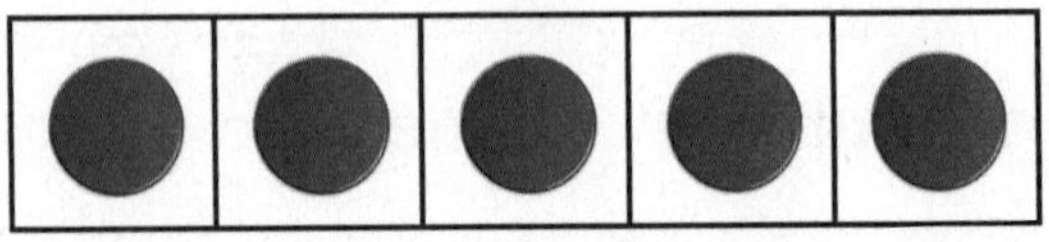

five frame [cinco marco]

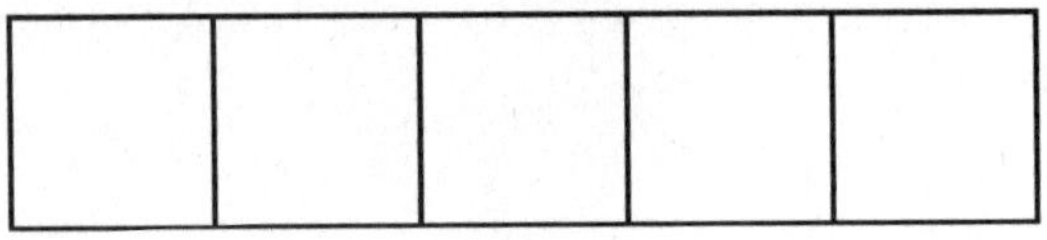

flat surface [superficie plana]

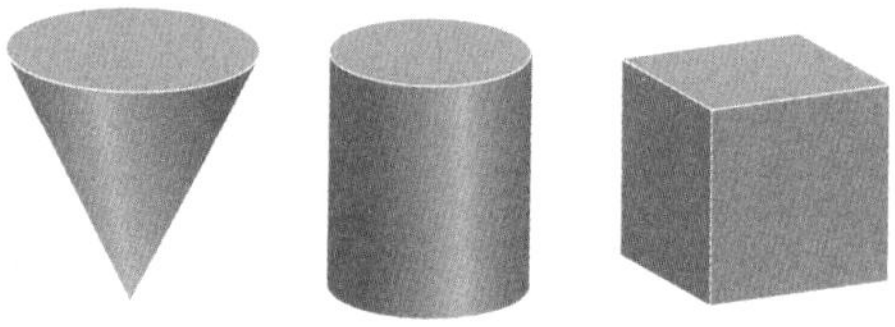

four [cuatro]

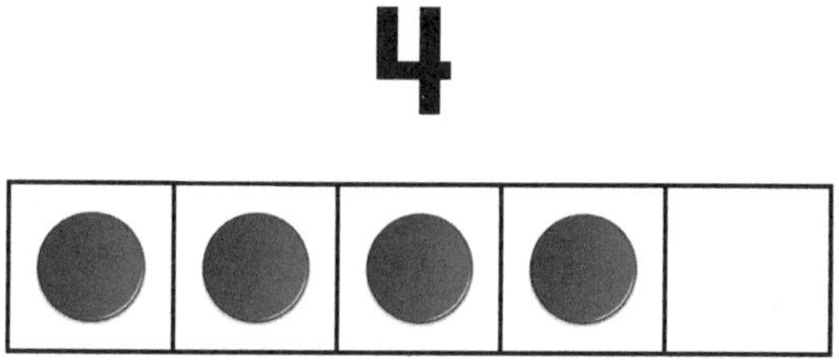

fourteen [catorce]

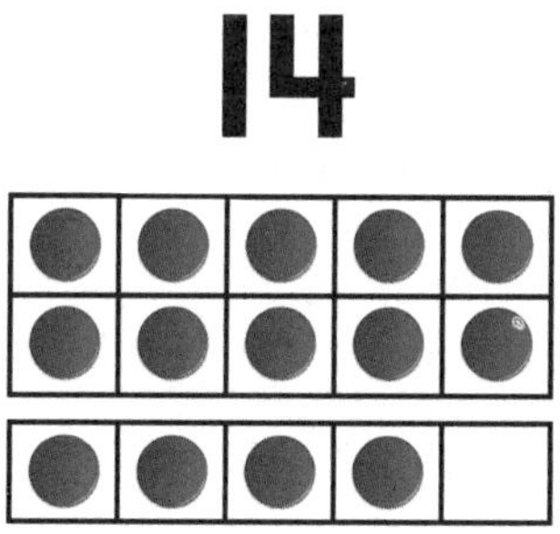

G

greater than [mas grande que]

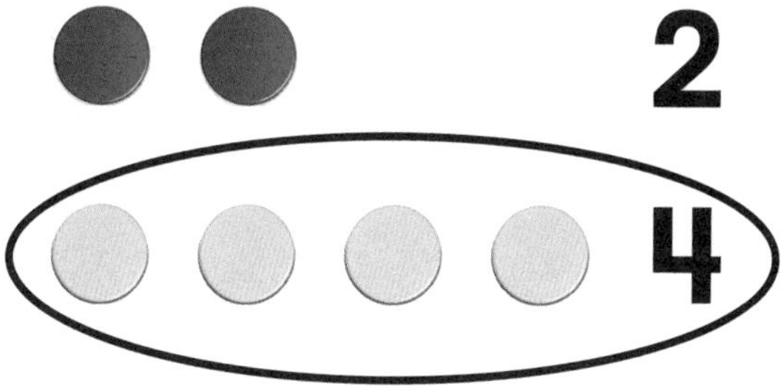

H

heavier [más pesado]

height [altura]

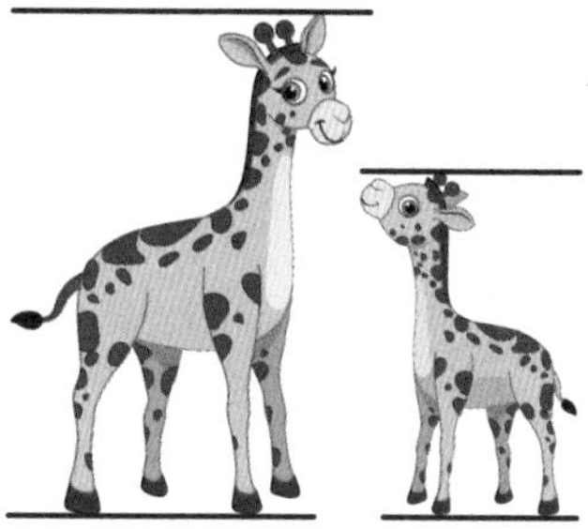

hexagon [hexágono]

hundred chart [cientos de cartas]

1	2	3	4	5	6	7	8	9	10
11	12	13	14	15	16	17	18	19	20
21	22	23	24	25	26	27	28	29	30
31	32	33	34	35	36	37	38	39	40
41	42	43	44	45	46	47	48	49	50
51	52	53	54	55	56	57	58	59	60
61	62	63	64	65	66	67	68	69	70
71	72	73	74	75	76	77	78	79	80
81	82	83	84	85	86	87	88	89	90
91	92	93	94	95	96	97	98	99	100

I

in all [en todo]

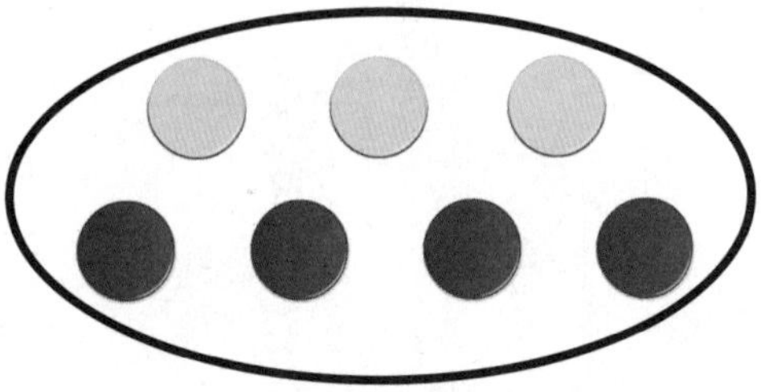

in front of [delante de]

J

join [unirse]

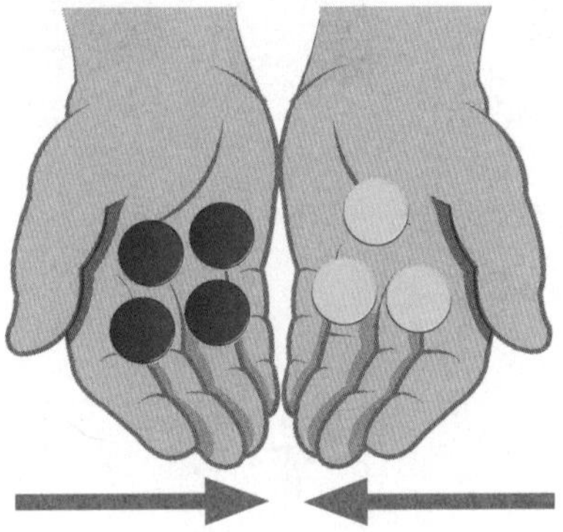

L

left [izquierda]

length [longitud]

less than [menos que]

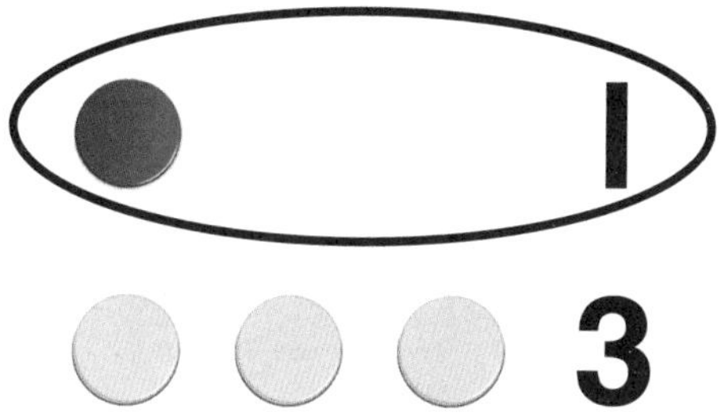

lighter [más liviano]

longer [más largo]

M

mark [marca]

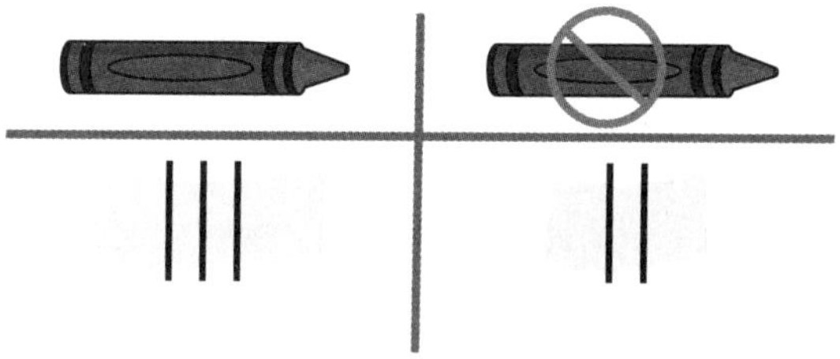

measurable attribute [atributo mensurable]

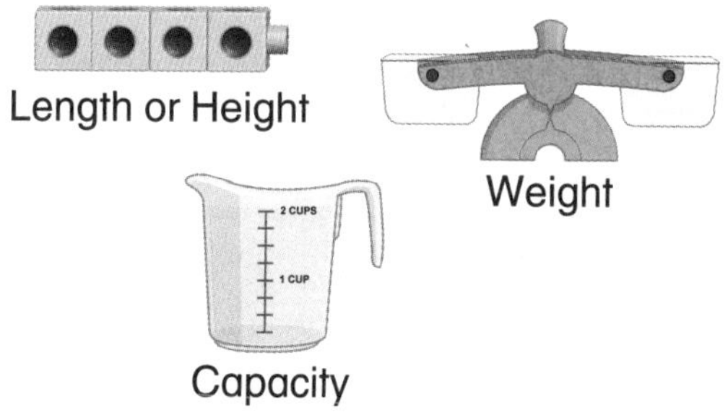

minus sign [signo menos]

$$3 - 2 = 1$$

more [más]

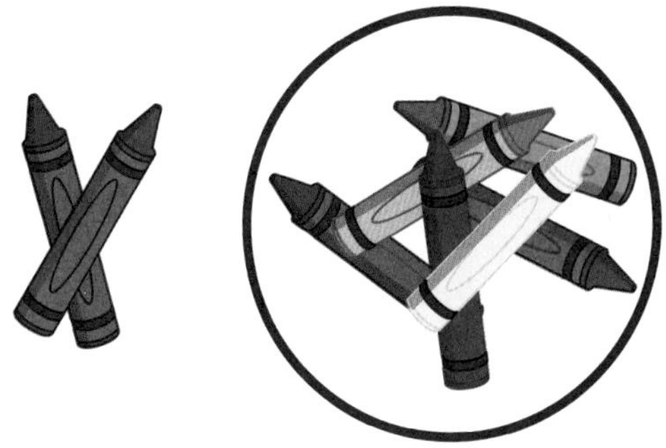

N

next to [al lado de]

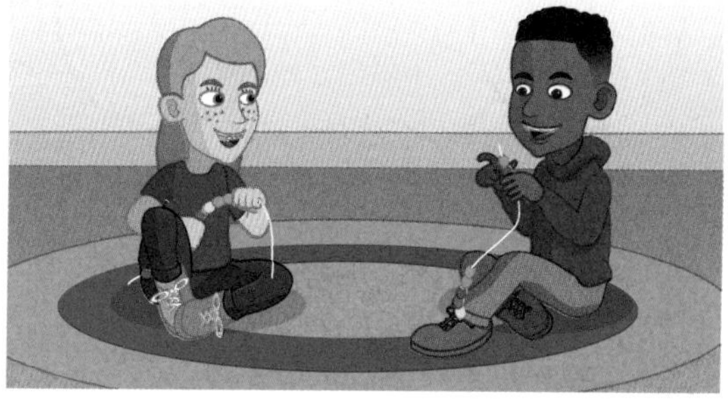

nine [nueve]

9

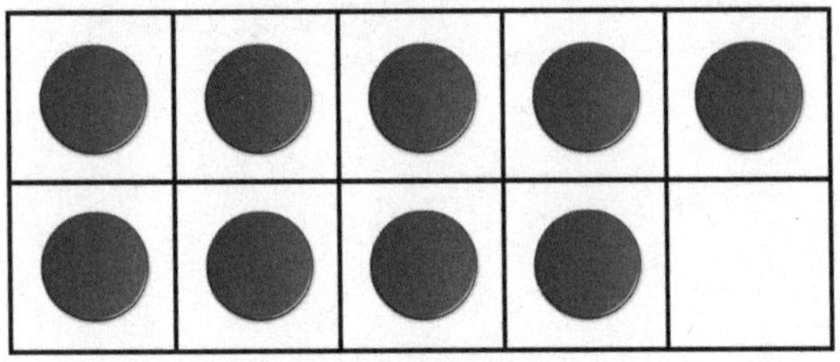

nineteen [diecinueve]

19

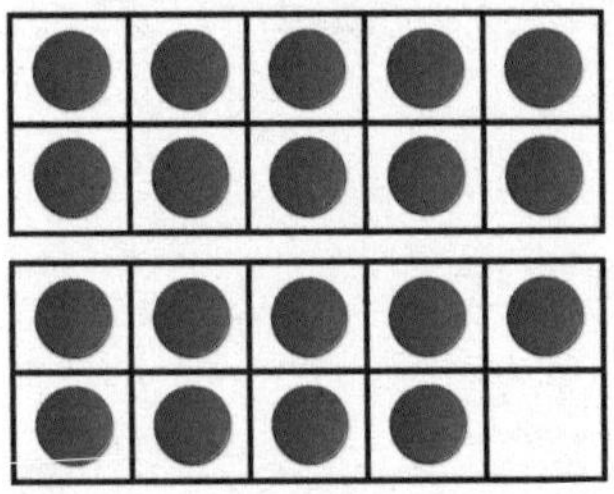

number [número]

1 2 3 4 5

number bond [número de bonos]

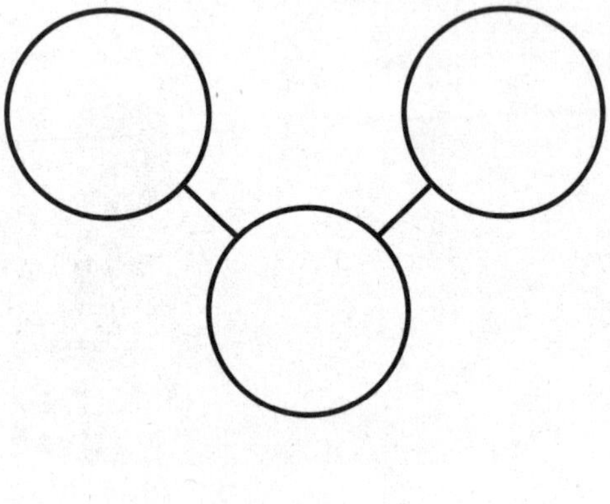

O

one [uno]

1

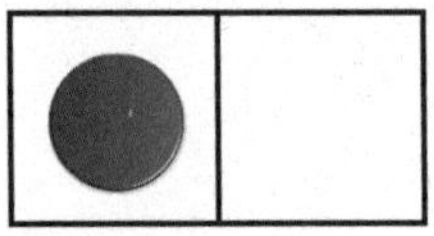

order [ordenar]

1 → 2 → 3 → 4 → 5

P

part [parte]

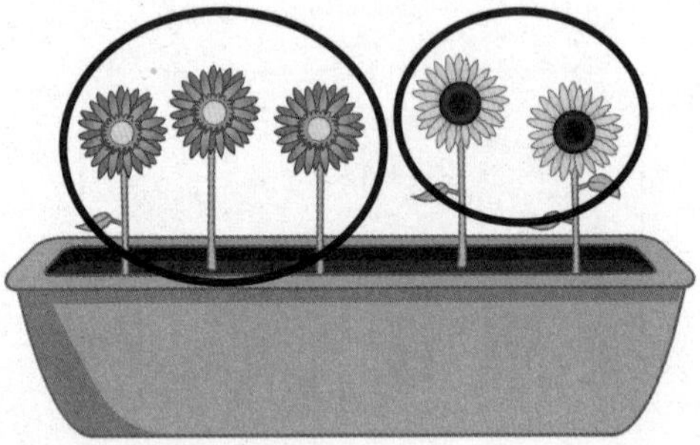

partner numbers
[números de socio]

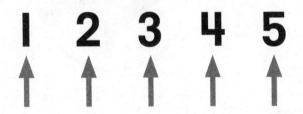

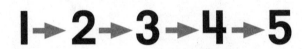

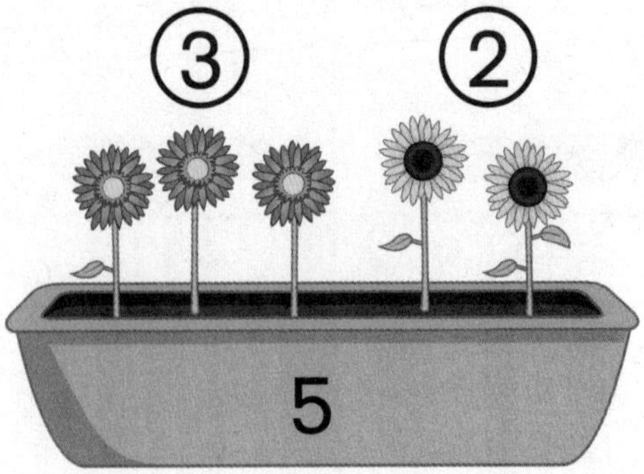

pattern [patrón]

1 + 1 = 2 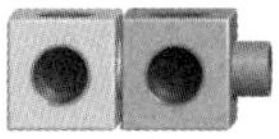

2 + 1 = 3 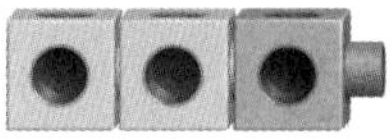

3 + 1 = 4 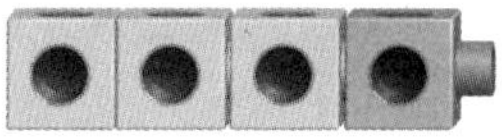

plus sign [signo de más]

2 + 1 = 3

put together [juntar]

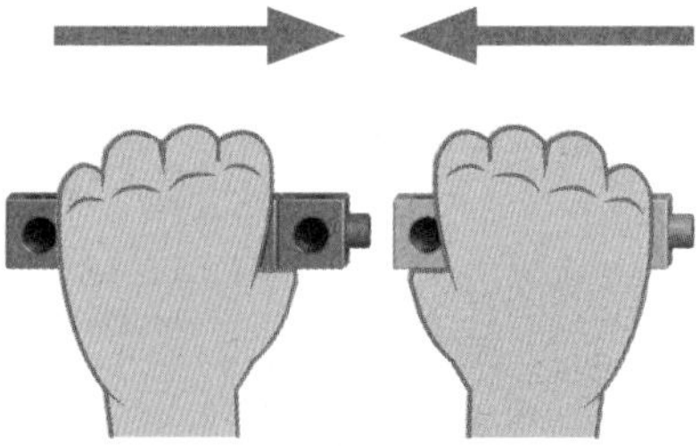

R

rectangle [rectángulo]

roll [rodar]

row [fila]

1	2	3	4	5	6	7	8	9	10
11	12	13	14	15	16	17	18	19	20
21	22	23	24	25	26	27	28	29	30
31	32	33	34	35	36	37	38	39	40
41	42	43	44	45	46	47	48	49	50
51	52	53	54	55	56	57	58	59	60
61	62	63	64	65	66	67	68	69	70
71	72	73	74	75	76	77	78	79	80
81	82	83	84	85	86	87	88	89	90
91	92	93	94	95	96	97	98	99	100

S

same as [igual que]

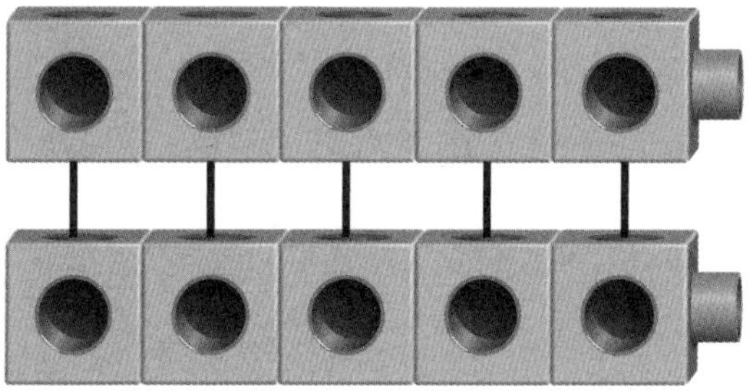

separate [separar]

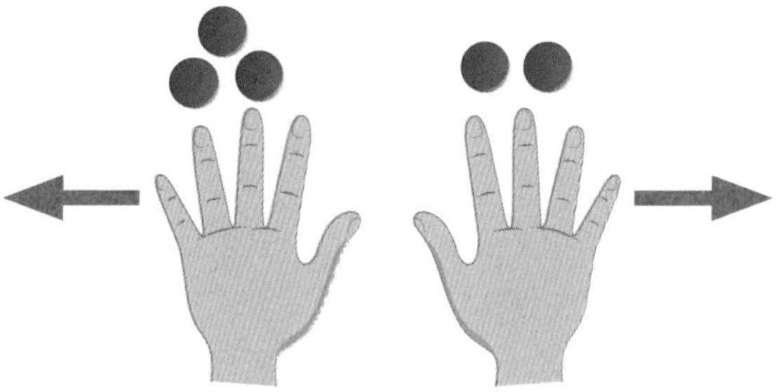

seven [siete]

7

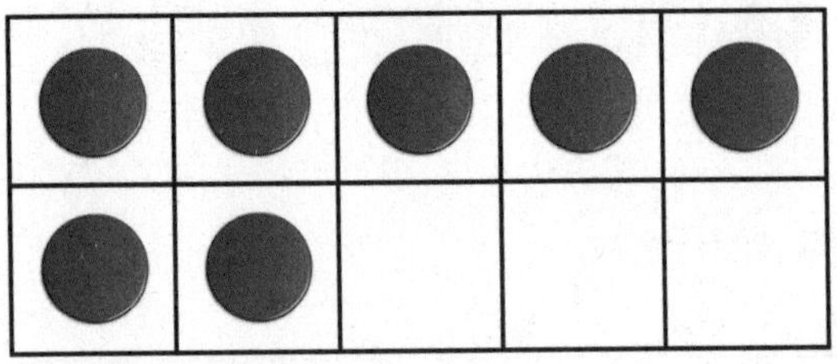

seventeen [diecisiete]

17

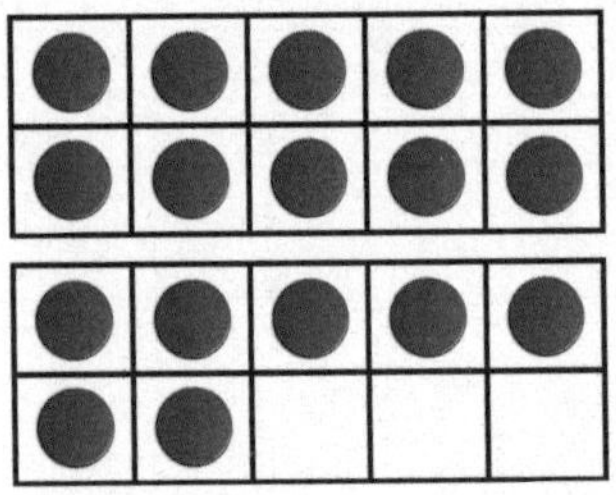

shorter [corta]

side [lado]

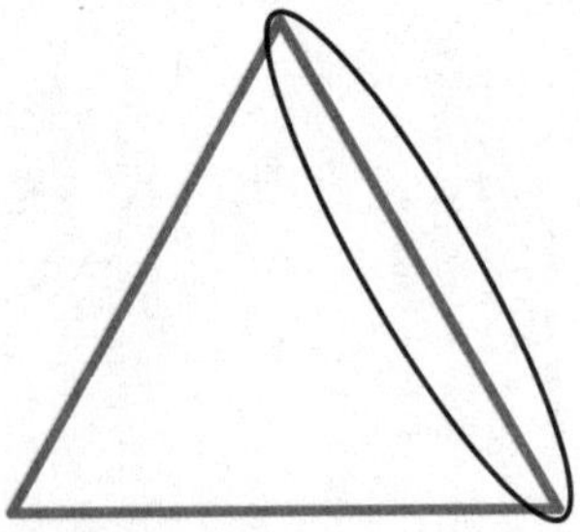

six [seis]

6

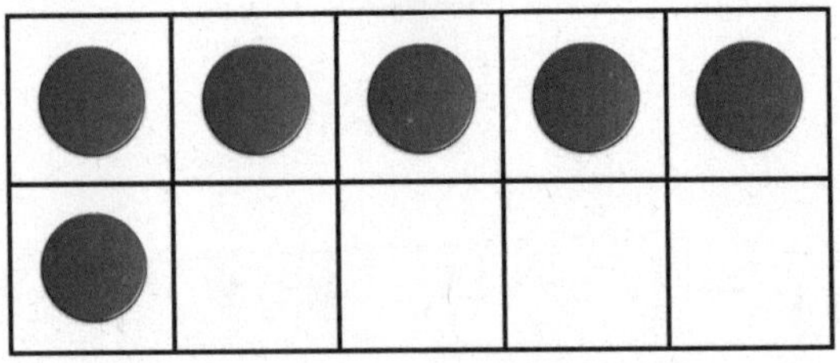

sixteen [dieciséis]

16

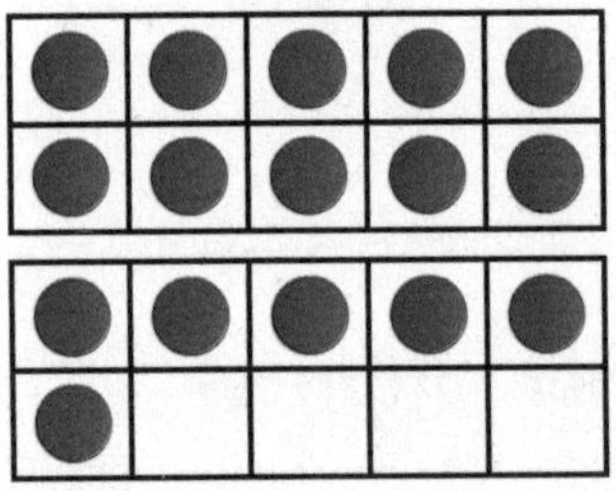

slide [deslizar]

sort [ordenar]

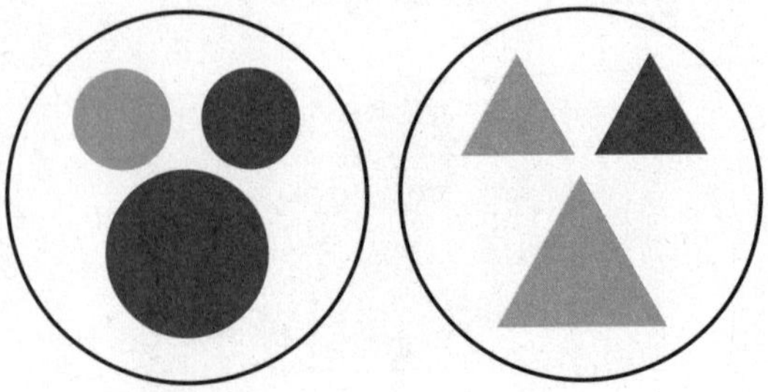

sphere [esfera]

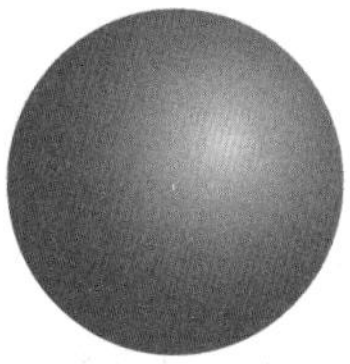

square [cuadrado]

stack [apilar]

subtract [restar]

$$3 - 1 = 2$$

subtraction sentence
[oración de resta]

$$4 - 1 = 3$$

T

take apart [desmontar]

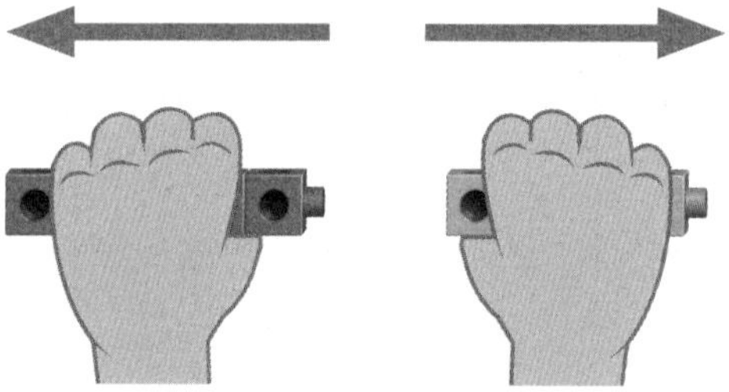

take away [quitar]

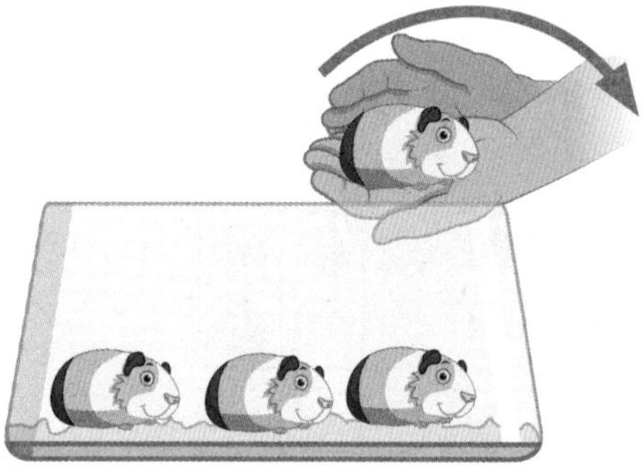

taller [más alto]

ten [diez]

10

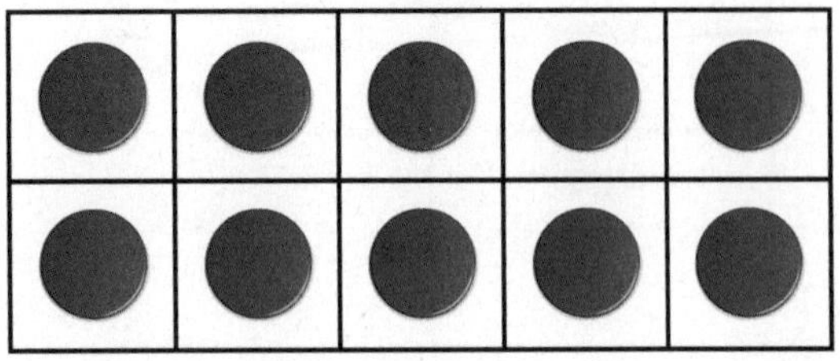

ten frame [diez marco]

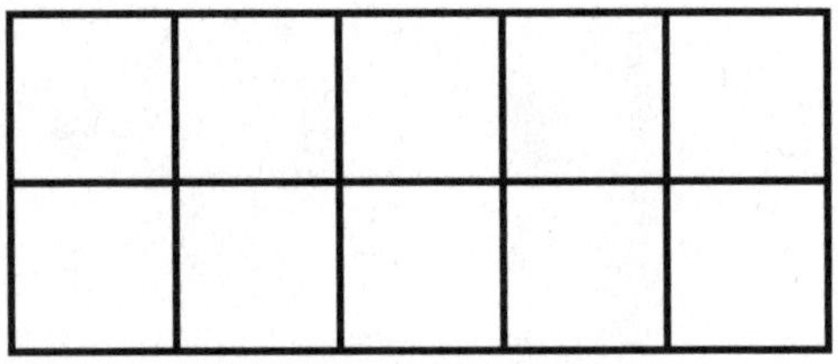

thirteen [trece]

13

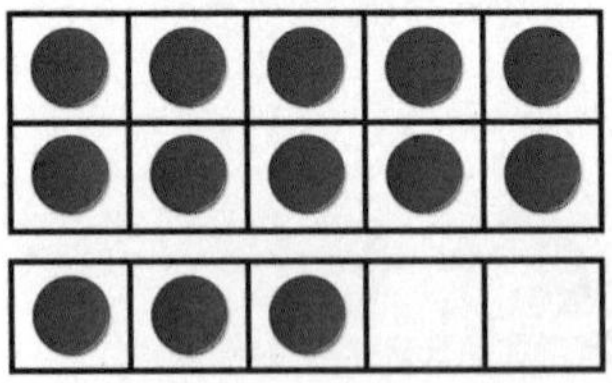

three [tres]

3

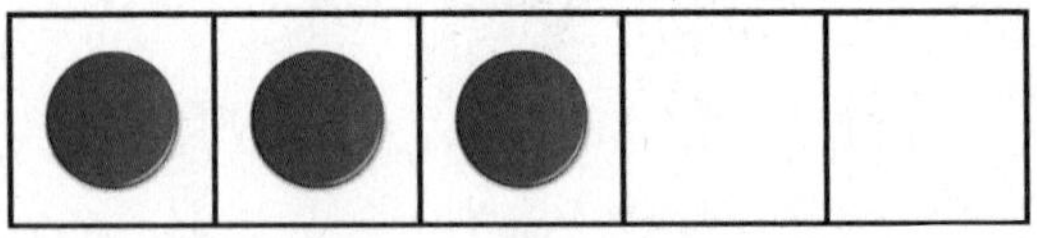

three-dimensional shape
[forma tridimensional]

triangle [triángulo]

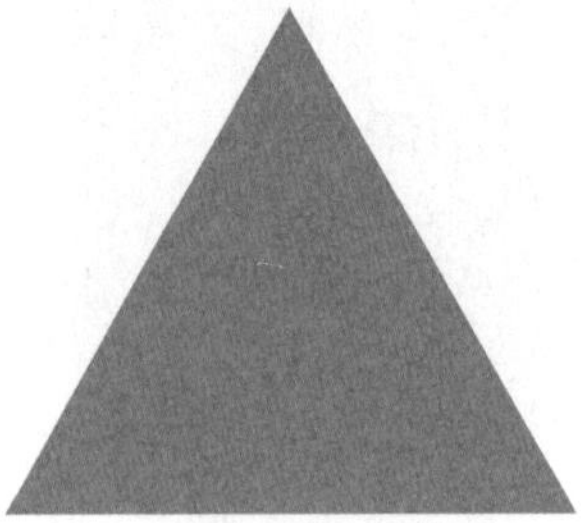

twelve [doce]

12

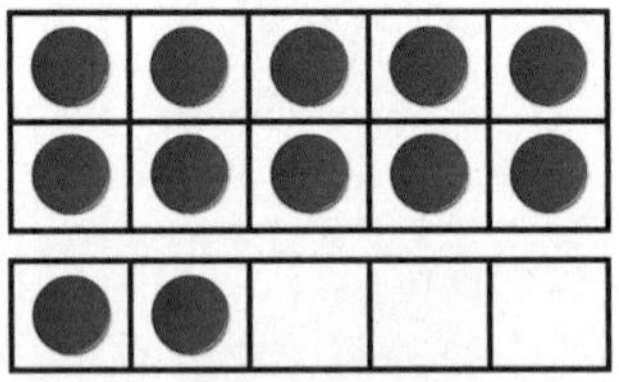

twenty [veinte]

20

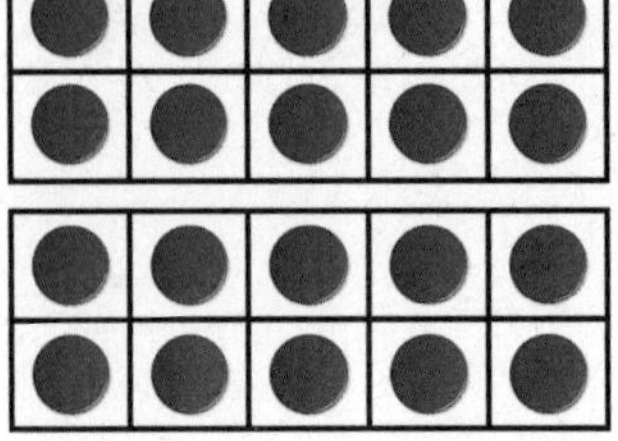

two [dos]

2

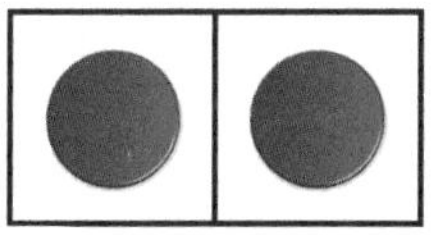

two-dimensional shape
[forma bidimensional]

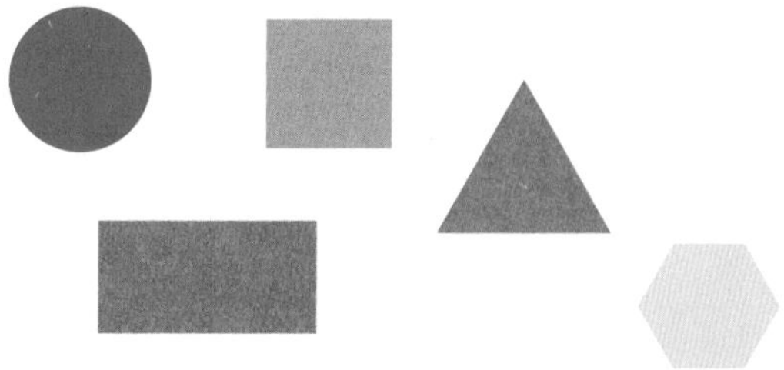

V

vertex [vértice]

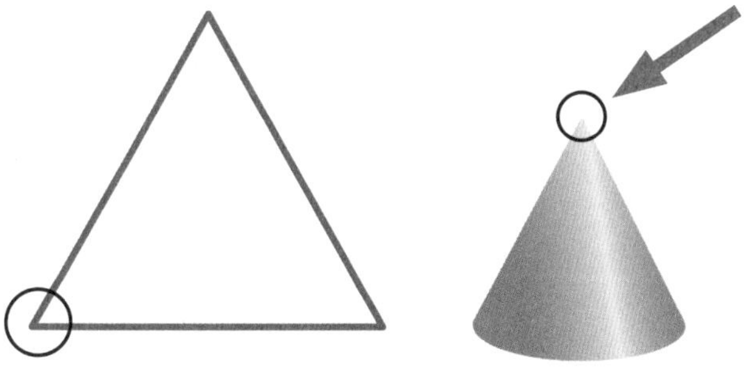

vertices [vértices]

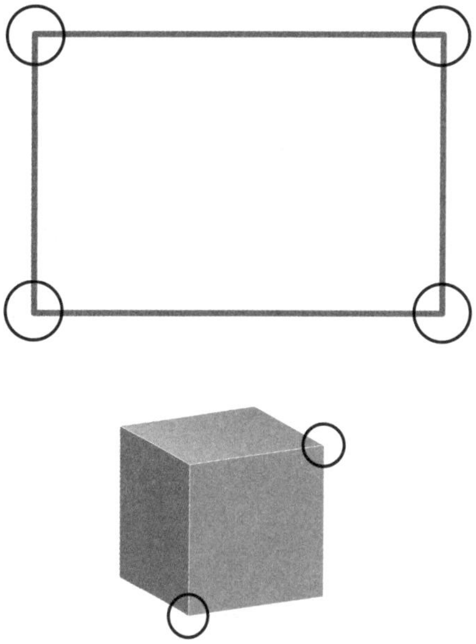

W

weight [peso]

whole [todo]

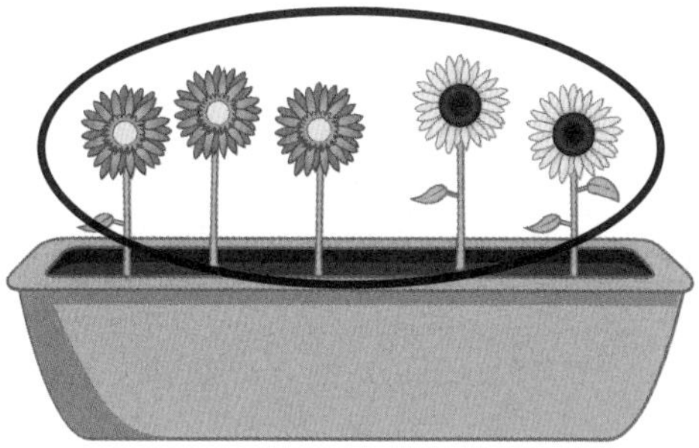

Z

zero [cero]

0

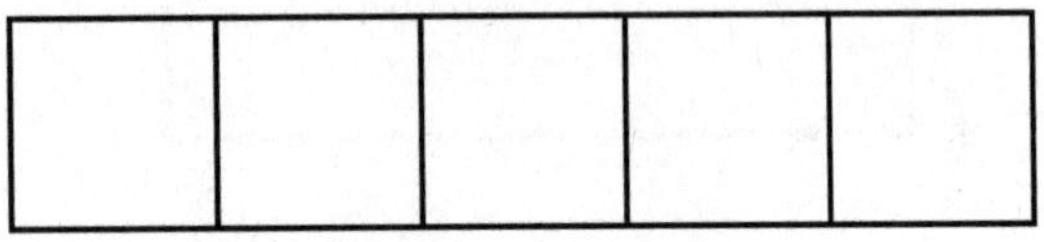

Index

A

Above (position), 628–630, 632
Addition
add to, 275–280
using group of 5, 305–310
partner numbers in
to 5, 299–304
finding numbers for, 287–292
to make 10, 311–316
practicing, 299–304
put together, 281–286
using related facts within 5, 361–366
understanding, 269–274
Addition patterns, with 0 and 1, 293–298
Addition sentence, 275–280 (*See also* Addition)
***Ants at the Picnic* (story),** 461–466
Apply and Grow: Practice, *In every lesson. For example, see:* 5, 61, 99, 173, 215, 271, 327, 381, 457, 501
***At the Pond* (story),** 33–38
Attributes, measurable
capacities, 671–676
describing objects by, 677–682
height, 641–646
length, 647–658
weight, 659–670

B

Balance scale, 665–670
Behind (position), 628–631
Below (position), 628–632
Beside (position), 628–632
***Bugs, Bugs, Bugs* (story),** 127–132
Building
three-dimensional shapes, 621–626
two-dimensional shapes, 583–588

C

Capacities
comparing, 671–676
describing objects by, 677–682
Castle tower, building
with three-dimensional shapes, 624
with two-dimensional shapes, 588
Cat, drawing with two-dimensional shapes, 576
Categories
classifying objects into, 189–194
comparing number of objects in, 195–200
Chapter Practice, *In every chapter. For example, see:* 53–56, 91–94, 165–168, 203–206, 263–266, 319–322, 369–372, 447–452, 493–496, 537–540
Chart, hundred
for counting by ones, 511–516, 523, 524, 527
for counting by tens
to 100, 517–522
within 100, 523, 524, 527
from number within 100, 529–534
Circles
building, 583, 585
drawing cat with, 576
drawing robot with, 574
identifying and describing, 571–576, 597
Classifying
comparing numbers of objects in, 195–200
objects into categories, 189–194
Column, on hundred chart, 511
Common Errors, *Throughout. For example, see:* T-10, T-140, T-172, T-216, T-332, T-386, T-569

Common Misconceptions, *Throughout. For example, see:* 189, T-192, T-294, T-344, T-671
Comparing capacities, 671–676
Comparing heights, 641–646
Comparing lengths, 647–652
using numbers, 653–658
Comparing numbers
to 5 (up to 5), 83–88
to 10 (up to 10), 183–188
to 20 (up to 20), 485–490
equal groups, 59–64
in groups to 5
using counting, 77–82
greater than, 65–70
less than, 71–76
in groups to 10
using counting, 177–182
using matching, 171–176
objects in categories, 195–200
Comparing weights, 659–664
using numbers, 665–670
Composing
6, 225–230
7, 231–236
8, 237–242
9, 243–248
10, 249–254
numbers to 5, 213–218
numbers to 10, using group of 5, 255–260
Cones
building, 621–626
identifying and describing, 597–602, 615–620
position, based on other objects, 627–632
roll, stack, or slide sorting of, 603–608
Counting
1 and 2, 3–8
3 and 4, 15–20
5, 27–32
6, 97–102
7, 109–114
8, 121–126
9, 133–138
10, 145–150
11 and 12, 385–390
13 and 14, 397–402
15, 409–414
16 and 17, 421–426
18 and 19, 433–438
20, 455–460
comparing using
for groups to 5, 77–82
for groups to 10, 177–182
for numbers to 20, 485–490
for objects in categories, 195–200
finding how many using, 467–472
forward to 20, from any number, 473–478
by ones
to 30, 499–504
to 50, 505–510
to 100, 511–516
within 100, 523–528
by tens, 523–528
to 100, 517–522
from number within 100, 529–534
Counting and ordering
to 20, 479–484
numbers to 5, 45–50
numbers to 10, 157–162
Cross-Curricular Connections, *In every lesson. For example, see:* T-7, T-75, T-131, T-253, T-341, T-443, T-527, T-587, T-613, T-645
Cubes
building, 621–626
identifying and describing, 597–602, 609–614
position, based on other objects, 627–632
roll, stack, or slide sorting of, 603–608
Cumulative Practice, 207–210, 373–376, 541–544, 689–692
Curved surfaces
of cones, 616–620
of cylinders, 616–620
of spheres, 610–614

Curves
of circles, 572–576
of two-dimensional shapes, 547–552
Cylinders
building, 621–626
identifying and describing, 597–602, 615–620
position, based on other objects, 627–632
roll, stack, or slide sorting of, 603–608

D

Decomposing
6, 225–230
7, 231–236
8, 237–242
9, 243–248
10, 249–254
numbers to 5, 213–218
numbers to 10, using group of 5, 255–260
taking apart in subtraction, 337–342
Differentiation, *See* Scaffolding Instruction
Drawing, with two-dimensional shapes
cat, 576
house, 568
robot, 574

E

Eight (8)
composing and decomposing, 237–242
modeling and counting, 121–126
understanding and writing, 127–132
Eighteen (18)
counting and writing, 433–438
understanding, 439–444
Eleven (11)
counting and writing, 385–390
understanding, 391–396
ELL Support, *In every lesson. For example, see:* T-3, T-59, T-98, T-174, T-261, T-340, T-445, T-517, T-580, T-650
Equal groups, showing and identifying, 59–64
Equal sign (=)
in add to problems, 276–280
in put together problems, 282–286
in take apart problems, 338–342
in take from problems, 332–336
Equations
addition, 269–274 (*See also* Addition)
subtraction, 331–336 (*See also* Subtraction)
Explore and Grow, *In every lesson. For example, see:* 3, 59, 97, 171, 213, 269, 325, 379, 455, 499

F

Fewer
in groups to 5, 65–70, 77–82
in groups to 10, 177–182
in numbers to 5, 83–88
in numbers to 10, 183–188
in numbers to 20, 485–490
Fifteen (15)
counting and writing, 409–414
understanding, 415–420
Fifty (50), counting by ones to, 505–510
Five (5)
comparing groups of objects (up to 5)
using counting, 77–82
greater than, 65–70
less than, 71–76
comparing numbers (up to 5), 83–88
counting and ordering numbers to, 45–50
group of
addition using, 305–310
composing and decomposing using, 255–260
subtraction using, 355–360
modeling and counting, 27–32
number bonds to represent numbers to, 219–224
partner numbers to, 213–218, 299–304
related facts within, adding or subtracting using, 361–366

Index

subtraction within, 349–354
understanding and writing, 33–38
Five frame
for adding partner numbers to 5, 299–300, 303
for addition patterns with 0 and 1, 293
for comparing number of objects, 65, 71, 77, 78
for concept of zero, 39, 40
for counting and ordering numbers, 46, 49
for modeling and counting
3 and 4, 15–20
5, 27–32
11 and 12, 385, 392–396
13 and 14, 397, 404, 405, 407, 408
15, 409
for showing partner numbers, 213
for subtraction patterns, 343, 344, 347
for subtraction within 5, 350, 354
Flat shapes, 598–602
Flat surfaces
of cones, 616–620
of cubes, 610–614
of cylinders, 616–620
Formative Assessment, *Throughout. For example, see:* T-6, T-130, T-174, T-228, T-284, T-350, T-386, T-470, T-568, T-624
Four (4)
modeling and counting, 15–20
understanding and writing, 21–26
Fourteen (14)
counting and writing, 397–402
understanding, 403–408

G

Games, *In every chapter. For example, see:* 52, 90, 164, 202, 262, 318, 368, 446, 492, 536
Greater than, 65–70
in groups to 5, 65–70, 77–82
in groups to 10, 177–182
in numbers to 5, 83–88
in numbers to 10, 183–188
in numbers to 20, 485–490
Groups
of 5
addition using, 305–310
composing and decomposing using, 255–260
subtraction using, 355–360
of 10, identifying, 379–384
addition in, 269–274
add to, 275–280
put together, 281–286
comparing numbers in
to 5, 83–88
using counting, for groups to 5, 77–82
using counting, for groups to 10, 177–182
equal, 59–64
greater than, 65–70
less than, 71–76
using matching, in groups to 10, 171–176
counting how many objects in, 467–472
equal, comparing and identifying, 59–64
subtraction in
take apart, 337–342
take away, 325–330
take from, 331–336

H

Heavier, 659–664
Heights
comparing, 641–646
describing objects by, 677–682
Hexagons
building, 583, 585
building house with, 586
drawing cat with, 576
drawing robot with, 574
identifying and describing, 571–576, 597
joining shapes to make, 578, 581
joining to make shapes, 579–582

Holds less
comparing capacities, 671–676
describing objects by, 677–682
Holds more
comparing capacities, 671–676
describing objects by, 677–682
House
building with two-dimensional shapes, 586
drawing with two-dimensional shapes, 568
How many, finding
addition for, 269–275
counting for, 467–472
subtraction for (how many left), 325–330
Hundred chart
for counting by ones, 511–516, 523, 524, 527
for counting by tens
to 100, 517–522
within 100, 523, 524, 527
from number within 100, 529–534

I

In all, addition for finding how many, 269–274
In front of (position), 627–630, 632
***In the Water* (story),** 151–156

J

Joining
in addition
add to, 275–280
put together, 281–286
two-dimensional shapes, 577–582

L

Learning Target, *In every lesson. For example, see:* 3, 59, 97, 171, 213, 269, 325, 379, 455, 499
Left, how many, 325–330 (*See also* Subtraction)
Lengths
comparing, 647–652
using numbers, 653–658
describing objects by, 677–682
Less, capacity (holds less)
comparing, 671–676
describing objects by, 677–682
Less than
in groups to 5, 71–82
in groups to 10, 177–182
in numbers to 5, 83–88
in numbers to 10, 183–188
in numbers to 20, 485–490
Lighter, 659–664
Linking cubes
for adding
partner numbers, 287–289, 291
partner numbers to make 10, 311, 313, 316
put together, 282, 283, 285
using related facts, 361
for comparing lengths, 653–658
for comparing numbers to 20, 485
for comparing weights, 666–670
for counting
1 and 2, 11, 13
3 and 4, 23, 25
5, 35, 37
6, 105, 107
7, 117, 119
8, 129, 131
9, 141, 143
10, 153, 155
11 and 12, 385, 387, 389
13 and 14, 397, 399, 401
15, 409, 411, 413
16 and 17, 421, 423, 425
18 and 19, 433, 435, 437
20, 455
for counting and ordering
numbers to 5, 45
numbers to 20, 479–484
for counting by tens
within 100, 524, 525, 527
from number within 100, 529
for counting forward to 20, 473

for counting to 100 by tens, 518, 519, 521
for finding how many, 467
for groups of 10, 379, 380, 383
for subtracting
using related facts, 361
take apart, 338, 339, 341, 342

Longer, 646–652

L-shaped vertices
of rectangles, 560–564
of squares, 566–570

M

"Make a 10" strategy, finding partner numbers in, 311–316

Mark, for classifying objects, 190–194

Matching, comparing groups to 10 by, 171–176

Mathematical Practices
Make sense of problems and persevere in solving them, *Throughout. For example, see:* T-36, T-62, T-130, T-186, T-228, T-328, T-442, T-530, T-650
Reason abstractly and quantitatively, *Throughout. For example, see:* T-74, T-106, T-192, T-237, T-270, T-333, T-380, T-474, T-572
Construct viable arguments and critique the reasoning of others, *Throughout. For example, see:* T-48, T-73, T-198, T-234, T-290, T-334, T-388, T-488, T-553
Model with mathematics, *Throughout. For example, see:* T-6, T-61,T-100, T-196, 225, T-270, T-422, T-520, T-630
Use appropriate tools strategically, *Throughout. For example, see:* T-40, T-77, T-106, T-177, T-256, T-284, T-356, T-578, T-668
Attend to precision, *Throughout. For example, see:* T-18, T-78, T-123, T-172, T-220, T-288, T-391, T-554, T-644
Look for and make use of structure, *Throughout. For example, see:* T-36, T-80, T-134, T-186, T-240, T-294, T-361, T-415, T-456
Look for and express regularity in repeated reasoning, *Throughout. For example, see:* T-28, T-85, T-100, T-184, T-222, T-293, T-343, T-439, T-456

Measurable attributes
capacities, 671–676
describing objects by, 677–682
height, 641–646
length, 647–658
weight, 659–670

Minus sign (−)
in take apart problems, 338–342
in take from problems, 331–336

Modeling
1 and 2, 3–8
3 and 4, 15–20
5, 27–32
6, 97–102
7, 109–114
8, 121–126
9, 133–138
10, 145–150
11 and 12, 385–390
13 and 14, 397–402
15, 409–414
16 and 17, 421–426
18 and 19, 433–438
20, 455–460

More
capacity (holds more)
comparing, 671–676
describing objects by, 677–682
in groups to 5, 65–70, 77–82
in groups to 10, 177–182
in numbers to 5, 83–88
in numbers to 10, 183–188
in numbers to 20, 485–490

Multiple Representations, *Throughout. For example, see:* 22, 256, 270, 276, 300, 312, 326, 332, 338, 428
***Music Class* (story),** 103–108
***My Baseball Game* (story),** 139–144
***My Pets* (story),** 9–14

N

Next to (position), 627, 628, 630, 631
Nine (9)
composing and decomposing, 243–248
modeling and counting, 133–138
understanding and writing, 139–144
Nineteen (19)
counting and writing, 433–438
understanding, 439–444
Number(s)
comparing (*See* Comparing numbers)
comparing lengths using, 653–658
comparing weights using, 665–670
counting and ordering
to 5, 45–50
to 10, 157–162
to 20, 479–484
modeling and counting
1 and 2, 3–8
3 and 4, 15–20
5, 27–32
6, 97–102
7, 109–114
8, 121–126
9, 133–138
10, 145–150
11 and 12, 385–390
13 and 14, 397–402
15, 409–414
16 and 17, 421–426
18 and 19, 433–438
20, 455–460
understanding and writing, 103–108
0, 40, 43
1 and 2, 9–14
3 and 4, 21–26
5, 33–38
6, 103–108
7, 115–120
8, 127–132
9, 139–144
10, 151–156
11 and 12, 385–396
13 and 14, 397–408
15, 409–420
16 and 17, 421–432
18 and 19, 433–444
20, 461–466
Number bonds
for 6, 226–230
for 7, 232–236
for 8, 238–242
for 9, 244–248
for 10, 250–254
for 11, 391
for 13, 403
for 15, 415
for 16, 427
for 18, 439
in addition, 270, 271, 273
for numbers to 5, 219–224
for numbers to 10, using group of 5, 256–260
in subtraction, 338, 339, 341
Number patterns
addition, 293–298
subtraction, 343–348

O

Objects
classifying, 189–194
in groups, addition of, 269–274
add to, 275–280
put together, 281–286
in groups, comparing numbers of
to 5, 83–88
using counting, in groups to 5, 77–82
using counting, in groups to 10, 177–182

Index

equal groups, 59–64
greater than, 65–70
less than, 71–76
using matching, in groups to 10, 171–176
in groups, counting to find how many, 467–472
in groups, subtraction of
take apart, 337–342
take away, 325–330
take from, 331–336
measurable attributes of
capacities, 671–676
describing, 677–682
height, 641–646
length, 647–658
weight, 659–670
One hundred (100)
counting by ones to, 511–516
counting by tens and ones within, 523–528
counting by tens to, 517–522
Ones (1)
in 11 and 12, 391–396
in 13 and 14, 403–408
in 15, 415–420
in 16 and 17, 427–432
in 18 and 19, 439–444
addition patterns with, 293–298
counting by
to 30, 499–504
to 50, 505–510
to 100, 511–516
within 100, 523–528
groups of ten and, 380–384
modeling and counting, 3–8
understanding and writing, 9–14
Ordering numbers
to 5, 45–50
to 10, 157–162
to 20, 479–484

P

Part(s)
in composing and decomposing
6, 225–230
7, 231–236
8, 237–242
9, 243–248
10, 249–254
numbers to 5, 213–218
numbers to 10, using group of 5, 255–260
number bonds and, 219–224
Partner numbers
adding
finding numbers for, 287–292
to make 10, 311–316
numbers to 5, 299–304
for composing and decomposing
6, 225–230
7, 231–236
8, 237–242
9, 243–248
10, 249–254
numbers to 5, 213–218
Pattern blocks, for making shapes, 578–582
Patterns
addition, with 0 and 1, 293–298
subtraction, 343–348
Performance Task, *In every chapter. For example, see:* 51, 89, 163, 201, 261, 317, 367, 445, 491, 535
Plus sign (+)
in add to problems, 275–280
in put together problems, 281–286
Positions, of solid shapes, 627–632
Practice, *In every lesson. For example, see:* 7–8, 63–64, 101–102, 175–176, 217–218, 273–274, 329–330, 383–384, 459–460, 503–504
Problem Types, *Throughout. For example, see:*
add to, result unknown, 278, 302, 319, 374, 378, 562, 683

put together,
both addends unknown, 290, 302, 304, 317, 320, 366, 372
total unknown, 282, 286, 302, 317, 320, 406, 445, 498, 568, 593
take apart,
both addends unknown, 337, 340, 354, 364, 367, 370, 372, 376
total unknown, 352
take from, result unknown, 332, 346, 348, 358, 360, 367
Put together
addition using, 281–286
composing using
6, 225–230
7, 231–236
8, 237–242
9, 243–248
10, 249–254
numbers to 5, 213–218
numbers to 10, using group of 5, 255–260

R

***Rainy Day* (story),** 115–120
Reading, *Throughout. For example, see:* T-7, T-149, T-181, T-235, T-279, T-359, T-431, T-515, T-607, T-663
Rectangles
building, 583, 584, 587
building house with, 586
drawing cat with, 576
drawing house with, 568
drawing robot with, 574
identifying and describing, 559–564, 597
joining squares to make, 577, 581
joining triangles to make, 579
Related facts, adding or subtracting using, 361–366
Response to Intervention, *Throughout. For example, see:* T-1B, T-61, T-211B, T-289, T-345, T-377B, T-457, T-497B, T-611, T-679
Robot, drawing with two-dimensional shapes, 574
Rocket shapes, creating with pattern blocks, 580
Roll/rolling, by solid shapes, 603–608
Row, on hundred chart, 511

S

Same as (equal groups), 59–64
Scaffolding Instruction, *In every lesson. For example, see:* T-5, T-79, T-111, T-233, T-283, T-363, T-405, T-513, T-549, T-649
Scale, for comparing weights, 665–670
Seven (7)
composing and decomposing, 231–236
modeling and counting, 109–114
understanding and writing, 115–120
Seventeen (17)
counting and writing, 421–426
understanding, 427–432
Shapes, *See also* specific shapes
three-dimensional
building, 621–626
describing, 597–608
identifying, 597–602
positions of, 627–632
roll, stack, or slide sorting of, 603–608
two-dimensional
building, 583–588
curves of, 547–552
describing, 547–552, 597–602
drawing cat with, 576
drawing house with, 568
drawing robot with, 574
identifying, 597–602
joining, 577–582
sides of, 548–552
vertices of, 548–552
Shorter
height, 641–646
length, 646–652

Index

Show how you know, 84, 94, 183, 205, 302, 654, 686
Sides
in building shapes, 583–588
of hexagons, 572–576
of rectangles, 560–564
of squares, 566–570
of triangles, 554–558, 584
of two-dimensional shapes, 548–552
Six (6)
composing and decomposing, 225–230
modeling and counting, 97–102
understanding and writing, 103–108
Sixteen (16)
counting and writing, 421–426
understanding, 427–432
Slide/sliding, by solid shapes, 603–608
Solid shapes, 598–602
building, 621–626
positions of, 627–632
roll, stack, or slide sorting of, 603–608
Sorting
measurable attributes, 677–682
rectangles, 559–564
squares, 565–570
three-dimensional shapes, 603–608
triangles, 553–558
two-dimensional shapes, 547–552
Spheres
building, 621–626
identifying and describing, 597–602, 609–614
position, based on other objects, 627–632
roll, stack, or slide sorting of, 603–614
Squares
building, 583, 587
building house with, 586
drawing house with, 568
identifying and describing, 565–570, 597
joining to make shapes, 577, 579–582
Stacks, of solid shapes, 603–608
Stories
Ants at the Picnic, 461–466
At the Pond, 33–38
Bugs, Bugs, Bugs, 127–132
Music Class, 103–108
My Baseball Game, 139–144
My Pets, 9–14
Rainy Day, 115–120
In the Water, 151–156
We Go Camping, 21–26
Straight sides
of hexagons, 572–576
of rectangles, 560–564
of squares, 566–570
of triangles, 554–558, 584
of two-dimensional shapes, 548–552
Subtraction
using group of 5, 355–360
practicing, within 5, 349–354
using related facts within 5, 361–366
take apart, 337–342
take away, 325–330
take from, 331–336
understanding, 325–330
Subtraction patterns, 343–348
Subtraction sentence, 331–336 (*See also* Subtraction)
Success Criteria, *In every lesson. For example, see:* T-3, T-65, T-189, T-237, T-299, T-361, T-421, T-511, T-583, T-647
Symbols
equal sign (=)
in add to problems, 276–280
in put together problems, 282–286
in take apart problems, 338–342
in take from problems, 332–336
minus sign (−)
in take apart problems, 338–342
in take from problems, 331–336
plus sign (+)
in add to problems, 275–280
in put together problems, 281–286

T

Take apart (decomposing)
6, 225–230
7, 231–236
8, 237–242
9, 243–248
10, 249–254
numbers to 5, 213–218
numbers to 10, using group of 5, 255–260
subtraction using, 337–342
Take away, 325–330
Take from, 331–336
Taller, 641–646
Ten frames
for adding
using group of 5, 305–310
partner numbers making 10, 312, 313, 315, 316
for comparing numbers up to 20, 485, 486, 489
for composing and decomposing, 256, 257
for counting and ordering numbers
to 5, 157–159
to 20, 479–484
for counting forward to 20, 473
for modeling and counting
6, 97–102
7, 109–114
8, 121–126
9, 133–138
10, 145–150
11 and 12, 385, 392–396
13 and 14, 397, 404–408
15, 409, 416–420
16 and 17, 421, 428–432
18 and 19, 433, 440–444
20, 455–460
for subtracting, using group of 5, 355–357, 359, 360
for subtraction patterns, 344–345
Tens (10)
in 11 and 12, 391–396
in 13 and 14, 403–408
in 15, 415–420
in 16 and 17, 427–432
in 18 and 19, 439–444
adding partner numbers to make, 311–316
comparing groups of objects (up to 10)
by counting, 177–182
by matching, 171–176
comparing numbers (up to 10), 183–188
composing and decomposing, 249–254
composing and decomposing numbers to, using group of 5, 255–260
counting and ordering numbers to, 157–162
counting by
to 100, 517–522
within 100, 523–528
from number within 100, 529–534
groups of, identifying, 379–384
modeling and counting, 145–150
understanding and writing, 151–156
Think and Grow, *In every lesson. For example, see:* 4, 60, 98, 172, 214, 270, 326, 380, 456, 500
Think and Grow: Modeling Real Life, *In every lesson. For example, see:* 6, 62, 100, 174, 216, 272, 328, 382, 458, 502
Thirteen (13)
counting and writing, 397–402
understanding, 403–408
Thirty (30), counting by ones to, 499–504
Three (3)
modeling and counting, 15–20
understanding and writing, 21–26
Three-dimensional shapes
building, 621–626
describing, 597–608
identifying, 597–602
positions of, 627–632
roll, stack, or slide sorting of, 603–608

Totem pole, building, 626
Triangles
  building, 583, 584, 586–588
  building house with, 586
  drawing cat with, 576
  drawing robot with, 574
  identifying and describing, 553–558, 597
  joining to make shapes, 578–582
Twelve (12)
  counting and writing, 385–390
  understanding, 391–396
Twenty (20)
  comparing numbers (up to 20), 485–490
  counting, 455–466
  counting forward from any number to, 473–478
  modeling, 455–460
  ordering numbers to, 479–484
  writing, 461–466
Two (2)
  modeling and counting, 3–8
  understanding and writing, 9–14
Two-dimensional shapes
  building, 583–588
  curves of, 547–552
  describing, 547–552, 597–602
  drawing cat with, 576
  drawing house with, 568
  drawing robot with, 574
  identifying, 597–602
  joining, 577–582
  sides of, 548–552
  vertices of, 548–552

V

Vertex (vertices)
  in building shapes, 583–588
  of hexagons, 572–576
  of rectangles, 560–564
  of squares, 566–570
  of triangles, 554–558, 584
  of two-dimensional shapes, 548–552

W

***We Go Camping* (story),** 21–26
Weights
  comparing, 659–664
    using numbers, 665–670
  describing objects by, 677–682
Whole
  composing and decomposing
    6, 225–230
    7, 231–236
    8, 237–242
    9, 243–248
    10, 249–254
    numbers to 5, 213–218
    numbers to 10, using group of 5, 255–260
  number bonds and, 219–224
Writing numbers
  0, 40, 43
  1 and 2, 9–14
  3 and 4, 21–26
  5, 33–38
  6, 103–108
  7, 115–120
  8, 127–132
  9, 139–144
  10, 151–156
  11 and 12, 385–390
  13 and 14, 397–402
  15, 409–414
  16 and 17, 421–426
  18 and 19, 433–438
  20, 461–466

Z

Zero (0)
  addition patterns with, 293–298
  concept of, 39–44
  writing, 40, 43

Credits

Chapter 1
1 BackyardProduction/iStock/Getty Images Plus, Liliya Drifan/iStock/Getty Images Plus, yotrak/iStock/Getty Images Plus, Tatomm/iStock/Getty Images Plus, kadmy/iStock/Getty Images Plus

Chapter 2
57 Mikael Dubois/iStock/Getty Images Plus

Chapter 3
95 PytyCzech/iStock/Getty Images Plus

Chapter 4
169 hugocorzo/iStock/getty Images Plus; **201** m_pavlov/iStock/Getty Images Plus

Chapter 5
211 borchee/iStock/Getty Images Plus; **262** billnoll/iStock/Getty Images Pus

Chapter 6
267 inusuke/iStock/Getty Images Plus, richcarey/iStock/Getty Images Plus, dwphotos/iStock/Getty Images Plus

Chapter 7
323 rustamank/iStock/Getty Images Plus

Chapter 8
377 wnjay_wootthisak/iStock/Getty Images Plus

Chapter 9
453 Big Ideas Learning

Chapter 10
497 Roman Pyshchyk /Shutterstock.com; **536** pixel_dreams/iStock/Getty Images Plus

Chapter 11
454 Paul Park/Moment Open/Getty Images

Chapter 12
595 Ian Lishman/Juice Images/Getty Images

Chapter 13
639 OlegDoroshin/Shutterstock.com

Cartoon Illustrations: MoreFrames Animation
Design Elements: oksanika/Shutterstock.com; icolourful/Shutterstock.com; Paul Lampard/123RF